SCOTTISH RAILWAY ATLAS
THEN AND NOW

Paul Smith and Paul Jordan

crecy.co.uk

THIS BOOK IS DEDICATED TO THE MEMORY OF
MISS ELLEN EARP
AND
KEVIN JORDAN

Jedburgh Station viewed on 1 June 1958. It was opened on 18 July 1856 by the Jedburgh Railway and became one of the earliest casualties following the creation of British Railways when the station closed to passengers on 13 August 1948. The engine shed, visible on the right, also closed on that date but the station remained open for goods until 10 August 1964.
WT (Bill) Stubbs Collection

First published 2021

© Paul Smith and Paul Jordan 2021

ISBN 9781800350342

Printed in Malta by Melita Press

Crécy Publishing Ltd
1a Ringway Trading Estate, Shadowmoss Rd, Manchester M22 5LH
www.crecy.co.uk

Front Cover: **Montrose North Signal Box** on 18 September 2015. It is a 51-lever box with a Stevens & Sons frame. Built in 1881 for the NBR it was "listed" 30 March 1999.

Rear Cover Background: Looking south at **Broughty Ferry Signal Box** on 15 September 2015. This preserved box was opened by the CR 27 November 1887 at the east end of the northbound platform but was relocated to the southbound platform in 2001 to facilitate the construction of a footbridge.

Rear Cover Inset: **Dundee Esplanade Station** viewed on 4 September 1964. It was opened in May 1899 by the NBR, closed 1 January 1917, reopened 1 February 1919 and closed by the L&NER 2 October 1939 when requisitioned by the War Department. It is still extant and in use as a base for the Tay Bridge maintenance engineers.
Neal Caplan/Online Transport Archive

Title Page: **Tay Bridge South Signal Box** viewed on 24 March 2018 with the iconic bridge stretching out northwards behind it. A brief resumé of the history of the structure can be found on Page 143.

Picture Credits
Every effort has been made to identify and correctly attribute photographic credits. Should any error have occurred this is entirely unintentional. Unless otherwise stated all photographs are by the authors.

INTRODUCTION

One of Scotland's newest stations, **Forres**, viewed on 24 March 2018.

This "Then and Now" atlas is based on the railway system as recorded on the Railway Clearing House map of Scotland, issued in 1920* and compares it to the lines and stations operational on 1 January 2021. The two maps are disposed on facing pages enabling easy reference between the two with the "Now" map featuring the modern use of the closed lines as walkways, roads etc. The "Then" map pages are illustrated with artefacts and photographs from the twentieth century and the "Now" from the twenty first. Unless stated all photographs are by the authors.

The RCH map is reproduced with no amendments or corrections and shows some stations that never reopened after the First World War as well as a line that was never built!

These are identified in the text and there is a comprehensive Index and Chronology detailing opening and closure dates as well as featuring photographs of all the stations currently open. Also included are small maps, OS References and the site status, where known, of all the standard gauge closed stations.

Previous and alternative station names are included in the text but space precludes us from presenting these in a separate and comprehensive alphabetical section.

Additionally there are summaries of principal railway walkways, preserved lines, Edinburgh Trams and the Glasgow Subway, a list of British Railways Scottish Region MPDs and a page of photographs of examples of Signal Boxes.

For clarity all tunnels have been omitted and where the terms "now" or "currently" are used in the text this refers to 2021.

We have assessed that a total of 1,617 stations feature, of which 1,223 have been closed and 394 are currently open.

Probably the smallest station on the Scottish network with a "fixed" facility - a wooden platform. This view of **Abbey of Deer Platform**, looking east, was taken in July 1954 and it can be assumed to be out of use as a wooden fence has been constructed across it and the path down to the platform has succumbed to nature! The site of this, located at NJ96640 48072, may be accessed by means of the Formantine and Buchan Way. *(See Map 16A B1).*
James Stevenson

* Official Railway Map of Scotland Prepared and Published At the Railway Clearing House, London 1920

Paul Jordan, **Wednesbury**, West Midlands and Paul Smith, **Redditch**, Worcestershire 2021

ABBREVIATIONS

The abbreviations used in this book will be familiar to many of those whose interests lie in railways but for clarification they are reproduced thus;
BR: British Railways, **CR:** Caledonian Railway, **G&SWR:** Glasgow & South Western Railway, **GNofSR:** Great North of Scotland Railway, **HR:** Highland Railway, **L&NER:** London & North Eastern Railway, **LM&SR:** London Midland & Scottish Railway, **NBR:** North British Railway.

KEY TO MAP PAGES

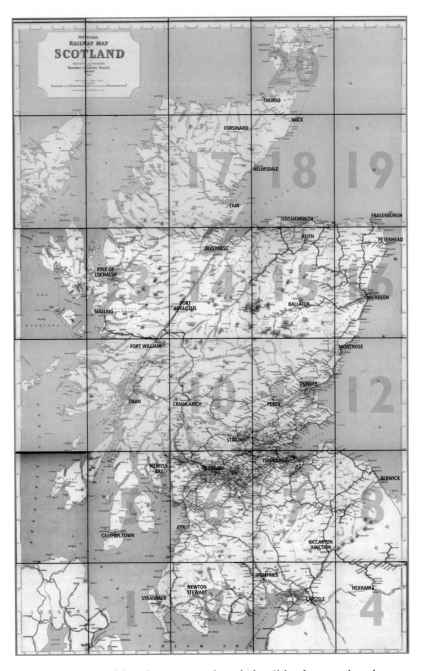

GLASGOW ENLARGEMENT

21 A

EDINBURGH ENLARGEMENT

22 A

Then' maps are indicated by the numeral and the '*Now*' maps by the numeral followed by the letter A
'*Then*' and '*Now*' maps are located opposite each other for easy reference

SCALE OF MAPS 1-20

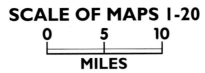

MILES

KEY - 1 JANUARY 2021 MAPS

Lines and stations shown on 1920 maps and operational .... **STRANRAER** ━━●━━

Lines and stations on 1920 maps closed to all traffic as of 1 January 2021 .... LYBSTER ──●──

Stations opened since 1920 but now closed .... HEADS OF AYR HOLIDAY CAMP ●

Stations opened since 1920 and operational .... WOODHALL ●

Stations opened prior to 1920, omitted from RCH map and operational .... FALLS OF CRUACHAN ●

Stations opened prior to 1920, omitted from RCH map and now closed .... AUCHLOCHAN HALT ●

Freight-only branches .... ━━━━━

Lines currently mothballed .... ════

Preserved stations and lines .... BOAT OF GARTEN ━━●━━

Planned extensions to Preserved lines .... ■■■■■■■■■■■

Trackbeds officially designated as bridle/cycle/walkways and
permissive footpaths .... ━━━━━

Trackbeds now roadways .... **A7** ━━━━━

Other Networks;

Edinburgh Trams .... ━━●━━

Glasgow Subway .... ━━●━━

Lines and stations closed or abandoned prior to 1920 are not shown.
Stations with * are/were non-timetabled.

CONTENTS

MAP 5

MAP 1
1920

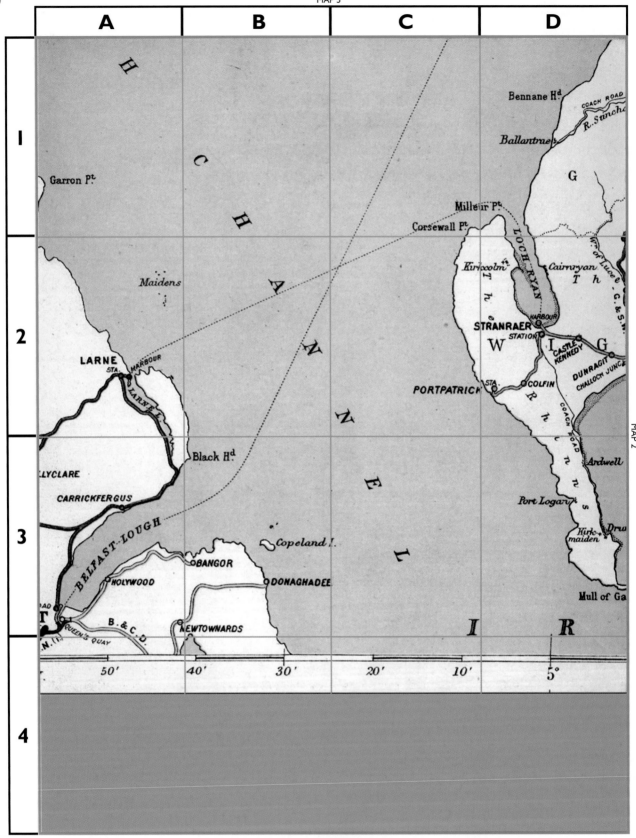

MAP 2

	A	B	C	D
1	Garron Pt			Bennane Hd / Ballantrae / G
2	Maidens / LARNE STA. / LARNE H.		LOCH RYAN / Kirkcolm / Corsewall Pt / Millair Pt / STRANRAER STATION / W / PORTPATRICK STA. / COLFIN	Cairnryan / Th / CASTLE KENNEDY / DUNRAGIT / CHALLOCH JUNCE / G
3	LLYCLARE / CARRICKFERGUS / BELFAST LOUGH / HOLYWOOD / BANGOR	Black Hd / Copeland I. / NEWTOWNARDS / DONAGHADEE / B. & C. D.		Ardwell / Port Logan Pt / Kirk-maiden / Mull of Ga / Drw
4				

Scale: 50' | 40' | 30' | 20' | 10' | 5°

Dunragit Signal Box viewed on 16 March 2017. It was built in 1927 for the LM&SR and has a 32-lever frame.

The station house and remains of the east-bound platform at the closed **Dunragit Station** on 16 March 2017.

BR Class 6P5F 4-6-2 No. 72006 *Clan Mackenzie* standing outside of the former Portpatrick Railway two-road building at **Stranraer MPD**.
Ken Fairey

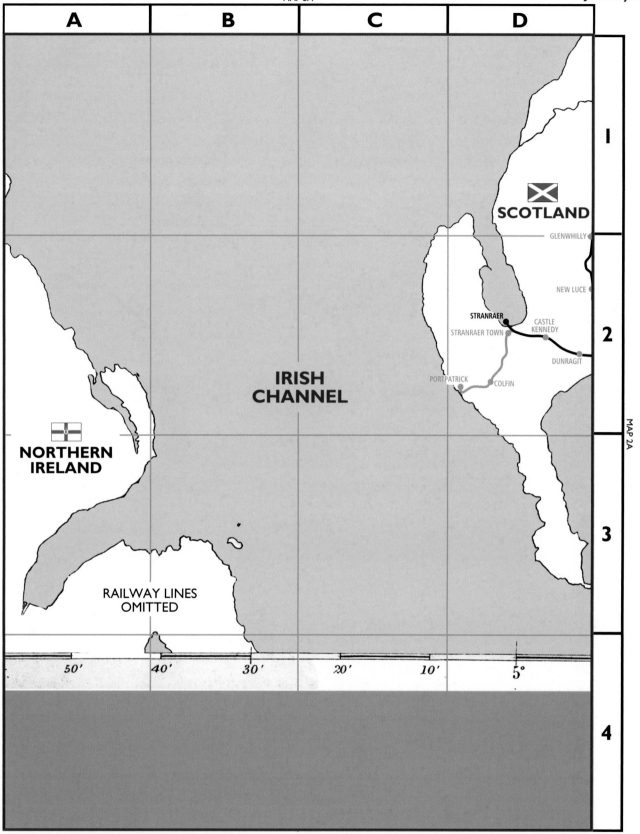

MAP 5A

	A	B	C	D
1				
2				
3				
4				

MAP 2A

SCOTLAND

GLENWHILLY

NEW LUCE

STRANRAER

CASTLE KENNEDY

STRANRAER TOWN

DUNRAGIT

PORTPATRICK

COLFIN

IRISH CHANNEL

NORTHERN IRELAND

RAILWAY LINES OMITTED

50' 40' 30' 20' 10' 5°

16 March 2107

Looking north towards the buffer stops at **Stranraer Station** on 16 March 2017.

Glenwhilly Signal Box a Type GSW7 box, built for the G&SWR in 1905 with a 20-lever frame viewed on 16 March 2017.

MAP 2
1920

MAP 6

	A	B	C	D

1

PINMORE
PINWHERRY
BARRHILL
L. Macaterick
Merrick
L. Enoch
A
Corscrine
YELLS RANGE
KIRKO
Trool
L. Dee
K
R. Dee
CW
U
COACH ROAD
Wr. or Ken
Dalry
NEW GALLOWAY
MONIAIVE CAIRN VALLEY
KIRKLAND
CROSSFORD
DUNSCORE
STEPFORD
NEWTONAIRDS
AULDG
IRO
Lochrutto
Milton L.
D B R I G

Maberry
L. Ochiltree
R. Cree
R. Badenoch
GLENWHILLY
Moors
NEW LUCE
L. Grennoch
Cairnsmore
NEWTON STEWART
WIGTOWNSHIRE JT.
PALNURE
CAL. G. & S.W.
L. & N.W. & MID.
GATEHOUSE OF FLEET
CREETOWN
L. Skerrow
L. Grenoch
Lawrieston
Wr. of Fleet
Wr. of Dee
PARTON
CROSSMICHAEL
CASTLE DOUGLAS
JUNO.
STA.
G. & S.W.
R. Dee
BRIDGE OF DEE
SOUT
DALBEATTI

2

PORTPATRICK & WIGTOWNSHIRE JT.
KIRKCOWAN
TOWN
GLENLUCE
Castle L.
Mochrum L.
WIGTOWN
WIGTOWN BAY
KIRKINNER
WHAUPHILL
SORBIE
MILLISLE
GARLIESTON
STA.
HARBOUR
Pier E.
GATEHOUSE
TARFF
Borgue
COACH ROAD
KIRKCUDBRIGHT
Auchencairn
Kirkandrigan B.
rough L.
Auchencairn Bay

3

LUCE BAY
COACH ROAD
The Machers
Port William
WHITHORN
Burrow Hd.
Isle of Whithorn
Abbey Head
nmore
lloway

I   S   H   S   E   A

From Dublin and

| 50' | 40' | 30' | 20' | 10' | 4° | 50' |

4

MAP 1

MAP 3

```
LEGEND FOR MAP 2
I CAIRN VALLEY LIGHT RAILWAY
    (See note on Page 134)
```

Newton Stewart Station viewed in BR days.
Neal Caplan/Online Transport Archive

Creetown Station viewed in April 1965.
Neal Caplan/Online Transport Archive

Crossmichael Station viewed in April 1965.
Neal Caplan/Online Transport Archive

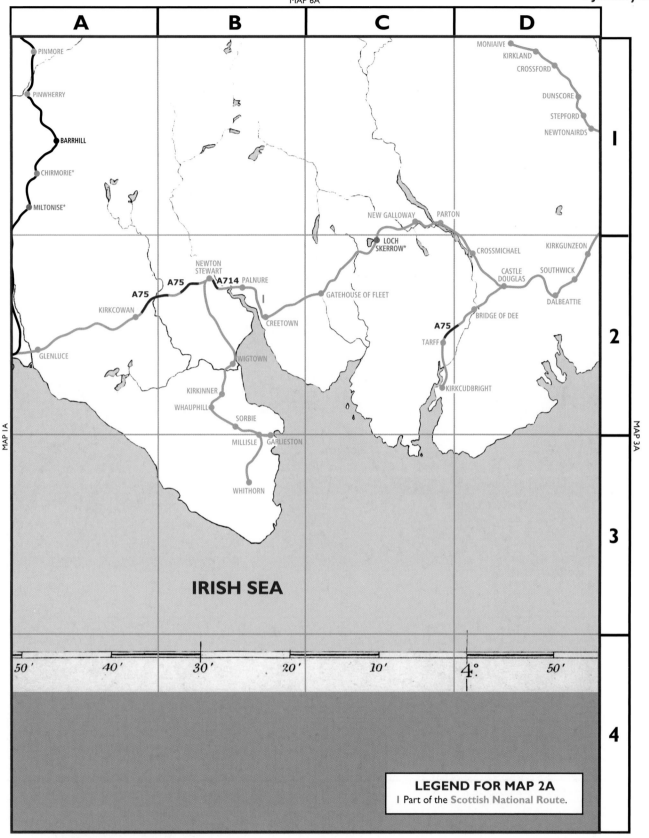

	A	B	C	D	

PINMORE

PINWHERRY

BARRHILL

CHIRMORIE*

MILTONISE*

MONIAIVE
KIRKLAND
CROSSFORD
DUNSCORE
STEPFORD
NEWTONAIRDS

1

NEW GALLOWAY   PARTON

LOCH
SKERROW*

KIRKGUNZEON

CROSSMICHAEL

SOUTHWICK

NEWTON
STEWART   **A714** PALNURE

CASTLE
DOUGLAS

A75   **A75**

GATEHOUSE OF FLEET

DALBEATTIE

KIRKCOWAN

CREETOWN

BRIDGE OF DEE

GLENLUCE

A75

WIGTOWN

TARFF

2

KIRKINNER

WHAUPHILL

KIRKCUDBRIGHT

SORBIE

MILLISLE GARLIESTON

WHITHORN

3

IRISH SEA

50'   40'   30'   20'   10'   4°   50'

4

LEGEND FOR MAP 2A
1 Part of the Scottish National Route.

MAP 1A

MAP 3A

16 March 2017

Looking north at **Barrhill Station** on 16 March 2017.

Barrhill Signal Box on 16 March 2017. This is the third box sited here – the previous two burned down!

MAP 3
1920

MAP 7

	A	B	C	D
I				
2				
3				
4				

MAP 2

MAP 3

GLASGOW
SHIELDHILL
AMISFIELD
HOLYWOOD
GRAY
CAIRN VALLEY JUNC.
OLOCHARBRIGGS
LOCAL
MAXWELLTOWN
G.&S.W.
DUMFRIES
RACKS
SOUTH
R. Nith
LOCHANHEAD
KILLYWHAN
SKILLYWHAN

NETHERCLEUGH
R | E S
LOCH-MABEN
Castle L.
LOCKERBIE
Dalton r.
CALEDONIAN
RUTHWELL
WESTERN
R. Annan
KIRTLEBRIDGE
ECCLEFECHAN
KIRKPATRICK

NEWCASTLETON
LANGHOLM
BRITI
North
KERSHOPE FOOT
Kershope Burn
GILNOCKIE
CANONBIE
PENTON
RIDDINGS
SCOTCH DYKE
GRETNA GREEN
JUNC. N.B.
LONGTOWN

New Abbey
KIRKGUNZEON
Criffell
WICK
Mainsriddle
Southerness Pt.
SOLWAY FIRTH
the Isle of Man

RUTHWELL
CUMMERTREES
SOLWAY VIADUCT
BOWNESS
WHITRIGG
MORICAMBE
JUNC. STA.
SILLOTH
BLACK DYKE
ABBEY TOWN
ABBEY HOLME
BROMFIELD
STATION JUNC.
BRAYTON
MARYPORT
STA. JUNC.
JUNC.
WORKINGTON
L. & N.W
From Whitehaven

ANNAN
CAL.
G.&S.W. JUNC.
DORNOCK
PORT CARLISLE DOCK
STA.
GLASSON PLATFORM
DRUM BURGH
KIRKBRIDE
N.B.
BURGH
KIRK ANDREWS
CAL.
CARWIGTON
&
CARLISLE
MARYPORT

RIGG
GRETNA
FLORISTON
ROCKCLIFFE
CARLISLE
CITADEL JOINT STA.
JUNCS.
ROME STR Jn.
PETTERIL JUNC.
LONDON & NORTH WESTERN
To London (Euston)
E

CLYNESIDE
HARKER
NORTH EAS
MIDLAND
N
To

40' 30' 20' 10' 3° 50' 40'

LEGEND FOR MAP 3
I **SOLWAY VIADUCT**
(See note on Page 134)

The site of the closed **Holywood Station** viewed on 20 March 2017 with one of the degraded platforms visible on the left.

Newcastleton Station viewed from a passing train on 9 October 1963.
Neal Caplan/Online Transport Archive

BR:
Dumfries to Gretna Green (Date Unknown)

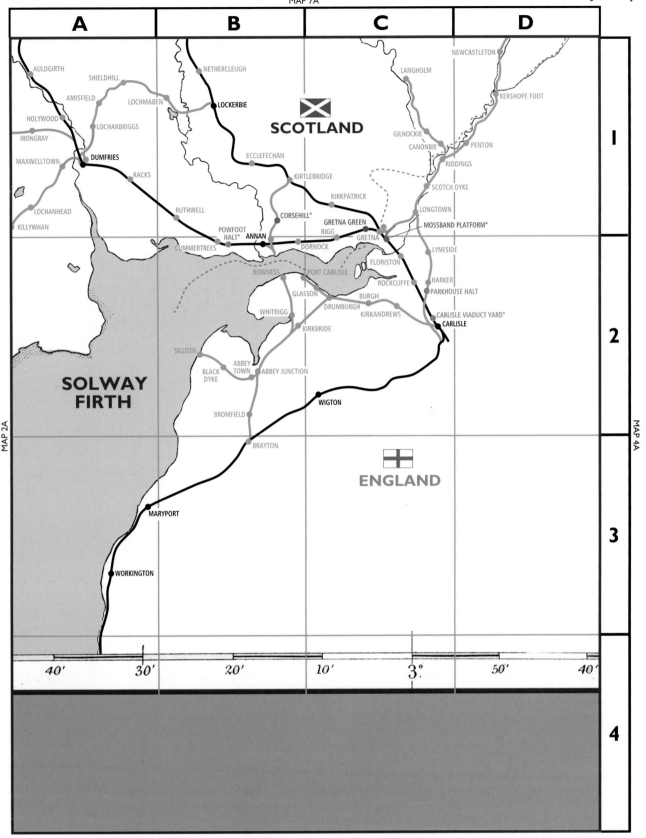

MAP 7A

	A	B	C	D	

AULDGIRTH
SHIELDHILL
AMISFIELD
HOLYWOOD
LOCHARBRIGGS
IRONGRAY
MAXWELLTOWN
DUMFRIES
RACKS
LOCHANHEAD
KILLYWHAN

NETHERCLEUGH
LOCKERBIE
LOCHMABEN

ECCLEFECHAN

KIRTLEBRIDGE

RUTHWELL

CORSEHILL*

POWFOOT
HALT*   ANNAN
CUMMERTREES

RIGG
DORNOCK

KIRKPATRICK

GRETNA GREEN

GRETNA

SCOTLAND

LANGHOLM

GILNOCKIE
CANONBIE

RIDDINGS

SCOTCH DYKE

LONGTOWN

MOSSBAND PLATFORM*

LYNESIDE

FLORISTON
ROCKCLIFFE
HARKER
PARKHOUSE HALT

CARLISLE VIADUCT YARD*
CARLISLE

NEWCASTLETON

KERSHOPE FOOT

PENTON

BOWNESS   PORT CARLISLE
GLASSON
WHITRIGG   DRUMBURGH   BURGH
KIRKBRIDE   KIRKANDREWS

SILLOTH

BLACK   ABBEY
DYKE   TOWN   ABBEY JUNCTION

WIGTON

BROMFIELD

BRAYTON

**SOLWAY
FIRTH**

ENGLAND

MARYPORT

WORKINGTON

MAP 2A

MAP 4A

1

2

3

4

40'   30'   20'   10'   3°   50'   40'

15 September 2015

Looking east at **Dumfries Station** on 16 March 2017.

Looking west at **Gretna Green Station** on 16 March 2017.

MAP 4
1920

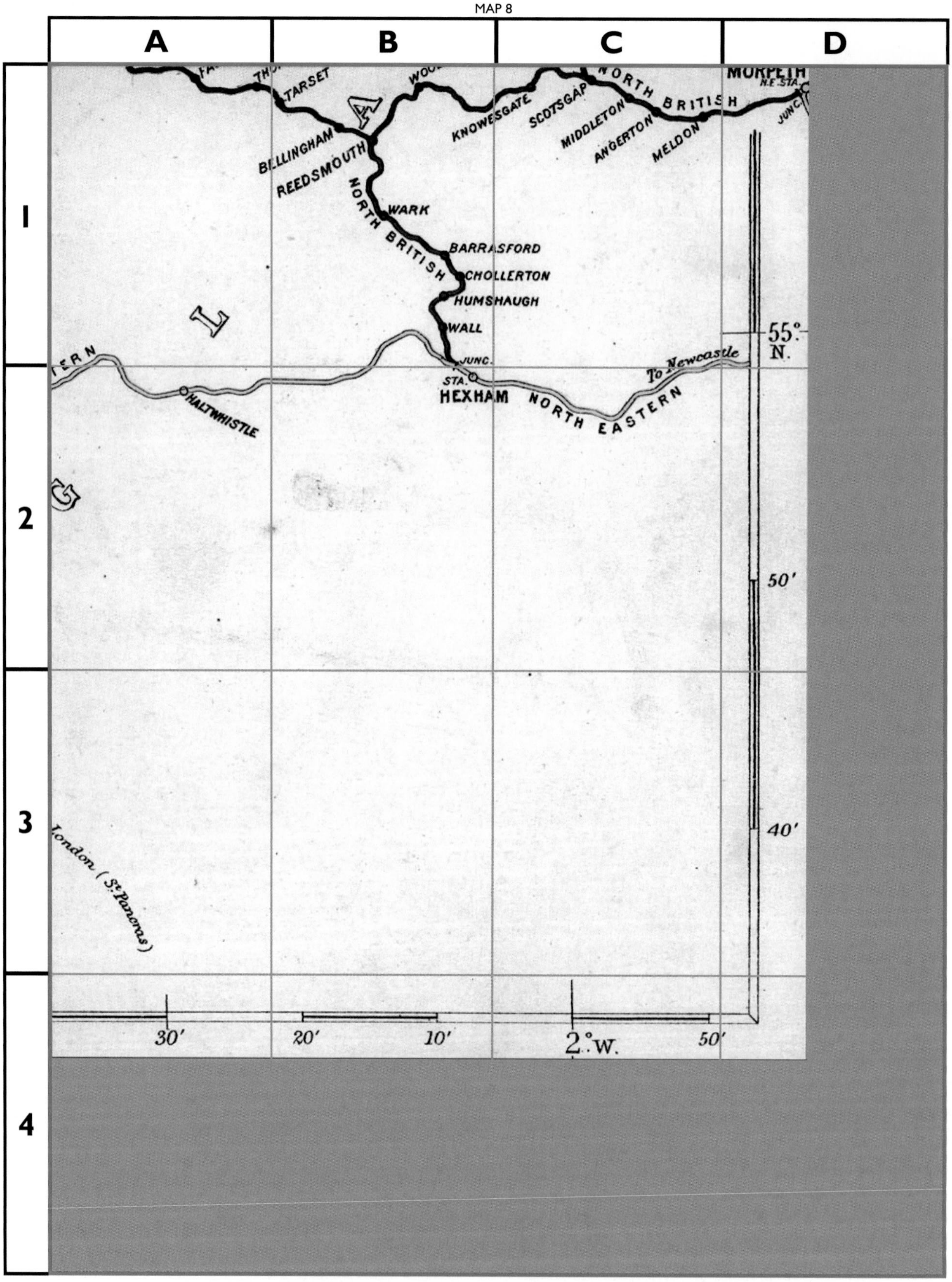

MAP 8

MAP 3

	A	B	C	D
1				
2				
3				
4				

TARSET

BELLINGHAM

REEDSMOUTH

WOO...

KNOWESGATE

SCOTSGAP

MIDDLETON

ANGERTON

MELDON

NORTH BRITISH

MORPETH
N.E.STA.

JUNC.

NORTH BRITISH

WARK

BARRASFORD

CHOLLERTON

HUMSHAUGH

WALL

JUNC.

STA.

HEXHAM

NORTH EASTERN

To Newcastle

...TERN

HALTWHISTLE

London (St. Pancras)

55°
N.

50'

40'

30' 20' 10' 2.°W. 50'

Tarset Station on 13 October 1956, the last day of passenger services. *Alan Brown Collection*

Ex-NER Class J21 0-6-0 No.65090 at **Wall Station** in the 1950s. *Alan Brown Collection*

Ex-NER Class J21 0-6-0 No.65117 at **Hexham MPD** on 22 September 1956. *WT Stubbs*

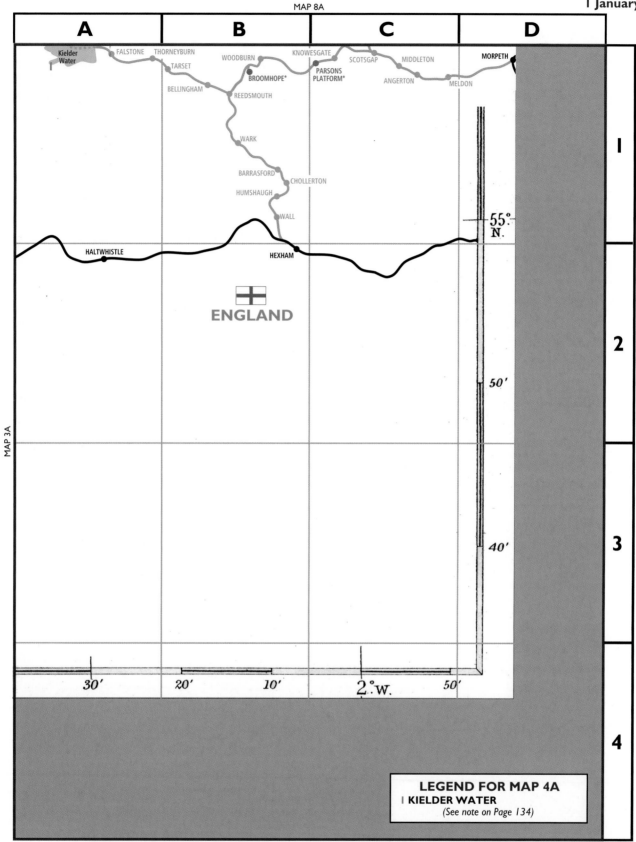

MAP 8A

A	B	C	D

Kielder Water   FALSTONE   THORNEYBURN   WOODBURN   KNOWESGATE   SCOTSGAP   MIDDLETON   MORPETH

TARSET   BROOMHOPE*   PARSONS PLATFORM*   ANGERTON   MELDON

BELLINGHAM   REEDSMOUTH

WARK

BARRASFORD   CHOLLERTON

HUMSHAUGH

WALL

HALTWHISTLE   HEXHAM

ENGLAND

55°. N.

50'

40'

1

2

3

4

MAP 3A

30'   20'   10'   2.°w.   50'

LEGEND FOR MAP 4A
1 KIELDER WATER
(See note on Page 134)

19 September 2015

Looking west at **Hexham Station** on 19 September 2015.

Looking west at **Morpeth Station** on 19 September 2015.

MAP 9

MAP 5
1920

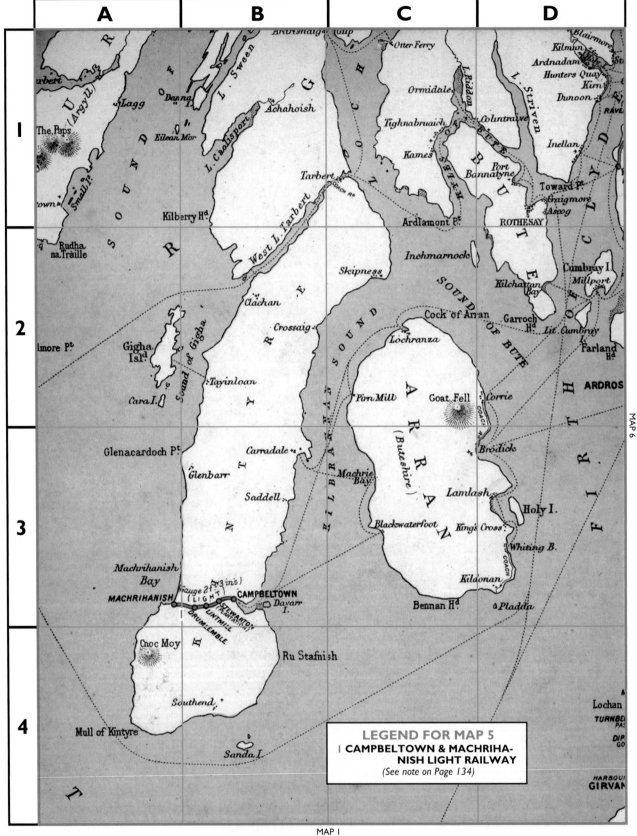

	A	B	C	D
1				
2				
3				
4				

MAP 1

The Paps
Tarbert (Argyll L.)
Lagg
Danna I.
Eilean Mor
Achahoish
L. Sween
Artilshaig Oup
Otter Ferry
Ormidale
L. Riddon
L. Striven
Blairmore
Kilmun
Ardnadam
Hunters Quay
Kirn
Dunoon
RAVE
SOUND OF JURA
Small I.
Kilberry Hd
West L. Tarbert
Tarbert
COACH Rd
Tighnabruaich
Kames
Coltraive
Port Bannatyne
KYLES OF BUTE
Toward Pt
Craigmore
Ascog
ROTHESAY
Rudha na Traille
Skipness
Clachan
Crossaig
Inchmarnock
Ardlamont Pt
Kilchattan Bay
SOUND OF BUTE
Garroch Hd
Lit. Cumbray
Cumbray I.
Millport
Farland Hd
Imore Pt
Gigha Isld
Sound of Gigha
Tayinloan
Cara I.
KINTYRE
Lochranza
ARRAN (Buteshire)
Fern Mill
Goat Fell
Corrie
COACH Rd
ARDROS
FIRTH OF CLYDE
Glenacardoch Pt
Glenbarr
Carradale
Saddell
KILBRANNAN SOUND
Machrie Bay
Brodick
Lamlash
Holy I.
Blackwaterfoot
King's Cross
Whiting B.
COACH Rd
Machrihanish Bay
Gauge 2ft 3 ins)
(LIGHT)
MACHRIHANISH
STEWARTON PLANTATION
LINTMILL
DRUMLEMBLE
CAMPBELTOWN
Davarr I.
Kilaonan
Bennan Hd
Pladda
Choc Moy
Ru Stafnish
Southend
Sanda I.
Mull of Kintyre
Lochan
TURNBE
PAS
DIP
GO
HARBOUI
GIRVAN

MAP 6

LEGEND FOR MAP 5

1 CAMPBELTOWN & MACHRIHANISH LIGHT RAILWAY
(See note on Page 134)

0-6-2T No.29 *Argyll* (Barclay 1049 of 1906), one of four locomotives used on the line, at **Machrihanish** on an unknown date.   *K Turner Collection*

Campbeltown, the eastern terminus of the Campbeltown & Machrihanish Light Railway, viewed in c1908.   *John Alsop Collection*

The entrance to **Wemyss Bay Station**, viewed in c1912.
John Alsop Collection

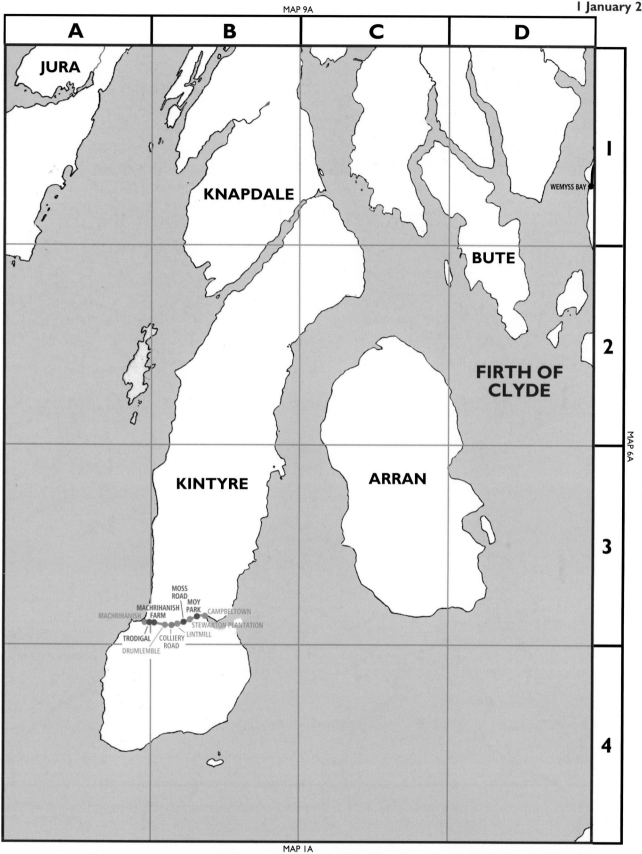

A	B	C	D

JURA

KNAPDALE

BUTE

1

FIRTH OF CLYDE

2

KINTYRE

ARRAN

3

WEMYSS BAY

MOSS ROAD
MOY PARK
MACHRIHANISH FARM
MACHRIHANISH
CAMPBELTOWN
STEWARTON PLANTATION
LINTMILL
TRODIGAL
COLLIERY ROAD
DRUMLEMBLE

4

17 March 2017

The concourse of Grade A listed **Wemyss Bay Station** viewed on 17 March 2017.

Class 385 Unit No.385001, then on test, parked on Platform 1 at **Wemyss Bay Station** on 17 March 2017.

MAP 6
1920

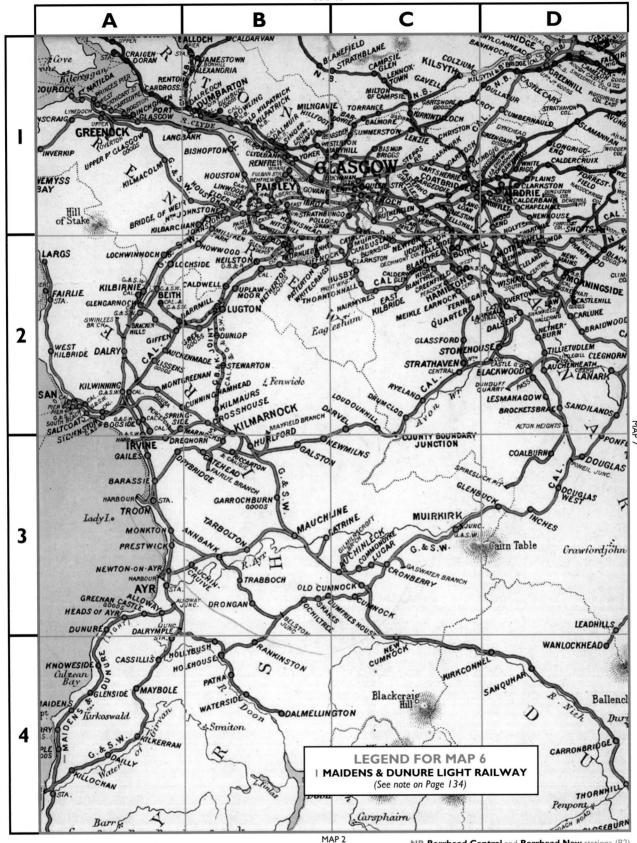

MAP 10

| A | B | C | D |

LEGEND FOR MAP 6
I MAIDENS & DUNURE LIGHT RAILWAY
(See note on Page 134)

MAP 2

MAP 7

NB **Barrhead Central** and **Barrhead New** stations (B2)
are incorrectly annotated and should be transposed.

Muirkirk Station in BR days.
Neal Caplan/Online Transport Archive

Inches Station in BR days.
Neal Caplan/Online Transport Archive

Looking west at **Thornhill Station** on 20
March 2017. Although it was closed by BR the
platforms were still extant and the station house
was in private use.

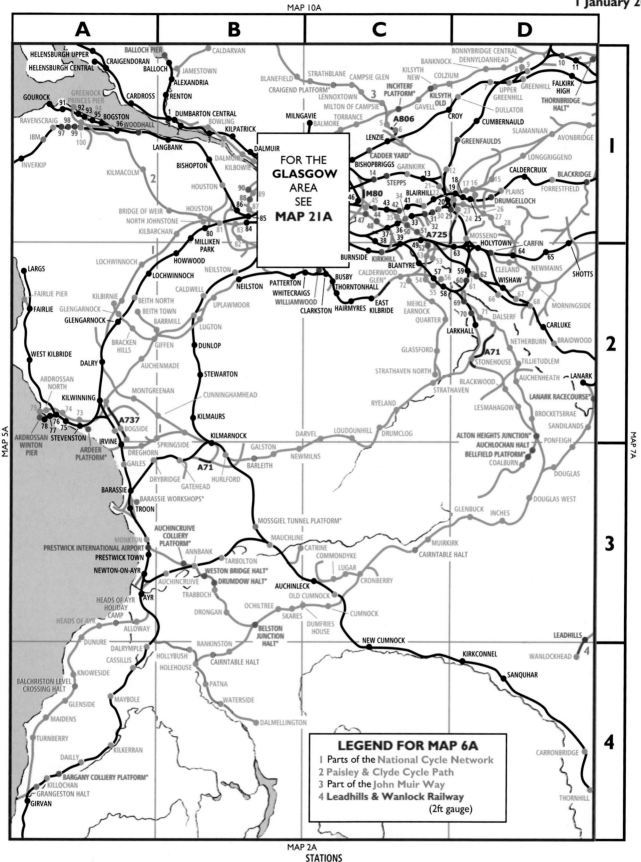

FOR THE
GLASGOW
AREA
SEE
MAP 21A

LEGEND FOR MAP 6A
1 Parts of the National Cycle Network
2 Paisley & Clyde Cycle Path
3 Part of the John Muir Way
4 **Leadhills & Wanlock Railway**
(2ft gauge)

MAP 2A

STATIONS

1. DALREOCH	16. RAWYARDS	31. KIRKWOOD	46. DUKE STREET
2. DUMBARTON EAST	17. COMMONHEAD	32. BARGEDDIE	47. PARKHEAD FOR
3. BOWLING	18. COATDYKE	33. BAILLIESTON	CELTIC PARK
4. OLD KILPATRICK	19. COATBRIDGE SUNNYSIDE	34. CALDERPARK HALT	48. TOLLCROSS
5. KIRKINTILLOCH	20. COATBRIDGE CENTRAL	35. MOUNT VERNON	49. UDDINGSTON
6. BACK O'LOCH HALT	21. GARTSHERRIE	36. MOUNT VERNON	50. BROOMHOUSE
7. CASTLECARY	22. COATBRIDGE CENTRAL	37. CARMYLE	51. UDDINGSTON WEST
8. BONNYBRIDGE	23. CALDER	38. CAMBUSLANG	52. UDDINGSTON EAST
9. BONNYBRIDGE HIGH	24. WHIFFLET	39. NEWTON	53. BOTHWELL
10. CAMELON	25. AIRDRIE	40. BARGEDDIE	54. BURNBANK
11. FALKIRK GRAHAMSTON	26. CALDERBANK	41. EASTERHOUSE	55. PEACOCK CROSS
12. GLENBOIG	27. CHAPELHALL	42. GARROWHILL	56. HAMILTON
13. GARTCOSH	28. NEWHOUSE	43. SHETTLESTON	57. HAMILTON WEST
14. ROBROYSTON	29. WHIFFLET	44. CARNTYNE	58. HAMILTON CENTRAL
15. WHITERIGG	30. LANGLOAN	45. PARKHEAD NORTH	59. MOTHERWELL

60. AIRBLES	75. SALTCOATS	89. SOUTH RENFREW
61. FLEMINGTON	76. ARDROSSAN SOUTH	90. RENFREW PORTERFIELD
62. SHIELDMUIR	BEACH	91. FORT MATILDA
63. BELLSHILL	77. ARDROSSAN TOWN	92. GREENOCK WEST
64. CLELAND	78. ARDROSSAN HARBOUR	93. GREENOCK CENTRAL
65. HARTSWOOD	79. ARDROSSAN PIER	94. LYNEDOCH GREENOCK
66. WISHAW SOUTH	80. JOHNSTONE	95. CARTSDYKE
67. OVERTOWN	81. ELDERSLIE	96. PORT GLASGOW
68. LAW JUNCTION	82. POTTERHILL	97. BRANCHTON
69. CHATELHERAULT	83. PAISLEY WEST	98. DRUMFROCHAR
70. MERRYTON	84. PAISLEY CANAL	99. WHINHILL
71. LARKHALL EAST	85. PAISLEY GILMOUR STREET	100. UPPER GREENOCK
72. HIGH BLANTYRE	86. PAISLEY ST JAMES	
73. STEVENSTON	87. PAISLEY ABERCORN	
74. SALTCOATS	88. SANDYFORD PLATFORM	

MAP 7
1920

MAP 11

| A | B | C | D |

MAP 6

MAP 8

MAP 3

The former CR **Broughton Station** viewed on 14 November 1964, some fourteen years after closure.
Neal Caplan/Online Transport Archive

Earlston Station viewed on 10 January 1965.
Neal Caplan/Online Transport Archive

Melrose Station viewed on 10 July 1964.
Neal Caplan/Online Transport Archive

MAP 11A

A	B	C	D

GRANGEMOUTH
BO'NESS
KINNIEL
POLMONT
MANUEL LOW LEVEL
PHILPSTOUN
SOUTH QUEENSFERRY HALT
Forth Bridge
NORTH QUEENSFERRY
DALMENY
ABERLADY
DREM
EAST FORTUNE
LONGNIDDRY
EAST LINTON
HADDINGTON
SETON MAINS HALT
PRESTONPANS
MANUEL
CAUSEWAYEND
LINLITHGOW
WINCHBURGH
BARNTON
TURNHOUSE
JOPPA
WALLYFORD
MACMERRY
BOWHOUSE
WESTFIELD
13
RATHO
INVERESK
WINTON
ORMISTON
SMEATON
PENCAITLAND
GIFFORD
BATHGATE UPPER
DECHMONT
UPHALL
16
WESTER HAILES
CURRIE HILL
RAVELRIG
CROSSGATEHALL HALT
SALTOUN
BANGOUR
BATHGATE
LIVINGSTON NORTH
LIVINGSTON SOUTH
KIRKNEWTON
BALERNO
CURRIE
DALKEITH
ESKBANK
NEWTONGRANGE
HUMBIE
ARMADALE
WHITBURN
NEWPARK
GOREBRIDGE
FUSHIEBRIDGE
BENTS
WEST CALDER
HARBURN
ESK BRIDGE
ROSSLYNLEE HOSPITAL HALT
PENICUIK
POMATHORN
TYNEHEAD
ADDIEWELL
BREICH
FAULDHOUSE
COBBINSHAW
LEADBURN
HERIOT
OXTON
HAYWOOD
WILSONTOWN
AUCHENGRAY
MACBIE HILL
BROOMLEE
LAMANCHA
FOUNTAINHALL JUNCTION
LAUDER
DUNSYRE
EDDLESTON
STOW
CARNWATH
CLEGHORN
NEWBIGGING
DOLPHINTON
BOWLAND
EARLSTON
CARSTAIRS
BANKHEAD
PEEBLES NBR
CARDRONA
GALASHIELS
TWEEDBANK
A68
THANKERTON
BIGGAR
LYNE
PEEBLES CR
STOBO
BROUGHTON
WALKERBURN
CLOVENFORDS
A6091
SYMINGTON
COULTER
INNERLEITHEN
THORNIELEE
ANGLING CLUB COTTAGE PLATFORM*
ABBOTSFORD FERRY
MELROSE
ST BOSWELLS
LAMINGTON
A7
LINDEAN
CHARLESFIELD HALT*
MAXTON
SELKIRK
BELSES
ABINGTON
CRAWFORD
HASSENDEAN
HAWICK
ELVANFOOT
STOBS CAMP
STOBS
BEATTOCK SUMMIT*
HARTHORPE*
SHANKEND
GRESKINE*
MOFFAT
WHITROPE SIDING*
RUTTONSIDE*
AUCHENCASTLE*
BEATTOCK
SAUGHTREE
RICCARTON JUNCTION
DEADWATER
WAMPHRAY
STEELE ROAD
CLOSEBURN
DINWOODIE

MAP 6A
MAP 8A

FOR THE
EDINBURGH
AREA
SEE
MAP 22A

LEGEND FOR MAP 7A
1 Bo'ness & Kinneil Railway
2 Edinburgh Trams
3 Parts of the Water of Leith Walkway
4 Pencaitland Railway Walk
5 Part of the Penicuik to Musselburgh Cycle-Walkway

MAP 3A

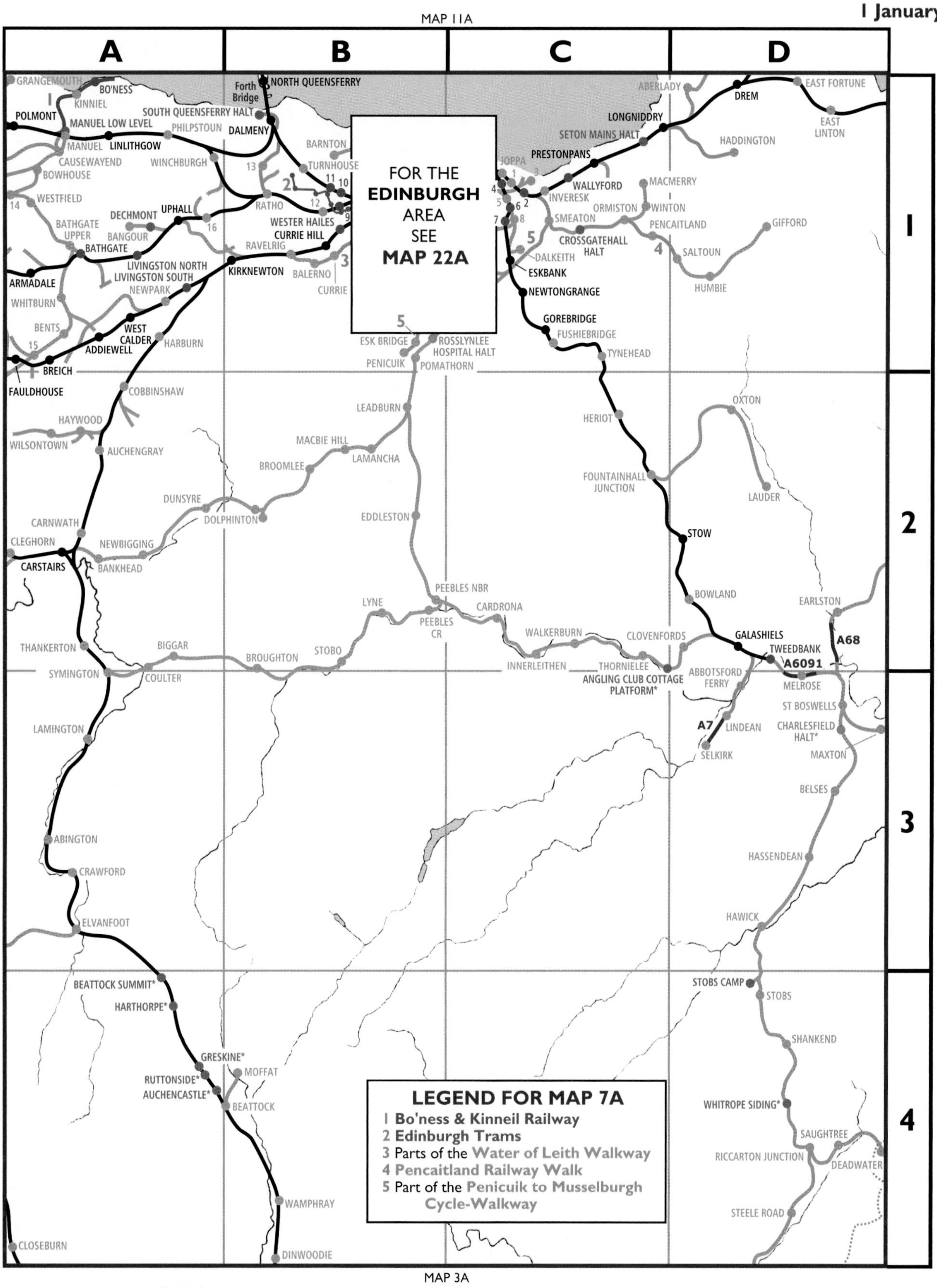

19 March 2017

Class 158 Unit No.158867 at the buffer stops at **Tweedbank Station** on 12 May 2017.

STATIONS

1. NEW HAILES
2. MUSSELBURGH
3. MUSSELBURGH
4. BRUNSTANE
5. NIDDRIE
6. NEWCRAIGHALL
7. SHAWFAIR
8. MILLERHILL
9. EDINBURGH PARK
10. SOUTH GYLE
11. EDINBURGH GATEWAY
12. GOGAR
13. KIRKLISTON
14. BLACKSTONE
15. FAULDHOUSE & CROFTHEAD
16. DRUMSHORELAND

MAP 8
1920

MAP 12

| A | B | C | D |

MAP 7

NORTH BRITISH

INNERWICK

COCKBURNSPATH

ST. ABB'S HEAD

GRANTSHOUSE

Coldingham

TON

HILLS

St Abb's Head

EYEMOUTH

BURNMOUTH

RESTON

AYTON

N.B.

formacus

Whiteadder W.

CHIRNSIDE

BERWICK

TWEEDMOUTH

R W I C K

EDROM

DUNS

R. Blackadder W.

N.B.

MARCHMONT

Swinton

VELVET HALL

NORHAM

NORTH EASTERN

Holy I.

GREENLAW

Leitholm

R. Tweed

TWIZELL

GORDON

Stichill

CARNAM

COLDSTREAM

SUNILAWS

Floors Cas.

SPROUSTON

STA.

N.E.

JUNC.

To Alnwick

To London (King's Cross)

50'

40'

KELSO

N.B.

ROXBURGH

Yetholm

H

RUTHER FORD

KIRKBANK

MAXTON

N'SRET

JEDFOOT

Morebattle

The Schel

The Cheviot

D

JEDBURGH

B U R G H

Hale Water

Windygate Hill

30'

Chesters

C H E V I O T

H I L L S

Brownhart Law

Carter Fell

20'

HEADWATER

N

ROTHBURY

BRINKBURN

KIELDER

FONTBURN

EWESLEY

PLASHETTS

LONGWITTON

ALSTONE

ORNEYBURN

ODBURN

MAP 4

Roxburgh Station on 3 August 1964.
Neal Caplan/Online Transport Archive

Chirnside Station viewed in BR days.
Neal Caplan/Online Transport Archive

Looking north at **Jedburgh Station** on 3 August 1964.
Neal Caplan/Online Transport Archive

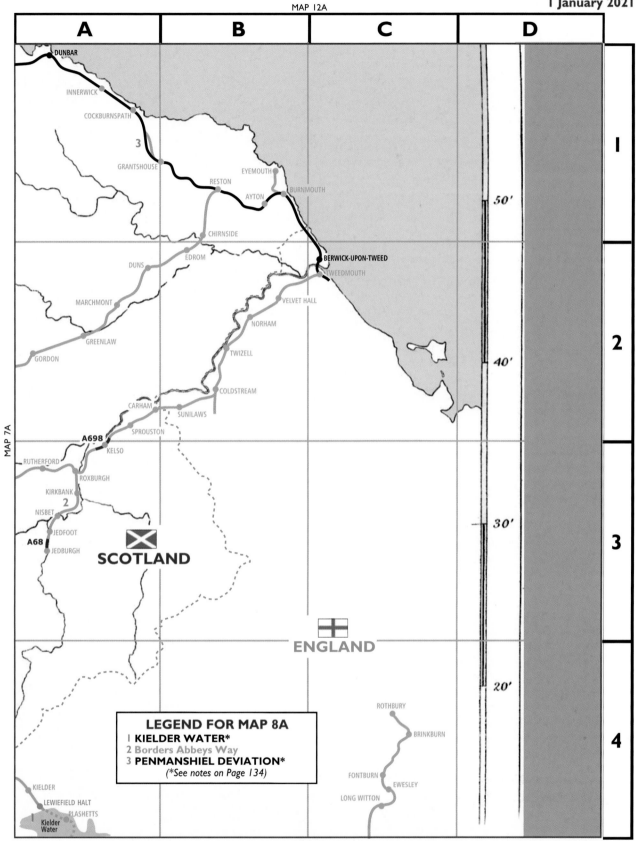

MAP 12A

| A | B | C | D |

DUNBAR
INNERWICK
COCKBURNSPATH
3
GRANTSHOUSE
RESTON
EYEMOUTH
AYTON
BURNMOUTH
CHIRNSIDE
EDROM
DUNS
BERWICK-UPON-TWEED
TWEEDMOUTH
MARCHMONT
VELVET HALL
GREENLAW
NORHAM
GORDON
TWIZELL
COLDSTREAM
CARHAM
SUNILAWS
SPROUSTON
A698
KELSO
RUTHERFORD
ROXBURGH
KIRKBANK
2
NISBET
JEDFOOT
A68
JEDBURGH

MAP 7A

SCOTLAND

ENGLAND

ROTHBURY
BRINKBURN
FONTBURN
EWESLEY
LONG WITTON

50'
40'
30'
20'

KIELDER
LEWIEFIELD HALT
PLASHETTS
Kielder Water

LEGEND FOR MAP 8A
1 **KIELDER WATER***
2 Borders Abbeys Way
3 **PENMANSHIEL DEVIATION***
    *(*See notes on Page 134)*

MAP 4A

1
2
3
4

19 September 2015

19 September 2015

Looking north at **Berwick-upon-Tweed Station** on 19 September 2015.

MAP 9
1920

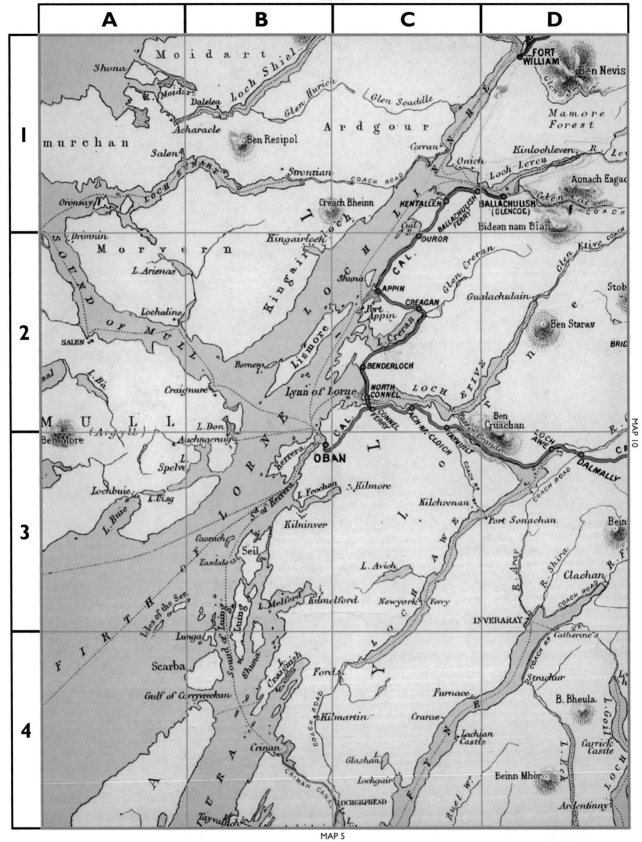

MAP 13

MAP 5

MAP 10

Looking east at **Dalmally Station**, probably in LM&SR days.
Allan Sommerfield Collection cty Engine Shed Society

Ex-L&NER Class K1 2-6-0 No.62012 amongst ex-LM&SR Class 5 4-6-0s in the yard at **Fort William MPD** on 16 August 1960. *Ken Fairey*

Ex-LM&SR Class 5 4-6-0 No.45153 standing outside of **Oban MPD**. It was opened by the Callander & Oban Railway on 30 June 1880 and closed by BR on 6 May 1963. *JF McEwan*

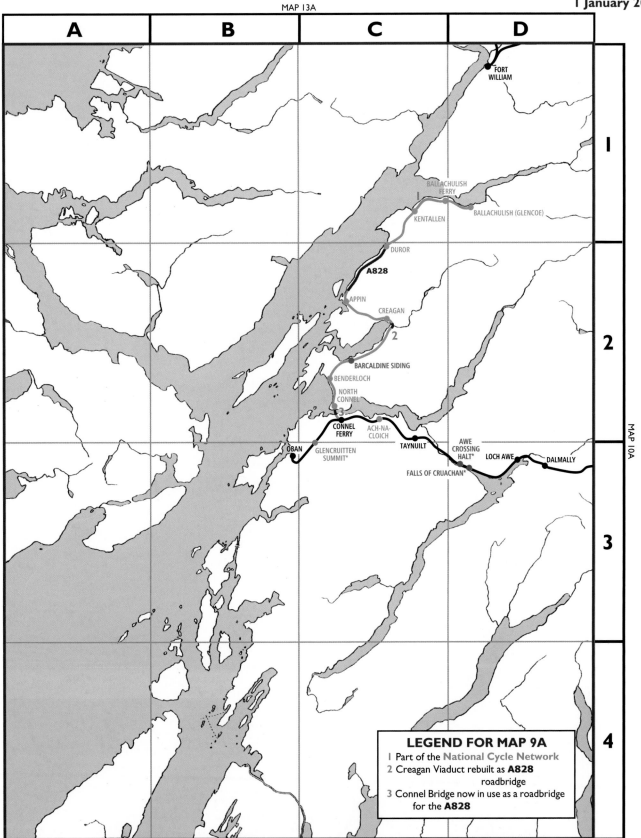

MAP 13A

	A	B	C	D	
				FORT WILLIAM	1
			BALLACHULISH FERRY		
			KENTALLEN	BALLACHULISH (GLENCOE)	
			DUROR		
			A828		2
			APPIN		
			CREAGAN		
			2		
			BARCALDINE SIDING		
			BENDERLOCH		
			NORTH CONNEL		
			3		
			CONNEL FERRY	ACH-NA-CLOICH	
		OBAN	GLENCRUITTEN SUMMIT*	TAYNUILT	AWE CROSSING HALT* LOCH AWE DALMALLY	3
			FALLS OF CRUACHAN*		
					4

MAP 10A

LEGEND FOR MAP 9A
1 Part of the National Cycle Network
2 Creagan Viaduct rebuilt as **A828** roadbridge
3 Connel Bridge now in use as a roadbridge for the **A828**

MAP 5A

14 September 2015

Looking south from the buffer stops at **Oban Station** on 14 September 2015.

Looking east at **Loch Awe Station** on 14 September 2015. The degraded former westbound platform can be seen on the right.

MAP 10
1920

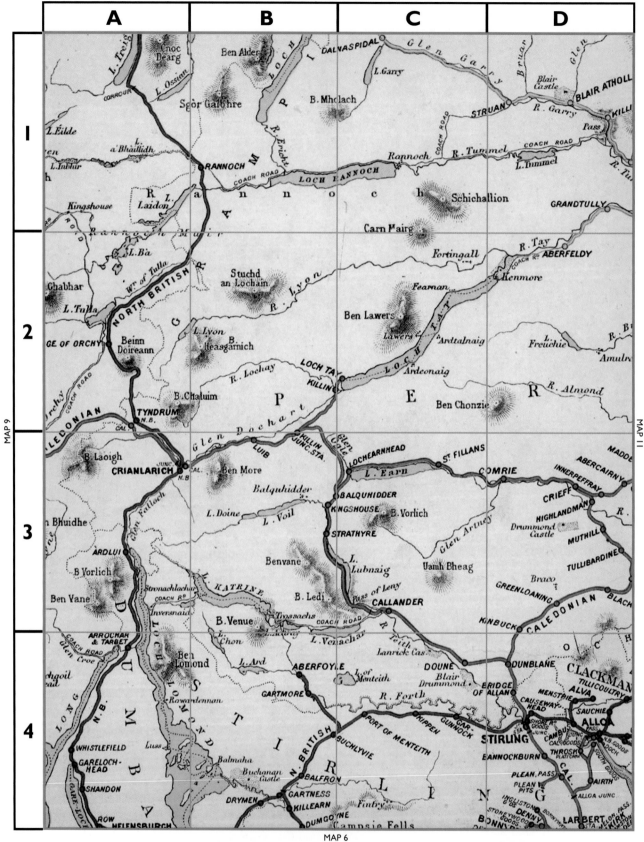

MAP 14

	A	**B**	**C**	**D**

MAP 9

MAP 11

MAP 6

Looking north at **Throsk Station** towards the Alloa Bridge on 24 March 1965.
Neal Caplan/Online Transport Archive

Ex-CR Class 2P 0-4-4T No.55207 at **Killin Station** on 20 June 1961.
Neal Caplan/Online Transport Archive

Ex-LM&SR Class 5 4-6-0 No.45084 at **Stirling Station** on 9 July 1965.
Neal Caplan/Online Transport Archive

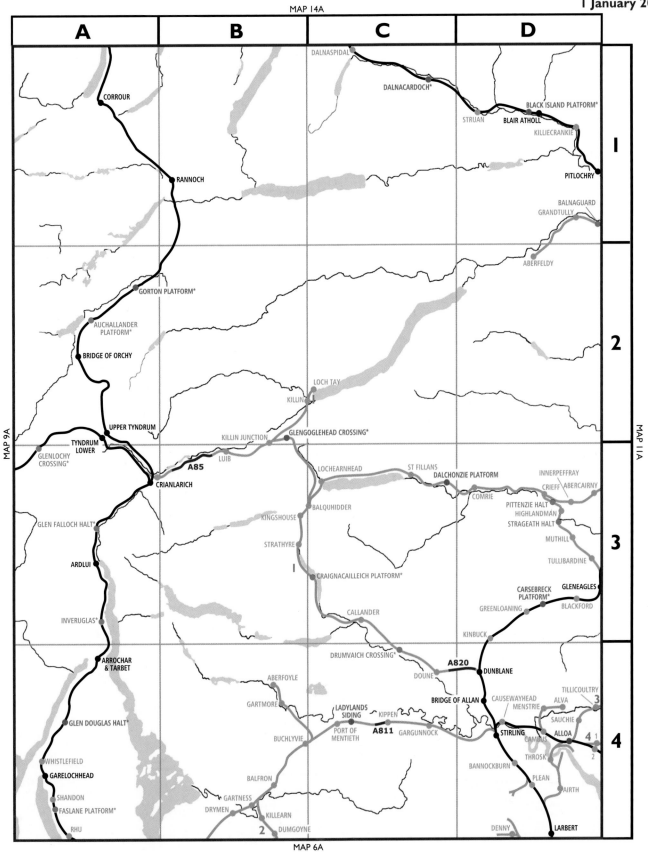

MAP 14A

	A	B	C	D	

MAP 9A

MAP 11A

CORROUR

DALNASPIDAL

DALNACARDOCH*

BLACK ISLAND PLATFORM*

STRUAN

BLAIR ATHOLL

KILLIECRANKIE

RANNOCH

PITLOCHRY

BALNAGUARD

GRANDTULLY

ABERFELDY

GORTON PLATFORM*

AUCHALLANDER
PLATFORM*

LOCH TAY

BRIDGE OF ORCHY

KILLIN

UPPER TYNDRUM

KILLIN JUNCTION

GLENGOGLEHEAD CROSSING*

TYNDRUM
LOWER

LUIB

A85

GLENLOCHY
CROSSING*

CRIANLARICH

LOCHEARNHEAD

ST FILLANS

DALCHONZIE PLATFORM

INNERPEFFRAY

CRIEFF ABERCAIRNY

COMRIE

PITTENZIE HALT
HIGHLANDMAN
STRAGEATH HALT

GLEN FALLOCH HALT*

KINGSHOUSE

BALQUHIDDER

MUTHILL

STRATHYRE

TULLIBARDINE

ARDLUI

CRAIGNACAILLEICH PLATFORM*

CARSEBRECK
PLATFORM*

GLENEAGLES

INVERUGLAS*

CALLANDER

GREENLOANING

BLACKFORD

KINBUCK

ARROCHAR
& TARBET

DRUMVAICH CROSSING*

A820

DOUNE

DUNBLANE

TILLICOULTRY

ABERFOYLE

BRIDGE OF ALLAN

CAUSEWAYHEAD

ALVA
MENSTRIE

3

GARTMORE

LADYLANDS
SIDING

KIPPEN

SAUCHIE

GLEN DOUGLAS HALT*

PORT OF
MENTIETH

A811

GARGUNNOCK

STIRLING

ALLOA

CAMBUS

4 1

BUCHLYVIE

THROSK

2

WHISTLEFIELD

BANNOCKBURN

GARELOCHHEAD

BALFRON

PLEAN

SHANDON

GARTNESS

FAIRTH

FASLANE PLATFORM*

DRYMEN

KILLEARN

DENNY

LARBERT

RHU

2 DUMGOYNE

MAP 6A

STATIONS
1. CLACKMANNAN ROAD
2. CLACKMANNAN & KENNET

RANNOCH
Raineach

15 September 2015

Class 156 Unit No.156447 departing south from
Corrour Station on 15 September 2015.

LEGEND FOR MAP 10A
1 Part of Rob Roy Way
2 Part of the West Highland Way
3 Part of the Devon Way
4 Part of the West Fife Cycleway

MAP 11
1920

MAP 15

A	B	C	D

MAP 10

MAP 12

1

Spital of Glenshee

R. Sth Esk

EDZELL

MARYI

STRACATHRO

CRA

CRANKIE

Ben Vrackie

R. Ardle

COACH ROAD

Kirkmichael

Glenisla

CARESTON

DUBTON

KINN

PITLOCHRY

R. Isla

TANNADICE

BRECHIN

BRIDGE OF DUN

JUSTINHAUGH

Kinnaird Cas.

FARNELL ROAD

BALLINLUIG

Br. of Cally

KIRRIEMUIR

GLASTERLAW

CAL.

GUAY

KIRRIEMUIR JUNC.

GLAMIS

FORFAR

FRIOCKHEIM

NTH.

LEYSMILL

LETH.

2

HIGHLAND

DALGUISE

ALYTH

EASSIE

Castle

KINGSMUIR

COLLISTON

CARMYLLIE

ST.

COACH ROAD

BLAIRGOWRIE

JORDANSTONE

MEIGLE

CALEDONIAN

KIRKBUDDO

DENHEAD

CARMYLLIE CAL. N.B.JT.

ELLIOT STA.

DUNKELD

R. Tay

ROSEMOUNT

ALYTH JUNC.

NEWTYLE

HILLS

CUTHLIE ARBIRLOT ELLIOT

MURTHLY

R. Isla

ARDLER

AUCHTERHOUSE

MONIKIE

Panmure Ho.

CAL.

BANKFOOT

CARGILL

COUPAR ANGUS

DRONLEY

ROSEMILL GOODS

KINGENNIE

DUNDEE & ARBROATH

EAST HAVEN

STANLEY STA. & JUNC.

BALLATHIE

WOODSIDE & BURRELTON

BALDRAGON

BARNHILL

CARNOUSTIE

T

H

CAL.

STRATHORD

LUNCARTY

LONGFORGAN

INVERGOWRIE

LOCHEE WEST

BALDOVAN

MARYFIELD

DUNDEE

EAST

WEST FERRY

BARRY LINKS

BUDDON

Buddon Ness

RUTHVEN ROAD

ALMOND BANK

INCHTURE VILLAGE

INCHTURE

ERROL

MAGDALEN GREEN

TAY BRIDGE

ESPLANADE

TAYPORT

MONIFIETH

BROUGHTY FERRY

METHVEN

TIBBERMUIR

METHVEN JUNC.

Scone Palace

INCHCOONANS GOODS

CAL.

FIRTH OF TAY

TAY BRIDGE PASS GOS

WEST NEWPORT

WORMIT

EAST NEWPORT

3

BALGOWAN

PERTH

ALMOND VALLEY JN.

GLEN CARSE

KILMANY

ST. FORT

LEUCHARS JUNC. STA.

OLD STA.

St. Andrews Bay

ST. ANDREWS

FORGANDENNY

N.B. GOODS

PRINCES STR.

GENERAL STA.

HARBOUR

HILTON JUNC.

KINFAUNS

NEWBURGH

LINDORES

Lindores L.

LUTHRIE

DAIRSIE

GUARD BRIDGE

Earn

FORTEVIOT

BRIDGE OF EARN

ABERNETHY

GLENBURNIE JUNC.

CUPAR

MT. MELVILLE

STRAVITHIE

DUNNING

N.B.

COLLESSIE

BRITISH

SPRINGFIELD

BOARHILLS

KINGSBARNS

AUCHTERARDER

GLENFARG

AUCHTER-MUCHTY

LADYBANK

LARGOWARD GOODS

LOCHTY GOODS

N.B.

CRAIL

GLENEAGLES

STRATHMIGLO

KINGSKETTLE

FORD

MAWCARSE

GATESIDE

FALKLAND ROAD

MONTRAVE GOODS

KILCONQUHAR

COLINSBURGH

ANSTRUTHER

MILNATHORT

MARKINCH

KENNOWAY GOODS

LARGO

ELIE

PITTENWEEM

ST. MONANS

4

KINROSS

KINROSS

Loch Leven

LESLIE

AUCHMUTY MILLS

CAMERON BRI.

LUNDIN LINKS

LEVEN

LUNDIN LINKS

Elie Ness

CROOK OF DEVON

BALADO

LOCH LEVEN

R. Leven

METHIL

RUMBLING BRIDGE

THORNTON

GLENCRAIG COL.

CARDENDEN

BUCKHAVEN

DOLLAR

R. Devon

N.B.

BLAIRADAM

KINGLASSIE COL.

WEST WEMYSS

Fidra

Craigleith

Bass R.

AN

BLACKMANNAN

LETHANS NO. 1 COL

STEELEND GOODS

KELTY

LADY HELEN

WEMYSS CASTLE

NORTH BERWICK

FOREST MILL

LETHANS No. 2

OAKLEY COL.

BLAIRENBATHIE

LOCH GELLY COL.

DYSART

BOGSIDE

EASTGRANGE

BALMULE COL.

NEW STA.

OLD STA.

SINCLAIRTOWN

N.B.

BLACKMANNAN

OAKLEY

WHITE...

COWDENBEATH

KIRKCALDY

KILBAGIE

UPPER

INVERTIEL JUNC.

KINCARDINE

DUNFERMLINE

HALBEATH

CROSSGATES

N.B.

KINGHORN

GULLANE

DIRLETON

CULROSS

TOWNHILL JN.

TORRYBURN

CHARLESTOWN

INVERKEITHING

BURNTISLAND

PETTYCUR

EAST FORTUNE

GRANGEMOUTH

BO'NESS

BRIDGENESS

NORTH

HARBOUR

ABERDOUR

Inchcolm

Inchkeith

OF

FORTH

MAP 7

Pittenweem Station viewed on 14 February 1965. *Neal Caplan/Online Transport Archive*

Dundee Esplanade Station viewed on 4 September 1964.
Neal Caplan/Online Transport Archive

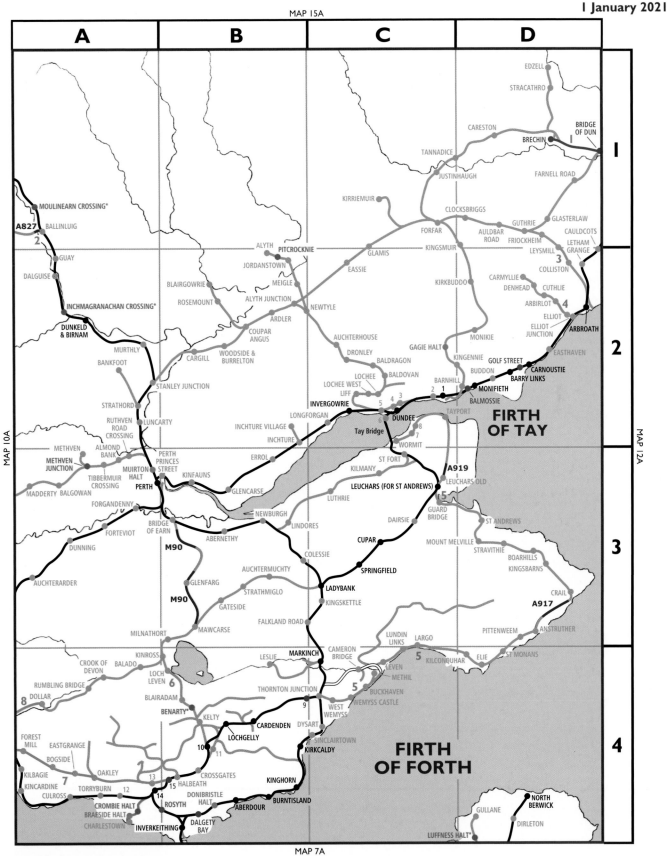

MAP 15A

A	B	C	D

MAP 10A

MAP 7A

MAP 12A

EDZELL
STRACATHRO
BRIDGE OF DUN
BRECHIN
CARESTON
TANNADICE
JUSTINHAUGH
FARNELL ROAD
CLOCKSBRIGGS
KIRRIEMUIR
GUTHRIE GLASTERLAW
FORFAR
AULDBAR ROAD CAULDCOTS
KINGSMUIR FRIOCKHEIM LETHAM GRANGE
GLAMIS LEYSMILL
PITCROCKNIE COLLISTON
ALYTH EASSIE CARMYLLIE
JORDANSTOWN DENHEAD CUTHLIE
MEIGLE KIRKBUDDO ARBIRLOT
BLAIRGOWRIE ELLIOT
ROSEMOUNT ALYTH JUNCTION ELLIOT JUNCTION ARBROATH
NEWTYLE MONIKIE
ARDLER EASTHAVEN
COUPAR ANGUS AUCHTERHOUSE GOLF STREET
WOODSIDE & BURRELTON DRONLEY KINGENNIE CARNOUSTIE
CARGILL BALDRAGON BUDDON BARRY LINKS
BANKFOOT BALDOVAN BARNHILL MONIFIETH
STANLEY JUNCTION LOCHEE BALMOSSIE
MURTHLY LOCHEE WEST 2 1
STRATHORD LIFF 5 4 3
LUNCARTY INVERGOWRIE DUNDEE
RUTHVEN ROAD CROSSING LONGFORGAN 6 TAYPORT
ALMOND BANK INCHTURE VILLAGE Tay Bridge 8
METHVEN INCHTURE WORMIT 7
METHVEN JUNCTION PERTH PRINCES STREET ERROL ST FORT
MUIRTON HALT KINFAUNS KILMANY A919
TIBBERMUIR CROSSING PERTH GLENCARSE LEUCHARS (FOR ST ANDREWS) LEUCHARS OLD
MADDERTY BALGOWAN LUTHRIE GUARD BRIDGE 5
FORGANDENNY NEWBURGH DAIRSIE ST ANDREWS
FORTEVIOT BRIDGE OF EARN LINDORES MOUNT MELVILLE STRAVITHIE
DUNNING ABERNETHY COLESSIE CUPAR BOARHILLS
M90 AUCHTERMUCHTY SPRINGFIELD KINGSBARNS
AUCHTERARDER GLENFARG LADYBANK CRAIL
M90 STRATHMIGLO KINGSKETTLE A917
GATESIDE FALKLAND ROAD PITTENWEEM ANSTRUTHER
MILNATHORT MAWCARSE LUNDIN LINKS
KINROSS LESLIE LARGO ELIE ST MONANS
CROOK OF DEVON BALADO MARKINCH KILCONQUHAR 5
RUMBLING BRIDGE LOCH LEVEN 6 CAMERON BRIDGE
DOLLAR BLAIRADAM LEVEN
8 BENARTY METHIL
FOREST MILL KELTY THORNTON JUNCTION BUCKHAVEN
EASTGRANGE 9 WEST WEMYSS WEMYSS CASTLE
BOGSIDE CARDENDEN WEST WEMYSS 5
KILBAGIE LOCHGELLY DYSART
KINCARDINE OAKLEY 10 SINCLAIRTOWN FIRTH OF FORTH
CULROSS 7 CROSSGATES 11 KIRKCALDY
TORRYBURN 12 HALBEATH KINGHORN
13 15 DONIBRISTLE HALT
CROMBIE HALT 14 ROSYTH BURNTISLAND
BRAESIDE HALT ABERDOUR
CHARLESTOWN INVERKEITHING DALGETY BAY
NORTH BERWICK
GULLANE
DIRLETON
LUFFNESS HALT

FIRTH OF TAY
FIRTH OF FORTH

A827
BALLINLUIG
2
GUAY
DALGUISE
MOULINEARN CROSSING*
INCHMAGRANACHAN CROSSING*
DUNKELD & BIRNAM

Perth
Peairt
ScotRail

18 September 2015

MAP 12
1920

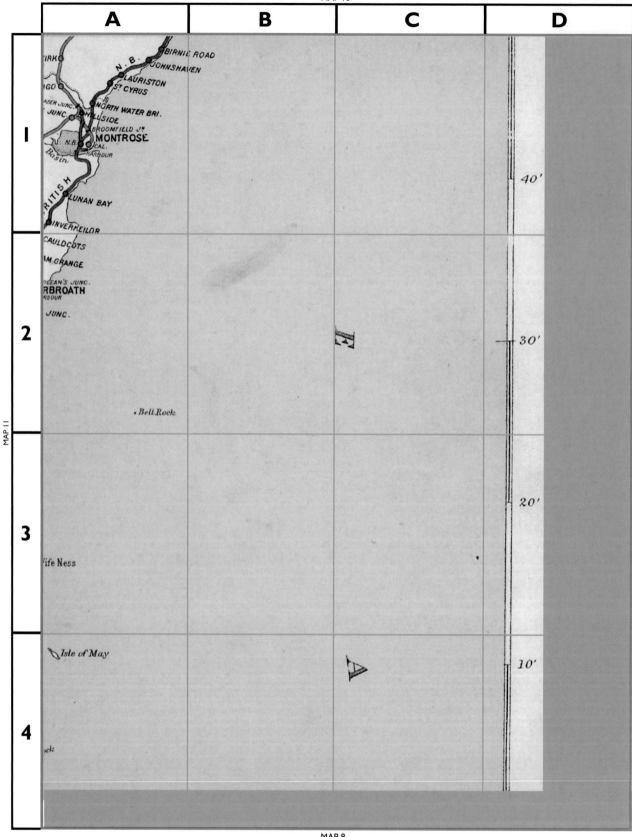

MAP 16

	A	B	C	D
1				
2				
3				
4				

MAP 11

MAP 8

BIRNIE ROAD
N. B. JOHNSHAVEN
LAURISTON
ST CYRUS
NORTH WATER BRI.
HILLSIDE
BROOMFIELD J^N
MONTROSE
CAL.
N.B.
HARBOUR
Basin
BRITISH
LUNAN BAY
INVERKEILOR
CAULDCOTS
AM GRANGE
GEAN'S JUNC.
RBROATH
JUNC.
Bell Rock
Fife Ness
Isle of May

40'
30'
20'
10'

Lunan Bay Station viewed in July 1950.
John Alsop Collection

Looking south at **Inverkeilor Station** in July 1950. *John Alsop Collection*

Montrose MPD viewed on 23 June 1957.
Allan Sommerfield Collection cty Engine Shed Society

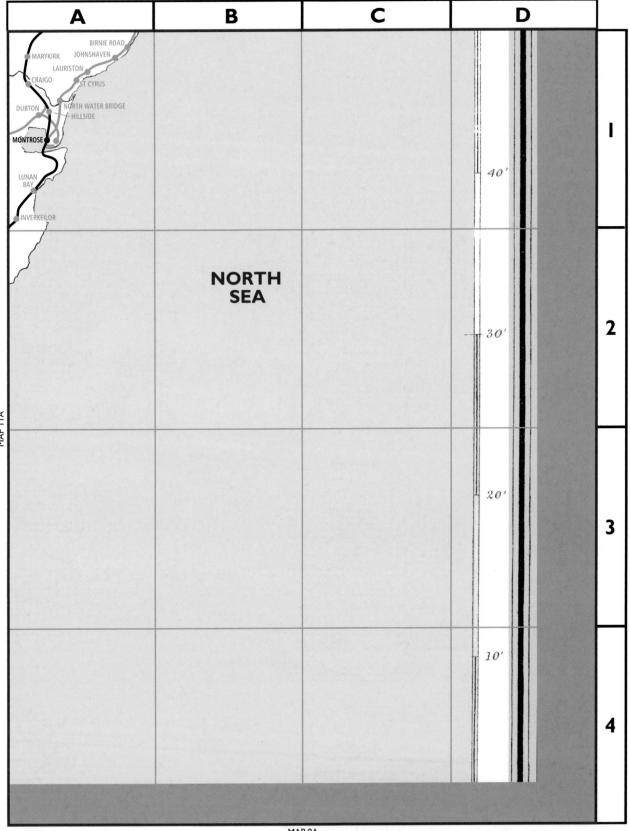

	A	B	C	D

MAP 11A

NORTH SEA

40'

30'

20'

10'

1

2

3

4

MAP 8A

18 September 2015

Looking south at **Montrose Station** on 18 September 2015.

MAP 13
1920

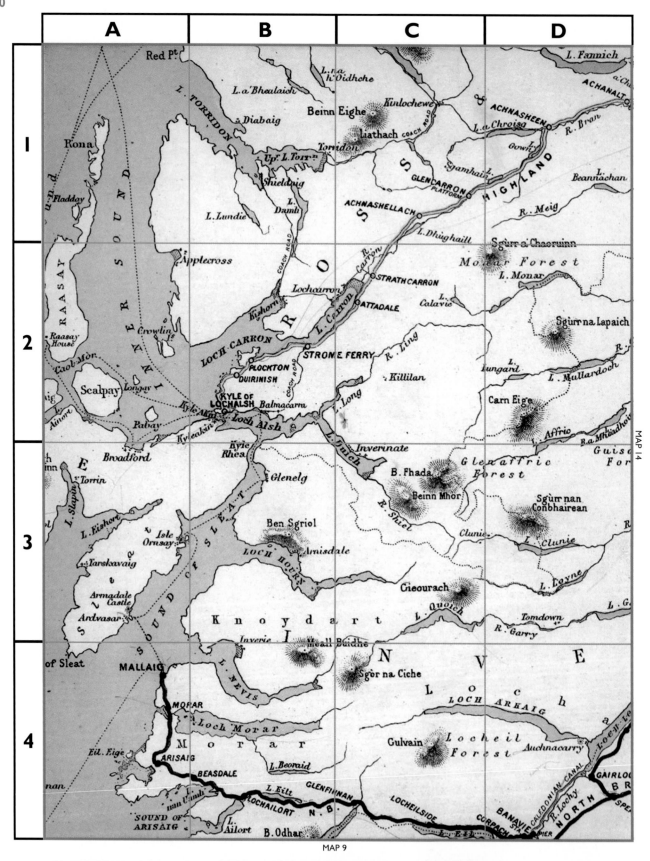

	A	B	C	D

1

2

3

4

MAP 14

MAP 9

Ex-LM&SR Class 5 4-6-0 No.44992 at **Kyle of Lochalsh MPD** on 11 September 1953.
Allan Sommerfield Collection cty The Engine Shed Society

The well-appointed **Gairlochy station** viewed in July 1914.
John Alsop Collection

Looking west along **Glencarron Platform** sometime after it had closed. *By Nigel Thompson CC BY-SA 2.0,https://commons.wikimedia.org/w/index php?curid=51354032*

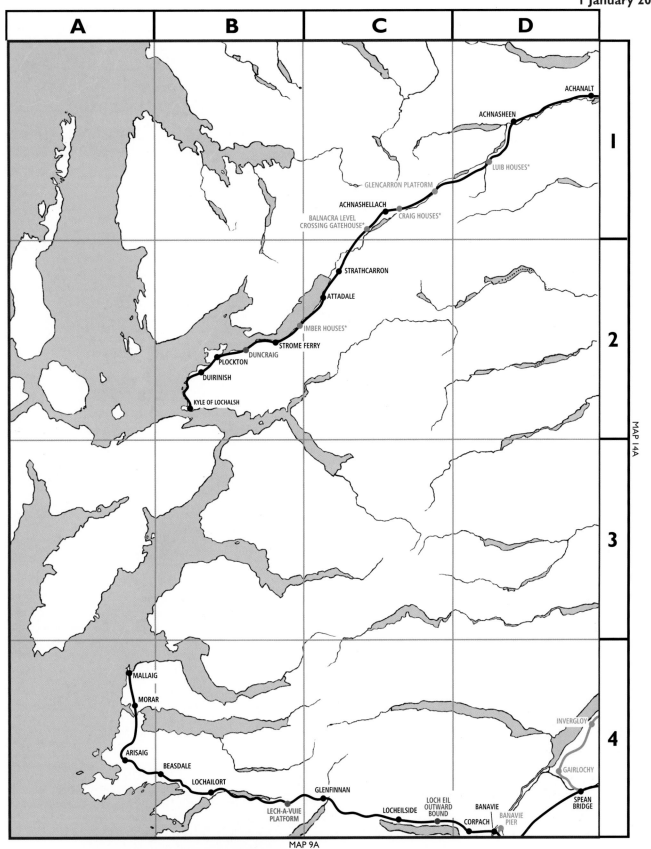

	A	B	C	D	

Map labels (grid):

D1: ACHANALT
C1/D1: ACHNASHEEN
D1: LUIB HOUSES*
C1: GLENCARRON PLATFORM
C1: ACHNASHELLACH
C1: CRAIG HOUSES*
B1/C1: BALNACRA LEVEL CROSSING GATEHOUSE*
C2: STRATHCARRON
C2: ATTADALE
C2: IMBER HOUSES*
B2: STROME FERRY
B2: DUNCRAIG
B2: PLOCKTON
B2: DUIRINISH
B2: KYLE OF LOCHALSH
A4: MALLAIG
A4: MORAR
A4: ARISAIG
B4: BEASDALE
B4: LOCHAILORT
B4: LECH-A-VUIE PLATFORM
B4: GLENFINNAN
C4: LOCHEILSIDE
C4: LOCH EIL OUTWARD BOUND
D4: BANAVIE
D4: BANAVIE PIER
D4: CORPACH
D4: INVERGLOY
D4: GAIRLOCHY
D4: SPEAN BRIDGE

MAP 14A

MAP 9A

14 September 2015

Looking west towards the buffer stops at **Kyle of Lochalsh Station** on 17 September 2015.

Looking east at **Attadale Station** on 17 September 2015.

MAP 14
1920

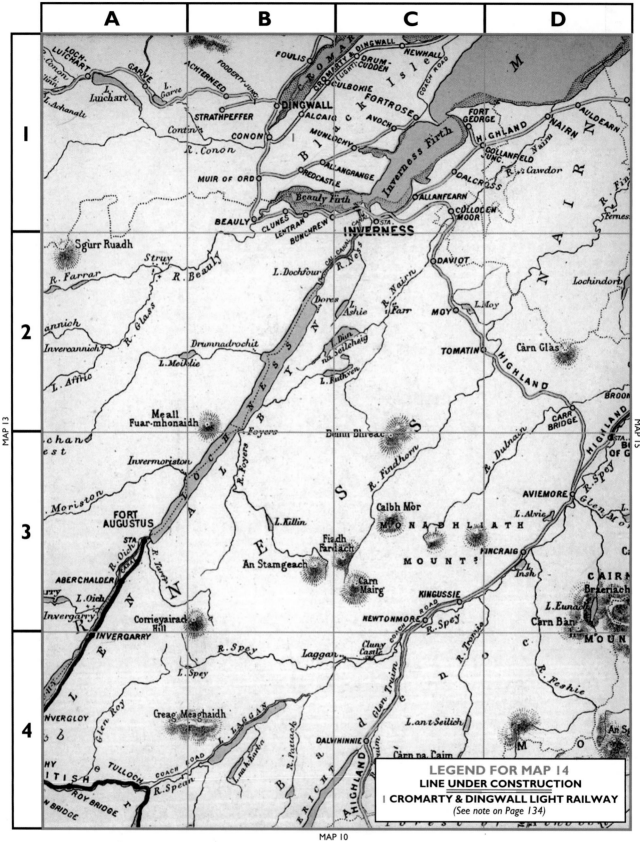

MAP 17

MAP 13

MAP 15

MAP 10

LEGEND FOR MAP 14
LINE UNDER CONSTRUCTION
I **CROMARTY & DINGWALL LIGHT RAILWAY**
(See note on Page 134)

Ex-CR Class 3P 4-4-0 No.54463 on the turntable at the semi-roundhouse **Inverness MPD** on 17 August 1960.   *Ken Fairey*

Looking south at **Boat of Garten Station**, complete with chicken, on 6 September 1958.   *Neal Caplan/Online Transport Archive*

Ex-CR Class 3P 4-4-0 No.54487 standing outside **Dingwall MPD** on 19 August 1960.   *Ken Fairey*

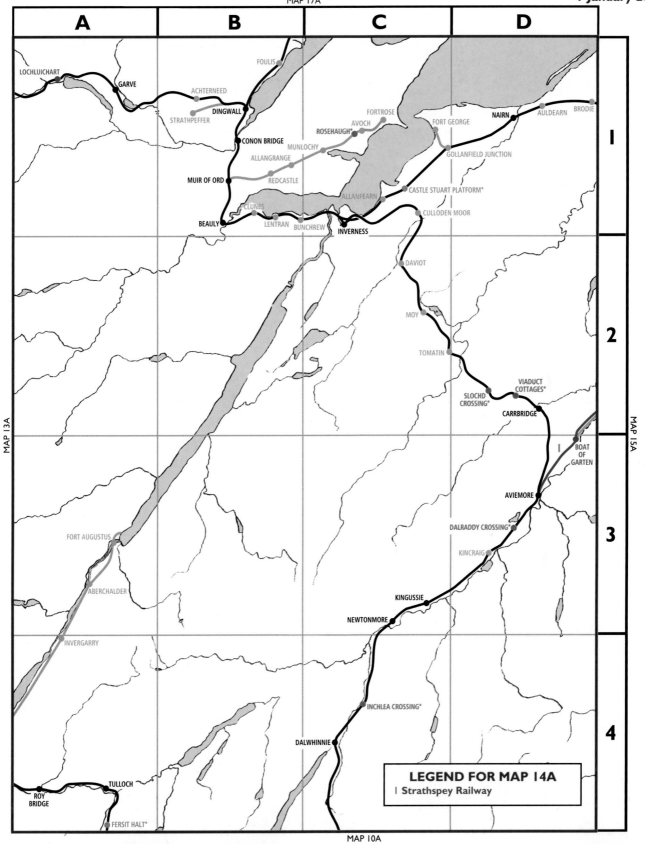

MAP 17A

| A | B | C | D |

MAP 13A

MAP 15A

LOCHLUICHART
GARVE
FOULIS
ACHTERNEED
DINGWALL
STRATHPEFFER
FORTROSE
AVOCH
ROSEHAUGH*
FORT GEORGE
NAIRN
AULDEARN
BRODIE
CONON BRIDGE
MUNLOCHY
GOLLANFIELD JUNCTION
ALLANGRANGE
MUIR OF ORD
REDCASTLE
ALLANFEARN
CASTLE STUART PLATFORM*
CLUNES
CULLODEN MOOR
BEAULY
LENTRAN
BUNCHREW
INVERNESS
DAVIOT
MOY
TOMATIN
VIADUCT COTTAGES*
SLOCHD CROSSING*
CARRBRIDGE
BOAT OF GARTEN
AVIEMORE
DALRADDY CROSSING*
FORT AUGUSTUS
KINCRAIG
ABERCHALDER
KINGUSSIE
INVERGARRY
NEWTONMORE
INCHLEA CROSSING*
DALWHINNIE
TULLOCH
ROY BRIDGE
FERSIT HALT*

LEGEND FOR MAP 14A
1 Strathspey Railway

MAP 10A

15 September 2015

Looking south at **Aviemore Station** on 15 September 2015.

Beauly Station viewed on 17 September 2015. At just 49.4ft long the platform is currently the shortest in Britain.

MAP 15
1920

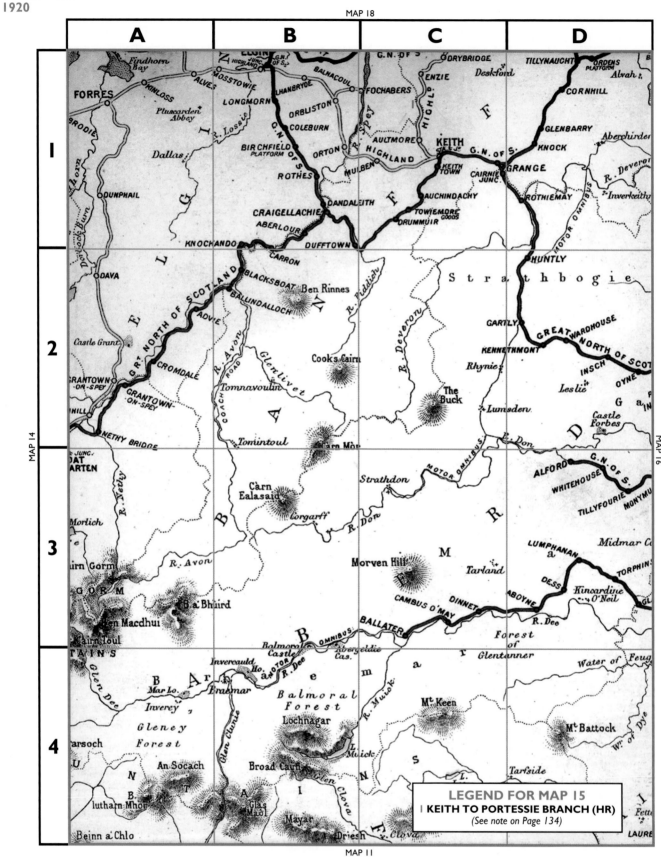

MAP 18

	A	B	C	D

MAP 14

MAP 16

MAP 11

LEGEND FOR MAP 15
I **KEITH TO PORTESSIE BRANCH (HR)**
(See note on Page 134)

The remains of **Kennethmont Station**, looking north on 17 September 2015. It was closed by BR on 6 May 1968.

Ballater station viewed in BR days.
J Joyce/Online Transport Archive

BR:
Ballater to Dinnet (Date Unknown)

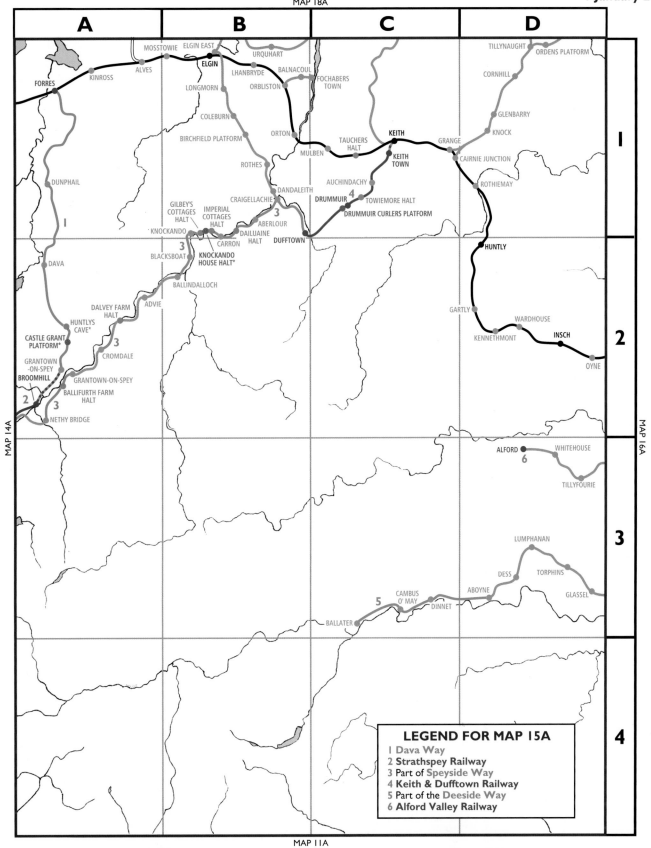

MAP 18A

	A	B	C	D	

1

MOSSTOWIE   ELGIN EAST
ELGIN
FORRES   KINROSS   ALVES   URQUHART
LHANBRYDE   BALNACOUL
LONGMORN   ORBLISTON   FOCHABERS TOWN
TILLYNAUGHT   ORDENS PLATFORM
CORNHILL
GLENBARRY   KNOCK
COLEBURN
BIRCHFIELD PLATFORM   ORTON   TAUCHERS HALT   **KEITH**   GRANGE   CAIRNIE JUNCTION
DUNPHAIL   MULBEN   **KEITH TOWN**
ROTHES   ROTHIEMAY
1
DAVA   DANDALEITH   AUCHINDACHY
GILBEY'S COTTAGES HALT   IMPERIAL COTTAGES HALT   CRAIGELLACHIE   **DRUMMUIR**   TOWIEMORE HALT
KNOCKANDO   ABERLOUR   **3**   **4**
DRUMMUIR CURLERS PLATFORM

2

CARRON   DAILUAINE HALT   **DUFFTOWN**
BLACKSBOAT   **KNOCKANDO HOUSE HALT***
HUNTLY
BALLINDALLOCH
DALVEY FARM HALT   ADVIE
HUNTLYS CAVE*
CASTLE GRANT PLATFORM*   CROMDALE   **3**
GARTLY   WARDHOUSE
KENNETHMONT   **INSCH**
GRANTOWN -ON-SPEY
BROOMHILL   GRANTOWN-ON-SPEY
2   BALLIFURTH FARM HALT   OYNE
3
NETHY BRIDGE

3

ALFORD   WHITEHOUSE
6
TILLYFOURIE

LUMPHANAN
DESS   TORPHINS
ABOYNE   GLASSEL
CAMBUS O' MAY
5   DINNET
BALLATER

MAP 14A

MAP 16A

4

LEGEND FOR MAP 15A
1 **Dava Way**
2 **Strathspey Railway**
3 Part of **Speyside Way**
4 **Keith & Dufftown Railway**
5 Part of the **Deeside Way**
6 **Alford Valley Railway**

MAP 11A

17 September 2015

Huntly Station viewed on 17 September 2015.

Looking west at **Keith Station** on 17 September 2015.

MAP 16
1920

MAP 19

	A	B	C	D

MAP 15

1

RIDGE
KING EDWARD
PLAIDY
Cuminestown
TURRIFF
G.N. OF S.
Hatton Castle
AUCHTERLESS
New Pitsligo
STRICHEN
BRUCKLAY
MAUD
New Deer
AUCHNAGATT
Buchan
N.
MINTLAW
Pitfour Ho.
LONGSIDE
LONMAY
MORMOND
L. of Strathbeg
St Fergus
NEWSEAT
INVERUGIE
BODDAM
LONGHAVEN
Rattray Head
PETERHEAD
STA.
HARBOUR
Buchan Ness

—30'

2

FYVIE
ROTHIE NORMAN
WARTLE
E
F o r m a r t i n e
LAND
FINGASK PLATF?M
PITCAPLE
MERAMSAY
INVERURIE
OLDMELDRUM
LETHENTY
PORT ELPHINSTONE GOODS
R. Ythan
Haddo Ho.
Tarves
ARNAGE
ESSLEMONT
B u c h a n
ELLON
R. Ythan
LOGIERIEVE
UDNY
NEW MACHAR
N. OF S.
HATTON
PITLURG
AUCHMACOY
Collieston
Newburgh
BULLERS O' BUCHAN PLATFORM
CRUDEN BAY
H

—20'

3

R. Don
KEMNAY
KINTORE
KINALDIE
PITMEDDEN
STONEYWOOD
BANKHEAD
BUCKSBURN
Cluny Cas.
Waterton
Dunecht Ho.
Skene
PARKHILL
DYCE
PERSLEY
WOODSIDE
DON
KITTYBREWSTER
HUTCHEON STR.
SCHOOLHILL
JOINT PASS. STA.
FERRYHILL JT.
HOLBURN STR.
ABERDEEN
WATERLOO GOODS
E. Aberdeen
Bay
Echt MOTOR OMNIBUS
RUTHRIE STON
PITFODELS
WEST CUTS
CULTS
BIELDSIDE
MURTLE
MILLTIMBER
CULTER
Castle
GREAT NORTH OF SCOTLAND
DRUM
PARK
CRATHES
BANCHORY
R. Dee
COVE BAY
PORTLETHEN
NEWTONHILL
CALEDONIAN
KINCARDINE

—10'

4

Strachan
Fetteresso Castle
STONEHAVEN
Dunnottar Cas.
CARMONT GOODS
DRUMLITHIE
Catterline
FORDOUN
Arbuthnott
rxairn
Bervie Wr.
NCEKIRK
BERVIE
GOURDON
MUCHALLS

—57°

—50

MAP 12

Ex-GNofSR Class D41 4-4-0 No. 62251 at **Peterhead MPD** on 2 August 1951. *Allan Sommerfield Collection cty Engine Shed Society*

Kittybrewster Station viewed on 3 September 1964. *Neal Caplan/Online Transport Archive*

Ex-NBR Class J36 0-6-0 No. 65338 in the yard at **Kittybrewster MPD**. *Ken Fairey*

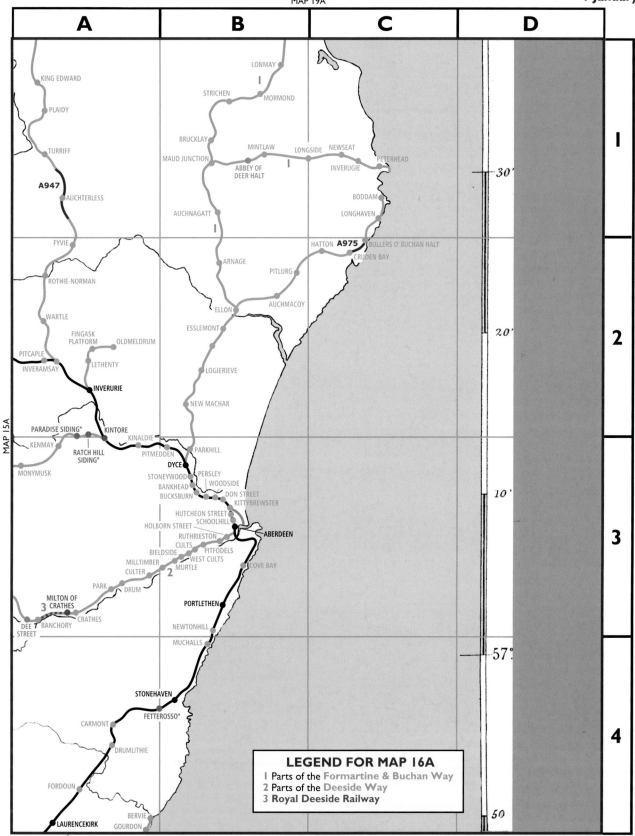

MAP 19A

	A	B	C	D

1

KING EDWARD

PLAIDY

TURRIFF

A947

AUCHTERLESS

LONMAY

STRICHEN

MORMOND

BRUCKLAY

MINTLAW

MAUD JUNCTION

ABBEY OF
DEER HALT

LONGSIDE

NEWSEAT

PETERHEAD

INVERUGIE

BODDAM

LONGHAVEN

2

FYVIE

ROTHIE-NORMAN

WARTLE

FINGASK
PLATFORM

OLDMELDRUM

PITCAPLE

INVERAMSAY

LETHENTY

INVERURIE

AUCHNAGATT

ARNAGE

PITLURG

ELLON

AUCHMACOY

ESSLEMONT

LOGIERIEVE

NEW MACHAR

HATTON **A975**

BULLERS O' BUCHAN HALT

CRUDEN BAY

3

MAP 15A

PARADISE SIDING*

KINTORE

KENMAY

RATCH HILL
SIDING*

KINALDIE

PITMEDDEN

PARKHILL

MONYMUSK

DYCE

PERSLEY

STONEYWOOD

WOODSIDE

BANKHEAD

DON STREET

BUCKSBURN

KITTYBREWSTER

HUTCHEON STREET

SCHOOLHILL

HOLBORN STREET

RUTHRIESTON

CULTS

ABERDEEN

BIELDSIDE

PITFODELS

MILLTIMBER

WEST CULTS

CULTER

2 MURTLE

PARK

DRUM

COVE BAY

MILTON OF
3 CRATHES

4

DEE **7** CRATHES
STREET BANCHORY

PORTLETHEN

NEWTONHILL

MUCHALLS

STONEHAVEN

CARMONT

FETTEROSSO*

DRUMLITHIE

FORDOUN

BERVIE

LAURENCEKIRK

GOURDON

30'

20'

10'

57°

50

LEGEND FOR MAP 16A
1 Parts of the Formartine & Buchan Way
2 Parts of the Deeside Way
3 Royal Deeside Railway

MAP 12A

18 September 2015

Class 170 Unit No. 170434 on Platform 6S at **Aberdeen Station** on 17 September 2015.

Looking north at **Stonehaven Station** on 18 September 2015.

MAP 17
1920

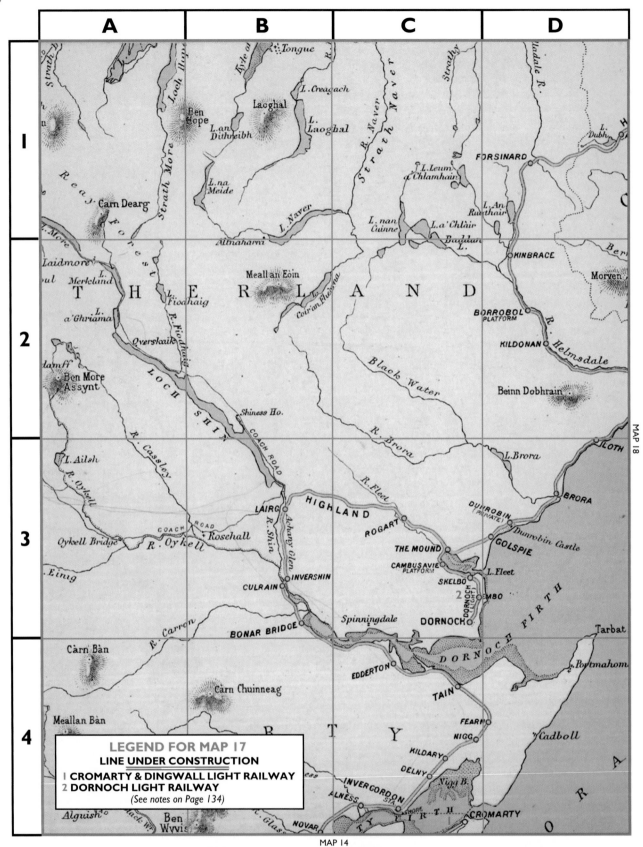

	A	B	C	D

MAP 18

MAP 14

LEGEND FOR MAP 17
LINE UNDER CONSTRUCTION
1 CROMARTY & DINGWALL LIGHT RAILWAY
2 DORNOCH LIGHT RAILWAY
(See notes on Page 134)

Ex-HR Class 0P 0-4-4T No.55051 outside of
Dornoch MPD on 10 September 1953 with the
station in view in the background.   *Allan
Sommerfield Collection cty Engine Shed Society*

Tain Station, looking north west.
Chris Bush Collection cty Engine Shed Society

LM&SR: (Issued by BR)
The Mound to Cambusavie (27 April 1952)

38

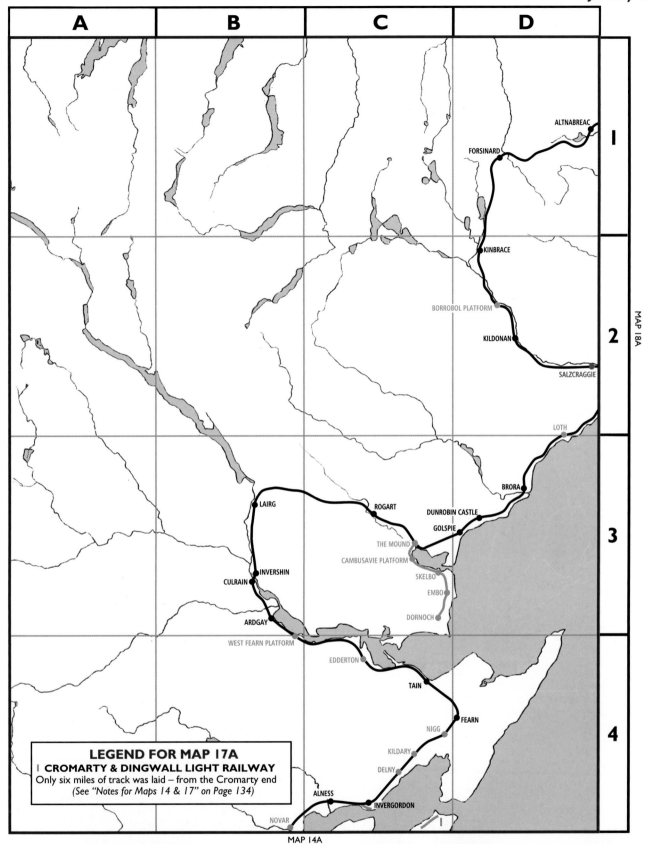

	A	B	C	D	
				ALTNABREAC	**1**
				FORSINARD	
				KINBRACE	**2**
				BORROBOL PLATFORM	
				KILDONAN	
				SALZCRAGGIE	
				LOTH	**3**
				BRORA	
		LAIRG	ROGART	DUNROBIN CASTLE	
				GOLSPIE	
			THE MOUND		
			CAMBUSAVIE PLATFORM	SKELBO	
		INVERSHIN		EMBO	
		CULRAIN		DORNOCH	
		ARDGAY			**4**
	WEST FEARN PLATFORM				
		EDDERTON			
			TAIN		
			NIGG	FEARN	
			KILDARY		
			DELNY		
		ALNESS			
	NOVAR		INVERGORDON		

MAP 18A

LEGEND FOR MAP 17A
1 CROMARTY & DINGWALL LIGHT RAILWAY
Only six miles of track was laid – from the Cromarty end
(See "Notes for Maps 14 & 17" on Page 134)

MAP 14A

16 September 2015

Rogart Station, complete with ginger station cat, viewed on 16 September 2015.

Looking south at **Dunrobin Castle Station** on 16 September 2015 with the former bay platform that housed the duke's private carriage visible in the fore-ground.

MAP 18
1920

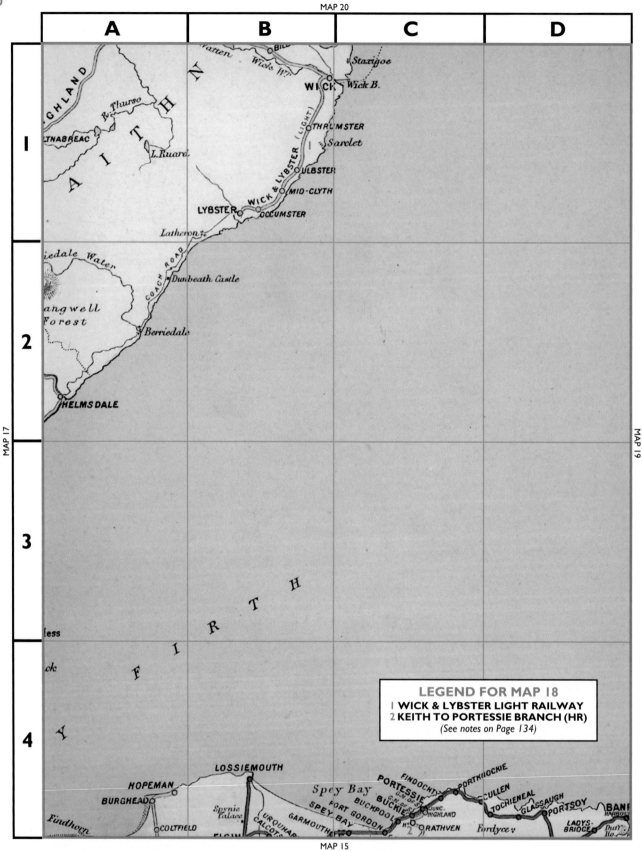

MAP 20

	A	B	C	D

MAP 17

MAP 19

LEGEND FOR MAP 18
1 **WICK & LYBSTER LIGHT RAILWAY**
2 **KEITH TO PORTESSIE BRANCH (HR)**
(See notes on Page 134)

MAP 15

The abandoned former Wick & Lybster Light Railway **Thrumster Station** viewed on 12 June 1961. It is now part of a community garden.
. *Neal Caplan/Online Transport Archive*

Banff MPD, with the station visible beyond, viewed in August 1957.
Allan Sommerfield Collection cty Engine Shed Society

L&NER: (Issued by BR)
Ladysbridge to Banff (2 September 1963)

MAP 18A

1 January 2021

MAP 20A

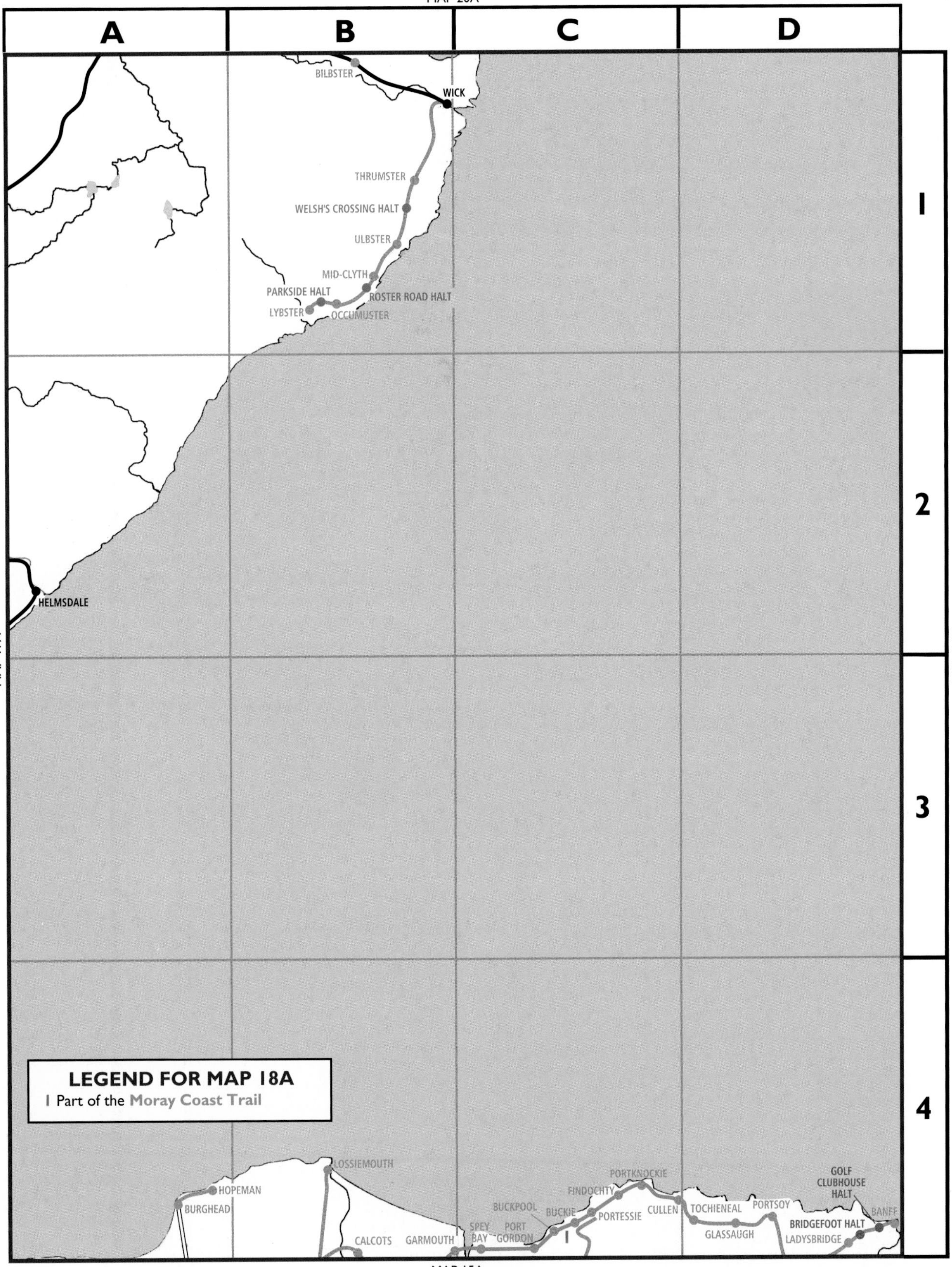

A
B
C
D
1
2
3
4
BILBSTER
WICK
THRUMSTER
WELSH'S CROSSING HALT
ULBSTER
MID-CLYTH
PARKSIDE HALT
ROSTER ROAD HALT
LYBSTER
OCCUMUSTER
HELMSDALE
LEGEND FOR MAP 18A
1 Part of the Moray Coast Trail
LOSSIEMOUTH
HOPEMAN
BURGHEAD
CALCOTS
GARMOUTH
SPEY BAY
PORT GORDON
BUCKPOOL
BUCKIE
FINDOCHTY
PORTKNOCKIE
PORTESSIE
CULLEN
TOCHIENEAL
GLASSAUGH
PORTSOY
GOLF CLUBHOUSE HALT
BRIDGEFOOT HALT
LADYSBRIDGE
BANFF
1

MAP 17A

MAP 19A

MAP 15A

Wick
Inbhir Ùige
ScotRail

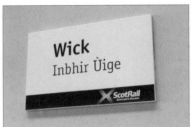

16 September 2015

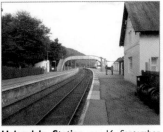

Helmsdale Station on 16 September 2015

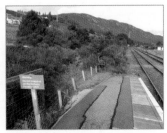

Looking north at **Helmsdale Station** on 16 September 2015 with the site of the former HR two-road engine shed on the left.

MAP 19
1920

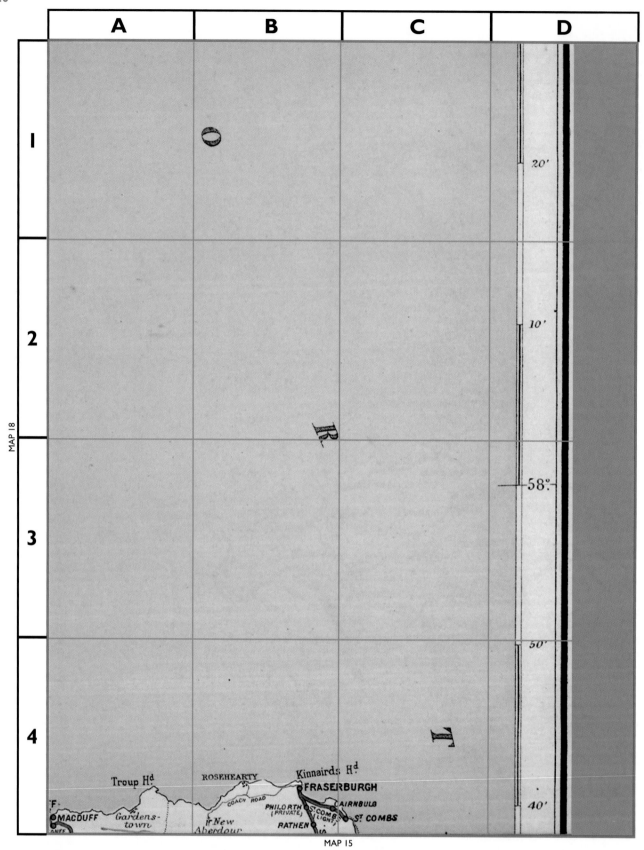

	A	B	C	D
1		O		20'
2				10'
3		R		58°
4			L	50'

MAP 18

Troup H.ᵈ
ROSEHEARTY   Kinnairds H.ᵈ
FRASERBURGH
F
MACDUFF   Gardens-town   COACH ROAD   CAIRNBULG
PHILORTH   ST COMB   ST. COMBS
(PRIVATE)   LIGHT
ir New   RATHEN
Aberdour

40'

MAP 15

Ex-GNofSR Class D40 4-4-0 No.62273 *George Davidson* at **Macduff MPD** on 1 August 1951.
Allan Sommerfield Collection cty Engine Shed Society

Banff Bridge Station viewed in 1961. *By Ben Brooksbank, CC BY-SA 2.0, https://commons.wikimedia. org/w/ index.php? curid =10098069*

Fraserburgh Station viewed on 28 July 1958 with ex-LM&SR Class 2P 4-4-0 No.40650 and BR Class 4 2-6-4T No.80114 visible in the shed yard.
Allan Sommerfield Collection cty Engine Shed Society

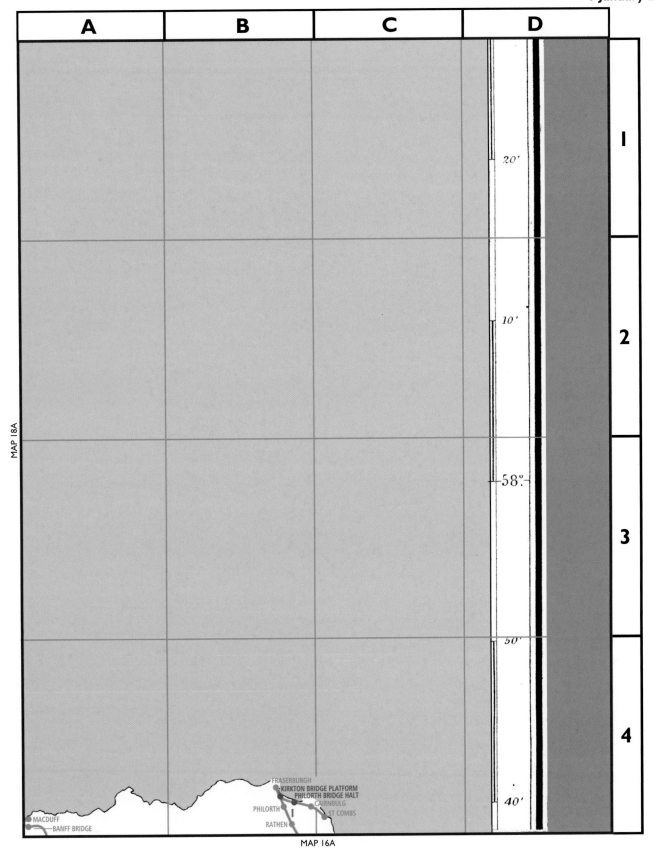

	A	B	C	D	
					1
				20'	
				10'	2
				-58°-	3
				50'	4
				40'	

MAP 18A

MAP 16A

FRASERBURGH
KIRKTON BRIDGE PLATFORM
PHILORTH BRIDGE HALT
CAIRNBULG
PHILORTH
ST COMBS
RATHEN
MACDUFF
BANFF BRIDGE

LEGEND FOR MAP 19A
1 Part of the Formartine & Buchan Way

MAP 20
1920

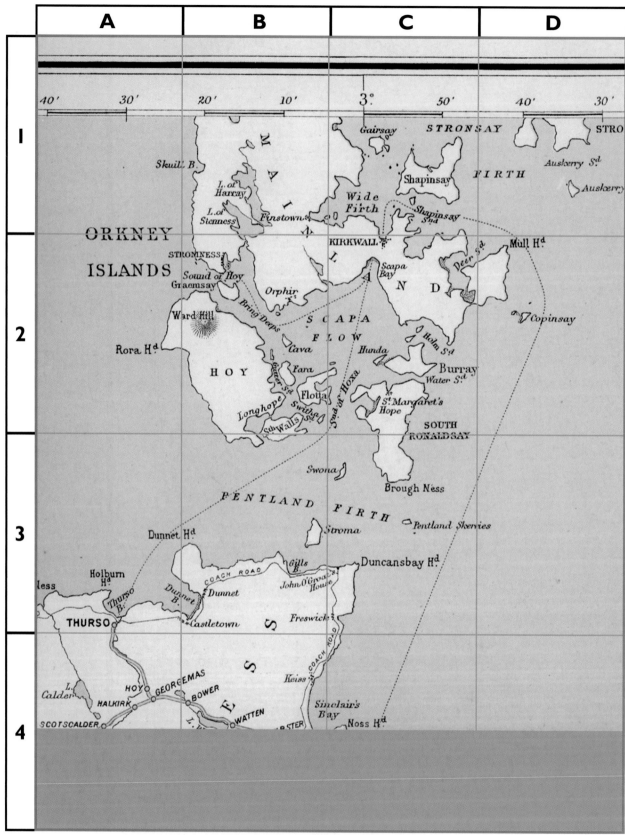

	A	B	C	D

40'   30'   20'   10'   3°   50'   40'   30'

1

Skull B.

MAINLAND

Gairsay   STRONSAY   STRO

L. of Harray

Shapinsay   FIRTH

Auskerry S.ᵈ

L. of Stenness   Finstown

Wide Firth

Shapinsay Snd.

Auskerry

ORKNEY

STROMNESS   KIRKWALL

Scapa Bay

Mull H.ᵈ

ISLANDS   Sound of Hoy   Graemsay   Orphir

MAINLAND

Deer Sᵈ

2

Ward Hill   Bring Deeps

SCAPA FLOW

Holm Sᵈ

Copinsay

Rora H.ᵈ   Cava   Hunda

Burray

HOY   Fara   Water Sᵈ

Flotta   St. Margaret's Hope

Longhope   Switha   Sud.of Hoxa

Sd. Walls   SOUTH RONALDSAY

3

Swona

PENTLAND FIRTH   Brough Ness

Dunnet H.ᵈ   Stroma   Pentland Skerries

Holburn Hᵈ   COACH ROAD   Gills B.   Duncansbay H.ᵈ

Ness   Thurso B.   Dunnet B.   Dunnet   John O'Groats House

THURSO   Castletown   Freswick

4

L. Calder   HOY   GEORGEMAS   BOWER   CAITHNESS   Keiss   COACH ROAD

HALKIRK   WATTEN   Sinclair's Bay

SCOTSCALDER   L. W...   ...STER   Noss H.ᵈ

MAP 18

Looking west at **Georgemas Junction Station** in 1963. The island platform, on the left, was removed in 2012 to allow for the construction of a freight terminal.   *Highland Railway Society Collection*

Bower Station viewed from a passing train on 25 May 1963.   *Highland Railway Society Collection*

Hoy Station viewed from a passing train on 25 May 1963.   *Highland Railway Society Collection*

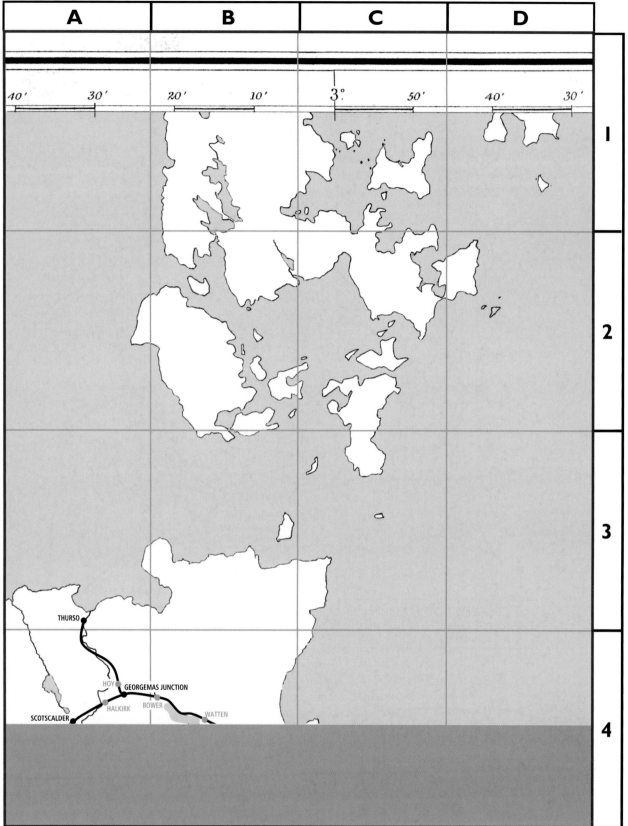

	A	B	C	D	

40'   30'   20'   10'   3°   50'   40'   30'

1

2

3

THURSO

HOY   GEORGEMAS JUNCTION
       BOWER
HALKIRK   WATTEN
SCOTSCALDER

4

MAP 18A

Thurso
Inbhir Theôrsa

16 September 2015

Looking south at **Scotscalder Station** on 16 September 2015.

Class 158 Unit No. 158705 about to depart from **Georgemas Junction Station** on 16 September 2015.

GLASGOW ENLARGEMENT

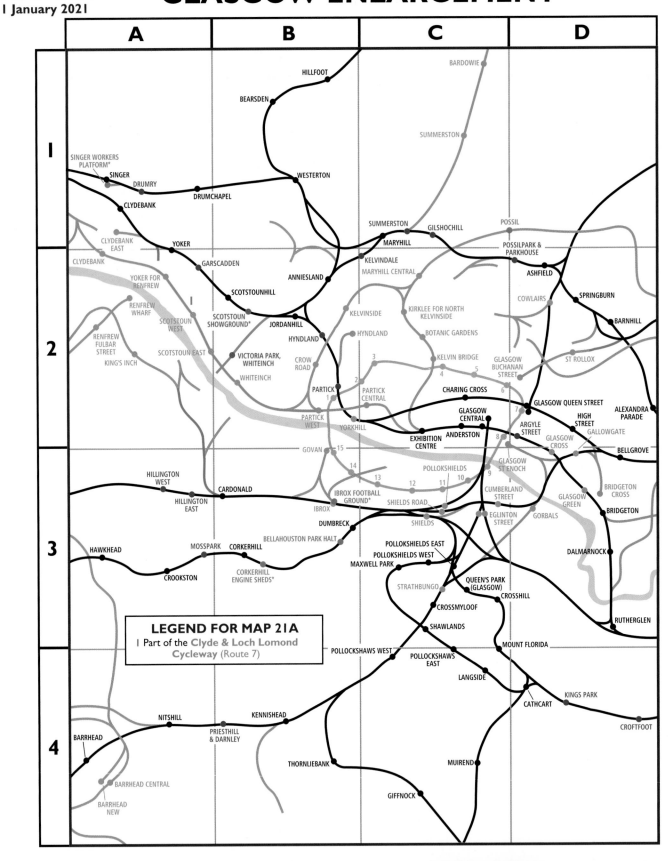

	A	B	C	D

1

BARDOWIE

HILLFOOT

BEARSDEN

SUMMERSTON

SINGER WORKERS PLATFORM*
SINGER
DRUMRY
CLYDEBANK
DRUMCHAPEL
WESTERTON

2

CLYDEBANK EAST
CLYDEBANK
YOKER
YOKER FOR RENFREW
RENFREW WHARF
RENFREW FULBAR STREET
KING'S INCH
SCOTSTOUN WEST
SCOTSTOUN EAST
GARSCADDEN
SCOTSTOUNHILL
SCOTSTOUN SHOWGROUND*
JORDANHILL
HYNDLAND
VICTORIA PARK, WHITEINCH
WHITEINCH
CROW ROAD
ANNIESLAND
SUMMERSTON
GILSHOCHILL
MARYHILL
KELVINDALE
MARYHILL CENTRAL
KELVINSIDE
HYNDLAND
KIRKLEE FOR NORTH KELVINSIDE
BOTANIC GARDENS
KELVIN BRIDGE
POSSIL
POSSILPARK & PARKHOUSE
ASHFIELD
COWLAIRS
SPRINGBURN
BARNHILL
ST ROLLOX
GLASGOW BUCHANAN STREET
PARTICK
PARTICK CENTRAL
PARTICK WEST
YORKHILL
CHARING CROSS
GLASGOW QUEEN STREET
ALEXANDRA PARADE

3

GOVAN 15
14
HILLINGTON WEST
CARDONALD
HILLINGTON EAST
13
IBROX FOOTBALL GROUND*
IBROX
DUMBRECK
BELLAHOUSTON PARK HALT
MOSSPARK
CORKERHILL
CORKERHILL ENGINE SHEDS*
HAWKHEAD
CROOKSTON
POLLOKSHIELDS
12 11 10
SHIELDS ROAD
SHIELDS
POLLOKSHIELDS EAST
POLLOKSHIELDS WEST
MAXWELL PARK
STRATHBUNGO
CROSSMYLOOF
SHAWLANDS
9
GLASGOW ST ENOCH
CUMBERLAND STREET
EGLINTON STREET
GORBALS
QUEEN'S PARK (GLASGOW)
CROSSHILL
GLASGOW CENTRAL
EXHIBITION CENTRE
ANDERSTON
ARGYLE STREET
GLASGOW CROSS
HIGH STREET
GALLOWGATE
BELLGROVE
8
7
GLASGOW GREEN
BRIDGETON CROSS
BRIDGETON
DALMARNOCK
RUTHERGLEN

LEGEND FOR MAP 21A
1 Part of the **Clyde & Loch Lomond Cycleway** (Route 7)

4

BARRHEAD
NITSHILL
PRIESTHILL & DARNLEY
KENNISHEAD
BARRHEAD CENTRAL
BARRHEAD NEW
THORNLIEBANK
POLLOCKSHAWS WEST
POLLOCKSHAWS EAST
LANGSIDE
MOUNT FLORIDA
CATHCART
KINGS PARK
CROFTFOOT
MUIREND
GIFFNOCK

GLASGOW SUBWAY STATIONS

1. PARTICK (MERKLAND STREET **UNTIL 1977**)
2. KELVINHALL (PARTICK CROSS **UNTIL 1977**)
3. HILLHEAD
4. KELVINBRIDGE
5. ST GEORGES CROSS
6. COWCADDENS
7. BUCHANAN STREET
8. ST ENOCH
9. BRIDGE STREET
10. WEST STREET
11. SHIELDS ROAD
12. KINNING PARK
13. CESSNOCK
14. IBROX (COPLAND ROAD **UNTIL 1977**)
15. GOVAN (GOVAN CROSS **UNTIL 1977**)

See Page 135 for a brief description of the Glasgow Subway.

Maxwell Park Station viewed on 18 March 2017.

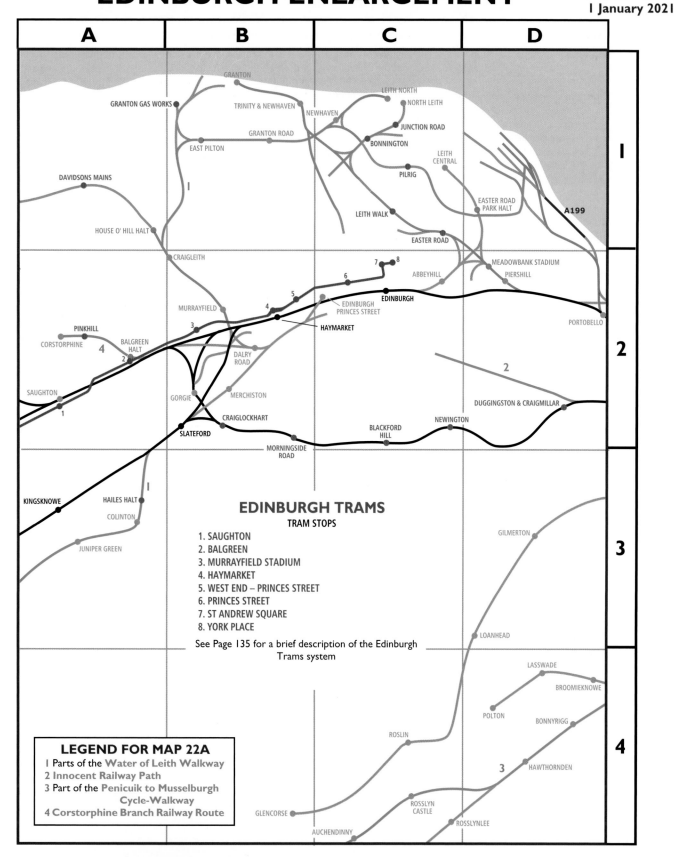

	A	B	C	D
1				
2				
3				
4				

GRANTON

GRANTON GAS WORKS

TRINITY & NEWHAVEN

NEWHAVEN

LEITH NORTH

NORTH LEITH

GRANTON ROAD

JUNCTION ROAD

BONNINGTON

EAST PILTON

PILRIG

LEITH CENTRAL

DAVIDSONS MAINS

LEITH WALK

EASTER ROAD PARK HALT

A199

HOUSE O' HILL HALT

EASTER ROAD

CRAIGLEITH

MEADOWBANK STADIUM

PIERSHILL

ABBEYHILL

7 8

6

EDINBURGH

MURRAYFIELD

5

EDINBURGH PRINCES STREET

PINKHILL

4

HAYMARKET

PORTOBELLO

CORSTORPHINE

3

BALGREEN HALT

4

DALRY ROAD

2

SAUGHTON

GORGIE

MERCHISTON

2

DUGGINGSTON & CRAIGMILLAR

1

CRAIGLOCKHART

SLATEFORD

BLACKFORD HILL

NEWINGTON

MORNINGSIDE ROAD

KINGSKNOWE

HAILES HALT

1

COLINTON

EDINBURGH TRAMS
TRAM STOPS
1. SAUGHTON
2. BALGREEN
3. MURRAYFIELD STADIUM
4. HAYMARKET
5. WEST END – PRINCES STREET
6. PRINCES STREET
7. ST ANDREW SQUARE
8. YORK PLACE

See Page 135 for a brief description of the Edinburgh Trams system

GILMERTON

JUNIPER GREEN

LOANHEAD

LASSWADE

BROOMIEKNOWE

POLTON

BONNYRIGG

ROSLIN

3

HAWTHORNDEN

LEGEND FOR MAP 22A
1 Parts of the **Water of Leith Walkway**
2 **Innocent Railway Path**
3 Part of the **Penicuik to Musselburgh Cycle-Walkway**
4 **Corstorphine Branch Railway Route**

GLENCORSE

AUCHENDINNY

ROSSLYN CASTLE

ROSSLYNLEE

12 May 2017

Class 158 Unit No.158706 passing through **Slateford Station** on 12 May 2017.

An Edinburgh-bound Virgin East Coast HST, with power car No.43274 trailing, at **Haymarket Station** on 12 May 2017.

INDEX OF STATIONS
(AND GOODS STATIONS, BRANCHES AND JUNCTIONS AS MARKED ON THE "THEN" MAPS)

The stations in this index are colour coded in a similar fashion to those on the "Now" maps and the Goods Stations, Branches and Junctions that are shown on the "Then" maps are reproduced in italics.

SOME NOTES ON THE TERMINOLOGY USED

Demolished: Where the station is of conventional construction with buildings and platforms etc., unless otherwise stated this term includes total removal and site clearance. With reference to stopping off points and similar locations, where there were no fixed facilities - perhaps merely utilising portable steps to gain access to a carriage - this refers to the facility being removed and unused.

In agricultural use: The site may be in use as a field or a location for farm buildings etc.

In commercial use: A general term covering uses from storage areas through to industrial and retail parks.

(a): Although not precisely established by mapping the site may be assumed to be within 100 yards of the point specified.

(e): The authors have not found any anecdotal or mapping information to accurately assess the location. This is particularly relevant where stations are connected to sites utilized by the Government or armed forces where, as a matter of policy, the areas are not defined on OS mapping. In these instances a map is not provided in this index.

* Private/untimetabled stations, employees platforms and stopping points.

THE MAPS DO NOT SHARE A COMMON SCALE BUT ARE INCLUDED FOR INFORMATION AND ILLUSTRATIVE PURPOSES.

ABBEYHILL   7 B1/22A C2
Opened 1 May 1869 by the NBR and closed 27 September 1964 by BR it had also been known as *Abbey Hill* and *Edinburgh Abbeyhill*.
Line lifted - One platform extant – Station site unused.
NT27207 74407

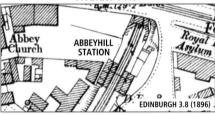
EDINBURGH 3.8 (1896)

ABBEY JUNCTION (CR)   3 B2
Opened 31 August 1870 by the Solway Junction Railway and closed 20 May 1921 by the CR.
Line lifted – Demolished – Station site unused.
NY18004 51586

ABBEY JUNCTION (NBR)   3 B2
Opened 8 August 1870 by the NBR and closed 20 May 1921.
Line lifted – Demolished – Station site unused.
NY17992 51574

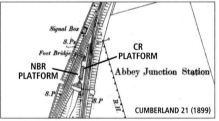
CUMBERLAND 21 (1899)

ABBEY OF DEER HALT*   16A B1
Opened by the L&NER c1930 and closed on an unrecorded date, possibly in the 1940s.
Line lifted - Demolished - The Formartine and Buchan Way passes through the station site. **NJ96640 48072**

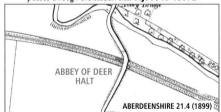
ABERDEENSHIRE 21.4 (1899)

ABBEY TOWN   3 B2
Opened 4 September 1856 by the Carlisle & Silloth Bay Railway as *Abbeyholme*, subsequently renamed by the NBR as *Abbey* and by 1889 as *Abbey Town*. It was closed by BR 7 September 1964.
Line lifted - Demolished - Station site in commercial use.
NY17346 50858

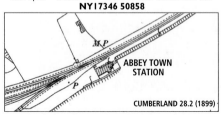
CUMBERLAND 28.2 (1899)

ABBOTSFORD FERRY   7 D3
Opened in May 1856 by the Selkirk & Galashiels Railway and closed 5 January 1931 by the L&NER.
Line lifted - Demolished – Station site landscaped area immediately on the north side of Boleside Road.
NT49742 33423

SELKIRKSHIRE 8.10 (1899)

ABERCAIRNY   10 D3
Opened 21 May 1866 by the Crieff & Methven Junction Railway as *Abbercairny*, renamed as *Abercairny* by the CR c1890 and closed 21 October 1951 by BR.
Line lifted - Station building and platform in private use.
NN92287 20951

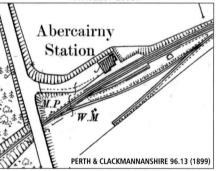
PERTH & CLACKMANNANSHIRE 96.13 (1899)

ABERCHALDER   14 A3
Opened 22 July 1903 by the HR, closed 1 November 1911 reopened 1 August 1913 and closed 1 December 1933 by the L&NER.
Line lifted – Demolished - Platform partially extant.
NH34433 03978

INVERNESS-MAINLAND 82.12 (1899)

ABERDEEN   16 B3
Opened by the CR and GNofSR 4 November 1867 as *Aberdeen Joint* and renamed as *Aberdeen* by the LM&SR and L&NER in 1938/9.

Class 158 Unit No.158702 at **Aberdeen Station** on 17 September 2015.

ABERDOUR   11 B4
Opened 2 June 1890 by the NBR.

Class 158 Units Nos 158712 and 158870 at **Aberdour Station** on 18 September 2015.

ABERFELDY   10 D2
Opened 3 July 1865 by the Inverness & Perth Junction Railway and closed 3 May 1965 by BR.
Line lifted - Demolished - Station site occupied by a car park and supermarket. **NN85835 49110**

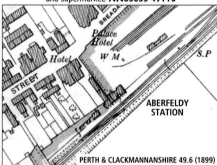
PERTH & CLACKMANNANSHIRE 49.6 (1899)

ABERFOYLE   10 B4
Opened 1 August 1882 by the Strathendrick & Aberfoyle Railway and closed 1 October 1951 by BR.
Line lifted – Demolished – Station site in use as a car park.
NN52106 00945

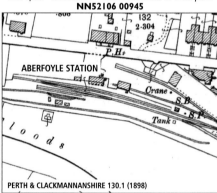
PERTH & CLACKMANNANSHIRE 130.1 (1898)

ABERLADY   7 D1
Opened 1 April 1898 by the Aberlady, Gullane & North British Railway and closed 12 September 1932 by the L&NER.
Line lifted – Demolished – Platform extant as part of the "Aberlady Caravan Park". **NT47015 79312**

NT47NE (1964)

ABERLOUR　15 B1
Opened 1 July 1863 by the Strathspey Railway and closed 18 October 1965 by BR.
Line lifted – Station building in use as the "Speyside Way Visitor Centre" - The Speyside Way passes through the station site. **NJ26511 42984**

ABERNETHY　11 B3
Opened 18 July 1848 by the Edinburgh & Northern Railway and closed 19 September 1955 by BR.
Line Operational – Demolished – One platform partially extant – No access. **NO19006 16681**

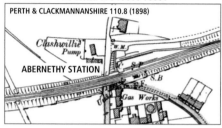

PERTH & CLACKMANNANSHIRE 110.8 (1898)

ABINGTON　7 A3
Opened 15 February 1848 by the CR and closed 4 January 1965 by BR.
Line Operational – Demolished – No access. **NS93593 23461**

LANARKSHIRE 43.13 (1896)

ABOYNE　15 D3
Opened 2 December 1859 by the Deeside Extension Railway and closed 28 February 1956 by BR.
Line lifted – Station building and platform in use as shops – The Deeside Way passes through the station site. **NO52979 98626**

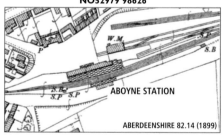

ABERDEENSHIRE 82.14 (1899)

ACHANALT　13 D1
Opened by the Dingwall & Skye Railway 19 August 1870 and worked from the outset by the HR.

*Looking west at **Achanalt** Station on 17 September 2015.*

ACH-NA-CLOICH　9 C2
Opened in June 1881 by the Callander & Oban Railway closed 1 January 1917 by the CR, reopened 1 March 1919 and closed 1 November 1965 by BR.
Line Operational – Platform extant – No access. **NM96105 33943**

ARGYLLSHIRE 87.11 (1897)

ACHNASHEEN　13 D1
Opened by the Dingwall & Skye Railway 19 August 1870 and worked from the outset by the HR.

*Looking east at **Achnasheen** Station on 17 September 2015.*

ACHNASHELLACH　13 C1
Opened by the Dingwall & Skye Railway 19 August 1870 as a private station and worked from the outset by the HR. In public use from 1 May 1871.

*Looking west at **Achnashellach** Station on 17 September 2015.*

ACHTERNEED　14 B1
Opened 19 August 1870 by the HR as *Strathpeffer*, renamed 1 June 1885 as *Achterneed* and closed 7 December 1964 by BR. It was reopened 8 February 1965 as an unadvertised and unstaffed halt. Date of final closure not recorded.
Line Operational – Demolished – Degraded platform extant - No access. **NH49046 59790**

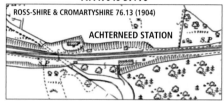

ROSS-SHIRE & CROMARTYSHIRE 76.13 (1904)
ACHTERNEED STATION

ADDIEWELL　7 A1
Opened by the CR 1 July 1882.

Addiewell Station on 19 March 2017.

ADVIE　15 A2
Opened 1 September 1868 by the GNofSR and closed 18 October 1965 by BR. This replaced an earlier GNofSR station sited ¾ mile east which opened 1 July 1863.
Line lifted - Demolished - Platform extant – The Speyside Way passes through the station site. **NJ12732 34606**

ELGINSHIRE 30.4 (1903)

AIRBLES　6A D2
Opened 15 May 1989.

*Looking north at **Airbles** Station on 19 March 2017.*

AIRDRIE (NBR)　6 D1
Opened by the Bathgate & Coatbridge Railway 11 August 1862 as *Airdrie South* and renamed by BR 3 March 1952 as *Airdrie*.

*A Class 320 Unit on Platform 1 at **Airdrie** Station on 12 May 2017.*

AIRDRIE (CR)　6 D1
Opened 1 June 1886 by the CR and 1 January 1917 reduced to the status of the terminus of a line from Newhouse that had been disconnected from the network. It was reconnected to the system 1 March 1919 with the reopening of the line through to Whifflet and closed 3 May 1943 by the LM&SR.
Line lifted – Demolished – Station site occupied by retail premises and a car park. **NS76266 65413**

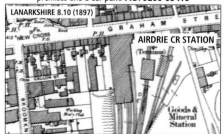

LANARKSHIRE 8.10 (1897)
AIRDRIE CR STATION

AIRTH　10 D4
Opened July 1852 by the CR as *Carnock Road*, renamed 1865 as *Airth Road*, in 1866 as *Airth* and closed 20 September 1954 by BR.
Line lifted – Demolished – Station site unused. **NS87085 87160**

STIRLINGSHIRE 24.2 (1896)
AIRTH STATION

ALCAIG　14 B1
Planned by the Cromarty & Dingwall Railway but never opened.

ALEXANDRA PARADE　21A D2
Opened by the City of Glasgow Union Railway in November 1877 as *Alexandra Park*, closed 1 January 1917, reopened 2 June 1919 and renamed by L&NER 1 July 1923 as *Alexandra Parade*.

Alexandra Parade Station on 13 May 2017.

ALEXANDRIA　6 B1
Opened by the Caledonian & Dunbarton-shire Junction Railway 15 July 1850.
Somewhat unusually, the station is sited in the middle of a large traffic island. *Looking north at Alexandria Station on 13 September 2015.*

ALFORD　15 D3/15A D3
Opened 21 March 1859 by the Alford Valley Railway, closed 2 January 1950 by BR and reopened in 1984 by the 2ft gauge Alford Valley Railway.

ALLANFEARN　14 C1
Opened 7 November 1855 by the Inverness & Nairn Railway as *Culloden*, renamed 1 November 1898 by the HR as *Allanfearn* and closed 3 May 1965 by BR.
Line Operational - Station building in private use – Platform extant. **NH71479 47581**

INVERNESS-MAINLAND 4.11 (1903)
Allanfearn Station

ALLANGRANGE　14 B1
Opened 1 February 1894 by the HR and closed 1 October 1951 by BR.
Line lifted – Demolished – Station site in commercial use. **NH60858 51900**

ROSS-SHIRE & CROMARTYSHIRE 100.2 (1904)
Allangrange Station

ALLOA　10A D4
Funded by the Scottish Executive and officially opened 15 May 2008, it is sited to the east of the original (NBR) station *(qv)*.

Alloa Station on 13 May 2017.

ALLOA DOCK　10 D4
ALLOA (NBR) GOODS　10 D4
ALLOA JUNCTION　10 D4
ALLOA (NBR)　10 D4
Opened 28 August 1850 by the Stirling & Dunfermline Railway as *Alloa*, renamed by the NBR in 1875 as *Alloa North* in 1882 as *Alloa* and closed by BR 7 October 1968.
Line Operational – Demolished - Part of station site occupied by the "Leisure Bowl". **NS88607 93090**

CLACKMANNANSHIRE 139.04 (1900)

ALLOA SOUTH 10 D4

Opened 2 September 1850 by the Scottish Central Railway as *Alloa*, renamed in 1854 as *Alloa South*, closed to passengers by the CR 1 October 1885 and to goods by BR 1 September 1950.

Line lifted – Demolished – Station site occupied by a car park.
NS88093 92574

CLACKMANNANSHIRE 139.06 (1900)

ALLOWAY 6 A3

Opened 17 May 1906 by the Maidens & Dunure Light Railway and closed 1 December 1930 by the LM&SR.

Line lifted – Demolished – Station site unused.
NS33392 18105

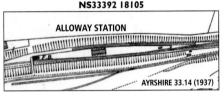

AYRSHIRE 33.14 (1937)

ALLOWAY JUNCTION 6 A3
ALMONDBANK 11 A3

Opened 1 January 1858 by the Perth, Almond Valley & Methven Railway as *Almond Bank*, renamed as *Almondbank* after 1890 and closed 1 October 1951 by BR.

Line lifted – Station House in private use – Remainder demolished. **NO06708 25120**

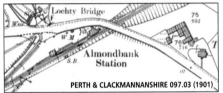

PERTH & CLACKMANNANSHIRE 097.03 (1901)

ALMOND JUNCTION 7 A1
ALMOND VALLEY JUNCTION 11 A3
ALNESS 17 C4

Opened 23 March 1863 by the Inverness & Ross-shire and Inverness & Aberdeen Junction Railways, closed by BR 13 June 1960 and reopened 7 May 1973.

Looking north at **Alness** Station on 16 September 2015.

ALTNABREAC 17 D1

Opened 28 July 1874 by the Sutherland and Caithness Railway.

Class 158 Unit No.158720 approaching **Altnabreac Station** on a northbound service on 16 September 2015.

ALTON HEIGHTS JUNCTION 6A D2

Opened in January 1893 by the CR and closed by BR c1956.
Line lifted – Demolished – Station site unused.
NS82925 37719 (a)

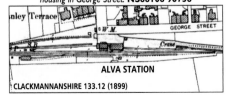

LANARKSHIRE 032.13 (1896)

ALVA 10 D4

Opened 3 June 1863 by the Alva Railway and closed 1 November 1954 by BR.

Line lifted – Station building in private use – Station site partially utilized as a small park and partially occupied by housing in George Street. **NS88108 96758**

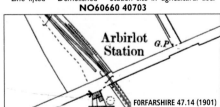

CLACKMANNANSHIRE 133.12 (1899)

ALVES 15 A1

Opened 25 March 1858 by the Inverness & Aberdeen Junction Railway and closed 3 May 1965 by BR.

Line Operational – Station building and platform in private use. **NJ13554 61789**

CLACKMANNANSHIRE 133.12 (1899)

ALYTH 11 B2

Opened 2 September 1861 by the Alyth Railway and closed 2 July 1951 by BR.

Line lifted – Demolished – Station site occupied by housing in Isla Place. **NO24852 48241**

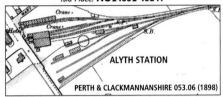

PERTH & CLACKMANNANSHIRE 053.06 (1898)

ALYTH JUNCTION 11 B2

Opened in 1861 by the Dundee, Perth & Aberdeen Junction Railway as *Meigle*, renamed 1 November 1876 by the CR as *Alyth Junction* and closed 4 September 1967 by BR.
Line lifted – Demolished – Station site unused.
NO29363 43018

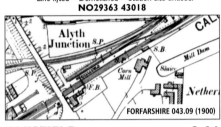

FORFARSHIRE 043.09 (1900)

AMISFIELD 3 A1

Opened 1 September 1863 by the Dumfries, Lochmaben & Lockerbie Junction Railway and used as a halt only for a period by the LM&SR. Closed 19 May 1952 by BR.
Line lifted – Demolished – Station site unused.
NX99866 82826

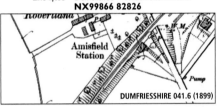

DUMFRIESSHIRE 041.6 (1899)

ANDERSTON 21A C2

Opened by the Glasgow Central Railway 10 August 1896 as *Anderston Cross*, closed by BR 3 August 1959 and re-opened 5 November 1979 as *Anderston*.

Looking east at **Anderston** Station on 13 May 2017.

ANGERTON 4 C1

Opened 23 July 1862 by the Blyth & Tyne Railway and closed 15 September 1952 by BR.
Line lifted – Station building and platform in private use.
NZ08686 83979

NORTHUMBERLAND (OLD SERIES) 71.5 (1896)

ANGLING CLUB COTTAGE PLATFORM 7A C2

Opened in 1898 by the NBR and closed by the L&NER after January 1947.

Line lifted – Demolished - Platform partially extant – Station site unused. **NT43222 35447**

SELKIRKSHIRE 007.07 (1897)

ANGLING CLUB COTTAGE PLATFORM

ANNAN (CR) 3 B2

Opened 1 October 1869 by the Solway Junction Railway, renamed by the LM&SR as *Annan Shawhill* 2 June 1924 and closed 27 April 1931.

Line lifted - Station building in private use – Platforms partially extant. **NY20074 66427**

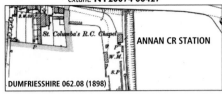

DUMFRIESSHIRE 062.08 (1898)

ANNAN (G&SWR) 3 B2

Opened 23 August 1848 by the Glasgow, Dumfries and Carlisle Railway and worked from the outset by the G&SWR.

Looking east at **Annan** Station on 16 March 2017.

ANNBANK 6 B3

Opened 1 September 1870 by the G&SWR and closed by BR 10 September 1951.
Line Operational – Demolished – No access.
NS40418 24814

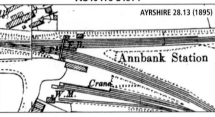

AYRSHIRE 28.13 (1895)

ANNIESLAND 21A B2

Opened by the NBR 15 March 1886 as *Great Western Road* and renamed by the L&NER 9 January 1931 as *Anniesland*.

Anniesland Station on 13 September 2015.

ANSTRUTHER 11 D3

Opened 1 September 1883 by the NBR and closed 6 September 1965 by BR.
Line lifted – Demolished – Station site occupied by an industrial estate. **NO56225 03617**

FIFESHIRE 22.12 (1893)

APPIN 9 C2

Opened 24 August 1903 by the Callander and Oban Railway and closed 28 March 1966 by BR.
Line lifted – Demolished – Platforms extant - A cycle/walkway passes through the station site. **NM92440 47289**

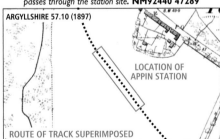

ARGYLLSHIRE 57.10 (1897)

LOCATION OF APPIN STATION

ROUTE OF TRACK SUPERIMPOSED

ARBIRLOT 11 D2

Opened 1 February 1900 by the Dundee & Arbroath Joint Railway, closed 1 January 1917, reopened Saturdays only from September 1917 and fully on 1 January 1918. Closed 2 December 1929 by the L&NER.
Line lifted – Demolished – Station site in agricultural use.
NO60660 40703

ARBIRLOT STATION

FORFARSHIRE 47.14 (1901)

ARBROATH
11 D2

Opened 14 December 1858 by the Dundee and Arbroath Joint Railway as *Arbroath Joint* and renamed as *Arbroath* at an unknown date.

*Looking south at **Arbroath** Station on 18 September 2015.*

ARBROATH HARBOUR
11 D2

ARDEER PLATFORM*
6A A2

Opened in 1896 by the G&SW and Lanarkshire Railways as *Ardeer Works Platform* for employees at the ICI works, subsequently renamed as *Ardeer Platform* and closed 3 October 1966 by BR.

Line lifted – Demolished – Degraded platform extant.
NS28252 40379

AYRSHIRE 16.11 (1895)

ARDGAY
17 B3

Opened by the Inverness and Aberdeen Junction Railway 1 October 1864 as *Bonar Bridge* and renamed by BR 2 May 1977 as *Ardgay*.

*Looking north at **Ardgay** Station on 16 September 2015.*

ARDLER
11 B2

Opened 24 February 1837 by the Newtyle & Coupar Angus Railway, closed 6 September 1847, reopened 2 August 1848 and closed 11 June 1956 by BR.

Line lifted – Demolished – Station site unused.
NO26030 41721

PERTH & CLACKMANNANSHIRE 64.7 (1898)

ARDLUI
10 A3

Opened by the West Highland Railway 7 August 1894 and worked from the outset by the NBR.

Ardlui Station on 13 September 2015.

ARDROSSAN HARBOUR
6 A2

Opened by BR 15 September 1986.

*Class 380 Unit No.380102 at **Ardrossan Harbour** Station on 16 March 2017.*

ARDROSSAN NORTH
6 A2

Opened 4 September 1848 by the Lanarkshire & Ayrshire Railway as *Ardrossan*, renamed by the CR as *Ardrossan Town* 1 October 1906, closed 1 January 1917, reopened 1 February 1919 and renamed as *Ardrossan North* by the LM&SR in 1924 and closed 4 July 1932.

Line lifted – Demolished – Station site occupied by housing in Montgomery Street. **NS23002 42594**

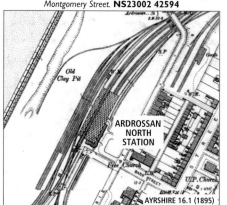

AYRSHIRE 16.1 (1895)

ARDROSSAN PIER
6 A2

Opened 30 May 1890 by the Lanarkshire & Ayrshire Railway, closed 1 January 1917, reopened 1 February 1919 and renamed by the LM&SR as *Ardrossan Montgomery Pier* 2 June 1924. Not being used during the Second World War it reopened 16 June 1947 and was closed 25 September 1967 by BR.

Line lifted – Demolished – Station site landscaped.
NS22563 42331

AYRSHIRE 16.1 (1895)

ARDROSSAN SOUTH BEACH
6 A2

Opened by the G&SWR 1 January 1883.

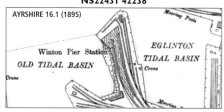

*Class 380 Unit No.380008 at **Ardrossan South Beach** Station on 16 March 2017.*

ARDROSSAN TOWN
6 A2

Opened by the Ardrossan and Johnstone Railway in 1831 as *Ardrossan*, renamed as *Ardrossan Town* by BR 28 February 1953, closed 1 January 1968 and reopened 19 January 1987.

*Looking north at **Ardrossan Town** Station on 16 March 2017.*

ARDROSSAN WINTON PIER
6 A2

Opened 27 July 1840 by the G&SWR as *Ardrossan*, renamed by the LM&SR as *Ardrossan Winton Pier* 2 June 1924 and by BR as *Ardrossan Harbour* 6 March 1967. It was closed 6 May 1967.

Line lifted – Demolished – Station site occupied by a car park.
NS22431 42238

AYRSHIRE 16.1 (1895)

ARGYLE STREET
21A D2

Opened 5 November 1979.

*Class 318 Unit No.318254 in the subterranean **Argyle Street** Station on 13 May 2017.*

ARISAIG
13 A4

Opened by the NBR 1 April 1901.

Arisaig Station on 14 September 2015.

ARMADALE
7 A1

The original station, sited on the opposite side of the road bridge to the replacement, was opened by the Bathgate & Coatbridge Railway 11 August 1862, closed by BR 9 January 1956 and reopened on the new site 4 March 2011.

Armadale Station on 12 May 2017.

ARMADALE COLLIERY
7 A1

ARNAGE
16 B2

Opened by the Formartine & Buchan Railway 18 July 1861 and closed by BR 4 October 1965.

Line lifted - Station building in private use – Platforms demolished - The Formartine and Buchan Way passes through the station site. **NJ93219 36176**

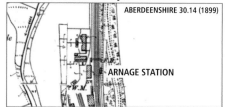

ABERDEENSHIRE 30.14 (1899)

ARROCHAR & TARBET
10 A4

Opened 7 August 1894 by the West Highland Railway and worked from the outset by the NBR.

*Looking north at **Arrochar & Tarbet** Station on 13 September 2015.*

ASHFIELD
21A D2

Opened 3 December 1993.

*Class 156 Unit No.156467 at **Ashfield** Station on 13 May 2017.*

ATTADALE
13 C2

Opened by the Dingwall & Skye Railway 1875/77 as a private station and worked from the outset by the HR. It became available for public use by December 1877, renamed c1880 as *Attadale Platform* and 1893 as *Attadale*.

*Looking east at **Attadale** Station on 17 September 2015.*

AUCHALLANDER PLATFORM*
10A A2

Opened prior to 1929 by the L&NER and closed at an unknown date.

Line Operational – Demolished. **NN32330 43705 (a)**

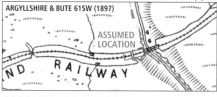

ARGYLLSHIRE & BUTE 61SW (1897)

AUCHENCASTLE*
7A A4

Opened 3 January 1900 by the CR and closed after 1926 by the LM&SR.

Line Operational – Demolished. **NT06621 04448**

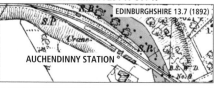

DUMFRIES-SHIRE 16.10 (1898)

AUCHENDINNY
7 B1/22A C4

Opened 2 September 1872 by the Penicuik Railway and closed by BR 5 March 1951. It was also known c1900 as *Auchendinny for Milton Bridge and Greenlaw Barracks*.

Line lifted – Demolished - Platforms partially extant - The Penicuik to Musselburgh Cycle-Walkway passes through the station site. **NT25141 61749**

EDINBURGHSHIRE 13.7 (1892)

AUCHENGRAY
7 A2

Opened 15 February 1848 by the CR and closed by BR 18 April 1966.

Line Operational – Demolished. **NS99085 53383**

LANARKSHIRE 20.7 (1896)

AUCHENHEATH
6 D2

Opened 1 December 1866 by the Linlithgow Railway and closed by BR 1 October 1951.

Line lifted – Station building in private use – Station site occupied by commercial garage premises. **NS80612 43645**

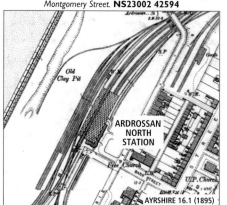

LANARKSHIRE 24.16 (1896)

AUCHENMADE 6 A2
Opened 4 September 1888 by the Lanarkshire & Ayrshire Railway, closed by the CR 1 January 1917, reopened 1 February 1919 and closed by the LM&SR 4 July 1932.
Line lifted – Demolished – Degraded platforms extant – Station site unused. **NS34265 48446**

AYRSHIRE 12.6 (1895)

AUCHINCRUIVE 6 B3
Opened in March 1897 by the G&SWR and closed by BR 10 September 1951.
Line Operational – Demolished. **NS37348 24118**

AYRSHIRE 33.3 (1895)

AUCHINCRUIVE COLLIERY 6A B3
PLATFORM*
Opened in 1898 by the G&SWR and closed by the LM&SR 3 March 1947.
Line lifted – Demolished – Station site unused.
NS39024 24709

AYRSHIRE 27.16 (1909)
AUCHINCRUIVE COLLIERY PLATFORM

AUCHINDACHY 15 C1
Opened 21 February 1862 by the Keith & Dufftown Railway as *Botriphnie*, renamed October 1862 as *Auchindachy* and closed by BR 6 May 1968.
Line Operated by the Keith & Dufftown Railway – Station building and platform in private use. **NJ40621 47551**

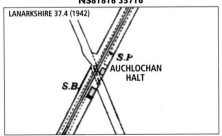
BANFFSHIRE 20.5 (1903)

AUCHINLECK 6 C3
Opened 9 August 1848 by the Glasgow, Paisley, Kilmarnock and Ayr Railway, closed by BR 6 December 1965 and reopened 14 May 1984.
Auchinleck Station on 20 March 2017.

AUCHLOCHAN HALT* 6A D3
A workmen's platform opened by the G&SWR sometime shortly after 23 September 1907 and closed by BR cMay 1957.
Line lifted – Demolished – Station site unused.
NS81818 35716

LANARKSHIRE 37.4 (1942)

AUCHMACOY 16 B2
Opened 2 August 1897 by the GNofSR and closed by the L&NER 31 October 1932.
Line lifted – Demolished – Station site unused. **NJ99550 31864**

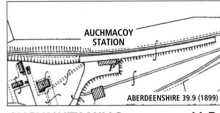
AUCHMACOY STATION
ABERDEENSHIRE 39.9 (1899)

AUCHMUTY MILLS 11 B4
AUCHNAGATT 16 B1
Opened 18 July 1861 by the Formartine & Buchan Railway and closed by BR 4 October 1965.
Line lifted - Station building in private use - Platforms extant - The Formartine and Buchan Way passes through the station site. **NJ93078 41830**

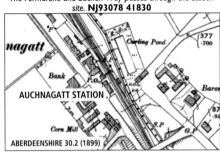
AUCHNAGATT STATION
ABERDEENSHIRE 30.2 (1899)

AUCHTERARDER 11 A3
Opened 23 May 1848 by the Scottish Central Railway and closed by BR 11 June 1956.
Line Operational - Station site in commercial use – One platform extant. **NN95505 12167**

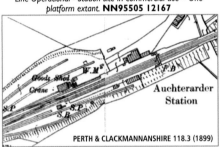
PERTH & CLACKMANNANSHIRE 118.3 (1899)

AUCHTERHOUSE 11 C2
Opened 1 November 1860 by the Dundee, Perth & Aberdeen Junction Railway and closed by BR 10 January 1955.
Line lifted – Demolished – Station site occupied by a dwelling. **NO33275 37618**

FORFARSHIRE 49.6 (1900)

AUCHTERLESS 16 A1
Opened 5 September 1857 by the Banff, Macduff & Turriff Junction Railway and closed by BR 1 October 1951.
Line lifted – Demolished – Station site partially occupied by a bungalow. **NJ74661 44255**

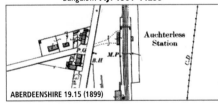
ABERDEENSHIRE 19.15 (1899)

AUCHTERMUCHTY 11 B3
Opened 8 June 1857 by the Fife & Kinross Railway and closed by BR 5 June 1950.
Line lifted – Station building incorporated into "Sterling Depot" – Platform demolished. **NO24187 11201**

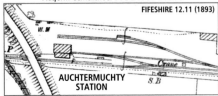
FIFESHIRE 12.11 (1893)
AUCHTERMUCHTY STATION

AUCHTERTOOL GOODS 11 B4
AULDBAR ROAD 11 D1
Opened by the Arbroath & Forfar Railway and in use by 25 February 1841, it was officially closed by BR 11 June 1956 but may have seen sporadic use until line closure 4 September 1967. It was also known as *Auldbar Road for Letham* in Bradshaw up until 1955.
Line lifted – Station House in private use – Platforms demolished. **NO53743 50947**

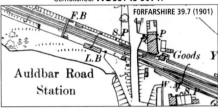
FORFARSHIRE 39.7 (1901)

AULDEARN 14 D1
Opened 9 December 1895 by the HR and closed by BR 6 June 1960.
Line Operational – Demolished – No access. **NH91922 56983**

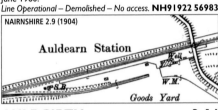
NAIRNSHIRE 2.9 (1904)

AULDGIRTH 3 A1
Opened 15 October 1849 by the Glasgow, Paisley, Kilmarnock & Ayr Railway and closed by BR 3 November 1952.
Line Operational – Station building in private use – Platforms demolished. **NX91477 86669**

DUMFRIES-SHIRE 40.8 (1899)

AULTMORE 15 B2
Opened 1 August 1884 by the HR as *Forgie*, renamed 1 January 1889 as *Aultmore*, closed to passengers 9 August 1915 and to goods by BR 3 October 1966.
Line lifted – Demolished – Station site partially occupied by a dwelling and partially unused. **NJ40195 53256**

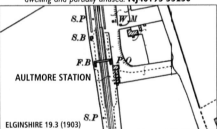
AULTMORE STATION
ELGINSHIRE 19.3 (1903)

AVIEMORE 14 D3
Opened 3 August 1863 by the Inverness and Perth Junction Railway and rebuilt in 1898. By 1997 the station was semi-derelict and all the buildings were refurbished and restored to full use again with the **Strathspey Railway**, a preserved line to Boat of Garten, taking over Platform 3.

Aviemore Station on 15 September 2015.

AVOCH 14 C1
Opened 1 February 1894 by the HR and closed by BR 1 October 1951.
Line lifted – Demolished – Station site occupied by housing in Station Road. **NH69467 55382**

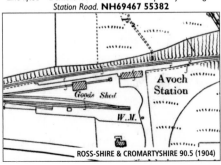
ROSS-SHIRE & CROMARTYSHIRE 90.5 (1904)

AVONBRIDGE 6 D1
Opened 5 August 1840 by the Slamannan Railway and closed by the L&NER 1 May 1930.
Line lifted – Demolished – Station site unused.
NS91058 72900

STIRLINGSHIRE 35.8 (1896)

AWE CROSSING HALT* 9A D3
Opened for railwaymen at an unknown date by the CR, shown in working timetable 15 September 1952 and subsequently closed by BR.
Line Operational – Demolished. **NN07693 26939 (a)**

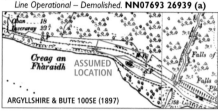
ARGYLLSHIRE & BUTE 100SE (1897)

AYR HARBOUR BRANCH 6 A3
AYR 6 A3
Opened 12 January 1886 by the G&SWR.

Class 380 Unit No.380004
on Platform 2 at
Ayr Station on 16 March 2017.

AYTON 8 B1
Opened 22 June 1846 by the NBR and closed by BR 5 February 1962.
Line Operational – Demolished – No access.
NT92967 60495

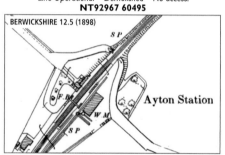
BERWICKSHIRE 12.5 (1898)

BACK O'LOCH HALT 6A C1
Opened 21 September 1925 by the L&NER and closed by BR 7 September 1964.
Line lifted – Demolished – The A806 passes through the station site. **NS65750 73400**

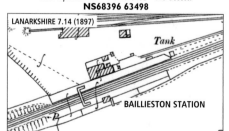
DUMBARTONSHIRE 33.6 (1896)

BAILLIESTON 6 C1
Opened 8 January 1866 by the CR and closed by BR 5 October 1964.
Line Operational – Demolished – No access.
NS68396 63498

LANARKSHIRE 7.14 (1897)

BAILLIESTON 6A C1
Opened 4 October 1993. The original station *(qv)* was sited some 1000 yards to the east.

Baillieston Station on 12 May 2017.

BALADO 11 A4
Opened 1 May 1863 by the Devon Valley Railway as *Cleish Road*, renamed 1878 as *Balado* and closed by BR 15 June 1964.
Line lifted - Demolished – Station site in commercial use.
NO08520 01363

KINROSS-SHIRE 25.4 (1894)

BALCHRISTON LEVEL 6A A4
CROSSING HALT*
Opened 17 May 1906 by the G&SWR and closed by the LM&SR 1 December 1930.
Line lifted – Demolished – Railway Crossing Cottage in private use. **NS25415 11214**

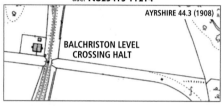
AYRSHIRE 44.3 (1908)

BALDOVAN 11 C2
Opened 16 December 1831 by the Dundee & Newtyle Railway as *Flour Depot St Marys Road*, subsequently renamed as *Baldovan*, as *Baldovan & Downfield* by the CR on 1 September 1905 and closed by BR 10 January 1955.
Line lifted – Demolished – Station site occupied by housing.
NO38706 33753

FORFARSHIRE 50.13 (1900)

BALDRAGON 11 C2
Opened 16 December 1831 by the Dundee & Newtyle Railway, closed by the CR 1 January 1917, reopened 1 February 1919 and closed by BR 10 January 1955.
Line lifted – Demolished – Station site unused.
NO37730 35027

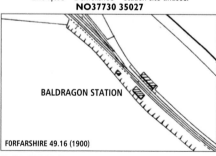
FORFARSHIRE 49.16 (1900)

BALERNO 7 B1
Opened 1 August 1874 by the CR and closed by the LM&SR 1 November 1943.
Line lifted – Demolished – Station site infilled and partially occupied by housing. **NT16517 67057**

EDINBURGHSHIRE 6.8 (1893)
BALERNO STATION

BALFRON 10 B4
Opened 26 May 1856 by the Edinburgh & Glasgow Railway and closed by BR 1 October 1951.
Line lifted – Demolished – A service road runs through the station site. NS52253 89337

STIRLINGSHIRE 14.16 (1896)

BALGOWAN 11 A3
Opened 21 May 1866 by the Crieff & Methven Junction Railway and closed by BR 1 October 1951.
Line lifted – Demolished – Station site partially in use as a sewage works. **NN99104 22673**

PERTH & CLACKMANNANSHIRE 96.12 (1899)

BALGREEN 22A A2
Opened 29 January 1934 by the L&NER, partially on the site of *Edinburgh Exhibition (NB) Halt*, and closed by BR 1 January 1968.
Line lifted – Demolished – The Corstorphine Branch Railway Route passes through the station site. **NT21820 72389**

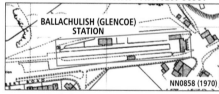
NT27SW (1947)
BALGREEN HALT

BALLACHULISH (GLENCOE) 9 D1
Opened 24 August 1903 by the Callander & Oban Railway as *Ballachulish* and closed by BR 28 March 1966. It was also known as *Ballachulish & Glencoe*, *Ballachulish (Glencoe) for Kinlochleven* and *Ballachulish Glencoe for Bridge of Coe* in various timetables.
Line lifted - Platforms demolished - Station building in use as the "Ballachulish Medical Practice". **NN08289 58381**

BALLACHULISH (GLENCOE) STATION
NN0858 (1970)

BALLACHULISH FERRY 9 C1
Opened 24 August 1903 by the Callander & Oban Railway closed by the CR 1 January 1917, reopened 1 March 1919 and closed by BR 28 March 1966.
Line lifted – Platform extant – A cycle/walkway passes through the station site. **NN05300 59374**

BALLACHULISH FERRY STATION
NN0559 (1970)

BALLATER 15 C3
Opened 17 October 1866 by the Aboyne & Braemar Railway, renamed as *Ballater for Balmoral and Braemar* by the L&NER, as *Ballater* by BR in 1955 and closed 28 March 1966.
Line lifted – Station building preserved and in commercial use.
NO36976 95943

ABERDEENSHIRE 91.7 (1900)
Terminus

BALLATHIE   11 B2
Opened 2 August 1848 by the Scottish Midland Junction Railway, closed to passengers by the CR in July 1868 and to goods by BR 7 September 1964.
Line lifted – Demolished – Station site unused.
NO13465 36468

PERTH & CLACKMANNANSHIRE 74.6 (1899)

BALLIFURTH FARM HALT   15A A2
Opened 15 June 1959 by BR and closed 18 October 1965.
Line lifted - Demolished – The Speyside Way passes through the station site. **NJ01409 23599**

ELGINSHIRE 32.16 (1904)

BALLINDALLOCH   15 B2
Opened 1 July 1863 by the Strathspey Railway and closed by BR 18 October 1965.
Line lifted - Station building in use as a hostel - Platform extant – The Speyside Way passes through the station site.
NJ16670 36604

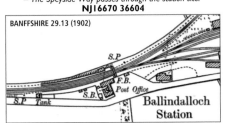
BANFFSHIRE 29.13 (1902)

BALLINLUIG   11 A1
Opened 1 June 1863 by the Inverness & Perth Junction Railway and closed by BR 3 May 1965.
Line Operational – Demolished – No access. **NN97948 52040**

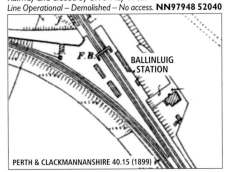
PERTH & CLACKMANNANSHIRE 40.15 (1899)

BALLOCH   6 B1
Opened 15 July 1850 by the Caledonian and Dumbartonshire Junction Railway as *Balloch*, renamed by BR 30 June 1952 as *Balloch Central* and closed 24 April 1988.
Line lifted - Station building in use as "Balloch Tourist Information Centre" – Station site in use as a car park.
NS38959 81951

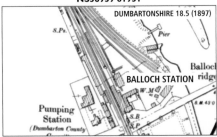
DUMBARTONSHIRE 18.5 (1897)

BALLOCH   6A B1
Opened 24 April 1988 as *Balloch Central* and renamed 15 May 1989 as *Balloch*. The original station building *(qv)* is still extant and sited on the opposite side of the road.

Class 320 Unit No.320305 at **Balloch Station** on 13 September 2015.

BALLOCH PIER   6 B1
BALLOCH PIER   6A B1
Opened 15 July 1850 by the Caledonian and Dumbartonshire Junction Railway as *Balloch Wharf*, subsequently renamed as *Balloch Pier* and closed by BR 29 September 1986.
Line lifted - Station building and platform extant.
NS38561 82534

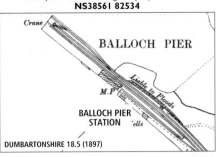
DUMBARTONSHIRE 18.5 (1897)

BALMORE   6 C1
Opened in April 1866 by the Kelvin Valley Railway and closed by BR 2 April 1951.
Line lifted – Demolished – Station site occupied by a bungalow.
NS60010 73569

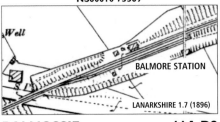
LANARKSHIRE 1.7 (1896)

BALMOSSIE   11A D2
Opened 18 June 1962 as *Balmossie Halt* and renamed as *Balmossie* 16 May 1983.

Looking north at **Balmossie Station** on 18 September 2015.

BALMULE COLLIERY BRANCH   11 A4
BALNACOUL   15 B1
Opened 23 October 1893 by the HR as *Balnacoul Platform*, renamed January 1894 as *Balnacoul*, by the LM&SR in 1922 as *Balnacoul Halt* and closed 14 September 1931.
Line lifted – Demolished – The A96 passes through the station site. **NJ32734 59796**

ELGINSHIRE 13.4 (1903)

BALNACRA LEVEL CROSSING GATEHOUSE*   13A C1
Opened 3 December 1951 by BR and last appeared in a working timetable 14 May 1984.
Line Operational – Demolished. **NG98417 46477**

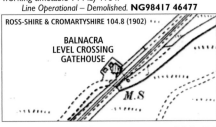
ROSS-SHIRE & CROMARTYSHIRE 104.8 (1902)

BALNAGUARD   10A D1
Opened 2 December 1935 by the LM&SR and closed by BR 3 May 1965. It was shown as *Balnaguard Halt* in some timetables.
Line lifted – Demolished – Station site in agricultural use.
NN94571 52039

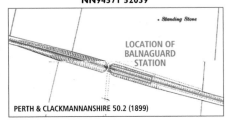
PERTH & CLACKMANNANSHIRE 50.2 (1899)

BALQUHIDDER   10 B3
Opened 1 May 1905 by the CR and closed by BR 28 September 1965.
Line lifted – Demolished – Station site occupied by "Balquhidder Braes Holiday Park". **NN57388 21010**

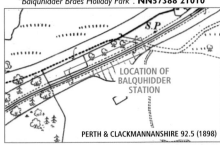
PERTH & CLACKMANNANSHIRE 92.5 (1898)

BANAVIE   13 D4
Opened 1 April 1901 by the NBR.

Looking west at **Banavie Station** on 14 September 2015.

BANAVIE PIER   13 D4
Opened 1 June 1895 by the NBR as *Banavie*, renamed 1 April 1901 as *Banavie Pier* and closed by the L&NER 16 September 1939.
Line lifted - Station building and platform in private use.
NN11564 77127

INVERNESS-MAINLAND 139.16 (1899)

BANCHORY   16 B3
Opened 8 September 1853 by the Deeside Railway and re-sited 20 chains west by the GNofSR 2 December 1859 when the line was extended. Closed by BR 28 February 1966.
Line lifted – Demolished – Station site occupied by housing in Glebe Park. **NO70399 95660**

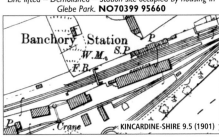
KINCARDINE-SHIRE 9.5 (1901)

BANFF   18 D4
Opened 1 May 1860 by the Banff, Portsoy and Strathisla Railway as *Banff Harbour*, renamed by the GNofSR as *Banff* in 1922 and closed by BR 6 July 1964.
Line lifted – Demolished – Station site unused.
NJ68763 64647

BANFFSHIRE 4.12 (1902)

BANFF BRIDGE   19 A4
Opened 1 July 1872 by the GNofSR and closed by BR 1 October 1951.
Line lifted – Station site in commercial use. **NJ69626 63731**

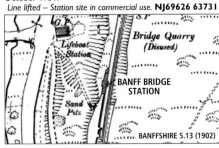
BANFFSHIRE 5.13 (1902)

BANFF HARBOUR   **18 D4**

BANGOUR   7 A1

Opened 19 June 1905 by the Edinburgh District Lunacy Board, a private line but publicly available and worked by the NBR. It closed 1 August 1921.

Line lifted – Demolished – Station site in private use.
NT03241 70718

BANKFOOT   11 A2

Opened 7 May 1906 by the CR and closed by the LM&SR 13 April 1931.

Line lifted – Demolished – Station site occupied by housing in Innewan Gardens. **NO06991 35131**

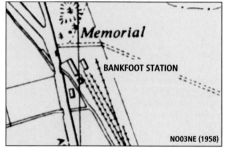

BANKHEAD   7 A2

Opened in November 1867 by the CR, closed by the LM&SR 12 September 1932, reopened 17 July 1933 and closed 4 June 1945.

Line lifted – Demolished – Station site occupied by housing in Bollan Court. **NS98150 44662**

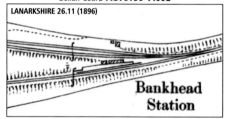

BANKHEAD   16 B3

Opened 1 July 1887 by the GNofSR and closed by the L&NER 5 April 1937.

Line Operational – Demolished – No access. **NJ89372 10331**

BANKNOCK   6 D1

Opened 2 July 1888 by the Kilsyth & Bonnybridge Joint Railway and closed by the L&NER 1 February 1935.

Line lifted – Demolished – A pathway passes through the station site. **NS78054 79328**

BANNOCKBURN   10 D4

Opened 1 March 1848 by the Scottish Central Railway and closed by BR 2 January 1950.

Line Operational – Demolished – No access. **NS81885 90420**

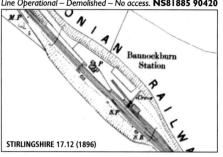

BARASSIE   6 A3

Opened in June 1848 by the G&SWR.

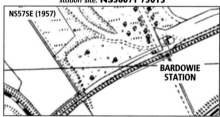

Barassie Station on 16 March 2017.

BARASSIE WORKSHOPS*   6A A3

Opened prior to 1926 by the LM&SR and closed by BR c1966.
Line lifted – Demolished – Station site occupied by housing.
NS32995 32252 (e)

BARCALDINE SIDING   9A C2

Opened cJuly 1914 by the CR as *Barcaldine Siding*, possibly closed for the duration of the Second World War, renamed by BR as *Barcaldine Halt* in 1960 and closed 28 March 1966.
Line lifted – Demolished – Station site in commercial use.
NM96308 42317

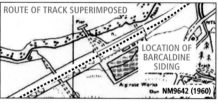

BARDOWIE   6 C1/21A C1

Opened 1 June 1905 by the NBR and closed by the L&NER 20 July 1931.

Line lifted – Demolished – A farm track passes through the station site. **NS58671 73013**

BARGANY COLLIERY PLATFORM*   6A A4

Opened prior to 1926 by the G&SWR, closure date unknown.
Line Operational – Demolished. **NS24908 01545 (e)**

BARGEDDIE   6 C1

Opened in February 1871 by the NBR as *Cuilhill*, renamed 1 April 1904 as *Bargeddie*, closed 1 January 1917, reopened 1 February 1919 and closed by the L&NER 26 September 1927.
Line Operational – Demolished – No access. **NS70018 64832**

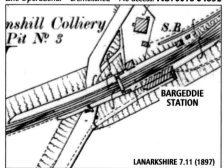

BARGEDDIE   6A C1

Opened 4 October 1993 and is built on the site of *Drumpark* station which was opened by the LM&SR 1 May 1934 and closed by BR 5 October 1964.

Bargeddie Station on 12 May 2017.

BARLEITH   6A B3

Opened in 1904 by the G&SWR for private use only, used for regular traffic by the LM&SR from June 1927 and closed by BR 6 April 1964.
Line lifted – Demolished – Station site unused within a Commercial Estate. **NS45696 36063**

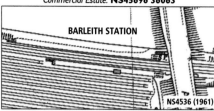

BARNHILL (CR)   11 D2

Opened in October 1874 by the CR as *Barnhill*, renamed by BR 30 June 1952 as *Barnhill Angus* and closed 10 January 1955.
Line lifted – Demolished – Station site occupied by housing in Guthrie Terrace. **NO47918 31703**

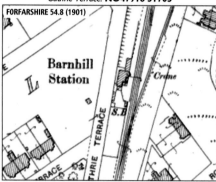

BARNHILL (NBR)   21A D2

Opened 1 October 1883 by the City of Glasgow Union Railway, closed by the NBR 1 January 1917 and reopened 2 June 1919.

Barnhill Station on 13 May 2017.

BARNTON FOR CRAMOND BRIG   7 B1

Opened 1 March 1894 by the CR as *Cramond Brig*, renamed 1 April 1903 as *Barnton for Cramond Brig* and closed by BR 7 May 1951.

Line lifted – Demolished – Station site occupied by housing in Barnton Grove. **NT18603 75062**

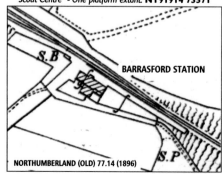

BARRASFORD   4 B1

Opened in June 1860 by the Border Counties Railway and closed by BR 15 October 1956.

Line lifted - Station building in private use as the "Barrasford Scout Centre" - One platform extant. **NY91914 73571**

BARRHEAD   6 B2/21A A4

Opened 27 September 1848 by the Glasgow, Barrhead & Neilston Direct Railway.

Class 156 Unit No.156493 on Platform 3 at Barrhead Station on 18 March 2017.

BARRHEAD CENTRAL 6 B2/21A A4
Opened 1 October 1902 by the G&SWR and closed 1 January 1917.
Line lifted – Demolished – Station site occupied by housing in South Park Avenue. **NS50007 59081**

BARRHEAD NEW 6 B2/21A A4
Built 1902 by the CR for a proposed suburban service that was never provided.
Line lifted – Demolished – Station site occupied by housing in Henry Street. **NS49881 58974**

BARRHILL 2 A1
Opened 19 September 1877 by the Girvan & Portpatrick Junction Railway, closed 7 February 1882, reopened 16 February 1882, closed 12 April 1886 and reopened 14 June 1886.
Barrhill Station on 16 March 2017.

BARRMILL 6 A2
Opened 26 June 1873 by the Glasgow, Barrhead and Kilmarnock Joint Railway and closed by BR 5 November 1962.
Line lifted – Demolished – Station site occupied by housing in Millbarr Grove. **NS36834 51568**

BARRY LINKS 11 D2
Opened in September 1851 by the Dundee & Arbroath Railway as *Barry* and renamed by the CR 1 April 1919 as *Barry Links.*

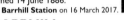

Looking south at **Barry Links Station** on 18 September 2015.

BATHGATE 7A A1
Opened 10 October 2010 and replaced the station sited some 750 yards to the west which was opened by BR 24 March 1986 and closed 10 October 2010 upon the opening of this one.
Bathgate Station on 13 May 2017.

BATHGATE LOWER 7 A1
Opened 1 March 1856 by the Monkland Railway as *Bathgate Monkland* and almost immediately closed as it did not have Board of Trade approval. Reopened 7 July 1856, subsequently renamed as *Bathgate Lower* and closed by the L&NER 1 May 1930.
Line lifted – Demolished – Newlands Court passes through the station site. **NS96925 69173**

BATHGATE UPPER 7 A1
Opened 12 November 1849 by the Edinburgh & Bathgate Railway and closed by BR 9 January 1956.
Line Operational – Demolished – No access. **NS97454 68498**

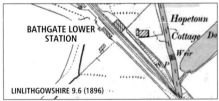

BEARSDEN 6 B1/21A B1
Opened 28 July 1863 by the Glasgow & Milngavie Junction Railway.

Looking south at **Bearsden Station** on 13 May 2017.

BEASDALE 13 B4
Opened 1 April 1901 by the NBR as a private station for Arisaig House, but was also available for public use. It was officially opened as a public station by BR 6 September 1965.
Beasdale Station on 14 September 2015.

BEATTOCK 7 B4
Opened 10 September 1848 by the CR and closed by BR 3 January 1972.
Line Operational – Demolished – No access. **NT07736 02394**

DUMFRIES-SHIRE 16.15 (1898)

BEATTOCK SUMMIT* 7A A4
Opened 3 January 1900 by the CR and closed by BR after 1952.
Line Operational – Demolished. **NS99550 15236 (a)**

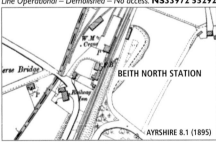

LANARKSHIRE 50.NE (1896)

BEAULY 14 B1
Opened 11 June 1862 by the Inverness & Ross-shire Railway, closed by BR 13 June 1960, and reopened 15 April 2002.
Looking south at **Beauly Station** on 17 September 2015.

BEITH NORTH (G&SWR) 6 A2
Opened 21 July 1840 by the Glasgow, Paisley, Kilmarnock & Ayr Railway as *Beith*, renamed by the LM&SR as *Beith North* 2 June 1924 and closed by BR 4 June 1951.
Line Operational – Demolished – No access. **NS33972 55292**

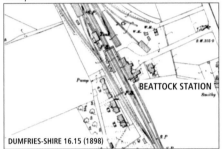

AYRSHIRE 8.1 (1895)

BEITH TOWN (CR) 6 A2
Opened 26 June 1873 by the Glasgow, Barrhead and Kilmarnock Joint Railway as *Beith*, renamed by BR as *Beith Town* 28 February 1953 and closed 5 November 1962.
Line lifted – Demolished – Station site occupied by housing in Balfour Avenue. **NS34499 53562**

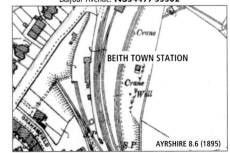

AYRSHIRE 8.6 (1895)

BELLAHOUSTON (See DUMBRECK)
BELLAHOUSTON PARK HALT 21A B3
Opened in May 1938 by the LM&SR for the Glasgow Exhibition and closed 1 January 1939.
Line Operational – Demolished. **NS55453 63231**

RENFREWSHIRE 13.1 (1893)

LOCATION OF BELLAHOUSTON PARK HALT

BELLFIELD PLATFORM* 6A D3
Opened c1912 by the CR and closed prior to 1922.
Line lifted – Demolished – Station site unused. **NS81467 34999 (a)**

LANARKSHIRE 37.4 (1896)

ASSUMED LOCATION

BELLGROVE 21A D3
Opened 23 November 1870 by the City of Glasgow Union Railway, it was also known as *Bellgrove Street* and *Bellgrove for Cattle Market.*

Bellgrove Station on 13 May 2017.

BELLINGHAM 4 B1
Opened 1 February 1861 by the Border Counties Railway as *Bellingham*, renamed as *Bellingham North Tyne* by the L&NER and closed by BR 15 October 1956.
Line lifted - Station building in use as council offices and tea rooms - Platforms still extant – Remainder of station site used as a car park. **NY84149 83325**

NORTHUMBERLAND (OLD) 68.6 (1895)

BELLSHILL (NBR) 6 C1
Opened 1 May 1879 by the Glasgow, Bothwell, Hamilton & Coatbridge Railway, closed, except for workmen's trains, 1 January 1917, reopened 2 June 1919 and closed by BR 10 September 1951.
Line lifted – Demolished – The A721, Gartcosh Walk, crosses the south end of the station site – Remainder of station site occupied by housing in Cochrane Street. **NS72866 60385**

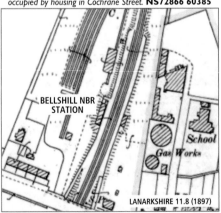

LANARKSHIRE 11.8 (1897)

BELLSHILL (CR) 6 C2
Opened 1 May 1879 by the CR.

Bellshill Station on 19 March 2017.

BELSES 7 D3

Opened 29 October 1849 by the NBR as *New Belses*, renamed c1862 as *Belses* and closed by BR 6 January 1969. It was also known as *Belses for Ancrum and Lilliesleaf* in some timetables.

Line lifted - Station buildings and platforms in private use.
NT57386 25190

ROXBURGHSHIRE 14.10 (1897)

BELSTON JUNCTION HALT* 6A B3

Opened in c1904 by the G&SWR and closed on an unknown date.

Line lifted – Demolished – A track passes through the station site. **NS48324 17708 (a)**

AYRSHIRE 34.16 (1894)

BELSTON JUNCTION 6 B3
BELTONFORD GOODS 8 A1
BENARTY* 11A B4

Opened after 1887 by the NBR for workmen's use and closed by the L&NER prior to September 1926. It was also known as *Benarty Siding.* **NT14877 95899**

Line lifted – Demolished - Station site unused.

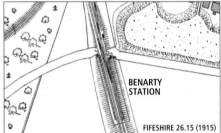

FIFESHIRE 26.15 (1915)

BENDERLOCH 9 C2

Opened 24 August 1903 by the CR and closed by BR 28 March 1966.

Line lifted – Demolished – A cycle/walkway passes through the station site. **NM90429 37992**

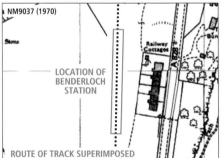

BENHAR EAST BRANCH 7 A1
BENTS 7 A1

Opened in February 1865 by the NBR and closed by the L&NER 1 May 1930.

Line lifted – Demolished - Station House in private use – A metalled pathway passes through the station site.
NS96707 62213

LINLITHGOWSHIRE 12.6 (1895)

BERVIE 16 A4

Opened 1 November 1865 by the Montrose & Bervie Railway as *Bervie*, renamed by the L&NER 5 July 1926 as *Inverbervie* and closed by BR 1 October 1951.

Line lifted – Demolished – Station site landscaped.
NO83254 72345

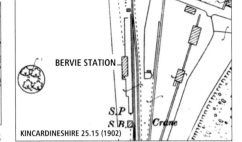

KINCARDINESHIRE 25.15 (1902)

BERWICK 8 C2

Opened 22 June 1846 by the NBR as *Berwick* and renamed as *Berwick-upon-Tweed* by BR 1 January 1955.

Looking north at **Berwick-upon-Tweed Station** on 19 September 2015.

BIELDSIDE 16 B3

Opened 1 June 1897 by the GNofSR and closed by the L&NER 5 April 1937.

Line lifted – Demolished - Platforms extant – The Deeside Way passes through the station site. **NJ88213 02304**

KINCARDINESHIRE 7.5 (1899)

BIGGAR 7 A2

Opened 6 November 1860 by the Symington, Biggar & Broughton Railway and closed by BR 5 June 1950.

Line lifted – Station building and platforms in commercial use. **NT03949 37259**

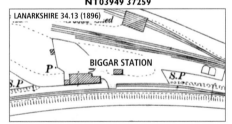

LANARKSHIRE 34.13 (1896)

BILBSTER 18 B1

Opened 28 July 1874 by the Sutherland & Caithness Railway and closed by BR 13 July 1960.

Line Operational - Station building in private use – Degraded platform extant. **ND28694 54197**

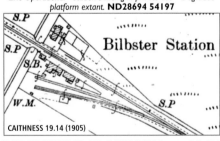

CAITHNESS 19.14 (1905)

BIRCHFIELD PLATFORM 15 B1

Opened in January 1871 by the GNofSR as *Birchfield*, renamed as *Birchfield Platform* in 1904, *Birchfield Halt* by the L&NER in 1939 and closed by BR 7 May 1956.

Line lifted – Demolished - Station House in private use – A track passes through the station site. **NJ25553 53179**

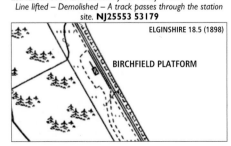

ELGINSHIRE 18.5 (1898)

BIRNIE ROAD 12 A1

Opened in November 1866 by the Scottish North Eastern Railway as *Birnie Road Siding*, subsequently renamed as *Birnie Road* and closed by BR in September 1951.

Line lifted – Demolished – A footpath passes through the station site. **NO81010 68398**

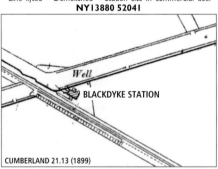

KINCARDINESHIRE 28.10 (1901)

BISHOPBRIGGS 6 C1

Opened 21 February 1842 by the Edinburgh & Glasgow Railway. This station, which was only temporary when first opened, was also known as *Bishopsbridge* and *Bishop-Briggs*.

Bishopbriggs Station on 13 May 2017.

BISHOPTON 6 B1

Opened 31 March 1841 by the Glasgow, Paisley & Greenock Railway.

Bishopton Station on 17 March 2017.

BLACKDYKE 3 B2

Opened in October 1856 by the Carlisle & Silloth Bay Railway as *Blackdyke*, renamed as *Blackdyke Halt* in c1920 and closed by BR 7 September 1964. It was also known as *Black Dykes* and *Black Dyke* in some timetables.

Line lifted – Demolished – Station site in commercial use.
NY13880 52041

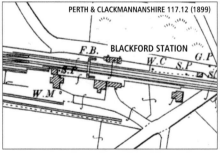

CUMBERLAND 21.13 (1899)

BLACKFORD 10 D3

Opened 23 May 1848 by the Scottish Central Railway and closed by BR 11 June 1956.

Line Operational - Station building in private use – Platforms demolished. **NN90025 09247**

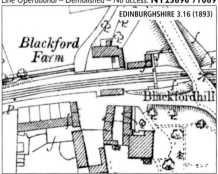

PERTH & CLACKMANNANSHIRE 117.12 (1899)

BLACKFORD HILL 22A C2

Opened 1 December 1884 by the Edinburgh Suburban & Southside Junction Railway, closed 1 January 1917, reopened 1 February 1919 and closed by BR 10 September 1962.

Line Operational – Demolished – No access. **NT25896 71089**

EDINBURGHSHIRE 3.16 (1893)

BLACKHALL GOODS 6 D2

BLACK ISLAND PLATFORM*   10A D1

Opened in June 1904 by the HR and closed by BR 11 April 1959.
Line Operational – Demolished. **NN85582 65590 (a)**

PERTH & CLACKMANNANSHIRE 21.14 (1898)

BLACKRIDGE   6A D1

Opened 12 December 2010.

Blackridge Station on 12 May 2017.

BLACKSBOAT   15 B2

Opened 1 July 1863 by the Strathspey Railway and closed by BR 18 October 1965.
Line lifted – Demolished – The Speyside Way passes through the station site. **NJ18331 38954**

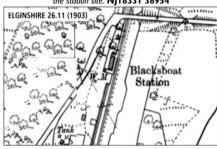

ELGINSHIRE 26.11 (1903)

BLACKSTONE   7 A1

Opened in January 1863 by the Monkland Railway as *Blackston*, renamed as *Blackston Junction* in 1865, as *Blackston* in 1890 and closed by the L&NER 1 May 1930. It was also known as *Blackstone* in some timetables.
Line lifted – Demolished – Platform partially extant – Station site unused. **NS92052 73037**

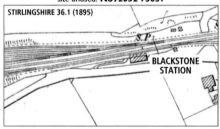

STIRLINGSHIRE 36.1 (1895)

BLACKWOOD   6 D2

Opened 1 December 1866 by the CR as a terminus, closed to passengers 1 July 1905 and subsequently used as a goods station.
Line lifted – Demolished – Station site occupied by Blackwood Primary School. **NS79227 43597**

LANARKSHIRE 24.15 (1896)

BLACKWOOD   6 D2

Opened 1 July 1905 by the CR, following construction of the Stonehouse to Lesmahagow line, and closed by BR 4 October 1969.
Line lifted – Demolished - Station site occupied by a church and housing in Southfield Close. **NS79502 43397**

NS74SE (1957)

BLAIR ATHOLL   10 D1

Opened 9 September 1863 by the Inverness and Perth Junction Railway as *Blair Athole* and renamed by the HR 7 September 1893 as *Blair Atholl*.

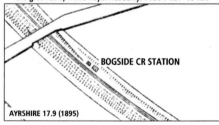

Looking north at **Blair Atholl Station** on 15 September 2015.

BLAIRADAM   11 B4

Opened 20 June 1860 by the Kinross-shire Railway and closed by the L&NER 22 September 1930. It was also used as a private station for Blairadam House.
Line lifted – Station building in private use – Platforms demolished – Station site in commercial use. **NT13243 97420**

KINROSS-SHIRE 26.10 (1896)

BLAIRENRATHIE COLLIERY   11 B4

BLAIRGOWRIE   11 B2

Opened 1 August 1855 by the Scottish Central Railway and closed by BR 10 January 1955.
Line lifted – Demolished – Station site occupied by a Tesco Supermarket and Welton Road. **NO18117 45066**

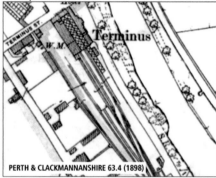

PERTH & CLACKMANNANSHIRE 63.4 (1898)

BLAIRHILL   6A C1

Opened in December 1888 by the NBR as *Drumpellier & Gartsherrie*, renamed 1 February 1899 as *Blairhill & Gartsherrie* and by BR 6 May 1968 as *Blairhill*.

Blairhill Station on 12 May 2017.

BLANEFIELD   6 B1

Opened in February 1868 by the Blane Valley Railway and closed by BR 1 October 1951.
Line lifted – Demolished – Station site unused - The John Muir Way by-passes the station site. **NS54958 79649**

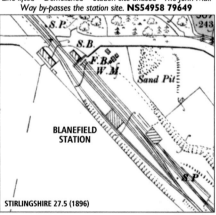

STIRLINGSHIRE 27.5 (1896)

BLANTYRE   6 C2

Opened 17 September 1849 by the Clydesdale Junction Railway.

Blantyre Station on 19 March 2017.

BOARHILLS   11 D3

Opened 1 September 1893 by the Anstruther & St Andrews Railway, closed 1 January 1917, reopened 1 February 1919 and closed by the L&NER 22 September 1930 but used occasionally afterwards for excursions.
Line lifted – Station House in private use – Platform demolished. **NO56603 13321**

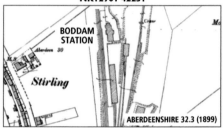

FIFESHIRE 15.4 (1893)

BOAT OF GARTEN   14 D3/14A D3

Opened 3 August 1863 by the Inverness & Perth Junction Railway and closed by BR 18 October 1965. The station, along with the line from Aviemore to Grantown, was purchased by the **Strathspey Railway Company** in 1972 and it reopened on 22 July 1978.

BODDAM   16 C1

Opened 2 August 1897 by the GNofSR and although closed by the L&NER 31 October 1932 some specials briefly ran during the Second World War.
Line lifted - Demolished – Station site in commercial use. **NK12901 42231**

ABERDEENSHIRE 32.3 (1899)

BOGSIDE (CR)   6 A2

Opened in June 1900 by the CR, closed 1 January 1917, reopened 1 February 1919, renamed by the LM&SR 2 June 1924 as *Bogside Moor* and closed 28 July 1930.
Line lifted – Demolished – Station site landscaped area within the grounds of Irvine Royal Academy. **NS31427 40426**

AYRSHIRE 17.9 (1895)

BOGSIDE (G&SWR)   6 A2

Opened in 1885 by the Glasgow, Paisley, Kilmarnock & Ayr Railway, renamed 30 June 1952 by BR as *Bogside Racecourse* reverted back to *Bogside* 14 June 1965 and closed 2 January 1967.
Line Operational – Station building extant – Northbound station site part of car park for Irvine Golf Club. **NS31010 40305**

AYRSHIRE 16.12 (1895)

BOGSIDE   11 A4

Opened in June 1851 by the Stirling & Dunfermline Railway as *Bogside*, renamed c1934 by the L&NER as *Bogside Fife* and closed by BR 15 September 1958.
Line lifted – Station building and platforms partially extant - The West Fife Cycleway passes through the station site. **NS97210 90138**

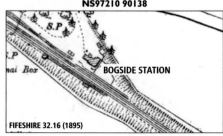

FIFESHIRE 32.16 (1895)

BOGSTON 6 A1

Opened in September 1878 by the CR, closed 1 January 1917 and reopened 1 March 1917.

Bogston Station on 17 March 2017.

BONAR BRIDGE (See ARDGAY)

BO'NESS 7 A1

Opened 1 March 1856 by the Monkland Railway but was closed immediately as it did not have Board of Trade approval. Reopened 10 June 1856 and closed by BR 7 May 1956.
Line lifted – Demolished – Station site occupied by a car park in Seaview Place. NS99704 81622

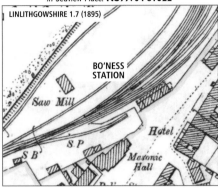

LINLITHGOWSHIRE 1.7 (1895)

BO'NESS 7A A1

Opened in 1981 by the Bo'ness & Kinneil Railway, it is sited about 0.25 miles from the original station (qv).

BONHILL BRANCH 6 B1
BONNINGTON 22A C1

Opened in October 1847 by the Edinburgh, Leith & Newhaven Railway, closed 1 January 1917, reopened 1 April 1919 and closed by the L&NER 16 June 1947.
Line lifted – Station building and platforms extant – The Water of Leith Walkway passes through the station site. NT25967 76148

EDINBURGHSHIRE 3.4 (1894)

BONNYBRIDGE (CR) 6 D1

Opened 2 August 1886 by the CR and closed by the LM&SR 28 July 1930.
Line lifted – Demolished – Station site in commercial use. NS82304 79879

STIRLINGSHIRE 30.1 (1896)

BONNYBRIDGE (NBR) 6 D1

Opened 1 May 1870 by the Edinburgh & Glasgow Railway, renamed 8 June 1953 by BR as *Bonnybridge High* and closed 6 March 1967.
Line Operational – Demolished – No access. NS83040 79259

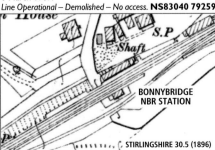

STIRLINGSHIRE 30.5 (1896)

BONNYBRIDGE CENTRAL 6 D1

Opened 2 July 1888 by the Kilsyth & Bonnybridge Junction Railway and closed by the L&NER 1 February 1935.
Line lifted – Demolished – Station site landscaped as a public garden. NS82280 80440

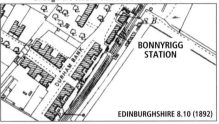

STIRLINGSHIRE 30.1 (1896)

BONNYRIGG C1/22A D4

Opened 1 August 1855 by the Esk Valley Railway as *Bonnyrigg*, renamed in 1866 by the NBR as *Bonnyrigg Road*, reverted back to *Bonnyrigg* 1 August 1868 and closed by BR 10 September 1962.
Line lifted - Demolished – Station site landscaped - Platforms partially extant - National Cycle Network Route No.1 passes through the station site. NT31167 64941

EDINBURGHSHIRE 8.10 (1892)

BORROBOL PLATFORM 17 D2

Opened in September 1876 by the Sutherland & Caithness Railway as *Borrobol Platform* but according to the HR no platforms were provided until 1880. It was renamed 10 September 1962 by BR as *Borrobol* and closed 29 November 1965. It was also known as *Borrobol Halt* in some timetables.
Line Operational – Demolished. NC87231 26475

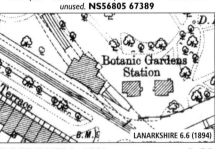

SUTHERLAND 66 (1904)

BOTANIC GARDENS 21A C2

Opened 10 August 1896 by the Glasgow Central Railway, closed by the CR 1 January 1917, reopened 2 June 1919 and closed by the LM&SR 6 February 1939.
Line lifted – Demolished – Platforms extant – Station site unused. NS56805 67389

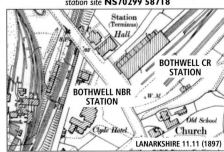

LANARKSHIRE 6.6 (1894)

BOTHWELL (CR) 6 C2

Opened 1 March 1877 by the CR and closed by BR 5 June 1950.
Line lifted – Demolished – Station site occupied by housing in Old Station Court. NS70397 58721

BOTHWELL (NBR) 6 C2

Opened 1 April 1878 by the Glasgow, Bothwell, Hamilton & Coatbridge Railway, closed by the NBR 1 January 1917 (except for workmen's trains), reopened 2 June 1919 and closed by BR 4 July 1955.
Line lifted – Demolished – A walkway passes through the station site NS70299 58718

LANARKSHIRE 11.11 (1897)

BOWER 20 B4

Opened 28 July 1874 by the Sutherland & Caithness Railway and closed by BR 13 June 1960.
Line Operational – Station building in private use – Degraded platforms partially extant. ND19873 58505

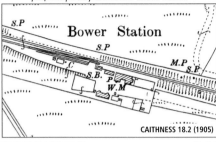

CAITHNESS 18.2 (1905)

BOWHOUSE 7 A1

Opened prior to July 1848 by the Slamannan Railway and closed by the L&NER 1 May 1930.
Line lifted – Demolished – Platform partially extant. NS94643 75129

STIRLINGSHIRE 31.14 (1896)

BOWLAND 7 D2

Opened 1 August 1848 by the NBR and closed by BR 7 December 1953.
Line Operational - Demolished – No access. NT45567 40156

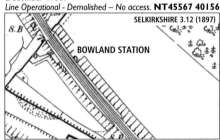

SELKIRKSHIRE 3.12 (1897)

BOWLING (NBR) 6 B1

Opened 31 May 1858 by the Caledonian and Dunbartonshire Junction Railway.

Looking west at **Bowling Station** on 13 September 2015.

BOWLING (CR) 6 B1

Opened 1 October 1896 by the Lanarkshire & Dumbartonshire Railway, closed by the CR 1 January 1917, reopened 1 February 1919 and closed by BR 5 February 1951.
Line lifted – Degraded platforms extant – Station site unused. NS44618 73770

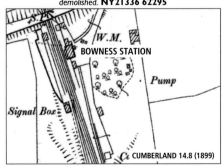

RENFREWSHIRE 4.9 (1896)

BOWNESS 3 B2

Opened 8 March 1870 by the Solway Junction Railway and closed in May 1921 by the CR.
Line lifted – Station building in private use – Platforms demolished. NY21336 62295

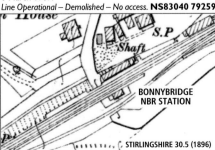

CUMBERLAND 14.8 (1899)

BRACKENHILLS 6 A2

Opened 1 September 1906 by the Lanarkshire & Ayrshire Railway and closed by the LM&SR 1 December 1930.
Line lifted – Demolished – Station site unused.
NS33682 51990

AYRSHIRE 8.9 (1895)

BRAESIDE HALT 11A A4

Opened 1 March 1921 by the NBR and closed by the L&NER in November 1926.
Line Mothballed – Demolished – Station site unused.
NT05975 83884 (a)

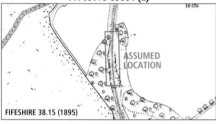

FIFESHIRE 38.15 (1895)

BRAIDWOOD 6 D2

Opened August 1848 by the CR and closed by BR 2 July 1962.
Line Operational – Station building in private use – Platforms demolished. **NS84946 48401**

LANARKSHIRE 25.1 (1896)

BRANCHTON 6A A1

Opened 5 June 1967 and replaced *Upper Greenock* station *(qv)*, sited about 1.2 miles to the east.

Branchton Station on 17 March 2017.

BRAYTON 3 B3

Opened in 1844 by the Maryport & Carlisle Railway as a private station, opened to the public 1 March 1848 and closed by BR 5 June 1950.
Line Operational – Demolished – No access. **NY16502 43619**

CUMBERLAND 36.2 (1899)

BRAYTON JUNCTION 3 B3

BRECHIN 11 D1/11A D1

Opened 1 February 1848 by the Aberdeen Railway, closed by BR 4 August 1952 and reopened in 1993 by the **Caledonian Railway (Brechin)**.

BREICH 7 A1

Opened 9 July 1869 by the Cleland & Midcalder Railway.

Looking west at **Breich Station** on 19 March 2017.

BRIDGEFOOT HALT 18A D4

Opened 1 October 1913 by the GNofSR and closed by BR 6 July 1964.
Line lifted – Demolished – A pathway passes through the station site. **NJ67004 64395**

BANFFSHIRE 4.11 (1928)

BRIDGE OF ALLAN 10 D4

Opened 1 June 1848 by the Scottish Central Railway and closed by BR 1 November 1965.
Line Operational – Demolished – Station House in private use.
NS78536 97828

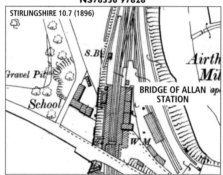

STIRLINGSHIRE 10.7 (1896)

BRIDGE OF ALLAN 10A D4

Opened 13 May 1985 and re-placed the original station that was sited a few hundred yards to the north *(qv)*.

Looking north at **Bridge of Allan Station** on 13 May 2017.

BRIDGE OF DEE 2 D2

Opened 18 April 1864 by the Kirkcudbright Railway and closed by BR 26 September 1949.
Line lifted – Station building in private use. **NX73238 60324**

KIRKCUDBRIGHTSHIRE 42.11 (1894)

BRIDGE OF DUN 11 D1/11A D1

Opened 1 February 1848 by the Aberdeen Railway, closed by BR 4 September 1967 and reopened in 1993 by the **Caledonian Railway (Brechin)**.

BRIDGE OF EARN 11 B3

Opened 18 July 1848 by the Edinburgh & Northern Railway resited 400 yards north by the NBR 1 February 1892 and closed by BR 15 June 1964.
Line Operational – Demolished – No access. **NO12827 18269**

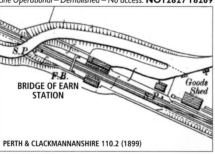

PERTH & CLACKMANNANSHIRE 110.2 (1899)

BRIDGE OF ORCHY 10 A2

Opened 7 August 1894 by the West Highland Railway.

Looking north at **Bridge of Orchy Station** on 13 September 2015.

BRIDGE OF WEIR 6 B1

Opened 23 December 1869 by the Greenock & Ayrshire Railway and closed by BR 10 January 1983.
Line lifted – Demolished – The Paisley and Clyde Cycle Path passes through the station site. **NS39086 65369**

RENFREWSHIRE 7.14 (1896)

BRIDGETON 21A D3

Opened 1 November 1895 by the Glasgow Central Railway as *Bridgeton Cross*, closed by BR 5 October 1964 and reopened 5 November 1979 as *Bridgeton*.

Bridgeton Station on 13 May 2017.

BRIDGETON CROSS 21A D3

Opened 1 June 1892 by the Glasgow City & District Railway as *Bridgeton Cross*, renamed by BR in 1954 as *Bridgeton Central*, 14 June 1965 as *Bridgeton* and closed 5 November 1979.
Line lifted – Demolished – Station site occupied by housing in Kerr Drive. **NS60676 64116**

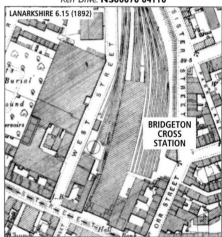

LANARKSHIRE 6.15 (1892)

BRINKBURN 8 C4

Opened 1 November 1870 by the Northumberland Central Railway as *Brinkburn*, renamed as *Brinkburn Halt* at an unknown date and closed by BR 15 September 1952.
Line lifted – Demolished – Station Master's House in use as holiday accommodation. **NZ08759 99571**

NORTHUMBERLAND (OLD) 45.13 (1896)

BROCKETSBRAE 6 D2

Opened 1 December 1866 by the Lesmahagow Railway as *Brocketsbrae*, renamed 1 June 1869 as *Lesmahagow*, reverted back to *Brocketsbrae* by the CR 1 June 1905 and closed by BR 1 October 1951.
Line lifted – Demolished – Station site occupied by housing in Brocketsbrae Road. **NS82387 39756**

LANARKSHIRE 31.8 (1896)

BRODIE 14 D1

Opened 22 December 1857 by the Inverness & Aberdeen Junction Railway and closed by BR 3 May 1965.
Line Operational – Station House in private use as the "Invercairn House B&B". **NH97833 57214**

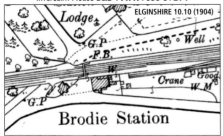

ELGINSHIRE 10.10 (1904)

BROMFIELD 3 B2

Opened 1 March 1873 by the Solway Junction Railway as *Broomfield*, renamed by the CR 1 November 1895 as *Bromfield* and closed in 1921.
Line lifted – Station building in private use. **NY17224 46615**

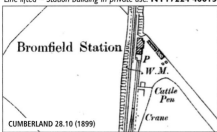

CUMBERLAND 28.10 (1899)

BROMFIELD JUNCTION 12 A1
BROOMHILL 15 A2/15A A2

Opened 3 August 1863 by the Inverness & Perth Junction Railway, closed by BR 18 October 1865 and reopened 31 May 2002 by the **Strathspey Railway**. It was also known as *Broomhill for Nethy Bridge* in some timetables.

BROOMHOPE* 4A B1

Opened c1900 by the NBR as a non-timetabled platform for the Vickers weapon-testing site and closed by BR in 1952.
Line lifted – Demolished – Station site in use as part of a field. **NY87611 83659**

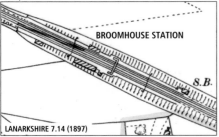

NORTHUMBERLAND (NEW) 66.9 (1921)
Broomhope Siding
BROOMHOPE PLATFORM

BROOMHOUSE 6A C1

Opened in December 1878 by the NBR, closed 1 January 1917, reopened 2 June 1919 and closed by the L&NER 26 September 1927.
Line lifted – Demolished – Station site unused. **NS67274 62827**

BROOMHOUSE STATION
S.B.
LANARKSHIRE 7.14 (1897)

BROOMIEKNOWE 7 C1/22A D4

Opened 15 April 1867 by the Esk Valley Railway as *Bonnyrigg*, renamed 1 August 1868 as *Broomieknowe*, closed by the NBR 1 January 1917, reopened 1 April 1919 and closed by BR 10 September 1951.
Line lifted – Demolished – Station site filled in and occupied by car park for "Bonnyrigg Health Centre". **NT30866 65555**

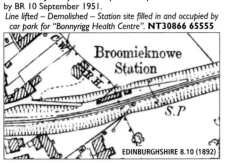

Broomieknowe Station
S.P.
EDINBURGHSHIRE 8.10 (1892)

BROOMLEE 7 B2

Opened 4 July 1864 by the Leadburn, Linton & Dolphinton Railway as *West Linton*, renamed in October 1864 as *Broomlee* and closed by the L&NER 1 April 1933.
Line lifted – Station building in private use - Platform demolished. **NT15480 50989**

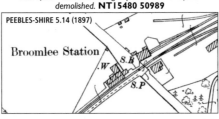

PEEBLES-SHIRE 5.14 (1897)
Broomlee Station

BROUGHTON 7 B2

Opened 6 November 1860 by the Symington, Biggar and Broughton Railway and closed by BR 5 June 1950.
Line lifted – Demolished - Degraded platforms extant – Station site in commercial use. **NT11092 36032**

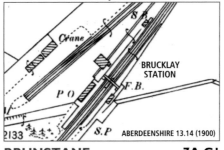

Broughton Station
PEEBLES-SHIRE 15.4 (1898)

BRORA 17 D3

Opened 1 November 1870 by the Sutherland Railway and worked from the outset by the Highland Railway.

Brora Station on 16 September 2015.

BROUGHTY FERRY 11 C2

Opened 8 October 1838 by the Dundee and Arbroath Railway.

Broughty Ferry Station on 18 September 2015 with the preserved signal box visible on the right.

BROUGHTY PIER BRANCH 11 C2
BROXBURN OIL WORKS 7 A1
BRUCKLAY 16 B1

Opened 24 April 1865 by the Formartine & Buchan Railway and closed by BR 4 October 1965.
Line lifted - Station building in private use - Platforms extant - The Formartine and Buchan Way passes through the station site. **NJ92679 50483**

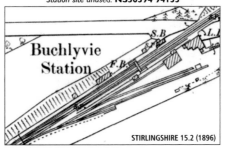

Crane
BRUCKLAY STATION
P.O.
F.B.
S.P.
ABERDEENSHIRE 13.14 (1900)

BRUNSTANE 7A C1

Opened 3 June 2002.

Looking north at **Brunstane Station** on 19 September 2015.

BUCHLYVIE 10 B4

Opened 26 May 1856 by the Edinburgh & Glasgow Railway and closed by BR 1 October 1951.
Line lifted – Demolished – Station House in private use – Station site unused. **NS56394 94133**

Buchlyvie Station
STIRLINGSHIRE 15.2 (1896)

BUCKHAVEN 11 C4

Opened 8 August 1881 by the Wemyss & Buckhaven Railway and closed by BR 10 January 1955.
Line lifted – Demolished – Station site in commercial use. **NT35586 98136**

BUCKHAVEN STATION
FIFESHIRE 28.11 (1893)

BUCKIE (GNofSR) 18 C4

Opened 1 May 1886 by the GNofSR and closed by BR 6 May 1968.
Line lifted – Demolished – The Moray Coast Trail passes through the station site. **NJ42834 65766**

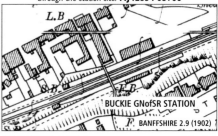

L.B.
BUCKIE GNofSR STATION
BANFFSHIRE 2.9 (1902)

BUCKIE (HR) 18 C4

Opened 1 August 1884 by the HR and closed 9 August 1915. *It can only be assumed that its appearance on the map was in anticipation of reopening at a later date.*
Line lifted – Demolished – An access road passes through the station site. **NJ42830 65344**

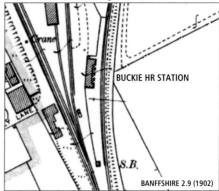

BUCKIE HR STATION
S.B.
BANFFSHIRE 2.9 (1902)

BUCKPOOL 18 C4

Opened 1 May 1886 by the GNofSR as *Nether Buckie*, renamed 1 January 1887 as *Buckpool* and closed by BR 7 March 1960.
Line lifted – Demolished – Station site occupied by housing in Great Western Court. **NJ41269 65223**

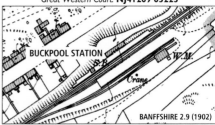

BUCKPOOL STATION
Crane
BANFFSHIRE 2.9 (1902)

BUCKSBURN 16 B3

Opened 20 September 1854 by the GNofSR as *Buxburn*, renamed as *Bucksburn* 1 January 1897 and closed by BR 5 March 1956.
Line Operational – Demolished – No access. **NJ89868 09738**

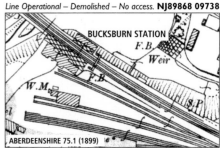

BUCKSBURN STATION
F.B.
W.M.
ABERDEENSHIRE 75.1 (1899)

BUDDON* 11 D2

Opened in 1890 by the Dundee & Arbroath Junction Railway for military use as *Barry Review Platform*. It was renamed 1 June 1893 as *Buddon* and used only intermittently until closure by BR c1957. At various times it was known as *Barry Review Siding, Barry Links Buddon Siding* and *War Dept B Siding*.
Line Operational – Demolished – No access.
NO52196 33066

FORFARSHIRE 55.2 (1920)

BULLERS O'BUCHAN HALT 16 C2

Opened in 1899 by the GNofSR as *Bullers O'Buchan Platform*, renamed 1914 as *Bullers O'Buchan Halt* and closed by the L&NER 31 October 1932.
Line lifted - Demolished – Station site unused.
NK10650 38062

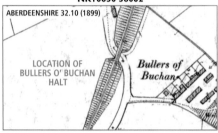
ABERDEENSHIRE 32.10 (1899)

BUNCHREW 14 B1

Opened 11 June 1862 by the Inverness & Ross-shire Railway and closed by BR 13 June 1960.
Line Operational – Station House in private use.
NH61655 45461

INVERNESS-MAINLAND 11.3 (1903)

BURGH 3 C2

Opened by the Port Carlisle Railway 22 June 1854 as *Burgh*, renamed 1 July 1923 by the LM&SR as *Burgh-by-Sands* and closed by BR 7 September 1964.
Line lifted – Station building and platform in private use – Remainder of station site occupied by housing in Southfield.
NY32238 58884

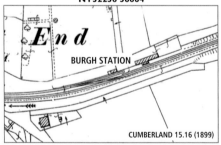
CUMBERLAND 15.16 (1899)

BURGHEAD 18 A4

Opened 22 December 1862 by the HR and closed by the LM&SR 14 September 1931.
Line lifted – Demolished – Station site unused.
NJ11518 68764

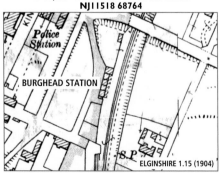
ELGINSHIRE 1.15 (1904)

BURNBANK (See GREENFIELD)

BURNMOUTH 8 B1

Opened prior to July 1848 by the NBR and closed by BR 5 February 1962.
Line Operational – Station building in private use – Platforms demolished. **NT95393 61097**

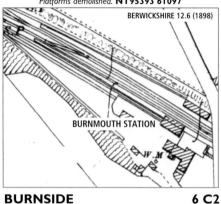
BERWICKSHIRE 12.6 (1898)

BURNSIDE 6 C2

Opened 1 August 1904 by the CR.

Burnside Station on 18 March 2017.

BURNTISLAND 11 B4

Opened 20 September 1847 by the Edinburgh and Northern Railway.

Looking east at **Burntisland Station** on 18 September 2015.

BUSBY 6 C2

Opened 1 January 1866 by the Busby Railway.

Looking north at **Busby Station** on 18 March 2017.

CADDER YARD* 6A C1

Opened c1900 by the NBR for railway staff and closed by BR in 1959.
Line Operational. **NS63006 71082 (e)**

CAIRNBULG 19 B4

Opened 1 July 1903 by the GNofSR as *Inverallochy*, immediately renamed as *Cairnbulg* and closed by BR 3 May 1965.
Line lifted - Demolished – Station site partially occupied by housing and partially unused. **NK04078 65050**

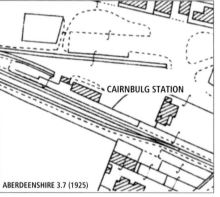
ABERDEENSHIRE 3.7 (1925)

CAIRNEYHILL 11 A4

Opened 2 July 1906 by the Kincardine & Dunfermline Railway and closed by the L&NER 7 July 1930.
Line Operational – Demolished – No access.
NT04101 86146

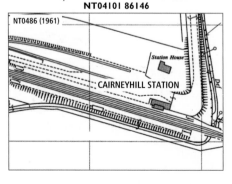
NT0486 (1961)

CAIRNIE JUNCTION 15 C1

Opened 1 June 1898 by the GNofSR initially as an exchange platform, became a public station by BR 14 June 1965 and closed 6 May 1968. It was also known as *Cairnie Platform, New Exchange Platform Cairnie Junction* and *Exchange Platform Cairnie Junction*.
Line Operational – Demolished – No access. **NJ50438 49691**

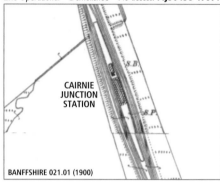
BANFFSHIRE 021.01 (1900)

CAIRNTABLE HALT 6A B4

Opened 24 September 1928 by the LM&SR and closed by BR 3 April 1950.
Line lifted – Demolished – A track passes through the station site. **NS43301 14023**

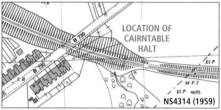
NS4314 (1959)

CAIRN VALLEY JUNCTION 3 A1
CALCOTS 18 B4

Opened 12 August 1884 by the GNofSR and closed by BR 6 May 1968.
Line lifted – Demolished – Part of one platform still extant - A track passes through the station site. **NJ25538 64249**

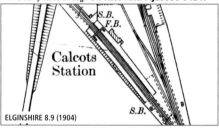
ELGINSHIRE 8.9 (1904)

CALDARVAN 6 B1

Opened 26 May 1856 by the Edinburgh & Glasgow Railway as *Kilmaronock*, renamed 1877 as *Caldarvan* and closed by the L&NER 1 October 1934.
Line lifted – Demolished – Station site occupied by housing in Auchincarroch Road. **NS43884 83280**

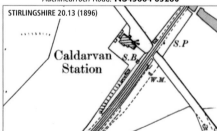
STIRLINGSHIRE 20.13 (1896)

CALDER 6 D1

Opened 1 June 1886 by the CR, closed 1 January 1917, reopened 1 March 1919 and closed by the LM&SR 3 May 1943.
Line lifted – Demolished - The North Calder Heritage Trail passes through the station site. **NS74559 64470**

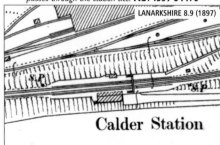
LANARKSHIRE 8.9 (1897)

CALDERBANK 6 D1

Opened 1 September 1887 by the CR and closed by the LM&SR 1 December 1930.
Line lifted – Demolished – Station site unused.
NS77071 63306

LANARKSHIRE 8.14 (1896)

CALDERCRUIX 6 D1

Opened 11 August 1862 by the Bathgate and Coatbridge Railway, closed by BR 9 January 1956 and reopened 13 February 2011.

Caldercruix Station on 12 May 2017.

CALDERPARK HALT 6A C1

Opened 5 July 1951 by BR and closed 4 July 1955.
Line lifted – Demolished – Station site occupied by flats and Calderpark Terrace. **NS67930 62510**

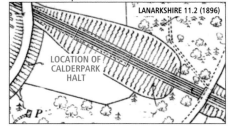

LANARKSHIRE 11.2 (1896)

LOCATION OF CALDERPARK HALT

CALDERWOOD GLEN 6 C2

Opened 11 February 1907 by the CR as an excursion platform for the Scottish Co-operative Wholesale Society's estate and only available for parties of 200 or more. Closed by the LM&SR in September 1939.
Line lifted – Demolished – Station site unused.
NS66231 56669

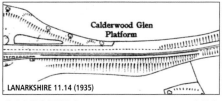

Calderwood Glen Platform

LANARKSHIRE 11.14 (1935)

CALDWELL 6 B2

Opened 27 March 1871 by the Glasgow, Barrhead and Kilmarnock Joint Railway as *Caldwell*, renamed 2 April 1962 by BR as *Uplawmoor* and closed 7 November 1966.
Line Operational – Demolished – House constructed on eastbound platform. **NS42903 55098**

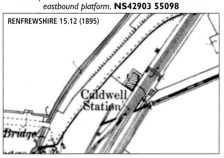

RENFREWSHIRE 15.12 (1895)

Caldwell Station

Bridge

CALLANDER 10 C3

Opened 1 June 1870 by the Callander & Oban Railway and closed by BR 1 November 1965.
Line lifted – Demolished – Station site in use as a car park.
NN62684 08124

PERTH & CLACKMANNANSHIRE 115.13 (1899)

CALLANDER & OBAN RAILWAY

CALLANDER STATION

Dreadnought Hotel

CAMBUS 10 D4

Opened in August 1854 by the Stirling & Dunfermline Railway as *Cambus*, renamed 1 December 1899 by the NBR as *Cambus for Tullibody* and closed by BR 7 October 1968.
Line Operational – Demolished – No access.
NS85566 94197

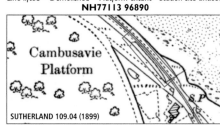

CLACKMANNANSHIRE 139.03 (1899)

Goods Yard

CAMBUS STATION

CAMBUSAVIE 17 C3

Opened 2 June 1902 by the HR and closed by BR 13 June 1960. It had also been known as *Cambusavie Halt* and *Cambusavie Platform* in some timetables.
Line lifted – Demolished – Platform extant - Station site unused.
NH77113 96890

Cambusavie Platform

SUTHERLAND 109.04 (1899)

CAMBUSLANG 6 C1

Opened by the CR 1 June 1849.

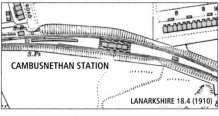

Cambuslang Station
on 18 March 2017.

CAMBUSNETHAN 6 D2

Opened 1 October 1901 by the CR and closed 1 January 1917.
Line lifted – Demolished – Station site occupied by housing in Fruin Drive. **NS81390 55490**

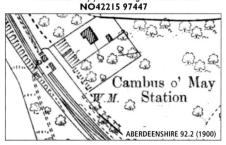

CAMBUSNETHAN STATION

LANARKSHIRE 18.4 (1910)

CAMBUS O'MAY 15 C3

Opened 4 October 1865 by the GNofSR as *Cambus O'May*, renamed 1935 by the L&NER as *Cambus O'May Halt* and closed by BR 28 February 1956.
Line lifted – Station building and platform in private use – The Deeside Way passes through the station site.
NO42215 97447

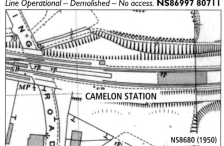

Cambus o' May W.M. Station

ABERDEENSHIRE 92.2 (1900)

CAMELON 6 D1

Opened 15 June 1903 by the NBR, closed 1 January 1917, reopened 1 February 1919 and closed by BR 4 September 1967. It was also known as *Falkirk Camelon* and *Camelon Falkirk*.
Line Operational – Demolished – No access. **NS86997 80711**

CAMELON STATION

NS8680 (1950)

CAMELON 6A D1

Opened 25 September 1994.

Camelon Station on 13 May 2017.

CAMERON BRIDGE 11 C4

Opened 10 August 1854 by the Edinburgh, Perth & Dundee Railway and closed by BR 6 October 1969.
Line Operational for Freight [Mothballed] – Demolished – Station site unused. **NO34835 00104**

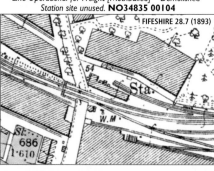

FIFESHIRE 28.7 (1893)

Sta

W.M.

686
1.610

CAMPBELTOWN 5 B3

Opened 18 August 1906 by the 2ft 3in gauge Campbeltown and Machrihanish Light Railway and closed prior to May 1932.

CAMPSIE GLEN 6 C1

Opened 1 July 1867 by the Blane Valley Railway, closed 1 January 1917, reopened 1 February 1919 and closed by BR 1 October 1951.
Line lifted – Demolished – Station House in private use – Newbridge crosses the station site. **NS61537 78635**

STIRLINGSHIRE 27.12 (1896)

W.M.

H

Campsie Glen Station

CAMPS BRANCHES 7 B1

CANAL (See PAISLEY CANAL)

CANONBIE 3 C1

Opened in May 1862 by the Border Union Railway as *Canobie*, renamed 1 February 1904 by the NBR as *Canonbie* and closed by BR 15 June 1964.
Line lifted - Station building in private use - Platforms partially extant. **NY40693 77089**

S.P.

DUMFRIES-SHIRE 54.9 (1898)

CANONBIE STATION

Pump

CARDENDEN 11 B4

Opened 4 September 1848 by the Edinburgh and Northern Railway.

Looking east at **Cardenden Station** on 18 September 2015.

CARDONALD 21A B3

Opened 1 July 1843 by the Glasgow & Paisley Joint Railway as *Moss Road*, closed 1849 and reopened in September 1879 as *Cardonald*.

Cardonald Station on 18 March 2017.

CARDRONA 7 C2

Opened 1 October 1864 by the Innerleithen & Galashiels Railway and closed by BR 5 February 1962.
Line lifted - Station building in use as Village Store and "Nashy's Coffeehouse" - Platforms partially extant. **NT30054 39062**

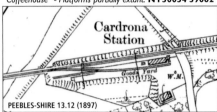

PEEBLES-SHIRE 13.12 (1897)

CARDROSS 6 A1

Opened 31 May 1858 by the Glasgow, Dumbarton and Helensburgh Railway.

Class 334 Unit No.334004 arriving at **Cardross Station** on 13 September 2015.

CARESTON 11 D1

Opened 1 June 1895 by the CR and closed by BR 4 August 1952.
Line lifted – Demolished – Station site in private and commercial use. **NO53751 60971**

FORFARSHIRE 26.11 (1900)

CARFIN 6A D2

Opened 1 October 1927 by the LM&SR as *Carfin Halt*, closed and then reopened by BR and subsequently renamed as *Carfin* 16 May 1983.

Carfin Station on 19 March 2017.

CARGILL 11 B2

Opened 2 August 1848 by the Scottish Central Railway and closed by BR 11 July 1956.
Line lifted – Station building in private use – Station site occupied by "Beech Hedge Caravan Park". **NO16238 37284**

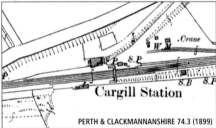

PERTH & CLACKMANNANSHIRE 74.3 (1899)

CARHAM 8 A2

Opened in July 1851 by the York, Newcastle & Berwick Railway and closed by BR 4 July 1955.
Lines lifted - Platforms extant – A rough roadway passes through the station site. **NT79148 37131**

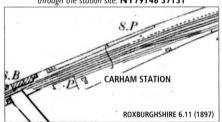

ROXBURGHSHIRE 6.11 (1897)

CARLISLE 3 C2

Opened 1 September 1847 by the Carlisle Station Joint Committee as *Carlisle Citadel* and renamed as *Carlisle* by BR.

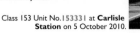

Class 153 Unit No.153331 at **Carlisle Station** on 5 October 2010.

CARLISLE VIADUCT YARD* 3A C2

Opened in July 1938 by the LM&SR for staff at Kingmoor MPD. Date of closure unknown.
Line Operational. **NY39900 55751 (e)**

CARLUKE 6 D2

Opened 15 February 1848 by the CR.

Carluke Station on 19 March 2017.

CARMONT 16 B4

Opened in September 1855 by the Aberdeen Railway as *New Mill Offset*, renamed 1866 as *Newmill Siding*, 1891 as *Newmill*, 1 October 1912 as *Carmont* and closed by BR 11 June 1956.
Line Operational - Demolished – No access. **NO78794 83138**

KINCARDINESHIRE 20.5 (1901)

CARMYLE 6 C1

Opened 8 January 1866 by the Rutherglen and Coatbridge Railway, and worked from the outset by the CR, it was closed by BR 5 October 1964 and reopened 4 October 1993.

Carmyle Station on 12 May 2017.

CARMYLLIE 11 D2

Opened 1 February 1900 by the Dundee and Arbroath Joint Railway, closed 1 January 1917, reopened 1 January 1918 and closed by the L&NER 2 December 1929.
Line lifted – Demolished – Station site unused. **NO56345 44162**

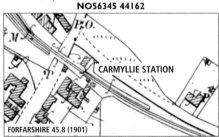

FORFARSHIRE 45.8 (1901)

CARNOUSTIE 11 D2

Opened c1900 by the Dundee & Arbroath Joint Railway. *This station is the second one here. The original one, opened by the Dundee & Arbroath Railway 6 October 1838, was sited further south.* **Carnoustie Station** on 18 September 2015.

CARNTYNE 6A C1

Opened June 1888 by the NBR, closed 1 January 1917 and reopened 1 April 1919. It was known as *Carntyne for Westmuir and Tollcross* in one timetable.

Carntyne Station on 12 May 2017.

CARNWATH 7 A2

Opened 15 February 1848 by the CR and closed by BR 18 April 1966.
Line Operational – Demolished – No access. **NS96995 46946**

LANARKSHIRE 26.6 (1896)

CARR BRIDGE 14 D2

Opened 8 July 1892 by the HR as *Carr Bridge* and renamed by BR 16 May 1983 as *Carrbridge*.

Carrbridge Station on 15 September 2015.

CARRON 15 B1

Opened 1 July 1863 by the Strathspey Railway and closed by BR 18 October 1965. It was also known as *Carron for Archiestown*.
Line lifted - Station building and partly-infilled platforms extant - The Speyside Way passes through the station site. **NJ22121 41311**

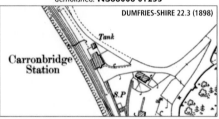

ELGINSHIRE 26.4 (1903)

CARRONBRIDGE 6 D4

Opened 1 March 1851 by the G&SWR and closed by BR 7 December 1953.
Line Operational – Station building in private use – Platforms demolished. **NS88008 01253**

DUMFRIES-SHIRE 22.3 (1898)

CARSEBRECK PLATFORM*10A D3

Opened in 1853 by the CR for Caledonian Curling Society meetings and closed by the LM&SR in 1935. It was also known as *Royal Curling Club Platform*.
Line Operational – Demolished – No access. **NN86943 09019**

PERTH & CLACKMANNANSHIRE 117.11 (1899)

CARSTAIRS 7 A2

Opened 15 February 1848 by the CR.

Looking west at **Carstairs Station** on 19 March 2017.

CARTSDYKE 6 A1

Opened in July 1870 by the CR.

Cartsdyke Station on 17 March 2017.

CASSILLIS 6 A4

Opened 13 October 1865 by the G&SWR and closed by BR 6 December 1954.
Line Operational – Station building in private use – Platforms demolished. **NS32874 13185**

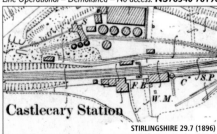

AYRSHIRE 39.10 (1894)

CASTLECARY 6 D1

Opened 21 February 1842 by the Edinburgh & Glasgow Railway and closed by BR 6 March 1967.
Line Operational – Demolished – No access. **NS78546 78196**

STIRLINGSHIRE 29.7 (1896)

CASTLE DOUGLAS 2 D2

Opened 7 November 1859 by the Castle Douglas & Dumfries Railway and closed by BR 14 June 1965.

Line lifted – Demolished – Station site in commercial use.
NX76908 62807

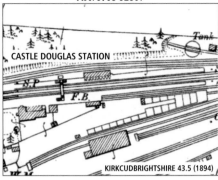

KIRKCUDBRIGHTSHIRE 43.5 (1894)

CASTLE DOUGLAS JUNCTION 2 D2

CASTLE GRANT PLATFORM* 15A A2

Opened in 1863 by the Inverness & Perth Junction Railway as a private station for the Grant Estate and closed by BR in 1949.

Line lifted – Demolished - The Dava Way passes through the station site. **NJ03279 30223**

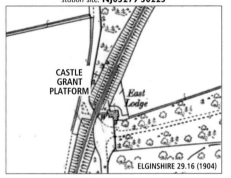

ELGINSHIRE 29.16 (1904)

CASTLEHILL GOODS 6 D2

CASTLE KENNEDY 1 D2

Opened 1 July 1861 by the Portpatrick & Wigtownshire Joint Railway and closed by BR 14 June 1965.

Line Operational – Station building in private use – Platforms demolished. **NX10822 59585**

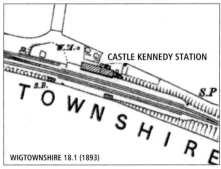

WIGTOWNSHIRE 18.1 (1893)

CASTLE STUART PLATFORM* 14A C1

Opened in 1938 by the LM&SR as a private station and closed by BR in 1949.

Line Operational - Demolished – No access. **NH74621 49269**

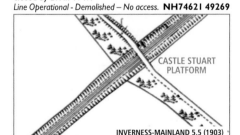

INVERNESS-MAINLAND 5.5 (1903)

CATHCART 6 C1/21A D4

Opened 18 March 1894 by the CR to replace the original station (opened by the Cathcart District Railway 25 May 1886) and establish an improved connection with the Cathcart Circle. Line.

Cathcart Station on 18 March 2017

CATHCART ST (See GREENOCK CENTRAL)

CATRINE 6 B3

Opened 1 September 1903 by the G&SWR, closed 1 January 1917, reopened in January 1919 and closed by the LM&SR 3 May 1943.

Line lifted – Demolished – Station site occupied by housing in Old Station Road. **NS53118 25720**

CATRINE STATION

NS5325 (1959)

CAULDCOTS 11 D2

Opened in October 1883 by the NBR and closed by the L&NER 22 September 1930.

Line Operational – Demolished – No access. **NO65717 47153**

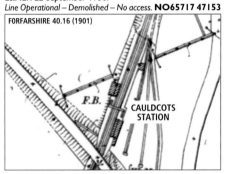

FORFARSHIRE 40.16 (1901)

CAULDCOTS STATION

CAUSEWAYEND 7 A1

Opened 5 August 1840 by the Slamannan Railway and closed by the L&NER 1 May 1930.

Line lifted - Demolished – Station site unused.
NS96260 76147

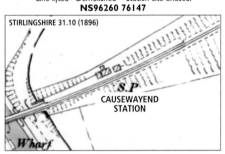

STIRLINGSHIRE 31.10 (1896)

CAUSEWAYEND STATION

CAUSEWAY HEAD 10 D4

Opened by the Stirling & Dunfermline Railway 1 July 1852, closed 1 January 1917, reopened 1 February 1919 and closed by BR 4 July 1955.

Line Operational – Demolished – No access. **NS80398 95301**

CAUSEWAY HEAD STATION

STIRLINGSHIRE 10.16 (1896)

CHALLOCH JUNCTION 2 A2

CHAPELHALL 6 D2

Opened 1 September 1887 by the CR and closed by the LM&SR 1 December 1930.

Line lifted – Demolished – Station site occupied by housing in Melrose Avenue. **NS78000 62817**

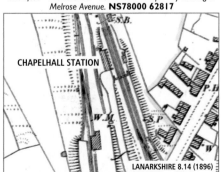

CHAPELHALL STATION

LANARKSHIRE 8.14 (1896)

CHARING CROSS 21A C2

Opened 15 March 1886 by the NBR.

Looking east at **Charing Cross Station** on 13 May 2017.

CHARLESFIELD HALT* 7A D3

Opened 10 August 1942 by the L&NER for employees at the Charlesfield Munitions Plant and closed by BR prior to June 1961.

Line lifted – Demolished - A farm track passes through the station site. **NT57780 29259**

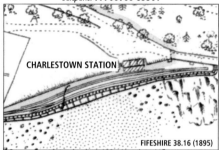

NT5729 (1961)

CHARLESFIELD HALT

CHARLESTOWN 11 A4

Opened 1 September 1894 by the NBR and closed by the L&NER 1 November 1926.

Line lifted – Demolished – Station site occupied by housing in Saltpans. **NT06966 83501**

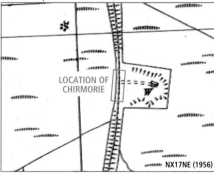

CHARLESTOWN STATION

FIFESHIRE 38.16 (1895)

CHATELHERAULT 6A D2

Opened 1 December 1866 by the Lesmahagow Railway as *Ferniegair*, it was rebuilt and reopened by the CR 2 October 1876, closed 1 January 1917 and rebuilt again and reopened by BR 12 December 2005 as *Chatelherault*.

Chatelherault Station on 19 March 2017.

CHIRMORIE* 2A A1

Opened in 1926 by the LM&SR for the use of railway staff and families and closed in 1938.

Line Operational – Demolished. **NX20088 77901**

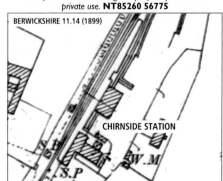

LOCATION OF CHIRMORIE

NX17NE (1956)

CHIRNSIDE 8 B1

Opened 15 August 1849 by the NBR and closed by BR 10 September 1951.

Line lifted – Station building and platform preserved in private use. **NT85260 56775**

BERWICKSHIRE 11.14 (1899)

CHIRNSIDE STATION

CHOLLERTON 4 B1

Opened in June 1860 by the Border Counties Railway and closed by BR 15 October 1956.

Line lifted - Station buildings and platforms in private use.
NY93053 71858

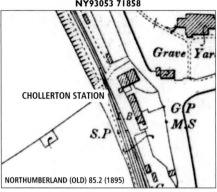

NORTHUMBERLAND (OLD) 85.2 (1895)

CHRYSTON 6 C1

Opened in 1839 by the Monkland Railway, closed to passengers 10 December 1851 and to goods by BR 4 January 1965.

Line lifted – Demolished – Station site in commercial use.
NS68948 70831

LANARKSHIRE 2.11 (1897)

CLACKMANNAN & KENNET 10 D4

Opened 18 December 1893 by the NBR and closed by the L&NER 7 July 1930 *(NB Incorrectly shown as Clackmannan on Map 10).*

Line Operational – Demolished – Station site occupied by housing in Hetherington Drive. **NS91581 91928**

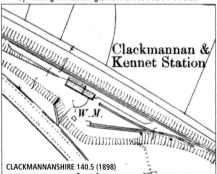

CLACKMANNANSHIRE 140.5 (1898)

CLACKMANNAN ROAD 10 D4

Opened 28 August 1850 by the Stirling & Dunfermline Railway as *Clackmannan*, renamed by the NBR 1 January 1894 as *Clackmannan Road*, closed 1 January 1917, reopened 2 June 1919 and closed by the L&NER 1 December 1921.

Line lifted – Demolished – Station site unused – The West Fife Cycle Way passes through the station site. **NS91991 92516**

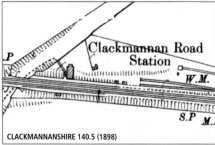

CLACKMANNANSHIRE 140.5 (1898)

CLARKSTON (CR) 6 C2

Opened 1 January 1866 by the Busby Railway as *Clarkston*, renamed 1 July 1877 *as Clarkston for Easlesham*, by BR 5 May 1952 as *Clarkston & Stamperland* and 7 May 1973 as *Clarkston*.
Clarkston Station on 18 March 2017.

CLARKSTON (NBR) 6 D1

Opened 11 August 1862 by the Bathgate & Coatbridge Railway as *Clarkston*, renamed by BR 8 June 1953 as *Clarkston Lanark* and closed 9 January 1956.

Line Operational – Demolished – Part of station site occupied by DRUMGELLOCH (qv). **NS78321 65669**

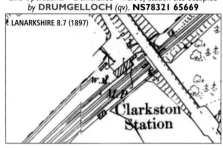

LANARKSHIRE 8.7 (1897)

CLEGHORN 7 A2

Opened 15 February 1848 by the CR as *Lanark*, renamed 1 January 1855 as *Cleghorn Junction*, 1 April 1864 as *Cleghorn* and closed by BR 4 January 1965.

Line Operational – Station building in private use – Platforms demolished. **NS90908 45611**

LANARKSHIRE 25.12 (1896)

CLELAND 6 D2

Opened 9 July 1869 by the CR as *Bellside*, renamed 1873 as *Bellside for Omoa*, 1 October 1879 as *Omoa* and by the LM&SR 1 October 1941 as *Cleland*.

Cleland Station on 19 March 2017.

CLELAND 6 D2

Opened 15 May 1867 by the CR, closed 1 January 1917, reopened 2 June 1919 and closed by the LM&SR 1 December 1930.

Line lifted – Demolished – Station site occupied by housing in Baxter Brae. **NS80024 57939**

LANARKSHIRE 12.11 (1896)

CLIM COLLIERY BRANCH 7 A2
CLOCKSBRIGGS 11 D1

Opened c1840 by the Arbroath & Forfar Railway, closed by the CR 1 January 1917, reopened 2 June 1919, renamed by the LM&SR in 1926 as *Clocksbriggs Halt*, 12 September 1932 as *Clocksbriggs* and closed by BR 5 December 1955.

Line lifted – Station House in private use – Platforms demolished. **NO49583 51933**

FORFARSHIRE 39.1 (1901)

CLOSEBURN 7 A4

Opened 15 October 1849 by the Glasgow, Paisley, Kilmarnock & Ayr Railway and closed by BR 11 September 1961.

Line Operational – Station building in private use – Platforms demolished. **NX89740 92299**

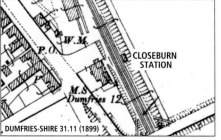

DUMFRIES-SHIRE 31.11 (1899)

CLOVENFORDS 7 D2

Opened 18 June 1866 by the Innerleithen & Galashiels Railway and closed by BR 5 February 1962.

Line lifted - Station building in private use – Station site occupied by housing in Station Yard. **NT45099 36660**

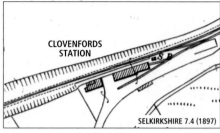

SELKIRKSHIRE 7.4 (1897)

CLUNES 14 B1

Opened in October 1863 by the Inverness & Aberdeen Junction Railway and closed by BR 13 June 1960.
Line Operational – Demolished – No access. **NH55836 46318**

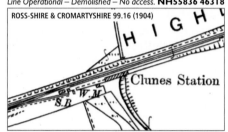

ROSS-SHIRE & CROMARTYSHIRE 99.16 (1904)

CLYDEBANK 6 B1/21A A1

Opened 17 May 1897 by the NBR as *Clydebank Central*, closed 1 January 1917, reopened 2 June 1919 and renamed by BR 14 June 1965 as *Clydebank*.

Clydebank Station on 13 September 2015.

CLYDEBANK 6 B1/21A A2

Opened 1 October 1896 by the Lanarkshire & Dumbartonshire Railway as *Clydebank*, renamed by BR 28 February 1953 as *Clydebank Riverside* and closed by BR 5 October 1964.

Line lifted – Demolished – Station site in commercial use.
NS49947 69589

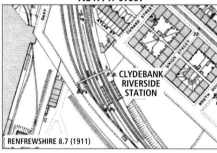

RENFREWSHIRE 8.7 (1911)

CLYDEBANK EAST 21A A1

Opened 1 December 1882 by the Glasgow, Yoker & Clydebank Railway as *Clydebank*, renamed by the NBR 17 May 1897 as *Clydebank East* and closed by BR 14 September 1959.

Line lifted – Demolished – Station site unused.
NS50052 69850

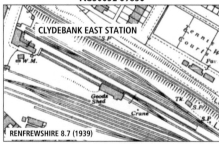

RENFREWSHIRE 8.7 (1939)

COALBURN 6 D3

Opened 2 November 1891 by the CR and closed by BR 4 October 1965.

Line lifted – Demolished – Station site unused.
NS81073 34544

LANARKSHIRE 37.8 (1896)

COATBRIDGE
CENTRAL (NBR)　　　　6 D1
Opened 26 October 1871 by the NBR, closed 1 January 1917 (except for workmen's trains), reopened 2 June 1919 and closed by BR 10 September 1951.
Line Operational – Demolished – No access. **NS73035 65138**

LANARKSHIRE 7.12 (1897)

COATBRIDGE
CENTRAL (CR)　　　　6 C1
Opened in February 1843 by the Garnkirk & Glasgow Railway as *Coatbridge*, and renamed by BR 8 June 1953 as *Coatbridge Central*.

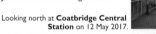
Looking north at **Coatbridge Central Station** on 12 May 2017.

COATBRIDGE SUNNYSIDE　6 D1
Opened 2 November 1863 by the Bathgate & Coatbridge Railway.

Looking west at **Coatbridge Sunnyside Station** on 12 May 2017.

COATDYKE　　　　6A D1
Opened in December 1890 by the Bathgate & Coatbridge Railway.

Coatdyke Station on 12 May 2017.

COBBINSHAW　　　　7 A2
Opened 4 October 1875 by the CR and closed by BR 18 April 1966.
Line Operational – Demolished – No access. **NT01191 57813**

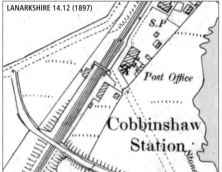
LANARKSHIRE 14.12 (1897)

COCKBURNSPATH　　　　8 A1
Opened 22 June 1846 by the NBR and closed by BR 18 June 1951.
Line Operational – Station building in private use – Platforms demolished. **NT77576 71680**

BERWICKSHIRE 1.10 (1898)

COLDSTREAM　　　　8 B2
Opened prior to July 1851 by the York, Newcastle & Berwick Railway as *Cornhill*, renamed by the NER 1 October 1873 as *Coldstream* and closed by BR 15 June 1964.
Line lifted – Demolished - Station site occupied by housing in Station Gardens. **NT86277 39447**

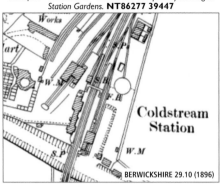
BERWICKSHIRE 29.10 (1896)

COLEBURN*　　　　15 B1
Opened 5 June 1863 by the Morayshire Railway, closed by the GNofSR in 1871 and retained for private use until at least 1926. It was also known as *Coleburns*.
Line lifted – Demolished – A track passes through the station site. **NJ24148 55260 (a)**

ELGINSHIRE 13.13 (1893)

COLFIN　　　　1 D2
Opened 28 August 1862 by the Portpatrick & Wigtownshire Joint Railway and closed by BR 6 February 1950.
Line lifted – Demolished – Degraded platform partially extant – Station site in private use as a garden area for an adjacent house. **NX03951 54739**

WIGTOWNSHIRE 17.15 (1893)

COLINTON　　　　7 B1/22A A3
Opened 1 August 1874 by the CR and closed by the LM&SR 1 November 1943.
Line lifted – Demolished - The Water of Leith Walkway passes through the station site. **NT21399 69081**

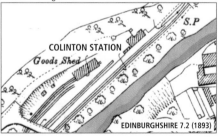
EDINBURGHSHIRE 7.2 (1893)

COLLESSIE　　　　11 B3
Opened prior to May 1848 by the Edinburgh & Northern Railway and closed by BR 19 September 1955.
Line Operational – Demolished – No access. **NO28515 13209**

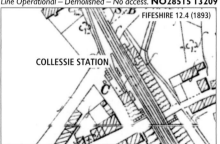
FIFESHIRE 12.4 (1893)

COLLIERY ROAD　　　　5A B3
Opened in May 1927 by the 2ft 3in gauge Campbeltown and Machrihanish Light Railway and closed after October 1927.

COLLISTON　　　　11 D2
Opened 24 November 1838 by the Arbroath & Forfar Railway and closed by BR 5 December 1955.
Line lifted – Station House in private use – Southbound platform extant – A footpath passes through part of the station site. **NO61863 45901**

FORFARSHIRE 46.2 (1901)

COLTFIELD　　　　18 A4
Opened 22 December 1862 by the Inverness and Aberdeen Junction Railway as *Wards*, renamed 1 January 1865 as *Coltfield*, in 1896 as *Coltfield Platform* and closed by the LM&SR 14 September 1931.
Line lifted – Demolished – Station site unused. **NJ12192 64360**

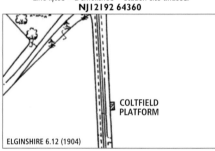
ELGINSHIRE 6.12 (1904)

COLZIUM　　　　6 C1
Opened 2 July 1888 by the Kilsyth & Bonnybridge Joint Railway, closed to passengers by the CR 1 March 1917 and to goods by BR 2 May 1955.
Line lifted – Demolished – Station site unused. **NS73476 78162**

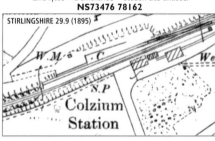
STIRLINGSHIRE 29.9 (1895)

COMMONDYKE　　　　6 C3
Opened 1 October 1897 by the Glasgow, Paisley, Kilmarnock & Ayr Railway and closed by BR 3 July 1950.
Line lifted – Platforms partially extant – Demolished – Station site unused. **NS57714 22189**

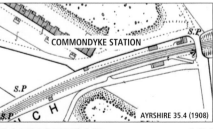
AYRSHIRE 35.4 (1908)

COMMONHEAD　　　　6 D1
Opened 5 August 1850 by the Slamannan Railway as *Commonhead*, renamed by the NBR 1 June 1886 as *Commonhead Airdrie North* and closed by the L&NER 1 May 1930.
Line lifted – Demolished – A walkway passes through the station site. **NS75850 66183**

LANARKSHIRE 8.5 (1897)

COMRIE
10 D3

Opened 1 June 1893 by the CR and closed by BR 6 July 1964.

Line lifted - Platforms partially extant - Station site part of "Comrie Holiday Park". **NN77812 22272**

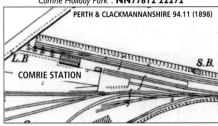

CONNEL FERRY
9 C2

Opened 1 July 1880 by the Callander and Oban Railway.

Looking west at **Connel Ferry Station** *on 14 September 2015.*

CONON BRIDGE
14 B1

Opened 11 June 1862 by the Inverness & Ross-shire Railway as *Conon*, closed by BR 13 June 1960 and rebuilt and reopened 8 February 2013 as *Conon Bridge*.

Looking north at **Conon Bridge Station** *on 17 September 2015.*

CORKERHILL
21A B3

Opened 1 December 1896 by the G&SWR as *Corkerhill Halt*, renamed as *Corkerhill* by LM&SR in 1933/4, closed by BR 10 January 1983 and reopened 30 July 1990.

Looking east at **Corkerhill Station** *on 18 March 2017.*

CORKERHILL ENGINE SHEDS*
21A B3

Opened by the LM&SR prior to 1942 for the use of engine shed staff and closed by BR after 1957.

Line Operational. **NS54274 62750 (e)**

CORNHILL
15 D1

Opened 30 July 1859 by the Banff, Portsoy & Strathisla Railway and closed by BR 6 May 1968.

Line lifted – Station building and platform privately preserved. **NJ58068 58855**

CORPACH
13 D4

Opened 1 April 1901 by the Mallaig Extension Railway.

Looking east at **Corpach Station** *on 14 September 2015.*

CORROUR
10 A1

Opened 7 August 1894 by the West Highland Railway as a private station for Sir John Stirling-Maxwell and opened for public use by the L&NER 11 September 1934.

Looking south at **Corrour Station** *on 15 September 2015.*

CORSEHILL*
3A B1

Opened by 1888 by the CR for use by quarry workers and closed by the LM&SR prior to July 1926.

Line lifted – Demolished – Station site in commercial use. **NY20511 70162 (a)**

CORSTORPHINE
7 B1/22A A2

Opened 1 February 1902 by the Edinburgh & Glasgow Railway and closed by BR 1 January 1968.

Line lifted – Demolished – Station site occupied by housing in The Paddockholm. **NT20244 72758**

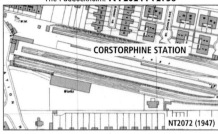

COTCASTLE GOODS
6 D2

COULTER
7 A2

Opened 6 November 1860 by the Symington, Biggar & Broughton Railway and closed by BR 5 June 1950.

Line lifted – Station building in private use – Platform extant. **NT01854 36324**

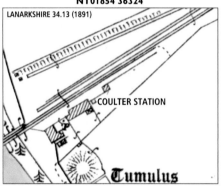

COUNTY BOUNDARY JUNCTION
6 C2

COUPAR ANGUS
11 B2

Opened 24 February 1837 by the Newtyle & Coupar Angus Railway, closed by the CR 6 September 1847, reopened 2 August 1848 and closed by BR 4 September 1967.

Line lifted – Booking Office extant – Demolished - Meadowside Close passes through the station site. **NO22479 40149**

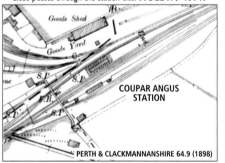

COVE BAY
16 B3

Opened 1 April 1850 by the Aberdeen Railway as *Cove*, renamed by the CR 1 October 1912 as *Cove Bay* and closed by BR 11 June 1956.

Line Operational – Demolished – No access. **NJ95321 00980**

COWDENBEATH (NEW)
11 B4

Opened 2 June 1890 by the NBR as *Cowdenbeath New* and renamed by BR 14 June 1965 as *Cowdenbeath*.

Cowdenbeath Station on 18 September 2015.

COWDENBEATH (OLD)
11 B4

Opened 4 September 1848 by the Edinburgh & Northern Railway as *Cowdenbeath*, renamed by the NBR 1 June 1890 as *Cowdenbeath Old* and although closed to passengers 31 March 1919 continued in use for miner's trains and goods traffic, the latter until closure by BR 1 January 1968.

Line lifted – Demolished – A cycle/walkway passes through the station site. **NT16676 91346**

COWLAIRS
21A D2

Opened 1 April 1858 by the Edinburgh & Glasgow Railway and closed by BR 7 September 1964.

Line Operational – Demolished – Platforms partially extant – No access. **NS60073 67757**

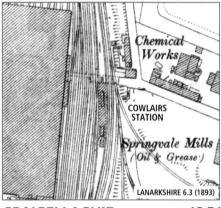

CRAIGELLACHIE
15 B1

Opened 1 July 1863 by the Strathspey Railway as *Strathspey Junction*, renamed by the GNofSR 1 June 1864 as *Craigellachie Junction*, c1878 as *Craigellachie* and closed by BR 6 May 1968.

Line lifted - Demolished – Platforms partially extant – The Speyside Way passes through the station site. **NJ29249 45156**

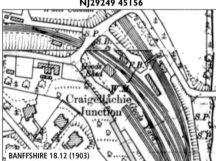

CRAIGENDORAN
6 A1

Opened 15 May 1882 by the NBR as *Craigendoran Pier* and renamed by the L&NER 1922/3 as *Craigendoran*.

Looking north at **Craigendoran Station** *on 13 September 2015.*

CRAIGENDORAN UPPER
6 A1

Constructed alongside Craigendoran (*qv*), opened by the West Highland Railway 7 August 1894 and closed by BR 14 June 1964.

Line Operational – Demolished – No access. **NS30992 81301**

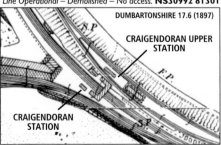

CRAIGEND PLATFORM*   6A C1
Opened in 1928 by the L&NER for workmen's trains and closed in 1942.

Line lifted – Demolished – The Paisley & Clyde Cycle Path passes through the station site. **NS59039 78792 (a)**

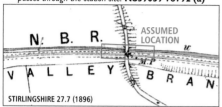

STIRLINGSHIRE 27.7 (1896)

CRAIGHEAD BRANCH   11 B4
CRAIG HOUSES*   13A C1
Opened 3 December 1951 by BR for the use of railwaymen's families and closed c1972.

Line Operational – Demolished. **NH04026 49207 (a)**

ROSS-SHIRE & CROMARTYSHIRE 94 (1902)

CRAIGLEITH   22A B2
Opened 1 August 1879 by the CR as *Craigleath*, renamed as *Craigleith for Blackhall* 1 July 1922 and closed by BR 30 April 1962.

Line lifted – Platforms extant - The Roseburn Path passes through the station site. **NT22425 74378**

EDINBURGHSHIRE 3.6 (1893)

CRAIGLOCKHART   22A B2
Opened 1 June 1887 by the Edinburgh Suburban & Southside Junction Railway, closed by the NBR 1 May 1890, reopened 1 January 1891, closed 1 January 1917, reopened 1 February 1919 and closed by BR 10 September 1962.

Line Operational – Demolished – Platforms partially extant – No access. **NT23326 71253**

EDINBURGHSHIRE 3.14 (1893)

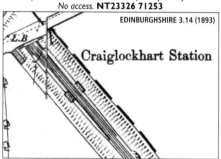

CRAIGNACAILLEICH PLATFORM*   10A C3
Opened c1922 by the LM&SR for use by railwaymen's families and closed by BR c1959.

Line lifted – Demolished – The Rob Roy Way passes through the station site. **NN58282 12195(a)**

PERTH & CLACKMANNANSHIRE 114NE (1898)

CRAIGO   12 A1
Opened in February 1851 by the Aberdeen Railway and closed by BR 11 June 1955.

Line Operational – Demolished – No access. **NO68830 64388**

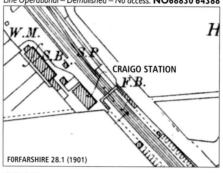

FORFARSHIRE 28.1 (1901)

CRAIL   11 D3
Opened 1 September 1883 by the Anstruther & St Andrews Railway and closed by BR 11 June 1956.

Line lifted – Station building in private use – Platforms demolished. **NO60928 07949**

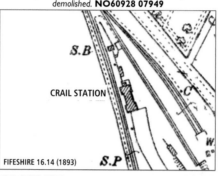

FIFESHIRE 16.14 (1893)

CRATHES   16 B3
Opened 1 January 1863 by the Deeside Railway and closed by BR 28 February 1966.

Line lifted –Station building extant – The Deeside Way passes through the station site. **NO74877 96345**

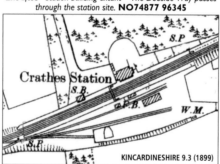

KINCARDINESHIRE 9.3 (1899)

CRAWFORD   7 A3
Opened 1 January 1891 by the CR and closed by BR 4 January 1965.

Line Operational – Demolished – No access. **NS95554 20933**

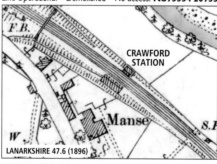

LANARKSHIRE 47.6 (1896)

CREAGAN   9 C2
Opened 24 August 1903 by the Callander & Oban Railway and closed by BR 28 March 1966.

Line lifted – Station building and platform restored as part of "Appin Holiday Homes" caravan site. **NM96936 44892**

NM9644 (1970)

CREETOWN   2 B2
Opened 12 March 1861 by the Portpatrick & Wigtownshire Joint Railway and closed by BR 14 June 1965.

Line lifted – Station building and platform in private use. **NX47517 59961**

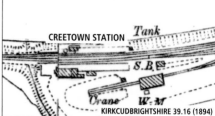

KIRKCUDBRIGHTSHIRE 39.16 (1894)

CRIANLARICH (CR)   10 A3
Opened 1 August 1873 by the Callander & Oban Railway as *Crianlarich*, renamed by BR in 1953 as *Crianlarich Lower* and closed 28 September 1965.

Line lifted – Demolished – Station site unused. **NN38663 25343**

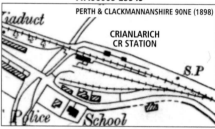

PERTH & CLACKMANNANSHIRE 90NE (1898)

CRIANLARICH (NBR)   10 A3
Opened 7 August 1894 by the West Highland Railway, renamed by BR in 1951 as *Crianlarich Upper* and reverted back to *Crianlarich* after 1965.

Looking north at **Crianlarich Station** on 13 September 2015.

CRIEFF   10 D3
Opened 1 June 1893 by the CR and closed by BR 6 July 1964.

Line lifted – Demolished – Station site occupied by "The Crieff Community Hospital" and Ambulance Station. **NN86219 21294**

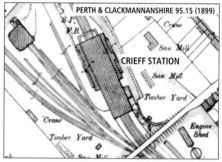

PERTH & CLACKMANNANSHIRE 95.15 (1899)

CROFTFOOT   21A D4
Opened by the LM&SR 1 January 1931.

Class 320 Unit No.320414 at **Croftfoot Station** on 18 March 2017.

CROMARTY   17 C4
Planned by the Cromarty & Dingwall Railway but never opened.

CROMBIE HALT*   11A A4
Opened in March 1916 by the NBR for use by workers at the adjacent Royal Ordnance Factory, it was closed by the L&NER prior to 1 November 1926.

Line Operational for Freight – Demolished. **NT06650 84533**

FIFESHIRE 38.15 (1895)

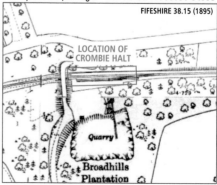

CROMDALE 15 A2

Opened 1 July 1863 by the Strathspey Railway and closed by BR 18 October 1965.

Line lifted - Station building and platform restored and in private use – The Speyside Way passes through the station site.
NJ07108 28649

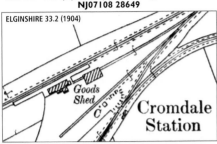

ELGINSHIRE 33.2 (1904)

CRONBERRY 6 C3

Opened 1 May 1876 by the Glasgow, Paisley, Kilmarnock & Ayr Railway and closed by BR 10 September 1951.

Line lifted – Demolished – Station site unused.
NS60763 22570

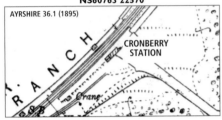

AYRSHIRE 36.1 (1895)

CROOK OF DEVON 11 A4

Opened 1 May 1863 by the Devon Valley Railway and closed by BR 15 June 1964. It was also known as *Crook of Devon for Fossoway* in some timetables.

Line lifted – Demolished – Station site occupied by housing in Station Road. **NO03748 00136**

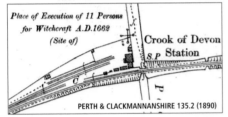

PERTH & CLACKMANNANSHIRE 135.2 (1890)

CROOKSTON 21A A3

Opened 1 July 1885 by the G&SWR, closed 1 January 1917, reopened 10 February 1919, closed by BR 10 January 1983 and reopened 30 July 1990.

Looking west at **Crookston Station** on 18 March 2017.

CROSSFORD 2 D1

Opened 1 March 1905 by the G&SWR and closed by the LM&SR 3 May 1943.

Line lifted – Demolished – Station site landscaped as part of garden for adjacent former Station Master's House.
NX83331 88209

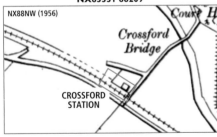

NX88NW (1956)

CROSSGATE HALL HALT 7A C1

Opened 1 August 1913 by the NBR, closed 1 January 1917, reopened 1 February 1919 and closed by the L&NER 22 September 1930.

Line lifted – Demolished – Station site unused.
NT36748 68911

EDINBURGHSHIRE 8.4 (1893)

CROSSGATES 11 B4

Opened 4 September 1848 by the Edinburgh & Northern Railway as *Crossgates*, renamed 1 July 1923 by the L&NER as *Crossgates Fife* and closed by BR 26 September 1949.

Line Operational – Demolished – Platforms partially extant – No access. **NT14744 89537**

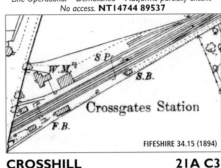

FIFESHIRE 34.15 (1894)

CROSSHILL 21A C3

Opened 1 March 1886 by the CR, closed 1 January 1917 and reopened 1 April 1919.

Crosshill Station on 18 March 2017.

CROSSHOUSE 6 B2

Opened in April 1873 by the Busby Railway and closed by BR 18 April 1966.

Line lifted – Demolished – Station site in commercial use - A cycle/walkway passes through part of the station site.
NS39967 39694

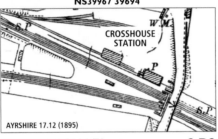

AYRSHIRE 17.12 (1895)

CROSSMICHAEL 2 D2

Opened 12 March 1861 by the Portpatrick & Wigtownshire Joint Railway and closed by BR 14 June 1965.

Line lifted – Station building and platform in private use.
NX72890 66894

KIRKCUDBRIGHTSHIRE 35.11 (1894)

CROSSMYLOOF 21A C3

Opened in June 1888 by the Glasgow, Barrhead & Kilmarnock Joint Railway.

Crossmyloof Station on 18 March 2017.

CROW ROAD 21A B2

Opened 1 October 1896 by the Lanarkshire & Dumbartonshire Railway and closed by BR 6 November 1960.

Line lifted – Demolished – Station site unused.
NS55161 67207

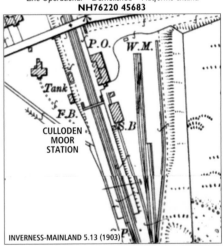

NS5567 (1949)

CROY 6 C1

Opened 21 February 1842 by the Edinburgh & Glasgow Railway.

Looking north at **Croy Station** on 13 May 2017.

CRUDEN BAY 16 C2

Opened 2 August 1897 by the GNofSR and closed by the L&NER 31 October 1932.

Line lifted – Demolished – Station site landscaped and incorporated into a field. **NK08313 36600**

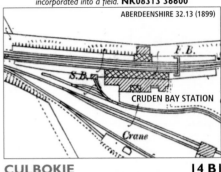

ABERDEENSHIRE 32.13 (1899)

CULBOKIE 14 B1

Planned by the Cromarty & Dingwall Railway but never opened.

CULLEN 18 C4

Opened 1 May 1886 by the GNofSR and closed by BR 6 May 1968.

Line lifted – Demolished – Station site occupied by housing in New View Court. **NJ51403 67219**

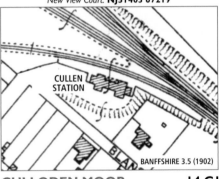

BANFFSHIRE 3.5 (1902)

CULLODEN MOOR 14 C1

Opened 1 November 1898 by the HR and closed by BR 6 May 1968.

Line Operational – Demolished – Platforms extant.
NH76220 45683

INVERNESS-MAINLAND 5.13 (1903)

CULRAIN 17 B3

Opened 1 July 1870 by the Sutherland Railway and worked by the HR from the outset.

Looking south at **Culrain Station** on 16 September 2015.

CULROSS 11 A4

Opened 2 July 1906 by the Keith & Dufftown Railway and closed by the L&NER 7 July 1930.

Line Operational – Demolished – No access. **NS99367 85999**

NS9985 (1961)

CULTER 16 A3

Opened 8 September 1853 by the Deeside Railway and closed by BR 28 February 1966.

Line lifted – Platform preserved extant - A roadway passes through the station site. **NJ84159 00487**

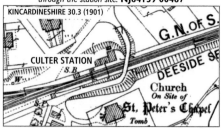

KINCARDINESHIRE 30.3 (1901)

CULTS 16 B3

Opened in 1855 by the Deeside Railway and closed by BR 28 February 1966.

Line lifted – Station building in private use – Platforms extant – The Deeside Way passes through the station site. **NJ89742 02979**

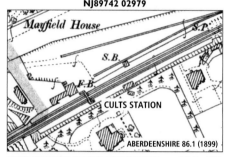

ABERDEENSHIRE 86.1 (1899)

CUMBERLAND STREET 21A C3

Opened 20 February 1900 by the G&SWR as *Eglinton Street*, renamed by the LM&SR 2 June 1924 as *Cumberland Street* and closed by BR 14 February 1966.

Line Operational – Demolished – No access. **NS58646 63993**

NS5863 (1952)

CUMBERNAULD 6 D1

Opened in May 1870 by the CR.

Cumbernauld Station on 13 May 2017.

CUMMERTREES 3 B2

Opened 23 August 1848 by the Glasgow, Paisley, Kilmarnock & Ayr Railway and closed by BR 19 September 1955.

Line Operational – Station building in private use – Platforms demolished. **NY13894 66560**

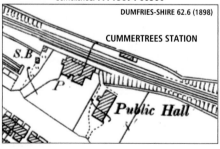

DUMFRIES-SHIRE 62.6 (1898)

CUMNOCK 6 C3

Opened 1 July 1872 by the G&SWR and closed by BR 10 September 1951.

Line lifted – Demolished – Station site occupied by housing in George McTurk Court. **NS57127 19401**

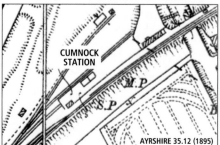

AYRSHIRE 35.12 (1895)

CUNNINGHAMHEAD 6 A2

Opened in September 1844 by the Glasgow, Paisley, Kilmarnock & Ayr Railway as *Stewarton*, closed 22 May 1848 reopened in November 1850, renamed by the G&SWR 1 September 1873 as *Cunninghamhead* and closed by BR 1 January 1951.

Line lifted – Demolished – Station site unused. **NS36937 41440**

AYRSHIRE 17.7 (1895)

CUPAR 11 C3

Opened 20 September 1847 by the Edinburgh and Northern Railway.

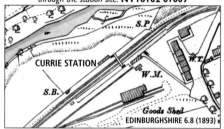

Cupar Station on 18 September 2015.

CURRIE 7 B1

Opened 1 August 1874 by the CR and closed by the LM&SR 1 November 1943.

Line lifted – Demolished - The Water of Leith Walkway passes through the station site. **NT18162 67669**

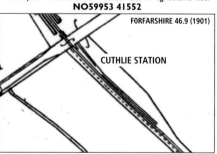

EDINBURGHSHIRE 6.8 (1893)

CURRIEHILL 7 B1

Opened 15 February 1848 by the CR as *Currie*, renamed as *Currie Hill* 1 May 1874, closed by BR 2 April 1951 and reopened 5 October 1987 as *Curriehill*.

Curriehill Station on 12 May 2017.

CUTHLIE 11 D2

Opened 1 February 1900 by the Dundee & Arbroath Joint Railway, closed 1 January 1917, reopened 1 January 1918 and closed by the L&NER 2 December 1929.

Line lifted – Demolished – Station site in agricultural use. **NO59953 41552**

FORFARSHIRE 46.9 (1901)

DAILLY 6 A4

Opened 24 May 1860 by the Maybole & Girvan Railway and closed by BR 6 September 1965.

Line Operational – Station building in private use – Platforms demolished. **NS26129 02222**

AYRSHIRE 50.7 (1894)

DAILUAINE HALT 15A B1

Opened 18 November 1933 by the L&NER and closed by BR 18 October 1965.

Line lifted - Platform extant – The Speyside Way passes through the station site. **NJ23667 41314**

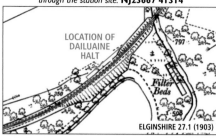

ELGINSHIRE 27.1 (1903)

DAIRSIE 11 C3

Opened 17 May 1848 by the Edinburgh, Perth & Dundee Railway and closed by BR 20 September 1954.

Line Operational – Demolished – No access. **NO41649 16687**

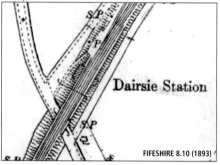

FIFESHIRE 8.10 (1893)

DALBEATTIE 2 D2

Opened 7 November 1859 by the Castle Douglas and Dumfries Railway and closed by BR 14 June 1965.

Line lifted – Demolished – Station site occupied by housing in Station Drive. **NX83105 61596**

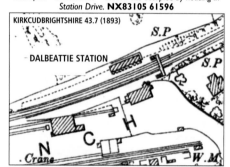

KIRKCUDBRIGHTSHIRE 43.7 (1893)

DALCHONZIE PLATFORM 10A C3

Opened 15 July 1903 by the CR and closed by BR 1 October 1951.

Line lifted – Station building and signal box in private use – Remainder demolished. **NN74052 23029**

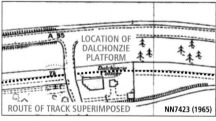

ROUTE OF TRACK SUPERIMPOSED NN7423 (1965)

DALCROSS 14 C1

Opened 7 November 1855 by the Inverness & Nairn Railway and closed by BR 3 May 1965.

Line Operational - Station building in private use - Platforms demolished. **NH76153 50426**

INVERNESS-MAINLAND 5.1 (1903)

DALGETY BAY 11A B4

Opened by Railtrack 28 March 1998.

Dalgety Bay Station
on 18 September 2015.

DALGUISE 11 A2

Opened 1 June 1863 by the Inverness & Perth Junction Railway and closed by BR 3 May 1965.
Line Operational – Station House in private use – Platforms demolished. **NN99506 47203**

PERTH & CLACKMANNANSHIRE 50.12 (1899)

DALKEITH 7 C1

Opened in 1839 by the Edinburgh & Dalkeith Railway, closed 1 January 1917, reopened 1 October 1919 and closed by the L&NER 5 January 1942.
Line lifted – Demolished – Station site occupied by a Morrisons Superstore. **NT32988 67160**

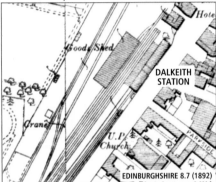

EDINBURGHSHIRE 8.7 (1892)

DALMALLY 9 D3

Opened by the Callander and Oban Railway 1 May 1877.

Looking west at **Dalmally Station** on 14 September 2015.

DALMARNOCK 21A D3

Opened by the Glasgow Central Railway 1 November 1895, closed by BR 5 October 1964 and reopened 5 November 1979.

The semi-subterranean **Dalmarnock Station** viewed on 12 May 2017.

DALMELLINGTON 6 B4

Opened by the Ayr & Dalmellington Railway 7 August 1856 and closed by BR 6 April 1964.
Line lifted – Demolished – Station site occupied by "Dalmellington Area Central". **NS47828 05888**

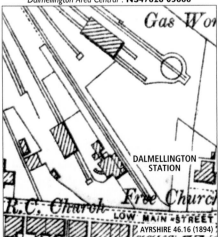

AYRSHIRE 46.16 (1894)

DALMENY 7 B1

Opened by the NBR 5 March 1890 as *Forth Bridge* and renamed 28 April 1890 as *Dalmeny.*

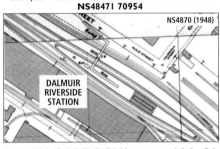

Class 158 Unit No. 158712
at **Dalmeny Station** on 12 May 2017.

DALMUIR 6 B1

Opened by the NBR 17 May 1897 as *Dalmuir*, renamed by BR May 1952 as *Dalmuir Park* and August 1973 as *Dalmuir.*

Looking west at **Dalmuir Station** on 13 September 2015.

DALMUIR RIVERSIDE 6 B1

Opened by the Lanarkshire & Dumbartonshire Railway 1 October 1896 as *Dalmuir*, renamed by BR in May 1952 as *Dalmuir Riverside* and closed 5 October 1964.
Line lifted – Demolished – Station site in commercial use. **NS48471 70954**

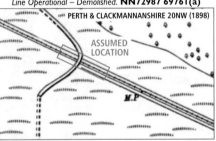

NS4870 (1948)

DALMUIR RIVERSIDE STATION

DALNACARDOCH* 10A C1

Opened 1 May 1905 by the HR. Closure date unknown.
Line Operational – Demolished. **NN72987 69761(a)**

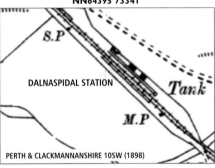

PERTH & CLACKMANNANSHIRE 20NW (1898)

ASSUMED LOCATION

M.P

DALNASPIDAL 10 C1

Opened in June 1864 by the HR and closed by BR 3 May 1965.
Line Operational – Demolished – Platforms extant – No access. **NN64395 73341**

S.P

DALNASPIDAL STATION

Tank

M.P

PERTH & CLACKMANNANSHIRE 10SW (1898)

DALRADDY CROSSING* 14A D3

Opened by the HR. Opening and closure dates unrecorded.
Line Operational – Demolished. **NH86011 08303 (a)**

Gravel Pits

ASSUMED LOCATION

INVERNESS-MAINLAND 73 (1900)

DALREOCH 6 B1

Opened 15 July 1850 by the Caledonian & Dumbartonshire Junction Railway.

Dalreoch Station
on 13 September 2015.

DALRY 6 A2

Opened 21 July 1840 by the Glasgow, Paisley, Kilmarnock & Ayr Railway.

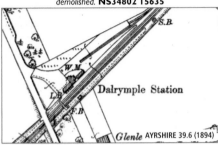

Dalry Station on 17 March 2017.

DALRYMPLE 6 A4

Opened 1 November 1856 by the Ayr & Maybole Railway and closed by BR 6 December 1954.
Line Operational – Station building in private use – Platforms demolished. **NS34802 15635**

S.B

W.M.

L.B
S.B

Dalrymple Station

Glenle AYRSHIRE 39.6 (1894)

DALRYMPLE JUNCTION 6 A3

DALRY ROAD 22A B2

Opened 2 July 1900 by the CR and closed by BR 30 April 1962.
Line lifted – One platform extant – A pathway passes through the station site. **NT23795 72672**

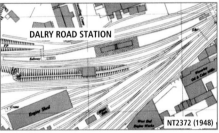

DALRY ROAD STATION

NT2372 (1948)

DALSERF 6 D2

Opened 1 December 1856 by the Lesmahagow Railway as *Ayr Road*, renamed by the CR 1 July 1903 as *Dalserf* and closed by BR 1 October 1951.
Line lifted – Demolished – Station site in commercial use. **NS78149 50931**

LANARKSHIRE 18.15 (1896)

DALSERF STATION

S.P

DALVEY FARM HALT 15A A2

Opened 15 June 1959 by BR and closed 18 October 1965.
Line lifted - Demolished – The Speyside Way passes through the station site. **NJ10966 32169**

LOCATION OF DALVEY FARM HALT

Bridge of Avon rantown

Bridge of Dalvey

ELGINSHIRE 30.11 (1903)

DALWHINNIE 14 C4

Opened by the Inverness & Perth Junction Railway 9 September 1863.

Looking south at **Dalwhinnie Station** on 15 September 2015.

DANDALEITH   15 B1

Opened 23 December 1858 by the Morayshire Railway as *Craigellachie*, renamed in 1864 as *Dandaleith* and closed by BR 5 March 1962.

Line lifted – Demolished – The A941 passes through the west side of the station site - Remainder unused. **NJ28713 45984**

ELGINSHIRE 23 (1903)

DARVEL   6 C2

Opened 1 June 1896 by the G&SWR and closed by BR 6 April 1964.

Line lifted – Demolished – Station site occupied by housing in Station Gate. **NS56294 37694**

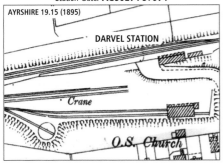

AYRSHIRE 19.15 (1895)

DAVA   15 A2

Opened 1 November 1864 by the Inverness & Perth Junction Railway and closed by BR 18 October 1965.

Line lifted – Station building in private use – Degraded platforms extant [The Dava Way by-passes the station]. **NJ00828 38940**

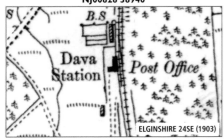

ELGINSHIRE 24SE (1903)

DAVIDSONS MAINS   22A A1

Opened 1 March 1894 by the CR as *Barnton Gate*, renamed 1 April 1903 as *Davidsons Mains* and closed by BR 7 May 1951.

Line lifted – Demolished – Station site occupied by housing in Barnton Avenue. **NT20416 75543**

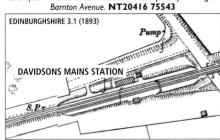

EDINBURGHSHIRE 3.1 (1893)

DAVIOT   14 C2

Opened 19 July 1897 by the HR and closed by BR 3 May 1965.

Line Operational – Demolished – Platforms extant. **NH73659 39872**

INVERNESS-MAINLAND 12.16 (1903)

DEADWATER   7 D4

Opened as a private station by the NBR prior to March 1877 as *Deadwater Foot Crossing* and opened to the public 1 March 1880 as *Deadwater*. Renamed by BR 9 September 1955 as *Deadwater Halt* and closed 15 October 1956.

Line lifted - Station building and platform in private use – The Kielder Forest Border Railway Trail passes through the station site. **NY60334 96763**

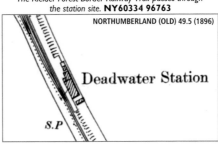

NORTHUMBERLAND (OLD) 49.5 (1896)

DECHMONT   7A A1

Opened 19 June 1905 by the Edinburgh District Lunacy Board, a private line but publicly available and worked by the NBR. It was closed 1 August 1921.

Line lifted – Demolished – Station site occupied by housing in Craiglaw. **NT04297 70818**

LINLITHGOWSHIRE 10.1 (1915)

DECHMONT COLLIERY   6 C2
DEE STREET   16A A3

Opened 6 February 1961 by BR and closed 28 February 1966.

Line lifted – Demolished – Station site unused. **NO69654 95548**

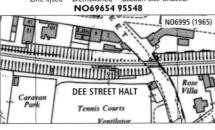

DELNY   17 C4

Opened 1 June 1864 by the Inverness & Aberdeen Junction Railway as *Delney*, renamed in 1856 as *Delny* and closed by BR 13 June 1960.

Line Operational – Station building and part-extant platform in private use. **NH74532 72558**

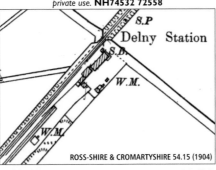

ROSS-SHIRE & CROMARTYSHIRE 54.15 (1904)

DENHEAD   11 D2

Opened 1 February 1900 by the Dundee & Arbroath Joint Railway, closed 1 January 1917, reopened 1 January 1918 and closed by the L&NER 2 December 1929.

Line lifted – Demolished – Station site in agricultural use. **NO57846 42406**

FORFARSHIRE 45.12 (1901)

DENNY   10 D4

Opened 26 March 1858 by the Scottish Central Railway and closed by the LM&SR 28 July 1930.

Line lifted – Station site – Station site occupied by a car park and landscaped area. **NS81271 82544**

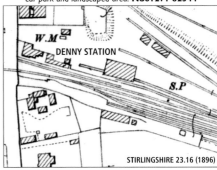

STIRLINGSHIRE 23.16 (1896)

DENNYLOANHEAD   6 D1

Opened 2 July 1888 by the Kilsyth & Bonnybridge Joint Railway and closed by the L&NER 1 February 1935.

Line lifted – Station building extant – Station site unused. **NS79896 79568**

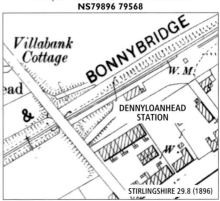

STIRLINGSHIRE 29.8 (1896)

DESS   15 D3

Opened 2 December 1859 by the Deeside Extension Railway and closed by BR 28 February 1966.

Line lifted – Station building and platform in private use. **NJ56453 00666**

ABERDEENSHIRE 82.11 (1899)

DEWSHILL PIT BRANCH   6 D1
DINGWALL   14 B1

Opened by the Inverness & Ross-shire Railway 11 June 1862.

Looking south at **Dingwall** Station on 17 September 2015.

DINNET   15 C3

Opened 17 October 1866 by the Aboyne & Braemar Railway and closed by BR 28 February 1966.

Line lifted – Station building in use as an office for the Dinnet and Kinnord Estate – Platforms extant – The Deeside Way passes through the station site. **NO46003 98749**

ABERDEENSHIRE 81.15 (1900)

DINWOODIE 7 B4
Opened in May 1853 by the CR and closed by BR 13 June 1960.
Line Operational – Station Master's House in private use – Platforms demolished. **NY10903 90623**

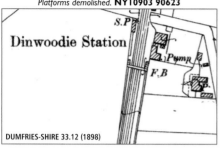
DUMFRIES-SHIRE 33.12 (1898)

DIPPLE GOODS 6 A4
DIRLETON 11 D4
Opened 17 June 1850 by the NBR and closed by BR 1 February 1954.
Line Operational – Station House in private use as the "Station House B&B". **NT52863 82705**

HADDINGTONSHIRE 2.15 (1892)

DOLLAR 11 A4
Opened 3 May 1869 by the Devon Valley Railway and closed by BR 15 June 1964.
Line lifted – Demolished – Platform extant - The Devon Way passes through the station site. **NS96260 97652**

CLACKMANNANSHIRE 134.7 (1899)

DOLPHINTON (CR) 7 B2
Opened 1 March 1867 by the CR, closed by the LM&SR 12 September 1932, reopened 17 July 1933 and closed 4 June 1945.
Line lifted – Demolished – Station site unused.
NT11213 47870

DOLPHINTON (NBR) 7 B2
Opened 4 July 1864 by the Leadburn, Linton & Dolphinton Railway and closed by the L&NER 1 April 1933.
Line lifted – Station building in private use. **NT11419 47837**

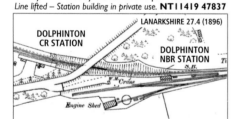
LANARKSHIRE 27.4 (1896)

DON STREET 16 B3
Opened 1 August 1887 by the GNofSR and closed by the L&NER 5 April 1937.
Line Operational – Demolished – No access. **NJ92736 08947**

ABERDEENSHIRE 75.2 (1899)

DONIBRISTLE HALT* 11A B4
Opened 2 March 1942 by the L&NER for admiralty workmen and closed by BR 2 November 1959.
Line Operational – Demolished – No access. **NT15586 84299**

NT1584 (1962)

DORNOCH 17 C3
Opened 2 June 1902 by the Dornoch Light Railway and closed by BR 13 June 1960.
Line lifted - Station building in use as a café – Platform extant - Remainder of station site occupied by Station Square.
NH79850 89917

SUTHERLAND 113.6 (1905)

DORNOCK 3 B2
Opened 23 August 1848 by the Glasgow, Paisley, Kilmarnock & Ayr Railway, closed October 1854, reopened 2 January 1865, renamed by the LM&SR 1 May 1923 as *Eastriggs* and closed by BR 6 December 1965.
Line Operational - Station building in private use – Platforms demolished. **NY24047 66405**

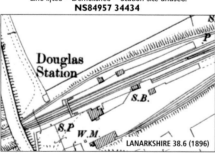
DUMFRIES-SHIRE 63.6 (1898)

DOUBA BRANCH 6 A2
DOUGLAS 6 D3
Opened 1 April 1864 by the CR as *Douglas*, renamed by the LM&SR 1 April 1931 as *Happendon* and closed by BR 5 October 1964.
Line lifted – Demolished – Station site unused.
NS84957 34434

LANARKSHIRE 38.6 (1896)

DOUGLAS WEST 6 D3
Opened 1 October 1896 by the CR and closed by BR 5 October 1964.
Line lifted – Demolished – Station site unused.
NS82029 30931

LANARKSHIRE 37.16 (1896)

DOUNE 10 C4
Opened 1 July 1858 by the Dunblane, Doune & Callander Railway and closed by BR 1 November 1965.
Line lifted – Station building in private use – Remainder of station site occupied by housing in Pistolmakers Row.
NN72452 01801

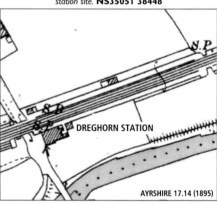
PERTH & CLACKMANNANSHIRE 125.13 (1899)

DREGHORN 6 A3
Opened 22 May 1848 by the G&SWR, closed in October 1850, reopened in May 1868 and closed by BR 6 April 1964.
Line lifted – Demolished – A cycle/walkway passes through the station site. **NS35051 38448**

AYRSHIRE 17.14 (1895)

DREM 7 D1
Opened 22 June 1846 by the NBR as *Drem Junction* and renamed in 1890 as *Drem.*

Looking west at **Drem Station** on 19 September 2015.

DRONGAN 6 B3
Opened in March 1875 by the G&SWR and closed by BR 10 September 1951.
Line Operational for Freight - Station building in private use – Platforms demolished. **NS44554 19018**

AYRSHIRE 34.14 (1894)

DRONLEY 11 C2
Opened 1 November 1860 by the Dundee, Perth & Aberdeen Junction Railway and closed by BR 10 January 1955.
Line lifted – Platform partially extant - "The Railway Path" passes through the station site. **NO34322 35960**

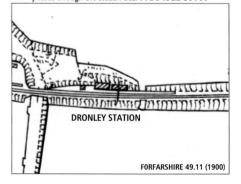
FORFARSHIRE 49.11 (1900)

DRUM 16 A3

Opened in January 1854 by the Deeside Railway and closed by BR 10 September 1951.

Line lifted – Station House in private use – Remainder of station site demolished **NO80683 99563**

ABERDEENSHIRE 85.10 (1899)

DRUMBURGH 3 C2

Opened 4 September 1856 by the Port Carlisle Railway and closed by BR 4 July 1955.

Line lifted – Demolished – Station site unused.
NY27263 59637

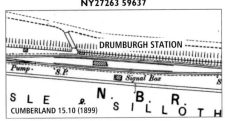

CUMBERLAND 15.10 (1899)

DRUMCHAPEL 6 B1/21A A1

Opened by the NBR 1 May 1890.

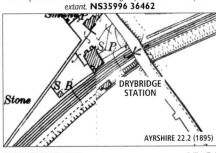

Drumchapel Station on 13 May 2017.

DRUMCLOG 6 C2

Opened 1 May 1905 by the CR, closed 1 July 1909, reopened 1 November 1909, closed 1 January 1917, reopened 4 December 1922 and closed by the LM&SR 11 September 1939.

Line lifted – Demolished - Station site unused.
NS63847 38626

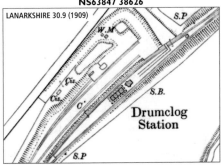

LANARKSHIRE 30.9 (1909)

DRUMCUDDEN 14 C1

Planned by the Cromarty & Dingwall Railway but never opened.

DRUMDOW HALT* 6A B3

Opened by the G&SWR prior to 1922 and closed by the LM&SR in 1928.

Line Operational for Freight – Demolished.
NS43383 22021 (a)

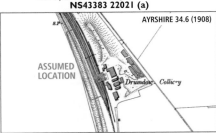

AYRSHIRE 34.6 (1908)

DRUMFROCHAR 6A A1

Opened 24 May 1998.

Drumfrochar Station on 17 March 2017.

DRUMGELLOCH 6A D1

Opened 6 March 2011. This station occupies the site of *Clarkston (NBR)* station *(qv)* and replaced a station sited 612 yards west which was opened by BR in 1989 and closed 9 May 2010.

Drumgelloch Station on 12 May 2017.

DRUMLEMBLE 5 B3

Opened 18 August 1906 by the 2ft 3in gauge Campbeltown and Machrihanish Light Railway and closed by May 1932.

DRUMLITHIE 16 A4

Opened 1 November 1849 by the Aberdeen Railway and closed by BR 11 June 1956.

Line Operational – Demolished – No access. **NO79064 80674**

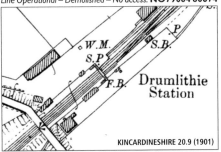

KINCARDINESHIRE 20.9 (1901)

DRUMMUIR 15 C1/15A C1

Opened 21 February 1862 by the Keith & Dufftown Railway, closed by BR 5 October 1964 and reopened in 2000 by the **Keith & Dufftown Railway**.

DRUMMUIR CURLERS PLATFORM* 15A C1

Opened prior to 1902 by the GNofSR and closed at an unknown date.

Line Operated by the Keith & Dufftown Railway – Demolished – A lineside shed occupies part of the station site.
NJ36248 43521

BANFFSHIRE 19.15 (1902)

DRUMRY 21A A1

Opened by BR 6 April 1953.

Looking west at **Drumry Station** on 13 September 2015.

DRUMSHORELAND 7 A1

Opened 12 November 1849 by the Edinburgh & Glasgow Railway as *Broxburn*, renamed by the NBR 1 May 1870 as *Drumshoreland for Broxburn* and closed by BR 18 June 1951.

Line Operational – Station building in private use – Platforms demolished. **NT08570 70725**

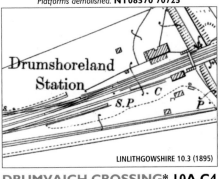

LINLITHGOWSHIRE 10.3 (1895)

DRUMVAICH CROSSING* 10A C4

Opened c1927 by the LM&SR and closed at an unknown date.

Line lifted – Signal box/house in private use.
NN67503 04286 (a)

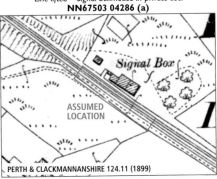

PERTH & CLACKMANNANSHIRE 124.11 (1899)

DRYBRIDGE 6 A3

Opened in July 1847 by the Kilmarnock & Troon Railway and closed by BR 3 March 1969.

Line Operational – Station building in private use – Platforms extant. **NS35996 36462**

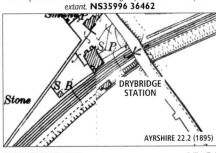

AYRSHIRE 22.2 (1895)

DRYBRIDGE 15 C1

Opened in May 1855 by the HR and closed 9 August 1915.

It can only be assumed that its appearance on the map was in anticipation of reopening at a later date.
Line lifted – Demolished – A road crosses the station site.
NJ43597 62942

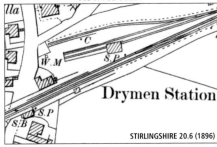

BANFFSHIRE 2.14 (1902)

DRYMEN 10 B4

Opened 26 May 1856 by the Forth & Clyde Junction Railway and closed by the L&NER 1 October 1934.

Line lifted – Station building in private use – Platforms demolished - A cycle/walkway passes through the station site.
NS47782 86267

STIRLINGSHIRE 20.6 (1896)

DUBTON JUNCTION 12 A1

Opened in May 1848 by the Aberdeen Railway as *Dubton* and closed by BR 4 August 1952. It was known as *Dubton Junction* in Bradshaw from 1849 to 1882.

Line lifted – Station building in private use – Platforms extant.
NO70085 60713

FORFARSHIRE 28.9 (1922)

DUDDINGSTON & CRAIGMILLAR 22A D2

Opened 1 December 1884 by the Edinburgh Suburban & Southside Junction Railway and closed by BR 10 September 1962.

Line Operational – Demolished – One platform extant – No access. **NT28765 71972**

EDINBURGHSHIRE 4.9 (1893)

DUFFTOWN 15 B1/15A B1
Opened 21 February 1862 by the Keith & Dufftown Railway as *Dufftown*, renamed by the L&NER in 1933 as *Dufftown for Tomintoul*, closed by BR 6 May 1968 and reopened in 2000 by the **Keith & Dufftown Railway**.

DUIRINISH 13 B2
Opened by the HR 2 November 1897.

Looking west at **Duirnish Station** on 17 September 2015.

DUKE STREET 6A C1
Opened in October 1883 by the City of Glasgow Union Railway, closed 1 January 1917 and reopened 2 June 1919.

Duke Street Station on 13 May 2017.

DULLATUR 6 D1
Opened in March 1876 by the Edinburgh & Glasgow Railway and closed by BR 5 June 1967.
Line Operational – Station building in private use – Platforms demolished – No access. **NS74538 77048**

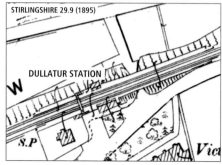
STIRLINGSHIRE 29.9 (1895)
DULLATUR STATION

DUMBARTON CENTRAL 6 B1
Opened by the Caledonian & Dumbartonshire Junction Railway 15 July 1850 as *Dumbarton* and renamed by BR 3 March 1952 as *Dumbarton Central*.

Dumbarton Central Station on 13 September 2015.

DUMBARTON EAST 6 B1
Opened by the Lanarkshire & Dumbartonshire Railway 1 October 1896.

Class 334 Unit No.334013 at **Dumbarton East Station** on 13 September 2015.

DUMBRECK 21A B3
Opened by the G&SWR 1 July 1885 as *Bellahouston*, closed 1 January 1917, reopened in August 1920, closed by BR 20 September 1954 and reopened 30 July 1990 as *Dumbreck*.

Dumbreck Station on 18 March 2017.

DUMBUCK GOODS 6 B1

DUMFRIES 3 A1
Opened by the G&SWR in September 1859.

Looking north at **Dumfries Station** on 16 March 2017.

DUMFRIES HOUSE 6 B3
Opened 1 July 1872 by the G&SWR and closed by BR 13 June 1949.
Line lifted - Demolished – Station site in agricultural use. **NS53903 19176**

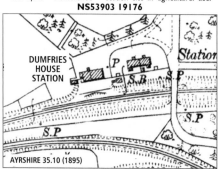
DUMFRIES HOUSE STATION
AYRSHIRE 35.10 (1895)

DUMGOYNE 10 B4
Opened 1 July 1862 by the Blane Valley Railway as *Killearn*, renamed by the NBR 1 October 1882 as *Killearn Old*, 1 April 1896 as *Dumgoyne Hill*, 28 September 1897 as *Dungoyne* and closed by BR 1 October 1951.
Line lifted – Station buildings in use as "The Beech Tree Inn" – The West Highland Way passes through the station site. **NS52296 83433**

STIRLINGSHIRE 20.16 (1896)
DUMGOYNE STATION

DUNBAR 8 A1
Opened by the NBR 22 June 1846.

Looking north at **Dunbar Station** on 19 September 2015.

DUNBLANE 10 D4
Opened by the Scottish Central Railway 23 May 1848.

Looking south at **Dunblane Station** on 13 May 2017.

DUNCRAIG 13A B2
Opened 2 November 1897 as a private station by the HR as *Duncraig Platform*, it was opened to the public by BR 23 May 1949, renamed as *Duncraig* 10 September 1962, closed 7 December 1964 and reopened 5 January 1976.
Looking west at **Duncraig Station** on 17 September 2015.

DUNDEE 11 C2
Opened by the NBR 1 June 1878 as *Dundee Tay Bridge* and renamed by BR 15 April 1966 as *Dundee*.

Class 170 Unit No.170472 at **Dundee Station** on 18 September 2015.

DUNDEE EAST 11 C2
Opened 14 December 1857 by the Dundee & Arbroath Railway and closed by BR 5 January 1959.
Line lifted – Demolished – An Arnold Clark car dealership occupies the station site. **NO40785 30434**

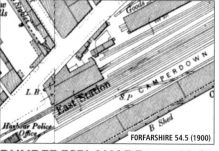
FORFARSHIRE 54.5 (1900)

DUNDEE ESPLANADE 11 C2
Opened in May 1899 by the NBR, closed 1 January 1917, reopened 1 February 1919 and closed by the L&NER 2 October 1939 when requisitioned by the War Department.
Line Operational – Station extant and in use as a base for Tay Bridge maintenance engineers. **NO39198 29305**

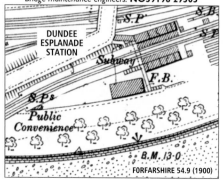
DUNDEE ESPLANADE STATION
FORFARSHIRE 54.9 (1900)

DUNDEE WEST 11 C2
Opened 24 May 1847 by the Dundee & Perth Railway as *Dundee*, renamed 1848 as *Dundee West*, 1853 by the CR as *Dundee Union Street*, 1866 as *Dundee West* and closed by BR 3 May 1965.
Line lifted – Demolished – The A991, South Marketgait, passes through part of the station site – Remainder of station site occupied by a car park. **NO40258 29949**

FORFARSHIRE 54.9 (1900)
DUNDEE WEST STATION

DUNDUFF QUARRY BRANCH 6 D2

DUNFERMLINE LOWER 11 A4
Opened by the NBR 1 November 1877 as *Comely Park*, renamed 4 March 1890 as *Dunfermline Lower*, renamed by BR 1968 as *Dunfermline*, May 1987 as *Dunfermline Lower*, May 1988 as *Dunfermline* and 26 January 2000 as *Dunfermline Town*.

Dunfermline Town Station on 18 September 2015.

DUNFERMLINE TOWN
(See **DUNFERMLINE LOWER**)

DUNFERMLINE QUEEN MARGARET 11A B4
Opened 26 January 2000.

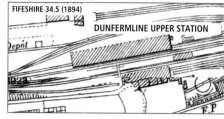
Dunfermline Queen Margaret Station on 18 September 2015.

DUNFERMLINE UPPER 11 A4
Opened 13 December 1894 by the Edinburgh, Perth & Dundee Railway as *Dunfermline*, renamed by the NBR in 1890 as *Dunfermline Upper* and closed by BR 7 October 1968.
Line lifted – Demolished – Station site occupied by the car park of a retail park. **NT09395 87704**

FIFESHIRE 34.5 (1894)
DUNFERMLINE UPPER STATION

DUNKELD 11 A2
Opened by the Perth & Dunkeld Railway 7 April 1856 as *Birnam & Dunkeld* and, following numerous name changes over the years, it was finally renamed by BR 13 May 1991 as *Dunkeld & Birnam*.

Looking north at **Dunkeld & Birnam Station** on 17 September 2015.

DUNLOP 6 B2
Opened by the Glasgow, Barrhead and Kilmarnock Joint Railway 27 March 1871, closed by BR 7 November 1966 and reopened 5 June 1967.

Dunlop Station on 19 March 2017.

DUNNING 11 A3
Opened 23 May 1848 by the Scottish Central Railway and closed by BR 11 June 1956.
Line Operational – Demolished – No access. **NO00344 16507**

NO01NW (1958)
Dunning Station

DUNPHAIL 15 A1
Opened 3 August 1893 by the Inverness & Perth Junction Railway and closed by BR 18 October 1965.
Line lifted – Station building and platform in private use [The Dava Way by-passes the station]. **NJ01550 48148**

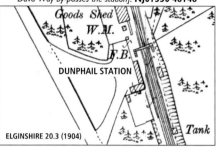
ELGINSHIRE 20.3 (1904)

DUNRAGIT 1 D2
Opened 1 July 1861 by the Portpatrick & Wigtownshire Joint Railway and closed by BR 14 June 1965.
Line Operational - Station building and platforms extant. **NX14797 57463**

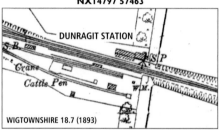
WIGTOWNSHIRE 18.7 (1893)

DUNROBIN 17 D3
Opened by the Duke of Sutherland's Railway 1 November 1870 as *Dunrobin*, closed to the public 19 June 1871, subsequently reopened, closed by BR 29 January 1965 and reopened 30 June 1985. It was renamed as *Dunrobin Castle* 17 May 1993.

Dunrobin Castle Station on 16 September 2015.

DUNS 8 A2
Opened 15 August 1849 by the NBR as *Dunse*, renamed in 1883 as *Duns* and closed by BR 10 September 1951.
Line lifted - Demolished - Station site part of "Duns Industrial Estate". **NT78824 53202**

BERWICKSHIRE 16.11 (1898)

DUNSCORE 2 D1
Opened 1 March 1905 by the Cairn Valley Light Railway and closed by the LM&SR 3 May 1943.
Line lifted – Demolished – Station site unused. **NX85800 84229**

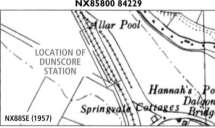
NX88SE (1957)

DUNSISTON COLLIERY BRANCH 6 D1
DUNSYRE 7 A2
Opened 1 March 1867 by the CR, closed by the LM&SR 12 September 1932, reopened 17 July 1933 and closed 4 June 1945.
Line lifted – Demolished – Part of station site occupied by housing – A walkway passes through the station site. **NT07455 48097**

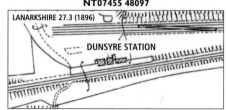
LANARKSHIRE 27.3 (1896)

DUNURE 6 A3
Opened 17 May 1906 by the Maidens & Dunure Light Railway and closed by the LM&SR 1 December 1930.
Line lifted – Demolished – Station site unused. **NS26334 16698**

AYRSHIRE 38.3 (1908)

DUROR 9 C2
Opened 24 August 1903 by the Callander & Oban Railway and closed by BR 28 March 1966.
Line lifted - Station building and platforms in private use. **NM97652 54183**

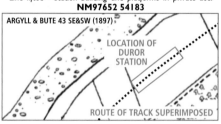
ARGYLL & BUTE 43 SE&SW (1897)

DYCE 16 B3
Opened 18 June 1861 by the GNofSR, closed by BR 6 May 1968 and reopened 15 September 1984.

Looking north at **Dyce** Station on 18 September 2015.

DYKEHEAD BRANCH 6 D1
DYSART 11 C4
Opened 20 September 1847 by the Edinburgh & Northern Railway and closed by BR 6 October 1969.
Line Operational – Demolished – No access. **NT30137 93394**

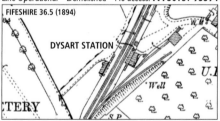
FIFESHIRE 36.5 (1894)

EARLSTON 7 D2
Opened 16 November 1863 by the Berwickshire Railway and closed by BR 13 August 1948.
Line lifted – Demolished – Station site occupied by the "Station Yard Industrial Estate". **NT57565 38367**

ROXBURGHSHIRE 4.10 (1897)

EASSIE 11 C2
Opened 4 June 1838 by the Newtyle & Glamis Railway, closed by the Dundee & Perth Railway in 1847, reopened 2 August 1848 and closed by BR 11 June 1956.
Line lifted – Station House extant – Platforms demolished. **NO34673 46961**

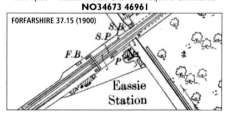
FORFARSHIRE 37.15 (1900)

EAST CALDER GOODS 7 A1
EASTERHOUSE 6 C1
Opened by the NBR 23 November 1870 as *Easterhouse*, renamed by the L&NER in 1933 as *Easterhouse for Baillieston* and by BR in 1949 as *Easterhouse*.

Easterhouse Station on 12 May 2017.

EASTER ROAD 22A C1
Opened 1 December 1891 by the NBR, closed 1 January 1917, reopened 1 February 1919 and closed by the L&NER 16 June 1947.
Line Out of Use – Demolished – Platforms extant - Station site unused. **NT27007 74878**

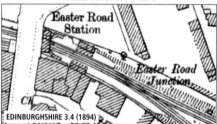
EDINBURGHSHIRE 3.4 (1894)

EASTER ROAD PARK HALT* 22A D1
Opened 8 April 1950 by BR for detraining only and although closed in December 1959 was used until 4 January 1964.
Line lifted – Demolished – Lochend Butterfly Way passes through the station site. **NT27528 74964**

NT2774 (1948)

EAST FORTUNE 7 D1
Opened in July 1848 by the NBR and closed by BR 4 May 1964.
Line Operational – Station building in private use – One platform extant. **NT55854 79554**

HADDINGTONSHIRE 5.8 (1892)

EASTGRANGE 11 A4
Opened in c1851 by the Stirling & Dunfermline Railway and closed by BR 15 September 1958.
Line lifted – Station building in private use - The West Fife Cycleway passes through the station site. **NT00001 89154**

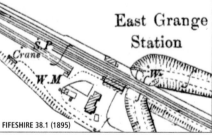
FIFESHIRE 38.1 (1895)

EASTHAVEN 11 D2
Opened 8 October 1838 by the Dundee & Arbroath Joint Railway and closed by BR 4 September 1967.
Line Operational – Demolished – No access. **NO58960 36135**

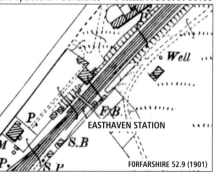
FORFARSHIRE 52.9 (1901)

EAST KILBRIDE 6 C2
Opened by the Busby Railway 1 September 1868 as *Kilbride* and renamed as *East Kilbride* at an unknown date.

Class 156 Unit No.156499 at **East Kilbride Station** on 18 March 2017.

EAST LINTON 7 D1
Opened 22 June 1846 by the NBR as *Linton*, renamed in 1864 as *East Linton* and closed by BR 4 May 1964.
Line Operational – Station building in private use – Platforms demolished. **NT59129 77105**

HADDINGTONSHIRE 6.13 (1892)

EAST LINTON STATION

EAST NEWPORT 11 C2
Opened 12 May 1879 by the Newport Railway as *East Newport*, renamed by BR in January 1956 as *Newport-on-Tay East* and closed 5 May 1969.
Line lifted – Station building in private use – East Station Place passes through the station site. **NO42453 27969**

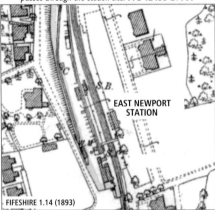

EAST NEWPORT STATION

FIFESHIRE 1.14 (1893)

EAST PILTON 22A B1
Opened 1 December 1934 by the LM&SR and closed by BR 30 April 1962. It was also known as *East Pilton Halt* during periods prior to 1948.
Line lifted – Demolished - The Ferry Road Path passes through the station site. **NT23347 76003**

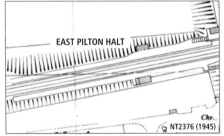

EAST PILTON HALT

NT2376 (1945)

ECCLEFECHAN 3 B1
Opened 10 September 1847 by the CR and closed by BR 13 June 1960.
Line Operational – Demolished – Station site occupied by an Engineeer's Yard. **NY18154 75422**

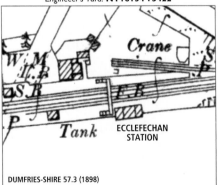

ECCLEFECHAN STATION

DUMFRIES-SHIRE 57.3 (1898)

EDDERTON 17 C4
Opened 1 October 1864 by the Inverness & Aberdeen Junction Railway and closed by BR 13 June 1960.
Line Operational – Station house in private use – Platforms demolished. **NH70795 85428**

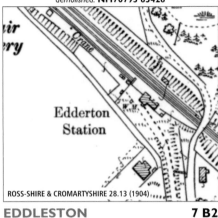

Edderton Station

ROSS-SHIRE & CROMARTYSHIRE 28.13 (1904)

EDDLESTON 7 B2
Opened 4 July 1855 by the Peebles Railway and closed by BR 5 February 1962.
Line lifted - Station building in private use – Station site occupied by housing in Station Lye. **NT24132 47102**

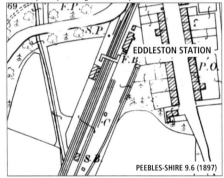

EDDLESTON STATION

PEEBLES-SHIRE 9.6 (1897)

EDINBURGH 7 B1/22A C2
Opened by the NBR 22 June 1846 as *Edinburgh North Bridge*, renamed in April 1866 as *Edinburgh Waverley* and by BR 18 April 1966 as *Edinburgh*.

The west end of **Edinburgh Station** viewed on 12 May 2017.

EDINBURGH GATEWAY 7A B1
Built as part of the Edinburgh to Glasgow Improvement Programme and opened on 11 December 2016.

Edinburgh Gateway Station on 12 May 2017.

EDINBURGH PARK 7A B1
Opened 4 December 2003.

Class 170 Unit No.170459 at **Edinburgh Park Station** on 12 May 2017.

EDINBURGH PRINCES STREET 7 B1/22A C2
Opened 2 May 1870 by the CR and closed by BR 6 September 1965.
Line lifted – Partially demolished and redeveloped. **NT24706 73533**

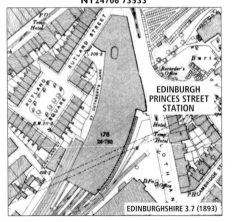

EDINBURGH PRINCES STREET STATION

EDINBURGHSHIRE 3.7 (1893)

EDROM 8 B2
Opened in May 1852 by the CR and closed by BR 10 September 1951.
Line lifted – Station building and platform restored. **NT83287 55018**

Edrom Station

BERWICKSHIRE 17.5 (1897)

EDZELL 11 D1
Opened 8 June 1896 by the Brechin & Edzell Railway, closed by the LM&SR 27 April 1931, reopened 4 July 1938 and closed 26 September 1938.
Line lifted – Demolished – Station site occupied by housing in The Drive. **NO60063 68574**

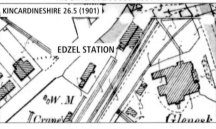

KINCARDINESHIRE 26.5 (1901)

EDZEL STATION

EGLINTON STREET (CR) 21A C3
Opened 1 July 1879 by the CR and closed by BR 1 February 1965.
Line Operational – Degraded platforms partially extant - Demolished – No access. **NS58489 63797**

EGLINTON STREET STATION

LANARKSHIRE 6.14 (1893)

ELDERSLIE 6 B1
Opened in August 1875 by the Glasgow, Paisley, Kilmarnock & Ayr Railway and closed by BR 14 February 1965.
Line Operational – Demolished – No access. **NS45156 63397**

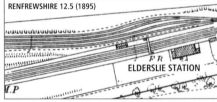

RENFREWSHIRE 12.5 (1895)

ELDERSLIE STATION

ELGIN 15 B1
Opened 25 March 1858 by the Inverness & Aberdeen Junction Railway.

Class 158 No.158702 at **Elgin Station** on 17 September 2015.

ELGIN EAST (GNofSR) 15 B1
Opened 10 August 1852 by the Morayshire Railway and closed by BR 6 May 1968.
Line Operational for Freight – Station building in use as offices. **NJ22077 62229**

ELGINSHIRE 7.16 (1904)

ELIE   11 D4

Opened 1 September 1863 by the Leven & East of Fife Railway and closed by BR 6 September 1965.
Line lifted - Demolished – Station site occupied by housing in Baird Place. **NO49576 00170**

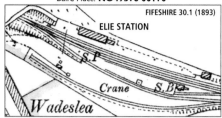

FIFESHIRE 30.1 (1893)

ELLIOT   11 D2

Opened 1 February 1900 by the CR and known as *Elliot Junction Light Railway Platform* it was used to accommodate Carmyllie branch trains if a platform in Elliot Junction Station *(qv)* was not available. It was closed by the LM&SR/L&NER Joint in 1929.
Line lifted – Demolished – The Elliott Nature Trail passes through the station site. **NO61995 39489 (a)**

ELLIOT JUNCTION   11 D2

Opened in October 1866 by the CR, closed 1 January 1917, reopened 1 February 1918 and closed by BR 4 September 1967.
Main Line Operational – Demolished – No access.
NO62178 39568

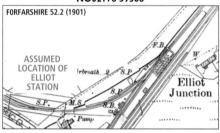

FORFARSHIRE 52.2 (1901)

ELLON   16 B2

Opened 18 July 1861 by the Formartine & Buchan Railway and closed by BR 4 October 1965.
Line lifted - Demolished - Platforms extant - The Formartine and Buchan Way passes through the station site. **NJ94955 30831**

ABERDEENSHIRE 38.15 (1899)

ELVANFOOT   7 A3

Opened in April 1848 by the CR and closed by BR 4 January 1965.
Line Operational – Demolished – No access. **NS95420 17175**

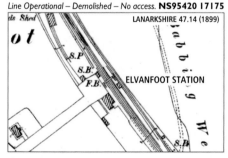

LANARKSHIRE 47.14 (1899)

EMBO   17 C3

Opened 2 June 1902 by the Dornoch Light Railway and closed by BR 13 June 1960.
Line lifted – Demolished – Station site occupied by Station Road. **NH81371 92934**

SUTHERLAND 110.14 (1904)

ENZIE   15 C1

Opened 1 August 1884 by the HR and closed 9 August 1915.
It can only be assumed that its appearance on the map was in anticipation of reopening at a later date.
Line lifted – Demolished – Station site in private use. **NJ41014 61033**

BANFFSHIRE 8.1 (1902)

ERROL   11 B3

Opened 24 May 1847 by the Dundee & Perth Railway and closed by BR 28 September 1985.
Line Operational - Station building in private use - Platforms extant. **NO25378 24538**

PERTH & CLACKMANNANSHIRE 99.3 (1898)

ESKBANK   7 C1

Opened 21 June 1847 by the NBR as *Gallowshall*, renamed as *Eskbank* in October 1850, as *Eskbank and Dalkeith* by BR in January 1954 and closed 6 January 1969.
Line Operational – Demolished – Degraded platforms extant - Station building converted into apartments. **NT32366 66647**

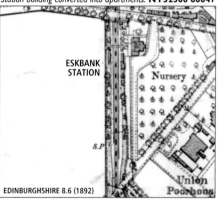

EDINBURGHSHIRE 8.6 (1892)

ESKBANK   7A C1

Opened 6 September 2015 and sited to the north of the original station *(qv)*.

Class 170 Unit No.170431 at **Eskbank Station** on 12 May 2017.

ESKBRIDGE   7 B1

Opened 1 July 1874 by the Penicuik Railway, closed by the NBR 1 January 1917, reopened 2 June 1919 and closed by the L&NER 22 September 1930.
Line lifted – Demolished - Platforms partially extant – The Penicuik to Musselburgh Cycle/Walkway passes through the station site. **NT24480 60458**

EDINBURGHSHIRE 13.7 (1892)

ESSLEMONT   16 B2

Opened 18 July 1861 by Formartine & Buchan Railway and closed by BR 15 September 1952.
Line lifted - Station building in private use - The Formartine and Buchan Way passes through the station site. **NJ93364 28867**

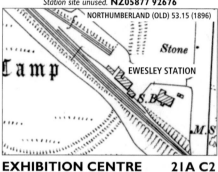

ABERDEENSHIRE 47.3 (1899)

EWESLEY   8 C4

Opened 1 November 1870 by the Northumberland Central Railway as *Ewesley*, subsequently renamed as *Ewesley Halt* and closed by BR 15 September 1952.
Line lifted – Demolished - Platforms partially extant – Station site unused. **NZ05877 92676**

NORTHUMBERLAND (OLD) 53.15 (1896)

EXHIBITION CENTRE   21A C2

Opened 10 August 1896 by the CR as *Stobcross*, closed by BR 3 August 1959, reopened 5 November 1979 as *Finnieston* and renamed as *Exhibition Centre* in 1986.

Looking west at **Exhibition Centre Station** on 13 May 2017.

EYEMOUTH   8 B1

Opened 13 April 1891 by the Eyemouth Railway, closed by BR 13 August 1948 due to extensive flooding, reopened 29 June 1949 and closed 5 February 1962.
Line lifted – Demolished – A car park occupies the west side of the station site - Remainder of station site unused.
NT94421 63957

BERWICKSHIRE 6.13 (1898)

FAIRLIE   6 A2

Opened by the G&SWR 1 June 1880 as *Fairlie*, renamed by BR 30 June 1952 as *Fairlie Town*, 2 March 1953 as *Fairlie High* and c1968 as *Fairlie*.

Fairlie Station on 17 March 2017.

FAIRLIE BRANCH   6 B3

FAIRLIE PIER   6 A2

Opened 1 July 1882 by the G&SWR and closed by BR 1 October 1971.
Line lifted – Station and pier demolished – Station site partially in use as a car park. **NS20700 55921**

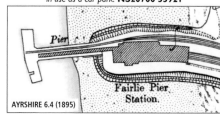

AYRSHIRE 6.4 (1895)

FALAHILL GOODS 7 C2

FALKIRK GRAHAMSTON 6 D1
Opened by the Edinburgh & Glasgow Railway 1 October 1850 as *Grahamston* and renamed by the NBR 1 February 1903 as *Falkirk Grahamston*.

Falkirk Grahamston Station on 13 May 2017.

FALKIRK HIGH 6 D1
Opened by the Edinburgh & Glasgow Railway 21 February 1842 as *Falkirk* and renamed by the NBR 1 February 1903 as *Falkirk High*.

Falkirk High Station on 13 May 2017.

FALKLAND ROAD 11 B3
Opened 20 September by the Edinburgh & Northern Railway and closed by BR 15 September 1958.
Line Operational – Demolished – No access. **NO28742 05740**

FIFESHIRE 20.5 (1894)

FALLSIDE 6 C1
Opened in August 1872 by the Clydesdale Junction Railway, closed by the CR 1 January 1917, reopened 1 May 1919 and closed by BR 3 August 1953.
Line Operational – Demolished – No access. **NS70942 60342**

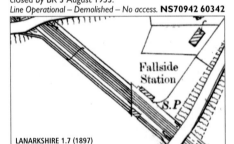

LANARKSHIRE 1.7 (1897)

FALLS OF CRUACHAN 9A D3
Opened by the Callander and Oban Railway 1 October 1893, closed by BR 1 November 1965 and reopened 20 June 1988.

Looking west at **Falls of Cruachan Station** on 14 September 2015.

FALSTONE 4 A1
Opened 2 September 1861 by the Border Counties Railway and closed by BR 15 October 1956.
Line lifted - Station building and platform in private use – A track passes through the station site. **NY72589 87290**

NORTHUMBERLAND (OLD) 59.10 (1896)

FARNELL ROAD 11 D1
Opened in May 1848 by the Aberdeen Railway and closed by BR 11 June 1956.
Line lifted – Station building in private use. **NO62871 55271**

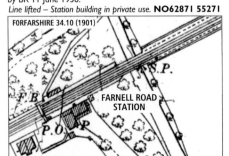

FORFARSHIRE 34.10 (1901)

FASLANE PLATFORM* 10A A4
Opened 26 August 1945 by the L&NER for workers on the Loch Sloy HEP scheme and probably closed by BR c1949.
Line Operational – Demolished. **NS25930 86148 (a)**

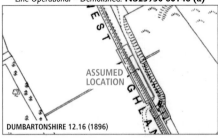

DUMBARTONSHIRE 12.16 (1896)

FAULDHOUSE 7 A1
Opened by the Cleland & Midcalder Railway 9 July 1869 as *Fauldhouse for Crofthead*, renamed by the CR 1 June 1872 as *Fauldhouse*, by BR 3 March 1952 as *Fauldhouse North* and 7 May 1973 as *Fauldhouse*.

Fauldhouse Station on 19 March 2017.

FAULDHOUSE & CROFTHEAD 7 A1
Opened 2 June 1845 by the Wilsontown, Morningside & Coltness Railway, closed by the NBR in 1848, reopened in August 1850, closed in December 1852, reopened 19 September 1864 as *Crofthead*, renamed 1 June 1899 as *Crofthead for Fauldhouse*, 1 September 1906 as *Fauldhouse & Crofthead* and closed by the L&NER 1 May 1930.
Line lifted – Demolished – Station site landscaped – A pathway passes through the station site. **NS93388 60407**

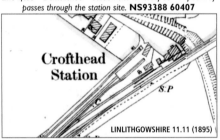

LINLITHGOWSHIRE 11.11 (1895)

FEARN 17 D4
Opened by the Inverness & Aberdeen Junction Railway 1 June 1864.

Looking north at **Fearn Station** on 16 September 2015.

FERNIEGAIR (See CHATELHERAULT)
FERRYHILL JUNCTION 16 B3
FERSIT HALT 14A A1
Opened 1 August 1931 by the L&NER and closed 31 December 1934.
Line Operational – Demolished. **NN35206 78183 (a)**

INVERNESS-MAINLAND 142 (1899)

FETTERESSO 16A A4
Opened at an unknown date by the CR and may have been for private use only. Closure date unknown.
Line Operational – Demolished. **NO85141 85428**

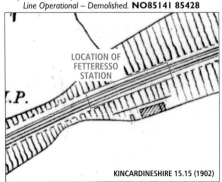

KINCARDINESHIRE 15.15 (1902)

FINDOCHTY 18 C4
Opened 1 May 1886 by the GNofSR and closed by BR 6 May 1968.
Lines lifted – Demolished – Station site occupied by housing in Dyce Crescent. **NJ46612 67791**

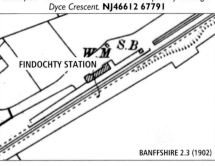

BANFFSHIRE 2.3 (1902)

FINGASK PLATFORM 16 A2
Opened 2 September 1867 by the Inverurie & Oldmeldrum Railway as *Muirtown*, renamed by the GNofSR in 1907 as *Fingask Platform*, in 1924 by the L&NER as *Fingask Halt* and closed 2 November 1931.
Line lifted – Demolished – Station site unused. **NJ77881 26884**

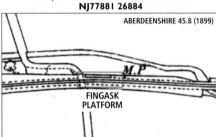

ABERDEENSHIRE 45.8 (1899)

FISHERROW 7 C1
Opened in 1831 by the Edinburgh & Dalkeith Railway, closed to passengers 14 July 1847 and closed to goods by BR 2 October 1961.
Line lifted – Demolished – Station site partially landscaped and partially occupied by a filling station. **NT33419 72885**

EDINBURGHSHIRE 4.7 (1893)

FLEMINGTON 6 D2
Opened 2 March 1891 by the CR and closed by BR 4 January 1965.
Line Operational – Demolished – No access. **NS76528 56090**

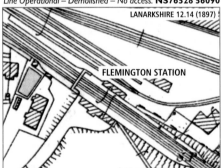

LANARKSHIRE 12.14 (1897)

FLORISTON 3 C2
Opened in May 1853 by the CR and closed by BR 17 July 1950.
Line Operational – Demolished. **NY35579 64073**

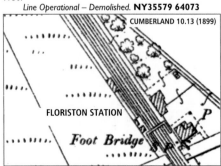

CUMBERLAND 10.13 (1899)

FOCHABERS 15 C1

Opened 23 October 1893 by the HR as *Fochabers Town* and closed by the LM&SR 14 September 1931.
Line lifted – Station building and platform in private use – Inchberry Place passes through the station site. **NJ33881 59546**

ELGINSHIRE 14.5 (1903)

FODDERTY JUNCTION 14 A1
FONTBURN 8 C4

Officially opened 1 June 1904 by the NBR as *Fontburn*, closed 3 October 1921, reopened 21 November 1921 as *Fontburn Halt* and closed by BR 15 September 1952.
Line lifted – Station site unused. **NZ05083 94128**

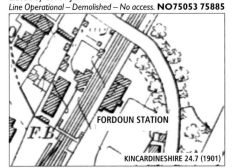

NORTHUMBERLAND (NEW) 58.4 (1921)

FORDOUN 16 A4

Opened in December 1849 by the Aberdeen Railway and closed by BR 11 June 1956.
Line Operational – Demolished – No access. **NO75053 75885**

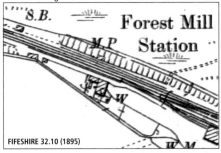

KINCARDINESHIRE 24.7 (1901)

FOREST MILL 11 A4

Opened 28 August 1850 by the Stirling & Dunfermline Railway as *Kincardine*, renamed by the NBR 1 January 1894 as *Forest Mill* and closed by the L&NER 22 September 1930.
Line lifted – Demolished – The West Fife Cycleway passes through the station site. **NS93773 92258**

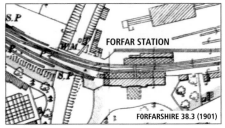

FIFESHIRE 32.10 (1895)

FORFAR 11 C1

Opened 2 August 1848 by the Aberdeen Railway as *Forfar Joint*, subsequently renamed as *Forfar* and closed by BR 4 September 1967.
Line lifted – Demolished – Station site occupied by housing in Esk Court. **NO45944 51346**

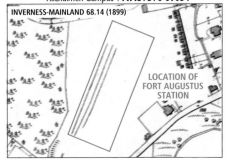

FORFARSHIRE 38.3 (1901)

FORGANDENNY 11 A3

Opened 23 May 1848 by the Scottish Central Railway and closed by BR 11 June 1956.
Line Operational – Station building in private use. **NO08825 19528**

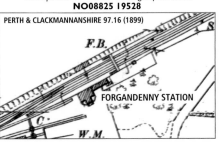

PERTH & CLACKMANNANSHIRE 97.16 (1899)

FORRES 15 A1

Opened 3 August 1863 by the Inverness & Aberdeen Junction Railway and closed 5 October 2017.
Line lifted – Demolished – Station site landscaped. **NJ02968 58925**

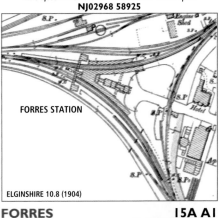

ELGINSHIRE 10.8 (1904)

FORRES 15A A1

Opened 20 October 2017 when the track was reconstructed on a new alignment by-passing the previous station *(qv)*.

Looking west at **Forres Station** on 24 March 2018.

FORRESTFIELD 6 D1

Opened 11 August 1862 by the Bathgate & Coatbridge Railway and closed by the L&NER 22 September 1930.
Line Operational – Demolished – A cycle/walkway runs parallel to the line and passes through the station site. **NS85424 67137**

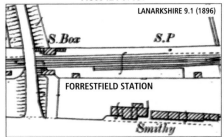

LANARKSHIRE 9.1 (1896)

FORSINARD 17 D1

Opened 28 July 1874 by the Sutherland & Caithness Railway.

Looking north at **Forsinard Station** on 16 September 2015.

FORT AUGUSTUS 14 A3

Opened 22 July 1903 by the Invergarry & Fort Augustus Railway, closed by the NBR 1 November 1911, reopened 1 August 1913 and closed by the L&NER 1 December 1933.
Line lifted - Demolished - Station site in use as part of the "Kilchuimen Campus". **NH37570 09054**

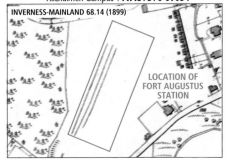

INVERNESS-MAINLAND 68.14 (1899)

FORTEVIOT 11 A3

Opened 23 May 1848 by the Scottish Central Railway and closed by BR 11 June 1956.
Line Operational – Station building in private use - Platforms demolished. **NO04638 17616**

PERTH & CLACKMANNANSHIRE 109.6 (1899)

FORTISSAT COLLIERY BRANCH 6 D1
FORT GEORGE 14 C1

Opened 1 July 1899 by the Inverness & Nairn Railway and although officially closed by the LM&SR 5 April 1943 military trains continued to use it until the line was abandoned by BR in 1958.
Line lifted - Station building in private use - Remainder of station site demolished. **NH78396 54960**

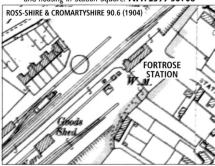

PERTH & CLACKMANNANSHIRE 109.6 (1899)

FORT MATILDA 6 A1

Opened by the CR 1 June 1889, it was closed temporarily by BR for tunnel repairs between 5 February and 20 April 1973 prior to permanent closure 3 October 1993 and reopening 27 March 1995.

Fort Matilda Station on 17 March 2017.

FORTROSE 14 C1

Opened 1 February 1894 by the HR and closed by BR 1 October 1951.
Line lifted - Demolished - Station site occupied by a car park and housing in Station Square. **NH72599 56708**

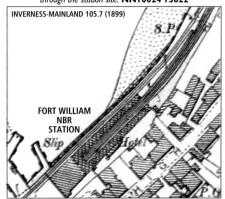

ROSS-SHIRE & CROMARTYSHIRE 90.6 (1904)

FORT WILLIAM (NBR) 9 D1

Opened by the West Highland Railway 7 August 1894 and closed by BR 9 June 1975.
Line lifted - Demolished – The A82, Argyll Coastal Road, passes through the station site. **NN10024 73822**

INVERNESS-MAINLAND 105.7 (1899)

FORT WILLIAM (BR)   9A D1

Opened 9 June 1975 and replaced the original station sited 880 yards to the south west. *(qv)*

Class 67 Locomotive No.67011
at **Fort William Station**
on 14 September 2015.

FOULIS   14 B1

Opened 23 March 1863 by the Inverness & Aberdeen Junction Railway as *Fowlis*, renamed by the HR 20 March 1916 as *Foulis* and closed by BR 13 June 1960.
Line Operational – Station building and platform in private use.
NH59654 63603

ROSS-SHIRE & CROMARTYSHIRE 77.5 (1904)

FOUNTAINHALL JUNCTION 7 C2

Opened 1 August 1848 by the NBR as *Burn House*, renamed in 1849 as *Fountainhall*, 2 July 1901 as *Fountainhall Junction*, by BR in 1959 as *Fountainhall* and closed 6 January 1969.
Line Operational - Station building extant – Platforms demolished.
NT42747 49792

EDINBURGHSHIRE 23.3 (1892)

FRASERBURGH   19 B4

Opened 24 April 1865 by the Formartine & Buchan Railway and closed by BR 4 October 1965.
Line lifted – Demolished – Station site in commercial use.
NJ99890 66688

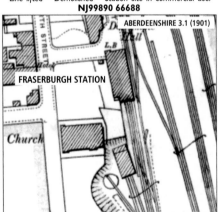

ABERDEENSHIRE 3.1 (1901)

FRIOCKHEIM   11 D1

Opened 25 February 1841 by the Aberdeen & Forfar Railway and closed by BR 5 December 1955.
Line lifted – Station House in private use – Platforms demolished. **NO58746 49435**

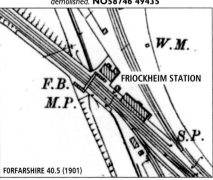

FORFARSHIRE 40.5 (1901)

FUSHIEBRIDGE   7 C1

Opened in 1849 by the NBR and, although closed by L&NER 4 October 1943, continued in use for workmen's trains until closed by BR 1 January 1951.
Line Operational – Demolished – No access. **NT35219 60391**

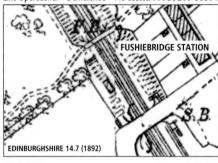

EDINBURGHSHIRE 14.7 (1892)

FYVIE   16 A2

Opened 5 September 1857 by the Banff, Macduff & Turriff Junction Railway and closed by BR 1 October 1951.
Line lifted – Demolished – Station site in commercial use.
NJ75733 39033

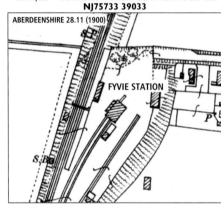

ABERDEENSHIRE 28.11 (1900)

GAGIE HALT   11A C2

Opened 2 September 1935 by the LM&SR and closed by BR 10 January 1955.
Line lifted – Demolished – Station site in commercial use.
NO46623 36420

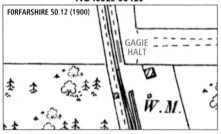

FORFARSHIRE 50.12 (1900)

GAILES   6 A3

Opened c1890 by the Glasgow, Paisley, Kilmarnock & Ayr Railway and closed by BR 2 January 1967.
Line Operational – Demolished – No access. **NS32268 35582**

AYRSHIRE 22.5 (1895)

GAIRLOCHY   13 D4

Opened 22 July 1903 by the Invergarry & Fort Augustus Railway, closed by the NBR 1 November 1911, reopened 1 August 1913 and closed by the L&NER 1 December 1933.
Line lifted – Demolished – Station site in use as the "Gairlochy Holiday Park". **NN18833 83547**

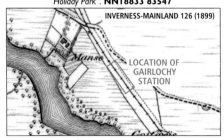

INVERNESS-MAINLAND 126 (1899)

GALASHIELS (NBR)   7 D2

Opened 20 February 1849 by the NBR and closed by BR 6 January 1969.
Line lifted – Demolished – Station site occupied by an Asda Supermarket. **NT49511 36143**

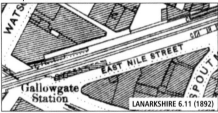

ROXBURGHSHIRE 3.15 (1897)

GALASHIELS   7A D2

Opened 6 September 2015 by the Borders Railway Project and sited to the north of the original station *(qv)*

Class 170 Unit No.170427 at
Galashiels Station on 12 May 2017.

GALASHIELS JUNCTION   7 D2

GALLOWGATE   21A D3

Opened 19 December 1870 by the Glasgow City & District Railway, closed 1 April 1870, reopened 17 May 1871 and although closed to the public 1 October 1902 workmen's trains continued to use it until closure by the L&NER in September 1926.
Line Operational – Demolished – No access. **NS59766 64849**

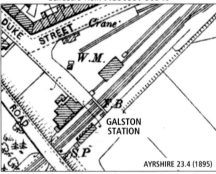

LANARKSHIRE 6.11 (1892)

GALSTON   6 B3

Opened 9 August 1848 by the Glasgow, Paisley, Kilmarnock & Ayr Railway and closed by BR 6 April 1964.
Line lifted – Demolished – Station site occupied by housing in Belvedere View. **NS50359 36346**

AYRSHIRE 23.4 (1895)

GARELOCHHEAD   10 A4

Opened by the West Highland Railway 7 August 1894.

**Garelochhead
Station** on 13 September 2015.

GARGUNNOCK   10 C4

Opened 26 May 1856 by the Edinburgh & Glasgow Railway and closed by the L&NER 1 October 1934.
Line lifted – Station House in private use – One platform extant.
NS71455 95101

PERTH & CLACKMANNANSHIRE 132.13 (1899)

GARLIESTON 2 B2
Opened 3 April 1876 by the Portpatrick & Wigtownshire Joint Railway as *Garliestown*, closed to passengers 1 March 1903 and to goods by BR 5 October 1965.
Line lifted – Demolished – Station site landscaped as part of the "Garlieston Caravan & Motorhome Club" site.
NX47744 46189

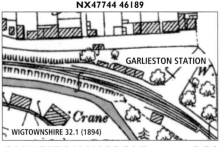

WIGTOWNSHIRE 32.1 (1894)

GARLIESTON HARBOUR 2 B2
GARMOUTH 18 B4
Opened 12 August 1884 by the GNofSR and closed by BR 6 May 1968.
Line lifted – Demolished – Site occupied by housing in The Sidings. **NJ33535 64055**

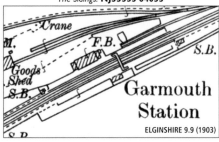

ELGINSHIRE 9.9 (1903)

GARNKIRK 6 C1
Opened c1837 by the Garnkirk & Glasgow Railway as *Chryston Road*, subsequently renamed as *Garnkirk Works*, by the CR in 1848 as *Garnkirk* and closed by BR 7 March 1960.
Line Operational – Demolished – No access. **NS68124 68384**

LANARKSHIRE 7.2 (1897)

GARROCHBURN GOODS 6 B3
GARROWHILL 6A C1
Opened by the L&NER 16 March 1936 as *Garrowhill Halt* and renamed by BR 11 September 1961 as *Garrowhill*.

Garrowhill Station on 12 May 2017.

GARSCADDEN 21A A2
Opened 7 November 1960.

Looking north at **Garscadden Station** on 13 September 2015.

GARTCOSH 6 C1
Opened by the Garnkirk and Glasgow Railway 1 June 1831, closed by BR 5 November 1962 and rebuilt and reopened 9 May 2005.

Gartcosh Station on 13 May 2017.

GARTLY 15 D2
Opened 20 September 1854 by the GNofSR and closed by BR 6 May 1968.
Line Operational – Station building in private use – Degraded platform extant. **NJ52260 32339**

GARTLY STATION

ABERDEENSHIRE 34.10 (1899)

GARTMORE 10 B4
Opened in October 1882 by the Strathendrick & Aberfoyle Railway and closed by BR 2 January 1950.
Line lifted – Demolished – Station site unused.
NS53249 98833

PERTH & CLACKMANNANSHIRE 130.5 (1898)

GARTNESS 10 B4
Opened 26 May 1856 by the Edinburgh & Glasgow Railway and closed by the L&NER 1 October 1934.
Line lifted – Demolished – Station site occupied by a house.
NS49889 86858

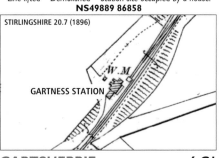

STIRLINGSHIRE 20.7 (1896)

GARTSHERRIE 6 C1
Opened in June 1832 by the Garnkirk & Glasgow Railway as *Gargill*, renamed by 1848 as *Gartsherrie*, closed by CR 1 January 1917, reopened 1 March 1919, renamed by the LM&SR in 1933 as *Gartsherrie Halt*, in 1935 as *Gartsherrie* and closed 28 October 1940.
Line Operational – Demolished – No access. **NS72148 66787**

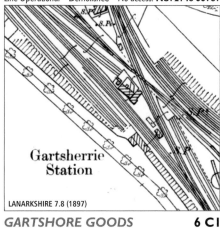

LANARKSHIRE 7.8 (1897)

GARTSHORE GOODS 6 C1
GARVE 14 A1
Opened by the Dingwall & Skye Railway 19 August 1870.

Garve Station on 17 September 2015.

GASK SIDINGS 11 A4
GASWATER BRANCH 6 C3
GATEHEAD 6 B3
Opened 1 March 1847 by the Kilmarnock & Troon Railway and closed by BR 3 March 1969.
Line Operational – Demolished – No access. **NS39174 36401**

GATEHEAD STATION

AYRSHIRE 22.4 (1895)

GATEHOUSE OF FLEET 2 C2
Opened in September 1861 by the Portpatrick & Wigtownshire Joint Railway as *Dromore*, renamed as *Gatehouse of Fleet* by 1 January 1912, closed by BR 5 December 1949 reopened 20 May 1950 and closed 14 June 1965.
Line lifted – Station building and platforms in private use.
NX54437 62434

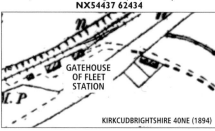

KIRKCUDBRIGHTSHIRE 40NE (1894)

GATESIDE 11 B3
Opened 15 March 1858 by the Fife & Kinross Railway and closed by BR 5 June 1950.
Line lifted – Station building in private use – Platform demolished. **NO18282 08890**

FIFESHIRE 11.16 (1894)

GAVELL 6 C1
Opened in December 1878 by the Kelvin Valley Railway as *Gavell*, renamed by the L&NER 29 September 1924 as *Twechar* and closed by the BR 6 August 1951.
Line lifted – Station House in private use - Demolished – Station site unused. **NS69571 76802**

STIRLINGSHIRE 20.7 (1896)

GEORGEMAS 20 A4
Opened by the Sutherland & Caithness Railway 28 July 1874 as *Georgemas* and renamed by BR as *Georgemas Junction*.

Looking west at **Georgemas Junction Station** on 17 September 2015.

GIFFEN 6 A2
Opened 4 September 1888 by the Lanarkshire & Ayrshire Railway as *Kilbirnie Junction*, renamed 1 October 1889 as *Giffen* and closed by the LM&SR 4 July 1932.
Line lifted – Demolished – Station site unused.
NS35998 50538

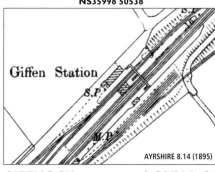

AYRSHIRE 8.14 (1895)

GIFFNOCK 6 C2/21A C4
Opened by the Busby Railway 1 January 1866.

Giffnock Station on 18 March 2017.

GIFFORD   7 D1
Opened 14 October 1901 by the Gifford & Garvald Light Railway and closed by the L&NER 3 April 1933.
Line lifted – Demolished – Station site occupied by housing.
NT52962 68466

HADDINGTONSHIRE 15.3 (1906)

GILBEY'S COTTAGES   15A B1
HALT
Opened 15 June 1959 by BR and closed 18 October 1965.
Line lifted - Demolished – The Speyside Way passes through the station site. **NJ19391 41496 (a)**

BANFFSHIRE 23.8 (1902)

GILMILNSCROFT BRANCH   6 C3
GILMERTON   7 C1/22A D3
Opened 23 July 1874 by the Edinburgh, Loanhead & Roslin Railway, closed by the NBR 1 January 1917 (except for workmen's trains), fully reopened 2 June 1919 and closed by the L&NER 1 May 1933.
Line lifted – Demolished – Station site unused.
NT29688 68067

EDINBURGHSHIRE 8.5 (1892)

GILMOUR STREET (See PAISLEY)
GILNOCKIE   3 C1
Opened 2 November 1864 by the Border Union Railway and closed by BR 15 June 1964.
Line lifted - Station building and platform in private use - A farm track passes through the station site. **NY39254 78477**

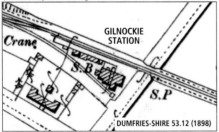
DUMFRIES-SHIRE 53.12 (1898)

GILSHOCHILL   21A C1
Opened 3 December 1993 as *Lambhill* and renamed as *Gilshochill* 24 May 1998.

Gilshochill Station on 13 May 2017.

GIRVAN   6 A4
Opened by the Girvan & Portpatrick Junction Railway 19 September 1877 as *Girvan New*, closed 7 February 1882, reopened 1 August 1883, closed 12 April 1886, reopened 14 June 1886, closed 2 September 1886, reopened 14 July 1890 and renamed by the G&SWR 1 April 1893 as *Girvan*.

Girvan Station on 16 March 2017.

GIRVAN HARBOUR   6 A4

GLAMIS   11 C1
Opened 4 June 1838 by the Newtyle & Glamis Railway, closed by the CR in July 1846, reopened 2 August 1848 and closed by BR 11 June 1956.
Line lifted – Demolished – Part of station site in use by the "Strathmore Vintage Vehicle Club". **NO37654 48899**

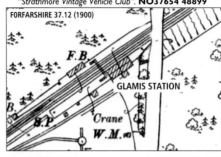
FORFARSHIRE 37.12 (1900)

GLASGOW   6 C1/21A D2
BUCHANAN STREET
Opened 1 November 1849 by the CR and closed by BR 7 November 1966.
Line lifted – Demolished – Station site occupied by the Glasgow Caledonian University. **NS59280 66060**

LANARKSHIRE 6.11 (1892)

GLASGOW   6 C1/21A C2
CENTRAL
Opened by the CR 1 August 1879.

Class 156 Unit No.156494 at **Glasgow Central (HL) Station** on 7 June 2011.

GLASGOW   6 C1/21A C2
CENTRAL
Opened by the Glasgow Central Railway 10 August 1896, closed by BR 5 October 1964 and reopened 5 November 1979.

Glasgow Central (LL) Station on 13 May 2017.

GLASGOW CROSS   21A D3
Opened 1 November 1895 by the Glasgow Central Railway and closed by BR 5 October 1964.
Line Operational – Demolished – Platforms partially extant - No access. **NS59633 64887**
SUBTERRANEAN

GLASGOW GREEN   21A D3
Opened 1 November 1895 by the Glasgow Central Railway, closed by the CR 1 January 1917, reopened 2 June 1919 and closed by BR 2 November 1953.
Line Operational – Demolished – No access. **NS60253 64244**

LANARKSHIRE 6.15 (1892)

GLASGOW QUEEN   6 C1/21A D2
STREET
Opened by the Edinburgh & Glasgow Railway 21 February 1842

Class 170 Unit No.170477 at **Glasgow Queen Street (HL) Station** on 7 June 2011.

GLASGOW QUEEN   6 C1/21A D2
STREET
Opened by the Glasgow City & District Railway 15 March 1886.

Looking west at **Glasgow Queen Street (LL) Station** on 13 May 2017.

GLASGOW   6 C1/21A C2
ST ENOCH
Opened 1 May 1876 by the G&SWR and closed by BR 27 June 1966.
Line lifted – Demolished – Station site occupied by the "St Enoch Shopping Centre". **NS59049 64968**

LANARKSHIRE 6.10 (1893)

GLASSAUGH   18 D4
Opened 1 April 1884 by the GNofSR and closed by BR 21 September 1953.
Line lifted – Demolished – Platforms partially extant – Station site unused. **NJ55889 65415**

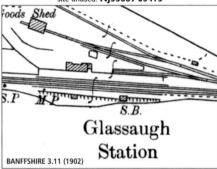
BANFFSHIRE 3.11 (1902)

GLASSEL   15 D3
Opened 2 December 1859 by the Deeside Extension Railway and closed by BR 28 February 1966.
Line lifted – Station building in private use – Remainder demolished. **NO65254 99193**

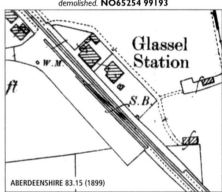
ABERDEENSHIRE 83.15 (1899)

GLASSFORD   6 C2
Opened 2 February 1863 by the Hamilton & Strathaven Railway, renamed by the LM&SR in 1933 as *Glassford Halt*, in 1938 as *Glassford* and closed 1 October 1945.
Line lifted – Demolished – Station site unused.
NS71131 47659

LANARKSHIRE 23.8 (1896)

GLASSON 3 C2

Opened in August 1854 by the Port Carlisle Railway, closed by the NBR 1 January 1917, reopened 1 February 1919 and closed by the L&NER 1 June 1932.

Line lifted – Demolished – Station site unused.
NY25368 60640

GLASTERLAW 11 D1

Opened in September 1880 by the CR and closed by BR 2 April 1951.

Line lifted – Platforms demolished - Station site occupied by private dwellings. **NO59693 51216**

GLENBARRY 15 D1

Opened 1 October 1859 by the Banff, Portsoy & Strathisla Railway, renamed by the GNofSR in 1872 as *Glenbarry* and closed by BR 6 May 1968.

Line lifted – Demolished – Station site unused.
NJ55423 54751

GLENBOIG 6 C1

Opened in February 1880 by the Scottish Central Railway and closed by BR 11 June 1956.

Line Operational – Demolished – No access. **NS72498 68628**

GLENBUCK 6 D3

Opened in October 1875 by the CR and closed by BR 4 August 1952.

Line lifted - Demolished – Station site unused – A pathway passes through the station site. **NS74930 28645**

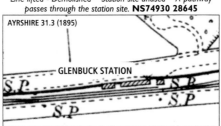

GLENBURNIE JUNCTION 11 B3
GLENCARRON PLATFORM 13 C1

Opened in 1871 by the Dingwall & Skye Railway as *Glencarron Platform*, renamed by BR 10 September 1962 as *Glencarron* and although closed 7 December 1964 was retained for a short period of time for non-timetabled use.

Line Operational - Demolished – No access. **NH06318 50812**

GLENCARSE 11 B3

Opened 24 May 1847 by the Dundee & Perth Railway and closed by BR 11 June 1956.

Line Operational – Station building in private use – Platforms demolished. **NO19668 21472**

GLENCORSE 7 B1/22A B4

Opened 2 July 1877 by the Edinburgh, Loanhead & Roslin Railway and closed by the L&NER 1 May 1933.

Line lifted – Demolished – Station site landscaped.
NT24587 61937

GLENCRAIG COLLIERY 11 B4
BRANCH
GLENCRUITTEN SUMMIT* 9A C3

Opened at an unknown date by the LM&SR and closed c1938.

Line Operational – Signal box/house in private use.
NM88231 31007

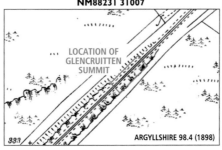

GLEN DOUGLAS HALT 10A A4

Opened in c1896 by the West Highland Railway as a non-timetabled stop for railway employees and families. Opened to the public 12 June 1961 by BR and although closed 15 June 1964 had intermittent use until c1973.

Line Operational – Demolished. **NS27433 99444**

GLENEAGLES 10 D3

Opened by the Scottish Central Railway 14 March 1856 as *Crieff Junction* and renamed by the CR 1 April 1912 as *Gleneagles*.

Looking south at **Gleneagles Station** on 13 May 2017.

GLEN FALLOCH HALT* 10A A3

Opened 10 April 1946 by the L&NER for workers on the Loch Sloy HEP scheme and probably closed by BR c1949.

Line Operational – Degraded platform partially extant.
NN31703 19908 (a)

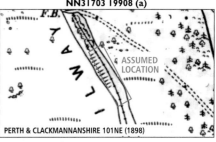

GLENFARG 11 B3

Opened 2 June 1890 by the NBR and closed by BR 15 June 1964.

Line lifted – Demolished - The M90 passes over the station site. **NO13551 10564**

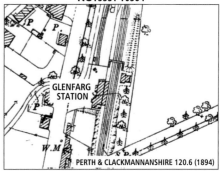

GLENFINNAN 13 C4

Opened by the NBR 1 April 1901 as *Glenfinnan for Loch Shiel* and renamed by BR 17 May 1982 as *Glenfinnan*.

Glenfinnan Station on 14 September 2015.

GLENGARNOCK (CR) 6 A1

Opened 2 December 1899 by the Lanarkshire & Ayrshire Railway as *Glengarnock*, renamed by the LM&SR 2 June 1924 as *Glengarnock High* and closed 1 December 1930.

Line lifted – Demolished – Station site unused.
NS31910 53294

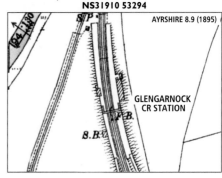

GLENGARNOCK (G&SWR)   6 A1

Opened by the Glasgow, Paisley, Kilmarnock & Ayr Railway 21 July 1840 as *Glengarnock and Kilbirnie* and renamed as *Glengarnock* by the G&SWR 1 June 1905.

Glengarnock Station on 17 March 2017.

GLENGRAIG COLLIERY   11 B4
GLENIFFER DEPOT BRANCH   6 B2
GLENLOCHY CROSSING*   10A A3

Opened at an unknown date by the LM&SR and closed by BR c1953.

Line Operational – Demolished. **NN25472 29476**

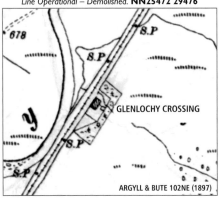

ARGYLL & BUTE 102NE (1897)

GLENLUCE   2 A2

Opened 12 March 1861 by the Portpatrick & Wigtownshire Joint Railway and closed by BR 14 June 1965.

Line lifted – Demolished – Station site occupied by housing in Fineview Crescent. **NX19891 57642**

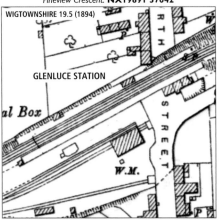

WIGTOWNSHIRE 19.5 (1894)

GLENOGLEHEAD CROSSING*   10A B2

Opened 1 June 1870 by the Callander & Oban Railway as *Killin*, renamed by the CR 1 April 1886 as *Glenoglehead Crossing* and closed by BR 28 September 1965.

Line lifted – Demolished – Station building in private use. **NN55808 28293**

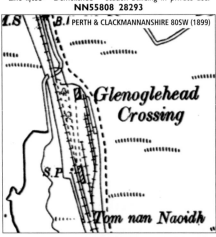

PERTH & CLACKMANNANSHIRE 80SW (1899)

GLENROTHES WITH THORNTON   11A C4

Opened 11 May 1992.

Class 170 Unit No. 170450 at **Glenrothes with Thornton Station** on 18 September 2015.

GLENSIDE   6 A4

Opened 17 May 1906 by the Maidens & Dunure Light Railway and closed by the LM&SR 1 December 1930.

Line lifted – Demolished – Station site occupied by the "Culzean Castle Camping and Caravanning Club" site. **NS24516 10137**

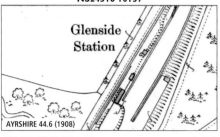

AYRSHIRE 44.6 (1908)

GLENWHILLY   1 D1

Opened 19 September 1877 by the Girvan & Portpatrick Joint Railway, closed 7 February 1882, reopened 16 February 1882, closed 12 April 1886, reopened 14 June 1886 and closed by BR 6 September 1965.

Line Operational – Station building in private use – One platform extant – No access. **NX17003 70928**

WIGTOWNSHIRE 6.8 (1893)

GOGAR   7 B1

Opened in July 1842 by the Edinburgh & Glasgow Railway and closed by the L&NER 22 September 1930.

Line Operational – Demolished – No access. **NT17393 71121**

EDINBURGHSHIRE 2.16 (1893)

GOLF CLUB HOUSE HALT   18A D4

Opened 1 October 1913 by the GNofSR and closed by BR 6 July 1964.

Line lifted – Demolished – A pathway passes through the station site. **NJ67665 64481**

NJ6764 (1963)

GOLF STREET   11A D2

Opened 7 November 1960 by BR as *Golf Street Halt* and renamed as *Golf Street* 16 May 1983.

Looking south at **Golf Street Station** on 18 September 2015.

GOLLANFIELD JUNCTION   14 C1

Opened 7 November 1855 by the Inverness & Nairn Railway as *Fort George*, renamed by the HR 1 July 1899 as *Gollanfield Junction*, by BR in 1959 as *Gollanfield* and closed 3 May 1965.

Line Operational - Station building in private use. **NH79747 52985**

INVERNESS-MAINLAND 1.15 (1903)

GOLSPIE   17 D3

Opened by the Sutherland Railway 13 April 1868.

Looking north at **Golspie Station** on 16 September 2015.

GORBALS   21A D3

Opened 1 September 1877 by the Glasgow, Barrhead & Kilmarnock Joint Railway and closed by the LM&SR 1 June 1928.

Line lifted – Demolished – Station site unused. **NS58977 64044**

LANARKSHIRE 6.14 (1893)

GORDON   8 A2

Opened 16 November 1863 by the Berwickshire Railway and closed by BR 13 August 1948.

Line lifted – Station building and platform in private use. **NT64733 43755**

BERWICKSHIRE 27.1 (1898)

GOREBRIDGE   7 C1

Opened by the NBR 14 July 1847, closed by BR 6 January 1969 and rebuilt and reopened by Network Rail and Transport for Scotland 6 September 2015.

Gorebridge Station on 12 May 2017.

GORGIE   22A B2

Opened 1 December 1884 by the Edinburgh Suburban & Southside Junction Railway as *Gorgie*, renamed by BR in May 1952 as *Gorgie East* and closed 10 September 1962.

Line Operational – Demolished – No access. **NT22834 71886**

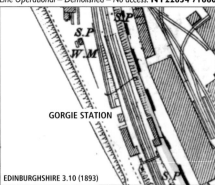

EDINBURGHSHIRE 3.10 (1893)

GORTON PLATFORM*   10A A2

Opened in July 1896 by the West Highland Railway as a non-timetabled stop for railway employees and families. Closed by BR c1970.

Line Operational – Demolished – Station site in use as Gorton Crossing Engineer's Siding. **NN39364 47917**

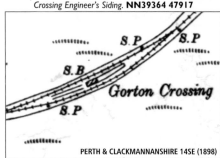

PERTH & CLACKMANNANSHIRE 14SE (1898)

GOURDON   16 A4

Opened 1 November 1865 by the Scottish North Eastern Railway and closed by BR 1 October 1951.

Line lifted – Demolished – Station site occupied by housing in Station Park. **NO82734 70839**

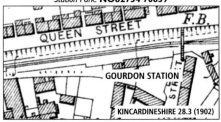

GOURDON STATION

KINCARDINESHIRE 28.3 (1902)

GOUROCK   6 A1

Opened by the CR 1 June 1899, closed by BR for tunnel repairs 5 February 1973, reopened 20 April 1973, closed 3 October 1993 and reopened 27 March 1995.

Class 380 Unit No.**380105** at **Gourock Station** on 17 March 2017.

GOVAN   6 B1/21A B3

Opened 2 December 1868 by the Glasgow & Paisley Joint Railway, closed by the G&SWR 1 July 1875, reopened 1 March 1880, closed in April 1899, reopened in May 1903, closed by May 1906, reopened in February 1911 and closed 9 May 1921.

Line lifted – Demolished – Station site in commercial use – Golspie Street crosses the station site. **NS55462 65612**

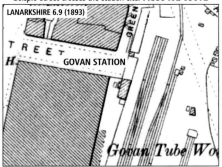

LANARKSHIRE 6.9 (1893)

GOVAN STATION

Govan Tube Wo

GRANDTULLY   10 D1

Opened 3 July 1865 by the Inverness & Perth Junction Railway and closed by BR 3 May 1965.

Line lifted – Demolished – Station site occupied by a car park for a caravan and camping site. **NN91339 53029**

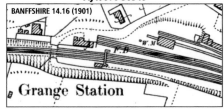

GRANDTULLY STATION

S.P.   M.P

PERTH & CLACKMANNANSHIRE 39.16 (1898)

GRANGE   15 C1

Opened 5 January 1857 by the GNofSR and closed by BR 6 May 1968.

Line Operational – Demolished – One platform partially extant. **NJ49670 50548**

BANFFSHIRE 14.16 (1901)

Grange Station

GRANGEMOUTH   7 A1

Opened 1 November 1861 by the CR and closed by BR 29 January 1968.

Line Operational for Freight – Demolished – Station site unused. **NS92551 82147**

GRANGEMOUTH STATION

Church

STIRLINGSHIRE 25.13 (1896)

GRANGESTON HALT*   6A A4

Opened 15 December 1941 by the LM&SR for ordnance factory workers and closed by BR in May 1957.

Line Operational – Demolished – One degraded platform extant. **NX20347 99675**

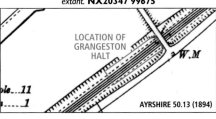

LOCATION OF GRANGESTON HALT

AYRSHIRE 50.13 (1894)

GRANTON (NBR)   7 B1/22A B1

Opened 19 February 1846 by the Edinburgh, Leith & Newhaven Railway, closed by the NBR 1 January 1917, reopened 1 February 1919 and closed by the L&NER 2 November 1925.

Line lifted – Demolished – Station site occupied by the "Royal Forth Yacht Club". **NT23771 77279**

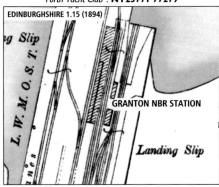

EDINBURGHSHIRE 1.15 (1894)

GRANTON NBR STATION

Landing Slip

GRANTON (CR) GOODS   7 B1
GRANTON GAS WORKS*   22A B1

Opened in 1902 by the CR for employees at the gas works and closed by the LM&SR in 1942.

Line lifted - Station building Grade B Listed and restored - Some platform still extant. **NT22637 76835**

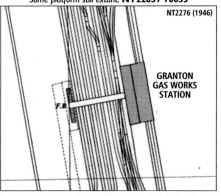

NT2276 (1946)

GRANTON GAS WORKS STATION

GRANTON ROAD   7 B1/22A B1

Opened 1 August 1879 by the CR and closed by BR 30 April 1962.

Line lifted – Demolished – Platforms extant – The Ferry Road Path passes through the station site. **NT24347 76147**

ROSE BAN

Granton Road Station

EDINBURGHSHIRE 3.3 (1894)

GRANTOWN ON SPEY   15 A2

Opened 1 July 1863 by the Strathspey Railway as *Grantown*, renamed by the GNofSR 1 June 1912 as *Grantown-on-Spey*, by BR 5 June 1950 as *Grantown-on-Spey East* and closed 18 October 1965.

Line lifted - Station buildings and platforms preserved as the "Highland Heritage & Culture Centre" – The Speyside Way passes through the station site. **NJ03849 26165**

ELGINSHIRE 33.5 (1904)

S.P.

Grantown Station

GRANTOWN ON SPEY   15 A2

Opened 3 August 1863 by the Inverness & Perth Junction Railway as *Grantown*, renamed by the HR 1 June 1912 as *Grantown-on-Spey*, by BR 5 June 1950 as *Grantown-on-Spey West* and closed 18 October 1965.

Line lifted – Station House in private use – Station site in commercial use. **NJ02435 26986**

ELGINSHIRE 32.8 (1903)

GRANTOWN ON SPEY STATION

Station Wood

Goods Shed

GRANTSHOUSE   8 A1

Opened in September 1846 by the NBR and closed by BR 4 May 1964.

Line Operational – Demolished – Station site in use as an Engineer's Yard. **NT80897 65477**

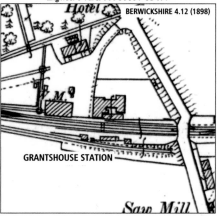

BERWICKSHIRE 4.12 (1898)

GRANTSHOUSE STATION

Saw Mill

GREE GOODS   6 B2
GREENAN CASTLE GOODS   6 A3
GREENGAIRS GOODS   6 D1
GREENFAULDS   6A D1

Opened 15 May 1989.

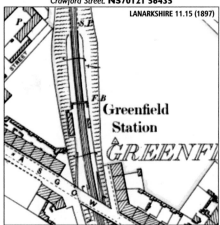

Greenfaulds Station on 13 May 2017.

GREENFIELD   6 C2

Opened in 1878 by the Glasgow, Rothwell, Hamilton & Coatbridge Railway as *Greenfield*, renamed by the NBR 1 May 1902 as *Burnbank*, closed 1 January 1917 (except for workmen's trains), reopened 2 June 1919 and closed by BR 15 September 1952.

Line lifted – Demolished – Station site occupied by housing in Crawford Street. **NS70121 56435**

LANARKSHIRE 11.15 (1897)

Greenfield Station

GREENF

GREENHILL   6 D1

Opened 1 March 1848 by the Scottish Central Railway and closed by BR 18 April 1966. It was also known as *Greenhill Junction, Caledonian Junction, Greenhill Lower Junction* and *Lower Greenhill* in various timetables.
Line Operational – Demolished – No access. **NS82183 79007**

GREENLAW   8 A2

Opened 16 November 1863 by the Berwickshire Railway and closed by BR 13 August 1948.
Line lifted – Station building in private use – Platforms demolished. **NT70873 45518**

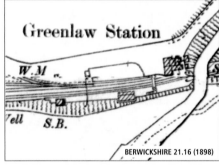

BERWICKSHIRE 21.16 (1898)

GREENLOANING   10 D3

Opened 23 May 1848 by the Scottish Central Railway and closed by BR 11 June 1956.
Line Operational - Station building in private use – Platforms demolished. **NN83524 07724**

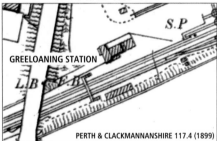

PERTH & CLACKMANNANSHIRE 117.4 (1899)

GREENOCK CENTRAL   6 A1

Opened by the CR 1 June 1899 as *Greenock Cathcart Street* and renamed 1 October 1898 as *Greenock Central.*

Greenock Central Station on 17 March 2017.

GREENOCK PRINCES PIER   6 A1

Opened 23 December 1869 by the Greenock & Ayrshire Railway as *Greenock Albert Harbour*, renamed by the G&SWR 1 May 1875 as *Greenock Princes Pier*, slightly resited 100 yards north 25 May 1894 and although closed by BR 2 February 1959 boat trains continued to use it until 20 November 1965.
Line lifted – Demolished – Station site part of "Clydeport Container Terminal". **NS27507 77149**

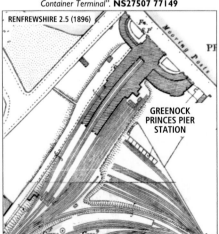

RENFREWSHIRE 2.5 (1896)

GREENOCK WEST   6 A1

Opened by the CR 1 June 1899.

Greenock West Station on 17 March 2017.

GRESKINE*   7A A4

Opened 3 January 1900 by the CR for railwaymen and families and closed by the LM&SR after 1926.
Line Operational – Demolished. **NT03973 09873 (a)**

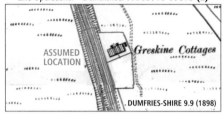

DUMFRIES-SHIRE 9.9 (1898)

GRETNA (CR)   3 C1

Opened 10 September 1847 by the CR and closed by BR 10 September 1951.
Line Operational – Station building in private use – Platforms demolished. **NY33332 67414**

GRETNA (NBR)   3 C1

Opened 1 November 1861 by the NBR, closed to passengers 9 August 1915 and closed to goods by BR 10 September 1951.
Line lifted – Demolished – Station House in private use. **NY33401 67469**

DUMFRIES-SHIRE 64.6 (1898)

GRETNA GREEN   3 C1

Opened by the Glasgow, Dumfries and Carlisle Railway 23 August 1848 as *Gretna*, renamed as *Gretna Green* by the G&SWR in April 1852 and closed by BR 6 December 1965.
Line Operational – Station building in private use – Platforms demolished. **NY32007 67902**

DUMFRIES-SHIRE 64.1 (1898)

GRETNA GREEN   3A C1

Opened 20 September 1993 and replaced the original one *(qv)* sited just to the east.

Looking west at **Gretna Green Station** on 13 September 2015.

GUARD BRIDGE   11 C3

Opened 1 July 1852 by the St Andrews Railway and closed by BR 6 September 1965.
Line lifted – Demolished – Station site occupied by housing in Kinnear Court. **NO45046 18956**

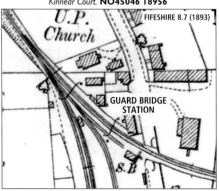

FIFESHIRE 8.7 (1893)

GUAY   11 A2

Opened 1 June 1863 by the Inverness & Perth Junction Railway and closed by BR 3 August 1959.
Line Operational – Demolished – Degraded platform partially extant – No access. **NN99760 49019**

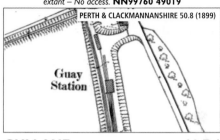

PERTH & CLACKMANNANSHIRE 50.8 (1899)

GULLANE   11 D4

Opened 1 April 1898 by the Aberlady, Gullane & North British Railway and closed by the L&NER 12 September 1932.
Line lifted – Demolished – Station site occupied by housing in Muirfield Station. **NT48802 82906**

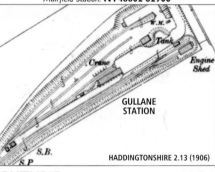

HADDINGTONSHIRE 2.13 (1906)

GUTHRIE   11 D1

Opened 4 December 1838 by the Arbroath & Forfar Railway and closed by BR 5 December 1955.
Line lifted – Demolished – Station site unused. **NO56699 50002**

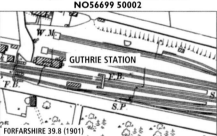

FORFARSHIRE 39.8 (1901)

HADDINGTON   7 D1

Opened 22 June 1846 by the NBR and closed by BR 5 December 1949.
Line lifted – Platform and one station building extant – Station site occupied by an Industrial Estate. **NT50748 73949**

HADDINGTONSHIRE 10.6 (1893)

HAILES HALT   22A A3

Opened 16 November 1908 by the CR, originally for golfers, and closed by the L&NER 1 November 1943.
Line lifted – Demolished - The Water of Leith Walkway passes through the station site. **NT21341 69712**

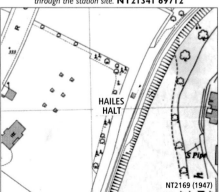

NT2169 (1947)

HAIRMYRES 6 C2

Opened by the Busby Railway 1 September 1868.

Hairmyres Station on 18 March 2017.

HALBEATH 11 B4

Opened 13 December 1849 by the Edinburgh, Perth & Dundee Railway, closed by the NBR 1 January 1917, reopened 1 April 1919 and closed by the L&NER 22 September 1930.

Line Operational - Station building in private use – Platforms partially extant. **NT12643 88779**

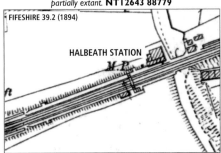

FIFESHIRE 39.2 (1894)

HALBEATH STATION

HALKIRK 20 A4

Opened 28 July 1874 by the Sutherland & Caithness Railway and closed by BR 13 June 1960.

Line Operational – Demolished. **ND13253 58347**

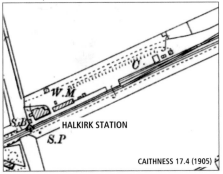

HALKIRK STATION

CAITHNESS 17.4 (1905)

HALLCRAIG BRANCH 6 D2

HALTWHISTLE 4 A2

Opened 18 June 1838 by the Newcastle & Carlisle Railway.

Looking east at **Haltwhistle Station** on 19 September 2015.

HAMILTON (NBR) 6 C2

Opened 1 April 1878 by the Glasgow, Rothwell, Hamilton & Coatbridge Railway, closed by the NBR 1 January 1917 (except for workmen's trains), reopened 2 June 1919 and closed by BR 15 September 1952.

Line lifted – Demolished – Station site partially occupied by a car park. **NS71935 55636**

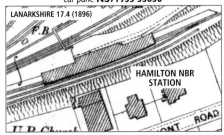

LANARKSHIRE 17.4 (1896)

HAMILTON NBR STATION

HAMILTON CENTRAL 6 C2

Opened by the CR 14 July 1876.

Hamilton Central Station on 19 March 2017.

HAMILTON WEST 6 C2

Opened by the Clydesdale Junction Railway 10 September 1849. *(Some reports suggest that the station may have closed 14 July 1876 when Hamilton Central opened and reopened 2 October 1876 when the link to Ferniegair was established).*

Class 318 Unit No.318268 at **Hamilton West Station** on 19 March 2017.

HARBURN 7 A1

Opened 15 February 1848 by the CR as *West Calder & Torphin*, renamed c1870 as *Harburn* and closed by BR 18 April 1966. It was also known as *West Calder & Harburn* in some timetables.

Line Operational – Demolished – No access. **NT04314 61653**

EDINBURGHSHIRE 11.7 (1893)

HARDENGREEN GOODS 7 C1

HARKER (NBR) 3 C2

Opened 29 October 1861 by the Border Union Railway and although officially closed by the L&NER 1 November 1929 it saw subsequent non-timetabled use serving the Ordnance Depot until c1941.

Line lifted – Station building in private use – Platforms demolished – A metalled roadway passes through the station site. **NY38613 60970**

HARKER (L&NER)* 3A C2

Opened by the L&NER 1 March 1943 for RAF personnel and closed by BR 6 January 1969.

Line lifted – Demolished – Station site unused – A metalled roadway passes through the station site. **NY38597 60890**

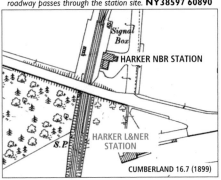

HARKER NBR STATION

HARKER L&NER STATION

CUMBERLAND 16.7 (1899)

HARTHOPE* 7A A4

Opened 3 January 1900 by the CR for railwaymen and families and closed by the LM&SR after 1926.

Line Operational – Demolished. **NT02683 12531**

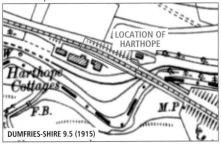

LOCATION OF HARTHOPE

DUMFRIES-SHIRE 9.5 (1915)

HARTWOOD HILL BRANCH 6 D2

HARTWOOD 6 D2

Opened by the CR 1 May 1889

Hartwood Station on 19 March 2017.

HASSENDEAN 7 D3

Opened in March 1850 by the NBR and closed by BR 6 January 1969.

Line lifted - Station building in use as "Hassendean Station B&B" - Platforms extant. **NT54798 20396**

ROXBURGHSHIRE 20.5 (1897)

HASSENDEAN STATION

HASSOCKRIGG COLLIERY 6 D1

HATTON 16 C2

Opened 2 August 1897 by the GNofSR and closed by the L&NER 31 October 1932.

Line lifted - Demolished – The A90 passes through the station site. **NK05392 36881**

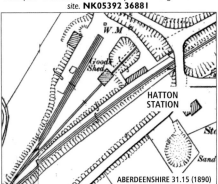

HATTON STATION

ABERDEENSHIRE 31.15 (1890)

HAWICK 7 D3

Opened 1 July 1862 by the NBR and closed by BR 6 January 1969.

Line lifted – Demolished – Station site occupied by the "Teviotdale Leisure Centre". **NT50524 15296**

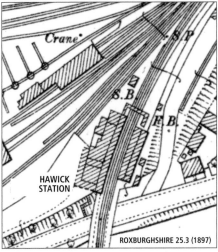

HAWICK STATION

ROXBURGHSHIRE 25.3 (1897)

HAWKHEAD 21A A3

Opened by the G&SWR 1 May 1894, closed 1 January 1917, reopened 10 February 1919, closed by BR 14 February 1966 and rebuilt and reopened 12 April 1991.

Hawkhead Station on 18 March 2017.

HAWTHORNDEN 7 C1/22A D4

Opened 4 July 1855 by the Peebles Railway as *Rosewell & Hawthornden* and closed by BR 10 September 1962. It was also known as *Hawthornden & Rosewell, Hawthornden for Rosewell, Hawthornden* and *Hawthornden Junction & Rosewell.*

Line lifted - Demolished - Platforms partially extant - The National Cycle Network Route No.1 passes through the station site. **NT28908 63213**

Hawthornden Station

EDINBURGHSHIRE 21.6 (1892)

HAYMARKET 7 B1/22A B2

Opened by the Edinburgh & Glasgow Railway 21 February 1842 as *Edinburgh* and renamed 22 June 1846 as *Haymarket* upon the opening of Edinburgh (Waverley) station.

Looking east at **Haymarket Station** on 12 May 2017.

HAYWOOD 7 A2

Opened in November 1867 by the CR as *Heywood*, renamed c1875 as *Haywood* and closed by BR 10 September 1951.

Line lifted – Demolished – Station site in industrial use. **NS97107 54912**

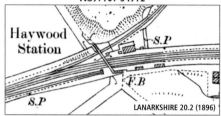

LANARKSHIRE 20.2 (1896)

HEADS OF AYR 6 A3

Opened 17 May 1906 by the Maidens & Dunure Light Railway and closed by the LM&SR 1 December 1930.

Line lifted – Demolished – Station site occupied by the "Heads of Ayr Caravan Park". **NS28498 18046**

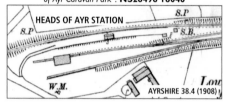

AYRSHIRE 38.4 (1908)

HEADS OF AYR HOLIDAY CAMP 6A A3

Opened 17 May 1947 by the LM&SR and closed by BR 14 September 1968.

Line lifted – Demolished – Station site part of "Craig Tara Caravans". **NS30255 18243**

NS3018 (1967)

HELENSBURGH CENTRAL 6 A1

Opened by the Glasgow, Dumbarton & Helensburgh Railway 31 May 1858 as *Helensburgh* and renamed by BR 8 June 1953 as *Helensburgh Central*.

Looking west at **Helensburgh Central Station** on 13 September 2015.

HELENSBURGH UPPER 6 A1

Opened by the West Highland Railway 7 August 1894.

Looking west at **Helensburgh Upper Station** on 13 September 2015.

HELMSDALE 18 A2

Opened by the Duke of Sutherland's Railway 16 May 1871.

Looking north at **Helmsdale Station** on 16 September 2015.

HERIOT 7 C2

Opened 1 August 1848 by the NBR and closed by BR 6 January 1969.

Line Operational - Station building in private use – Platforms demolished. **NT40337 54590**

EDINBURGHSHIRE 21.6 (1892)

HEXHAM 4 B2

Opened 10 March 1835 by the Newcastle & Carlisle Railway.

Looking east at **Hexham Station** on 19 September 2015.

HEXHAM JUNCTION 4 B1

HIGH BLANTYRE 6 C2

Opened 2 February 1863 by the Hamilton & Strathaven Railway and closed by the LM&SR 1 October 1945.

Line lifted – Demolished – Station site occupied by housing in Craigmuir Gardens. **NS67856 56604**

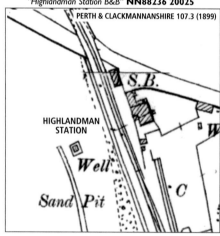

LANARKSHIRE 11.14 (1896)

HIGHLANDMAN 10 D3

Opened in July 1856 by the Crieff Junction Railway, closed by the CR 1 January 1917, reopened 1 February 1919 and closed by BR 6 July 1964.

Line lifted - Station building and platform in private use as the "Highlandman Station B&B" **NN88236 20025**

PERTH & CLACKMANNANSHIRE 107.3 (1899)

HIGH STREET 21A D2

Opened by the Glasgow City & District Railway 1 April 1871 as *College*, renamed as *High Street* by the NBR 1 January 1914, closed 1977 by BR and reopened 5 October 1981.

High Street Station on 13 May 2017.

HILLFOOT 6 C1/21A B1

Opened by the NBR 1 May 1900.

Hillfoot Station on 13 May 2017.

HILTON JUNCTION 11 B3

HILLINGTON EAST 21A A3

Opened by the LM&SR 19 March 1934 as *Hillington* and renamed 1 April 1940 as *Hillington East*.

Hillington East Station on 18 March 2017.

HILLINGTON WEST 21A A3

Opened by the LM&SR 1 April 1940 as *Hillington* and renamed by BR 3 March 1952 as *Hillington West*.

Hillington West Station on 18 March 2017.

HILLSIDE 12 A1

Opened 1 May 1883 by the NBR and closed by the L&NER in February 1927.

Line Operational – Demolished – No access. **NO71102 61155**

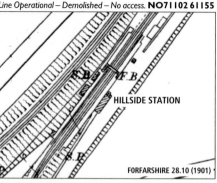

FORFARSHIRE 28.10 (1901)

HOLBURN STREET 16 B3

Opened 2 July 1894 by the GNofSR and closed by the L&NER 5 April 1937.

Line lifted – Demolished – Platforms extant – The Deeside Way passes through the station site. **NJ93080 04444**

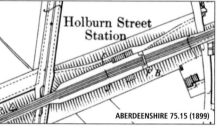

ABERDEENSHIRE 75.15 (1899)

HOLEHOUSE 6 B4

Opened 2 December 1895 by the G&SWR and closed by BR 3 April 1950.

Line Operational for Freight – Demolished. **NS40651 13530**

LOCATION OF HOLEHOUSE STATION

AYRSHIRE 40.9 (1894)

HOLLYBUSH 6 B4

Opened 7 August 1856 by the Ayr & Dalmellington Railway and closed by BR 6 April 1964.

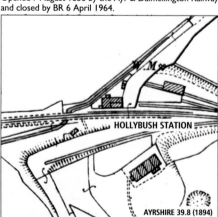

AYRSHIRE 39.8 (1894)

HOLYGATE GOODS 7 A1

HOLYTOWN 6 D2

Opened by the CR 1 June 1880 as *Carfin*, renamed 1 January 1882 as *Carfin Junction*, 1 June 1882 as *Holytown Junction* and 1 October 1901 as *Holytown*.

Holytown Station on 19 March 2017.

HOLYWOOD 3 A1
Opened 15 October 1849 by the Glasgow, Paisley, Kilmarnock & Ayr Railway as *Killylung*, renamed 28 October 1850 as *Holywood* and closed by BR 26 September 1949.
Line Operational - Platforms extant – No access.
NX95351 81428

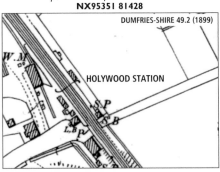

HOPEMAN 18 A4
Opened 10 October 1892 by the HR, closed 1 January 1917, reopened for limited school use 13 January 1917, reopened totally 2 June 1919 and closed by the LM&SR 14 September 1931.
Line lifted – Station building and platform extant as part of the "Station Caravan Park". **NJ14485 69666**

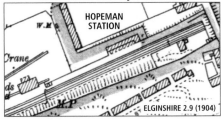

HOUSE O' HILL HALT 22A A1
Opened 1 February 1937 by the LM&SR and closed by BR 7 May 1951.
Line lifted – Demolished - The Blackhall Path passes through the station site. **NT21446 75296**

HOUSTON (CR) 6 B1
Opened 31 March 1841 by the Glasgow, Paisley & Greenock Railway as *Houston*, renamed by the LM&SR 1 May 1926 as *Georgetown* and closed by BR 2 February 1959.
Line Operational – Demolished – No access. **NS45378 67531**

HOUSTON (G&SWR) 6 B1
Opened in March 1871 by the G&SWR as *Windyhill*, subsequently renamed as *Crosslee*, *Houston & Crosslee*, *Houston for Crosslee*, then by BR 7 May 1973 as *Houston* and closed 10 January 1983.
Line lifted – Demolished – One degraded platform extant - The Paisley and Clyde Cycle Path passes through the station site. **NS42149 64556**

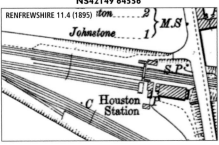

HOWWOOD 6 B2
Opened by the G&SWR 1 December 1876, closed by BR 7 March 1955 and reopened 12 March 2001.

Howwood Station on 17 March 2017.

HOY 20 A4
Opened 1 October 1874 by the Sutherland & Caithness Railway and closed by BR 29 November 1965.
Line Operational – Demolished. **ND14794 60413**

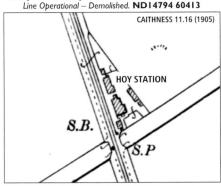

HUMBIE 7 D1
Opened 14 October 1901 by the Gifford & Garvald Light Railway and closed by the L&NER 3 April 1933.
Line lifted – Demolished – Station site unused.
NT48114 65094

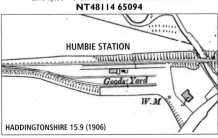

HUMSHAUGH 4 B1
Opened 5 April 1858 by the Border Counties Railway as *Chollerford*, renamed by the NBR 1 August 1919 as *Humshaugh* and closed by BR 15 October 1956.
Line lifted - Station building and platform in private use.
NY92094 70483

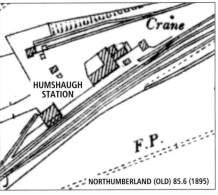

HUNTLY 15 D2
Opened by the GNofSR 20 September 1854.

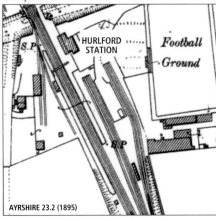

Class 158 Unit No.158710 at **Huntly Station** on 17 September 2015.

HUNTLYS CAVE* 15A A2
Opened prior to 29 May 1937 by the LM&SR for use by railwaymen's families and closed by BR after 1957.
Line lifted – Demolished – The Dava Way passes through the station site. **NJ02389 32582**

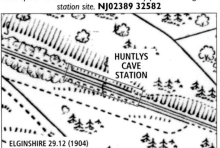

HURLFORD 6 B3
Opened 9 August 1848 by the Glasgow, Paisley, Kilmarnock & Ayr Railway and closed by BR 7 March 1955.
Line Operational – Demolished – No access. **NS4489136729**

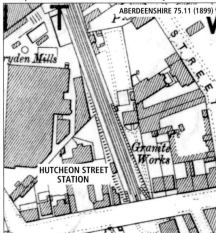

HUTCHEON STREET 16 B3
Opened 1 December 1887 by the GNofSR and closed by the L&NER 5 April 1937.
Line Operational – Demolished – No access. **NJ93408 06981**

HYNDLAND (BR) 21A B2
Opened 5 November 1960.

Hyndland Station on 13 May 2017.

HYNDLAND (NBR) 21A B2
Opened 15 March 1886 by the Glasgow City & District Railway and closed by BR 5 November 1960.
Line lifted – Demolished – Station site in use as the "Old Station Park". **NS55821 67629**

IBM 6A A1
Opened 9 May 1978 as *IBM Halt*, renamed 16 May 1983 as *IBM* and was effectively, although not officially, closed from 8 December 2018 after which date trains ceased to call here.

Looking east at **IBM Station** on 17 March 2017.

IBROX 6 B1/21A B3
Opened 6 November 1843 by the Glasgow, Paisley, Kilmarnock & Ayr Railway as *Bellahouston*, closed in 1845 and reopened 2 December 1868 by the Glasgow & Paisley Joint Railway as *Ibrox*. Following the closure to passengers of the Govan line on 9 May 1921 the Govan branch line platforms were designated as *Ibrox Football Ground (qv)* and used for workmen's and football traffic. The station was closed by BR 6 February 1967.
Line Operational – Demolished – No access. **NS55306 64296**

FOR MAP SEE PAGE 92

IBROX FOOTBALL GROUND*　　21A B3

Opened following the closure of the Govan branch on 9 May 1921 and utilized the branch platforms of *Ibrox* station *(qv)* for occasional workmen's trains and football traffic. It was closed by BR in c1965.
Line lifted – Demolished – Station site unused.
NS55273 64325

IMBER HOUSES*　　13A B2

Opened 3 December 1951 by BR for the use of railwaymen's families and closed c1972.
Line Operational – Demolished – No access.
NG89663 36578 (a)

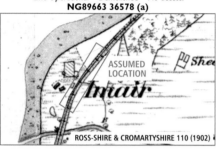

IMPERIAL COTTAGES HALT　　15A B1

Opened 15 June 1959 by BR and closed 18 October 1965.
Line lifted - Demolished – The Speyside Way passes through the station site. **NJ21576 41527**

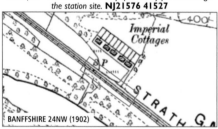

INCHCOONANS GOODS　　11 B3
INCHES　　6 D3

Opened 1 June 1874 by the CR and closed by BR 5 October 1964.
Line lifted – Demolished – Station site unused.
NS78793 28376

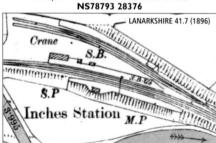

INCHGREEN GOODS　　6 A1
INCHLEA CROSSING*　　14A C4

Date unknown but possibly opened by the HR to take railwaymen's children to school. This may have continued into BR days.
Line Operational – Demolished. **NN67577 89930 (a)**

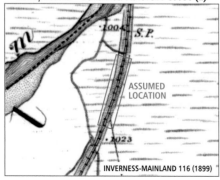

INCHMAGRANACHAN CROSSING*　　11A A2

Opening and closing dates unknown but possibly opened by the HR for use by railwaymen and their families.
Line Operational – Demolished. **NO00377 43830**

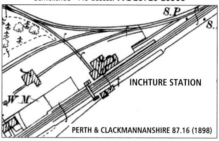

INCHTERF PLATFORM*　　6A C1

Opened by 1917 by the NBR for employees at the Inchterf Firing Range and closed at an unknown date.
Line lifted – Demolished – Station site unused.
NS67984 76097 (e)

INCHTURE　　11 B2

Opened 24 May 1847 by the Dundee & Perth Railway and closed by BR 11 June 1956.
Line Operational – Station building in private use – Platforms demolished - No access. **NO28726 26508**

INCHTURE VILLAGE　　11 B2

Opened 1 February 1848 by the CR (as a horse-drawn roadside tramway) and closed 1 January 1917.
Line lifted – Demolished – The A90 crosses the station site.
NO27662 28563

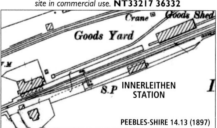

INGLISTON GOODS BRANCH　10 D4
INGLISTON COLLIERY BRANCH　7 B1
INNERLEITHEN　　7 C2

Opened 1 October 1864 by the Innerleithen & Galashiels Railway and closed by BR 5 February 1962.
Line lifted - Station building and one platform extant – Station site in commercial use. **NT33217 36332**

INNERPEFFRAY　　10 D3

Opened 21 May 1866 by the Crieff & Methven Junction Railway, closed by the CR 1 January 1917, reopened 2 June 1919 and closed by BR 1 October 1951.
Line lifted – Station building in private use as "Peveryl House" – Platform demolished. **NN89366 20216**

INNERWICK　　8 A1

Opened in July 1848 by the NBR and closed by BR 18 June 1951.
Line Operational – Station building in private use – Platforms demolished. **NT74151 74345**

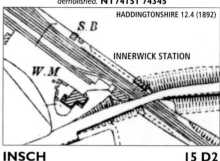

INSCH　　15 D2

Opened by the GNofSR 20 September 1854.

Insch Station on 17 September 2015.

INVERAMSAY　　16 A2

Opened 5 September 1857 by the GNofSR and closed by BR 1 October 1951.
Line Operational – Demolished – No access. **NJ73681 25290**

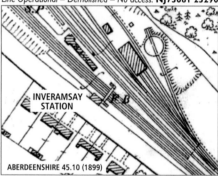

INVERBERVIE (See BERVIE)
INVERESK　　7 C1

Opened in September 1846 by the NBR as *Musselburgh*, renamed in 1847 as *Inveresk*, 1 October 1876 as *Inveresk Junction*, 12 June 1890 as *Inveresk* and closed by BR 4 May 1964.
Line Operational – Demolished – No access. **NT34984 71427**

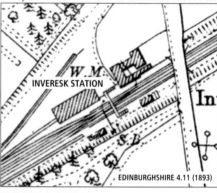

INVERGARRY　　14 A4

Opened 22 July 1903 by the Invergarry & Fort Augustus Railway, closed by the NBR 1 November 1911, reopened 1 August 1913 and closed by the L&NER 1 December 1933.
Line lifted - Station building in private use - Platform restored and remainder of station site occupied by a Forestry Commission car park - The Great Glen Way passes through the station site. **NN30426 98463**

INVERGLOY 13 D4

Opened in June 1904 by the Invergarry & Fort Augustus Railway, closed by the NBR 1 November 1911, reopened 1 August 1913 and closed by the L&NER 1 December 1933.
Line lifted – Demolished – Station site in the garden of an adjacent hotel "Invergloy Halt". **NN22942 88558**

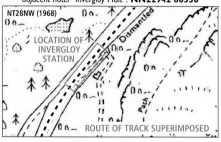

INVERGORDON 17 C4

Opened by the Inverness & Aberdeen Junction Railway 23 March 1863.

Looking north at Invergordon Station on 16 September 2015.

INVERGORDON SHORE BRANCH 17 C4

INVERGOWRIE 11 C2

Opened by the Dundee & Perth Railway 24 May 1847.

Invergowrie Station on 18 September 2015.

INVERKEILOR 12 A1

Opened 1 May 1883 by the NBR as *Inverkeillor*, renamed by the NBR in 1896 as *Inverkeilor* and closed by the L&NER 22 September 1930.
Line Operational - Station demolished – No access. **NO66722 49091**

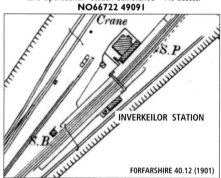

FORFARSHIRE 40.12 (1901)

INVERKEITHING 11 B4

Opened by the NBR 2 June 1890.

Inverkeithing Station on 18 September 2015.

INVERKEITHING HARBOUR BRANCH 11 B4

INVERKIP 6 A1

Opened by the Greenock & Wemyss Bay Railway 15 May 1865.

Inverkip Station on 17 March 2017.

INVERNESS 14 C1

Opened by the Inverness & Nairn Railway 7 November 1855.

Inverness Station on 15 September 2015.

INVERNESS CANAL BRANCH 14 C1

INVERSHIN 17 B3

Opened by the Sutherland Railway 13 April 1868

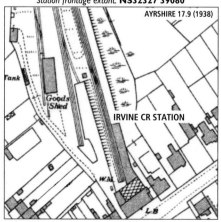

Looking north at Invershin Station on 16 September 2015.

INVERTIEL JUNCTION 11 B4
INVERUGIE 16 C1

Opened 3 July 1862 by the Formartine & Buchan Railway and closed by BR 3 May 1965.
Line lifted - Demolished - The Formartine and Buchan Way passes through the station site. **NK09814 47367**

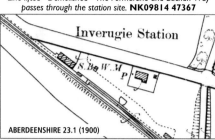

ABERDEENSHIRE 23.1 (1900)

INVERUGLAS* 10A A3

Opened 29 October 1945 by the L&NER for workers on the Loch Sloy HEP scheme and probably closed by BR c1949
Line Operational – Demolished. **NN31739 09255 (a)**

STIRLINGSHIRE 1SE (1896)

INVERURIE 16 A2

Opened by the GNofSR 8 February 1902.

Class 158 Unit No.158702 at Inverurie Station on 17 September 2015.

IRONGRAY 3 A1

Opened 1 March 1905 by the Cairn Valley Light Railway and closed by the LM&SR 3 May 1943.
Line lifted – Demolished – Station site unused – Station Masters House in private use. **NX91854 80397**

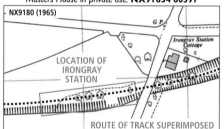

ROUTE OF TRACK SUPERIMPOSED

IRVINE (CR) 6 A2

Opened 2 June 1890 by the Lanarkshire & Ayrshire Railway as *Irvine*, closed by the CR 1 January 1917, reopened 1 February 1919, renamed by the LM&SR 2 June 1924 as *Irvine Bank Street* and closed 28 July 1930.
Line lifted – Demolished – Station site in commercial use – Station frontage extant. **NS32327 39080**

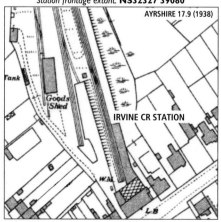

AYRSHIRE 17.9 (1938)

IRVINE (G&SWR) 6 A2

Opened by the Glasgow, Paisley, Kilmarnock & Ayr Railway 5 August 1839.

Looking north at Irvine Station on 16 March 2017.

IRVINE HARBOUR BRANCH 6 A3

JAMESTOWN 6 B1

Opened 26 May 1856 by the Forth & Clyde Junction Railway and closed by the L&NER 1 October 1934.
Line lifted – Demolished – Levenbank Road passes through the station site. **NS39777 81255**

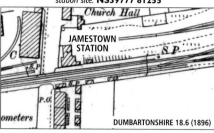

DUMBARTONSHIRE 18.6 (1896)

JEDBURGH 8 A3

Opened 18 July 1856 by the Jedburgh Railway and closed by BR 13 August 1948.
Line lifted - Demolished - Station site occupied by an Industrial Estate. **NT65653 21512**

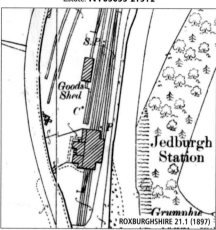

ROXBURGHSHIRE 21.1 (1897)

JEDFOOT 8 A3

Opened 18 July 1856 by the Jedburgh Railway as *Jedfoot Bridge*, renamed by the NBR in 1913 as *Jedfoot* and closed by BR 13 August 1948.
Line lifted – Demolished – St Cuthbert's Way and Borders Abbeys Way pass through the station site. **NT66125 24070**

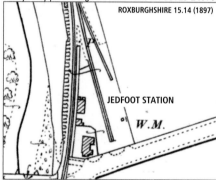

ROXBURGHSHIRE 15.14 (1897)

JOHNSHAVEN 12 A1

Opened 1 November 1865 by the Montrose & Bervie Railway and closed by BR 1 October 1951.
Line lifted – Demolished – Station site unused. **NO79419 67065**

KINCARDINESHIRE 28.13 (1901)

JOHNSTONE 6 B1

Opened by the Glasgow, Paisley, Kilmarnock & Ayr Railway 21 July 1840 as *Johnstone*, renamed by BR 18 June 1951 as *Johnstone High* and 10 September 1962 as *Johnstone*.

Johnstone Station on 17 March 2017.

JOINT PASS STATION (See ABERDEEN)

JOPPA
7 C1

Opened 16 May 1859 by the NBR and closed by BR 7 September 1964.

Line Operational – Station building extant – Platforms demolished. **NT31290 73212**

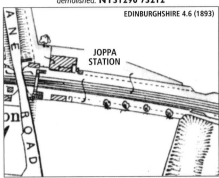

EDINBURGHSHIRE 4.6 (1893)

JORDANHILL
21A B2

Opened by the Glasgow City & District Railway 1 August 1847.

Jordanhill Station on 13 September 2015.

JORDANSTONE
11 B2

Opened in October 1861 by the Alyth Railway and closed by BR 2 July 1951.

Line lifted – Station building in private use – Platform extant. **NO27758 47756**

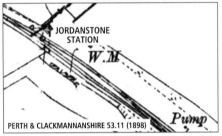

PERTH & CLACKMANNANSHIRE 53.11 (1898)

JUNCTION ROAD
22A C1

Opened 1 May 1869 by the Edinburgh, Leith & Newhaven Railway as *Junction Road*, closed by the NBR 1 January 1917, reopened 1 April 1919, renamed by the L&NER 1 July 1923 as *Junction Bridge* and closed 16 June 1947.

Line lifted – Demolished – The Water of Leith Walkway passes through the station site. **NT26507 76404**

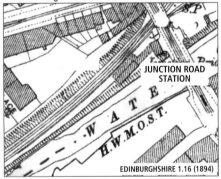

EDINBURGHSHIRE 1.16 (1894)

JUNIPER GREEN
7 B1/22A A3

Opened 1 August 1874 by the CR and closed by the LM&SR 1 November 1943.

Line lifted – Demolished - The Water of Leith Walkway passes through the station site. **NT19848 68522**

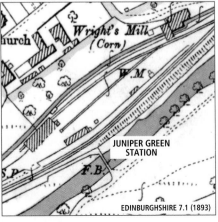

EDINBURGHSHIRE 7.1 (1893)

JUSTINHAUGH
11 C1

Opened 1 June 1895 by the CR and closed by BR 4 August 1952.

Line lifted – Demolished – Station site in commercial use. **NO46143 56800**

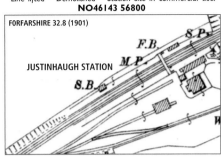

FORFARSHIRE 32.8 (1901)

KEITH
15 C1

Opened by the Inverness & Aberdeen Junction Railway 18 August 1858 as *Keith*, renamed by BR 1952 as *Keith Junction* and 12 May 1980 as *Keith*.

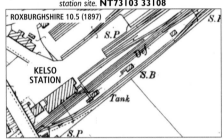

Looking east at **Keith Station** on 17 September 2015.

KEITH TOWN
15 C1/15A C1

Opened in April 1862 by the Keith & Dufftown Railway as *Earlsmill*, renamed by the GNofSR 1 May 1897 as *Keith Town*, closed by BR 6 May 1968 and reopened in 2000 by the **Keith & Dufftown Railway**.

KELSO
8 A3

Opened 27 January 1851 by the NBR and closed by BR 15 June 1964.

Line lifted – Demolished - Station site partially occupied by the "Station Yard Industrial Area" – The A698 passes through the station site. **NT73103 33108**

ROXBURGHSHIRE 10.5 (1897)

KELSO JUNCTION
7 D3

KELTY
11 B4

Opened 20 June 1860 by the Kinross-shire Railway and closed by the L&NER 22 September 1930.

Line lifted – Demolished - Station site part of "Lochore Meadows Country Park". **NT15272 94875**

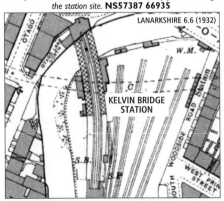

FIFESHIRE 34.3 (1894)

KELVIN BRIDGE
21A C2

Opened 10 August 1896 by the Glasgow Central Railway, closed by the CR 1 January 1917, reopened 2 June 1919 and closed by BR 4 August 1952.

Line lifted – Demolished – The Kelvin Walkway passes through the station site. **NS57387 66935**

LANARKSHIRE 6.6 (1932)

KELVINSIDE
21A B2

Opened 1 April 1897 by the Lanarkshire & Dumbarton Railway, closed by the CR 1 January 1917, reopened 2 June 1919 and closed by the LM&SR 1 July 1942.

Line lifted – Platforms demolished – Station House in use as the "1051 GWR Restaurant". **NS55634 68066**

NS5568 (1949)

KELVINDALE
21A C2

Opened 26 September 2005.

Kelvindale Station on 13 May 2017.

KEMNAY
16 A3

Opened 21 March 1859 by the Alford Valley Railway and closed by BR 2 January 1950.

Line lifted – Demolished – Station site redeveloped. **NJ73119 16088**

ABERDEENSHIRE 64.2 (1890)

KENNETHMONT
15 D2

Opened 20 September 1854 by the GNofSR and closed by BR 6 May 1968.

Line Operational - Station building in private use - Platform partially extant. **NJ55375 29345**

ABERDEENSHIRE 43.3 (1899)

KENNISHEAD
6 B2/21A B4

Opened by the Glasgow, Barrhead & Kilmarnock Joint Railway 27 September 1848 as *Crofthead*, renamed 1 August 1850 as *Kennishead (Thornliebank)*, 1 May 1852 as *Kennishead & Spierbridge* and 1 May 1859 as *Kennishead*.

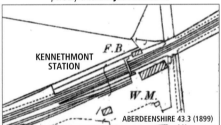

Kennishead Station on 18 March 2017.

KENNOWAY GOODS
11 C4

KENTALLEN
9 C1

Opened 24 August 1903 by the Callander & Oban Railway and closed by BR 28 March 1966.

Line lifted – Station building and platforms now part of "Holly Tree Hotel". **NN01325 58347**

NN05SW (1970)

LOCATION OF KENTALLEN STATION

ROUTE OF TRACK SUPERIMPOSED

KERSHOPE FOOT 3 D1

Opened 1 March 1862 by the Border Union Railway and closed by BR 6 January 1969.
Line lifted – Demolished - A track passes through the station site. **NY47525 82875**

ROXBURGHSHIRE 48.2 (1896)

KIELDER 8 A4

Opened 1 January 1862 by the Border Counties Railway as *Kielder*, renamed by BR 1 October 1948 as *Kielder Forest* and closed 15 October 1956.
Line lifted - Station building in private use - Platform demolished.
NY62628 93524

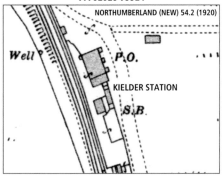

NORTHUMBERLAND (NEW) 54.2 (1920)

KILBAGIE 11 A4

Opened 17 September 1894 by the NBR and closed by the L&NER 7 July 1930.
Line Operational – Demolished – No access. **NS93088 89969**

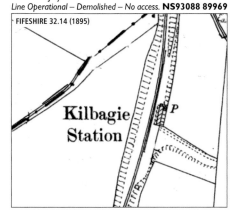

FIFESHIRE 32.14 (1895)

KILBARCHAN 6 B1

Opened 1 June 1905 by the G&SWR and closed by BR 27 June 1966.
Line lifted – Demolished – Platform extant – A cycle/walkway passes through the station site. **NS40786 62842**

NS4062 (1949)

KILBIRNIE (CR) 6 A2

Opened 2 December 1889 by the Lanarkshire & Ayrshire Railway as *Kilbirnie*, renamed by the LM&SR 2 June 1924 as *Kilbirnie South* and closed by the LM&SR 1 December 1930.
Line lifted – Demolished – Station site occupied by a Tesco store. **NS31776 54717**
SEE MAP IN NEXT COLUMN

KILBIRNIE (G&SWR) 6 A2

Opened 1 June 1905 by the G&SWR and closed by BR 27 June 1966.
Line lifted – Demolished – Platform extant - Station site unused – A cycle/walkway passes through the station site.
NS32020 54667

NS3254 (1965)

KILBOWIE 6 B1

Opened 1 October 1896 by the Lanarkshire & Dumbarton-shire Railway as *Kilbowie Road*, renamed by the CR 1 April 1908 as *Kilbowie* and closed by BR 5 October 1964.
Line lifted – Demolished – Station site in commercial use.
NS49652 70370

NS4970 (1948)

KILCONQUHAR 11 D4

Opened 11 August 1857 by the East of Fife Railway as *Kilconquhar & Elie*, renamed by the NBR in 1864 as *Kilconquhar* and closed by BR 6 September 1965.
Line lifted – Station building and platform in private use.
NO47888 01564

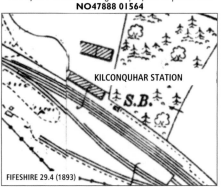

FIFESHIRE 29.4 (1893)

KILDARY 17 C4

Opened 1 June 1864 by the Inverness & Aberdeen Junction Railway as *Parkhill*, renamed by the HR in c1865 as *Kildary* and closed by BR 13 June 1960.
Line Operational – Demolished – No access. **NH76515 74612**

ROSS-SHIRE & CROMARTYSHIRE 54.8 (1904)

KILDONAN 17 D2

Opened by the Sutherland & Caithness Railway 28 July 1874.

Looking north at **Kildonan Station** on 16 September 2015.

KILKERRAN 6 A4

Opened 24 May 1860 by the Maybole & Girvan Railway and closed by BR 6 September 1965.
Line Operational - Station House extant - Platforms demolished.
NS29702 04352

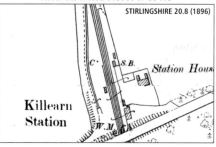

AYRSHIRE 50.4 (1894)

KILLEARN 10 B4

Opened 1 August 1882 by the Strathendrick & Aberfoyle Railway as *Killearn New*, renamed by the NBR 1 April 1896 as *Killearn* and closed by BR 1 October 1951.
Line lifted – Demolished – Station House in private use - Station site unused. **NS50947 85413**

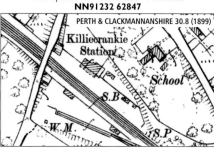

STIRLINGSHIRE 20.8 (1896)

KILLIECRANKIE 10 D1

Opened 1 July 1864 by the HR and closed by BR 3 May 1965
Line Operational – Demolished – No access.
NN91232 62847

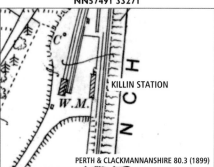

PERTH & CLACKMANNANSHIRE 30.8 (1899)

KILLIN 10 B2

Opened 1 April 1886 by the CR and closed by BR 28 September 1965.
Line lifted – Station site in use as a council depot and car park - The Rob Roy Way passes through the station site.
NN57491 33271

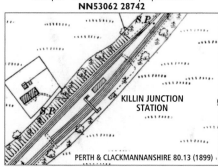

PERTH & CLACKMANNANSHIRE 80.3 (1899)

KILLIN JUNCTION 10 B2

Opened 1 April 1886 by the CR and closed by BR 28 September 1965.
Line lifted – Demolished – One platform extant.
NN53062 28742

PERTH & CLACKMANNANSHIRE 80.13 (1899)

KILLOCHAN 6 A4

Opened 24 May 1860 by the Maybole & Girvan Railway and closed by BR 1 January 1951.
Line Operational - Station building in private use – Platforms demolished. **NS22181 00610**

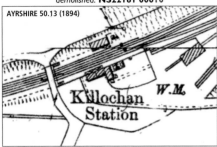

AYRSHIRE 50.13 (1894)

KILLYWHAN 3 A1

Opened 7 September 1859 by the Castle Douglas & Dumfries Railway and closed by BR 17 June 1963.
Line lifted – Station building and one platform in private use. **NX88863 69368**

KIRKCUDBRIGHTSHIRE 37.1 (1893)

KILMACOLM 6 A1

Opened 23 December 1869 by the Greenock & Ayrshire Railway as *Kilmalcolm*, renamed by the G&SWR 1 December 1904 as *Kilmacolm* and closed by BR 10 January 1983.
Line lifted – Station building in use as "The Pullman Diner" – The Paisley and Clyde Cycle Path passes through the station site. **NS35661 69789**

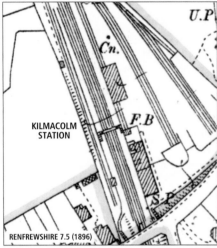

RENFREWSHIRE 7.5 (1896)

KILMANY 11 C3

Opened 25 January 1909 by the Newburgh & North Fife Railway and closed by BR 12 February 1951.
Line lifted – Demolished – Station site occupied by dwellings. **NO38397 21742**

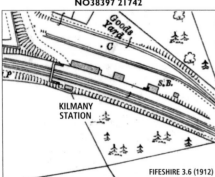

FIFESHIRE 3.6 (1912)

KILMARNOCK 6 B2

Opened by the Glasgow, Paisley, Kilmarnock & Ayr Railway 4 April 1843.

Kilmarnock Station on 19 March 2017.

KILMAURS 6 B2

Opened by the Glasgow, Barrhead and Kilmarnock Joint Railway 26 June 1873, closed by BR 7 November 1966 and reopened 12 May 1984.

Kilmaurs Station on 19 March 2017.

KILNKNOWE JUNCTION 7 D2
KILPATRICK 6 B1

Opened by the Glasgow, Dumbarton & Helensburgh Railway 31 May 1858.

Kilpatrick Station on 13 September 2015.

KILSYTH NEW 6 C1

Opened 2 July 1888 by the Kilsyth & Bonnybridge Joint Railway and closed by the L&NER 1 February 1935.
Line lifted – Demolished – Station site occupied by a garage [Miller Motors Ltd]. **NS71959 78092**

STIRLINGSHIRE 28.12 (1896)

KILSYTH OLD 6A C1

Opened 1 June 1878 by the Kelvin Valley Railway as *Kilsyth*, renamed by the NBR 2 July 1888 as *Kilsyth Old*, by the L&NER 1 January 1936 as *Kilsyth* and closed by BR 6 August 1951.
Line lifted – Demolished – Station site occupied by "Kilsyth Swimming Pool". **NS71490 78052**

STIRLINGSHIRE 28.12 (1896)

KILWINNING 6 A2

Opened by the Glasgow, Paisley, Kilmarnock & Ayr Railway 23 March 1840.

Kilwinning Station on 16 March 2017.

KILWINNING (CR) 6 A2

Opened 4 September 1888 by the Lanarkshire & Ayrshire Railway as *Kilwinning*, closed by the CR 1 January 1917, reopened 1 February 1919, renamed by the LM&SR 2 June 1924 as *Kilwinning East* and closed 4 July 1931.
Line lifted – Demolished – Station site landscaped. **NS29999 43399**

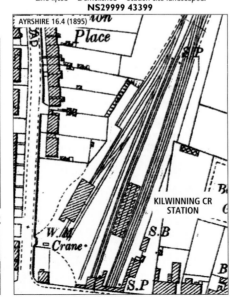

AYRSHIRE 16.4 (1895)

KILWINNING CR STATION

KINALDIE 16 A3

Opened 1 December 1854 by the GNofSR and closed by BR 7 December 1964.
Line Operational – Demolished – No access. **NJ83002 15312**

KINALDIE STATION

ABERDEENSHIRE 65.6 (1899)

KINBRACE 17 D2

Opened by the Sutherland & Caithness Railway 28 July 1874.

Class 158 Unit No.158705 at **Kinbrace** Station on 16 September 2015.

KINBUCK 10 D3

Opened 23 May 1848 by the Scottish Central Railway and closed by BR 11 June 1956.
Line Operational – Station building in private use – Platforms demolished – No access. **NN79342 04861**

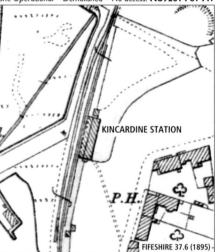

KINBUCK STATION

PERTH & CLACKMANNANSHIRE 125.8 (1899)

KINCARDINE 11 A4

Opened 18 December 1893 by the NBR and closed by the L&NER 7 July 1930.
Line Operational – Demolished – No access. **NS92814 87447**

KINCARDINE STATION

FIFESHIRE 37.6 (1895)

KINCRAIG 14 D3

Opened 9 September 1863 by the Inverness & Perth Junction Railway as *Boat of Insch*, renamed by the HR in 1871 as *Kincraig* and closed by BR 18 October 1965.
Line Operational – Station building in private use - Platforms demolished. **NH83218 05683**

INVERNESS-MAINLAND 88.1 (1899)

KINCRAIG STATION

KINFAUNS 11 B3

Opened 24 May 1847 by the Dundee & Perth Railway and closed by BR 2 January 1950.
Line Operational – Demolished – No access. **NO15756 21944**

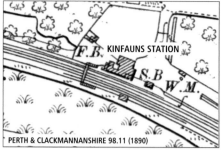

PERTH & CLACKMANNANSHIRE 98.11 (1890)

KING EDWARD 16 A1

Opened 4 June 1860 by the Banff, Macduff & Turriff Extension Railway and closed by BR 1 October 1951.
Line lifted – Demolished – Some buildings extant – Station site in commercial use. **NJ71676 57901**

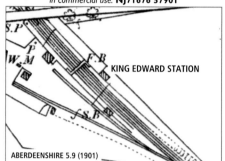

ABERDEENSHIRE 5.9 (1901)

KINGENNIE 11 D2

Opened 14 November 1870 by the CR and closed by BR 10 January 1955.
Line lifted – Station House in private use – Platforms demolished. **NO47533 34633**

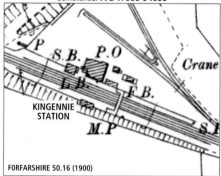

FORFARSHIRE 50.16 (1900)

KINGHORN 11 B4

Opened by the Edinburgh & Northern Railway 20 September 1847.

Looking north at **Kinghorn Station** on 18 September 2015.

KINGLASSIE COLLIERY BRANCH 11 B4

KINGSBARNS 11 D3

Opened 1 September 1883 by the Anstruther & St Andrews Railway and, although closed by the L&NER 22 September 1930, it saw further use during the Second World War for personnel working at RAF Kilduncan.
Line lifted – Demolished – Station site unused. **NO57977 11451**

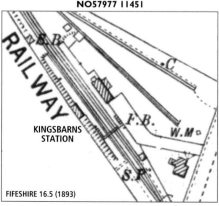

FIFESHIRE 16.5 (1893)

KINGSHOUSE 10 B3

Opened in June 1872 by the Callander & Oban Railway as *Kingshouse*, renamed by the CR in 1911 as *Kingshouse Platform*, renamed by BR 18 June 1962 as *Kingshouse* and closed by BR 28 September 1965.
Line lifted - Demolished – The Rob Roy Way passes through the station site. **NN56239 20287**

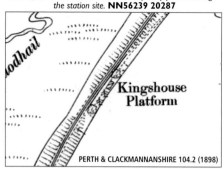

PERTH & CLACKMANNANSHIRE 104.2 (1898)

KING'S INCH 21A A2

Opened 1 June 1903 by the Glasgow & Renfrew District Railway as *Renfrew Central*, renamed by the end of 1903 as *Renfrew King's Inch*, closed by the LM&SR 5 June 1926, reopened 14 June 1926 and closed 19 July 1926.
Line lifted – Demolished – Station site occupied by housing in Anne Avenue. **NS50985 67739**

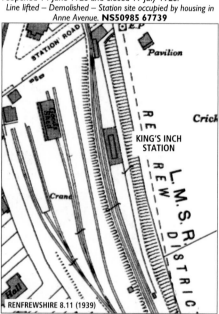

RENFREWSHIRE 8.11 (1939)

KINGSKETTLE 11 C3

Opened 20 September 1847 by the Edinburgh & Northern Railway, closed by the NBR 1 January 1917, reopened 1 February 1919 and closed by BR 4 September 1967.
Line Operational – Demolished – No access. **NO30750 08234**

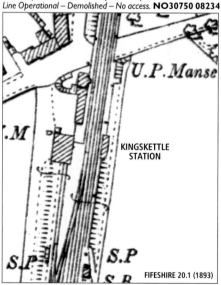

FIFESHIRE 20.1 (1893)

KINGSKNOWE 7 B1/22A A3

Opened by the CR 15 February 1848 as *Slateford*, renamed as *Kings Knowes* 1 January 1853, as *Kingsnowe* in same year, closed 1 January 1917, reopened 1 February 1919, closed by BR 6 July 1964 and reopened 1 February 1971.

Kingsnowe Station on 12 May 2017.

KINGSMUIR 11 D1

Opened 14 November 1870 by the CR and closed by BR 10 January 1955.
Line lifted – Demolished – Station site landscaped.
NO48602 48450

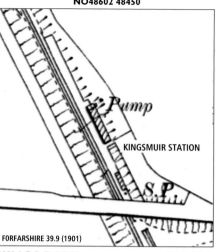

FORFARSHIRE 39.9 (1901)

KINGS PARK 21A D4

Opened by the LM&SR 6 October 1928

Kings Park Station on 18 March 2017.

KINGUSSIE 14 C3

Opened by the Inverness & Perth Junction Railway 9 September 1863.

Looking south at **Kingussie Station** on 15 September 2015.

KINLOSS 15 A1

Opened in 1904 by the HR, on the site of the original station which was opened 25 March 1858 by the Inverness & Aberdeen Junction Railway and closed by BR 3 May 1965.
Line Operational – Station building in private use.
NJ07066 61292

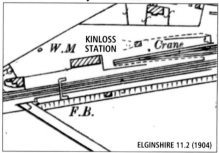

ELGINSHIRE 11.2 (1904)

KINNABER JUNCTION 12 A1

KINNEIL 7 A1

Opened 2 January 1899 by the NBR, closed 1 January 1917, reopened 1 September 1919 and closed by the L&NER 22 September 1930.
Line Operated by the Bo'ness & Kinneil Railway – Demolished – Station site unused. **NS98410 81086**

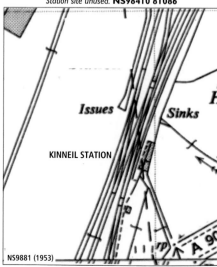

NS9881 (1953)

KINROSS 11 B4

Opened in 1890 by the NBR as *Kinross Junction* and closed by BR 5 January 1970.

Line lifted – Demolished – Station site unused.

NO11118 02752

KINTORE 16 A3

Opened 20 September 1854 by the GNofSR, closed by BR 7 December 1964 and re-opened on a new site. slightly to the north, on 15 October 2020.

Kintore Station in October 2020.

KIPPEN 10 C4

Opened 26 May 1856 by the Forth & Clyde Junction Railway and closed by the L&NER 1 October 1934.

Line lifted – Station buildings extant – Station site unused.

NS66474 95705

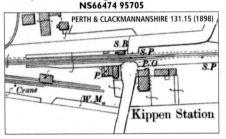

KIRKANDREWS 3 C2

Opened in August 1854 by the Port Carlisle Railway and closed by BR 7 September 1964.

Line lifted – Station building in private use – Platform demolished. **NY35217 58457**

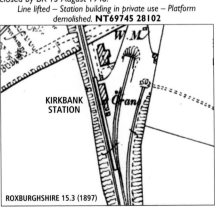

KIRKBANK 8 A3

Opened 18 July 1856 by the Jedburgh Railway as *Old Ormiston*, renamed by the NBR 20 May 1868 as *Kirkbank* and closed by BR 13 August 1948.

Line lifted – Station building in private use – Platform demolished. **NT69745 28102**

KIRKBRIDE 3 B2

Opened 4 September 1856 by the Carlisle & Silloth Bay Railway and closed by BR 7 September 1964.

Line lifted – Station building in private use – Platform demolished – Remainder of station site occupied by houses.

NY22925 56736

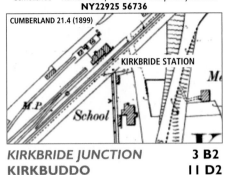

KIRKBRIDE JUNCTION 3 B2

KIRKBUDDO 11 D2

Opened 14 November 1870 by the CR and closed by BR 10 January 1955.

Line lifted – Station house and platform in private use.

NO49710 43679

KIRKCALDY HARBOUR BRANCH 11 C4

KIRKCALDY 11 B4

Opened by the Edinburgh & Northern Railway 20 September 1847.

Looking south at **Kirkcaldy Station** on 18 September 2015.

KIRKCONNEL 6 D4

Opened by the Glasgow, Paisley, Kilmarnock and Ayr Railway 28 October 1850.

Looking west at **Kirkconnel Station** on 20 March 2017.

KIRKCOWAN 2 A2

Opened 12 March 1861 by the Portpatrick Railway and closed by BR 14 June 1965.

Line lifted – Demolished – Station site partially occupied by a realigned B733, Station Road, and partially unused.

NX32262 60997

KIRKCUDBRIGHT 2 C2

Opened 7 March 1864 by the Kirkcudbright Railway and closed by BR 3 May 1965.

Lines lifted – Station house in use as a studio and art gallery, remainder of station site occupied by housing.

NX68572 51200

KIRKGUNZEON 2 D2

Opened 7 November 1859 by the Castle Douglas & Dumfries Railway and closed by BR 2 January 1950.

Line lifted – Station building in private use – Station site occupied by "Mossband Residential Park". **NX87201 66441**

KIRKHILL 6A C2

Opened by the Lanarkshire & Ayrshire Railway 1 August 1904.

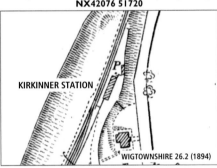

Kirkhill Station on 18 March 2017.

KIRKINNER 2 B2

Opened 2 August 1875 by the Portpatrick & Wigtownshire Joint Railway and closed by BR 25 September 1950.

Line lifted – Demolished – Station site occupied by housing.

NX42076 51720

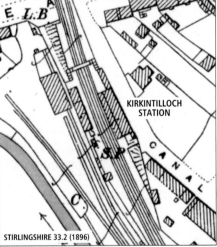

KIRKINTILLOCH 6 C1

Opened 5 July 1848 by the Edinburgh & Glasgow Railway and closed by BR 7 September 1964.

Line lifted – Demolished – Station site occupied by the "Campsie View Care Home". **NS65607 74122**

KIRKINTILLOCH BASIN BRANCH 6 C1

KIRKLAND 2 D1

Opened 1 March 1905 by the Cairn Valley Light Railway and closed by the LM&SR 3 May 1943.

Line lifted – Demolished – Station site unused.

NX81094 89701

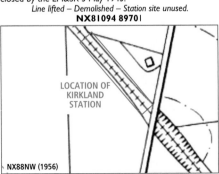

KIRKLEE FOR NORTH KELVINSIDE 21A C2

Opened 10 August 1896 by the Glasgow Central Railway as *Kirklee*, renamed by the CR in 1913 as *Kirklee for North Kelvinside*, closed 1 January 1917, reopened 2 June 1919 and closed by the LM&SR 1 May 1939.
Line lifted – Demolished – Platforms partially extant – Station site occupied by housing in Kirklee Place. **NS56697 67821**

KIRKLISTON 7 B1

Opened 1 March 1866 by the NBR and closed by the L&NER 22 September 1930.
Line lifted – Demolished – Auldgate passes through the station site. **NT12687 74392**

KIRKNEWTON 7 B1

Opened by the CR 15 February 1848 as *Kirknewton*, renamed in April 1848 as *Midcalder & Kirknewton*, 1849 as *Midcalder* and by BR 17 May 1982 as *Kirknewton*.

Kirknewton Station on 12 May 2017.

KIRKPATRICK 3 C1

Opened 10 September 1847 by the CR and closed by BR 13 June 1960.
Line Operational – Station building in private use – Platforms demolished. **NY27445 70429**

KIRKTON BRIDGE PLATFORM 19A B4

Opened in June 1904 by the GNofSR and closed by BR 3 May 1965.
Line lifted - Demolished – Station site partially absorbed into Fraserburgh Golf Club. **NK00411 65316**

KIRKWOOD 6A C1

Opened 4 October 1993.

Kirkwood Station on 12 May 2017

KIRRIEMUIR 11 C1

Opened in December 1854 by the Scottish North Eastern Railway and closed by BR 4 August 1952.
Line lifted – Demolished – Station site landscaped and occupied by housing in Marywell Gardens – Trackbed paved as a footpath and grassed platform survives. **NO38937 54001**

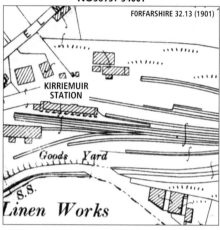

KIRRIEMUIR JUNCTION 11 C1
KIRTLEBRIDGE 3 B1

Opened in October 1869 by the CR and closed by BR 13 June 1960.
Line Operational – Demolished – No access. **NY23833 72726**

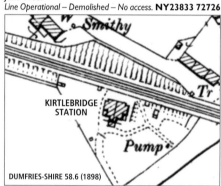

KITTYBREWSTER 16 B3

Opened 4 November 1867 by the GNofSR and closed by BR 6 May 1968.
Line Operational – Demolished – No access. **NJ93222 07760**

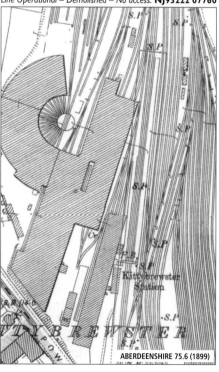

KNOCK 15 D1

Opened 30 July 1859 by the Banff, Portsoy & Strathisla Railway and closed by BR 6 May 1968.
Line lifted – Demolished – A track passes through the extant platforms – Station site owned by The Knockdhu Distillery. **NJ54640 52914**

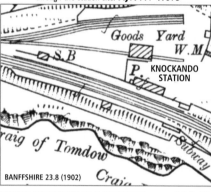

KNOCKANDO 15 B1

Opened 1 July 1899 by the GNofSR as *Dalbeallie*, renamed 1 May 1905 as *Knockando* and closed by BR 18 October 1965.
Line lifted - Station building and platforms preserved extant and owned by the Tandhu Distillery – The Speyside Way passes through the station site. **NJ19117 41675**

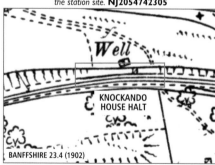

KNOCKANDO HOUSE HALT 15A B1

Opened 1 September 1869 by the GNofSR as *Knockando Halt*, a private station, renamed as *Knockando House Halt* after 1905 and closed by BR 18 October 1965.
Line lifted - Demolished – The Speyside Way passes through the station site. **NJ2054742305**

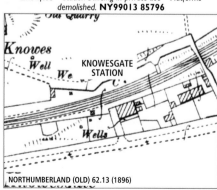

KNOWESGATE 4 C1

Opened 1 July 1864 by the NBR and closed by BR 15 September 1952.
Line lifted – Station building in private use – Platforms demolished. **NY99013 85796**

KNOWESIDE　6 A4
Opened 17 May 1906 by the Maidens & Dunure Light Railway and closed by the LM&SR 1 December 1930.
Line lifted – Demolished – Station site occupied by "Culzean Bay Holiday Park". **NS25373 12663**

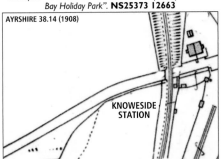

AYRSHIRE 38.14 (1908)

KNOWESIDE STATION

KYLE OF LOCHALSH　13 B2
Opened by the HR 2 November 1907.

Kyle of Lochalsh Station on 17 September 2015.

LADY HELEN COLLIERY　11 B4
LADYBANK　11 C3
Opened 20 September 1847 by the Edinburgh & Northern Railway.

Looking north at **Ladybank** Station on 18 September 2015.

LADYLANDS SIDING　10A C4
Opened 20 September 1861 by the Forth & Clyde Junction Railway as *Ladylands Siding*, renamed by the L&NER 11 July 1927 as *Ladylands Platform* and closed 1 October 1934.
Line lifted – Demolished – Station site in commercial use. **NS62945 95692**

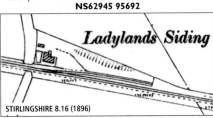

Ladylands Siding

STIRLINGSHIRE 8.16 (1896)

LADYSBRIDGE　18 D4
Opened 1 October 1859 by the Banff, Portsoy & Strathisla Railway and closed by BR 6 July 1964.
Line lifted – Demolished – A short access road passes through the station site. **NJ65089 63588**

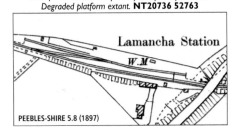

Ladysbridge Station

W.M

BANFFSHIRE 4.15 (1902)

LAIRG　17 B3
Opened by the Sutherland Railway 13 April 1868.

Looking south at **Lairg** Station on 16 September 2015.

LAMANCHA　7 B2
Opened in August 1864 by the Leadburn, Linton & Dolphinton Railway and closed by the L&NER 1 April 1933.
Line lifted – Station site partially occupied by a house - Degraded platform extant. **NT20736 52763**

Lamancha Station

W.M

PEEBLES-SHIRE 5.8 (1897)

LAMINGTON　7 A3
Opened in April 1848 by the CR and closed by BR 4 January 1965.
Line Operational – Demolished – No access. **NS97100 30770**

Cattle Pen

W.M.

F.B

LAMINGTON STATION

LANARKSHIRE 39.15 (1896)

LANARK　6 D2
Opened by the Lanark Railway 5 June 1855.

Looking west at **Lanark** Station on 19 March 2017.

LANARK RACECOURSE*　6A D2
Opened 9 August 1910 by the CR and although closed by BR 27 September 1964 it may have been retained for military use until 1968.
Line lifted – Demolished – Degraded platform partially extant – Station site unused. **NS89777 42700**

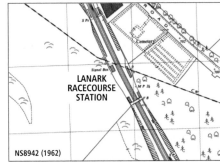

LANARK RACECOURSE STATION

NS8942 (1962)

LANGBANK　6 B1
Opened by the Glasgow, Paisley & Greenock Railway March 1841 as *Lang Bank* and renamed 1 May 1853 as *Langbank*.

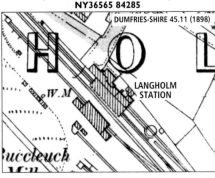

Langbank Station on 17 March 2017.

LANGHOLM　3 C1
Opened 11 April 1864 by the Border Counties Railway but closed almost immediately upon the collapse of the Byreburn Viaduct. Reopened 2 November 1864 and closed by BR 15 June 1964.
Line lifted - Demolished – Station site occupied by the "Townsfoot Residential and Industrial Development". **NY36565 84285**

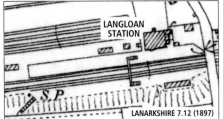

DUMFRIES-SHIRE 45.11 (1898)

H O L

W.M

LANGHOLM STATION

Buccleuch

LANGLOAN　6 C1
Opened 8 January 1866 by the CR and closed by BR 5 October 1964.
Line Operational – Demolished – No access. **NS72219 64228**

LANGLOAN STATION

S.P.

LANARKSHIRE 7.12 (1897)

LANGSIDE　21A C4
Opened by the Cathcart District Railway 2 April 1894 as *Langside & Newlands* and renamed by BR c1961 as *Langside*.

Langside Station on 18 March 2017.

LARBERT　10 D4
Opened by the Scottish Central Railway 1 March 1848.

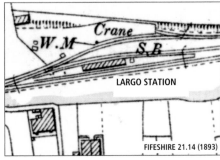

Larbert Station on 13 May 2017.

LARGO　11 C3
Opened 11 August 1857 by the East of Fife Railway and closed by BR 6 September 1965.
Line lifted – Demolished – Station site part of Station Park. **NO41815 02650**

Crane

W.M

S.B

LARGO STATION

FIFESHIRE 21.14 (1893)

LARGOWARD GOODS　11 C3
LARGS　6 A2
Opened by the G&SWR 1 June 1885.

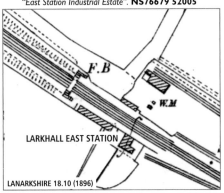

Largs Station on 17 March 2017.

LARKHALL CENTRAL　6 D2
Opened by the CR 1 July 1905 as *Larkhall Central*, renamed as *Larkhall* by BR 14 June 1965, closed 4 October 1965 and reopened 12 December 2005 as a terminus.

Larkhall Station on 19 March 2017.

LARKHALL EAST　6 D2
Opened 1 December 1866 by the Linlithgow Railway as *Larkhall*, renamed by the CR 1 June 1905 as *Larkhall East* and closed by BR 10 September 1951.
Line lifted – Demolished – Station site partially occupied by "East Station Industrial Estate". **NS76679 52005**

F.B

W.M

LARKHALL EAST STATION

LANARKSHIRE 18.10 (1896)

LASSWADE　7 C1/22A D4
Opened 12 October 1868 by the Esk Valley Railway and closed by BR 10 September 1951.
Line lifted – Demolished – Station site unused. **NT30262 65748**

Gas Works

W.M

LASSWADE STATION

S.P

EDINBURGHSHIRE 8.9 (1892)

LAUDER 7 D2
Opened 2 July 1901 by the Lauder Light Railway and closed by the L&NER 12 September 1932.
Line lifted – Demolished – Station site occupied by Whitlaw Road and Industrial Units. **NT52399 48095**

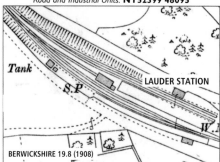

BERWICKSHIRE 19.8 (1908)

LAURENCEKIRK 16 A4
Opened by the Aberdeen Railway 1 November 1849, closed by BR 4 September 1967 and reopened 17 May 2009.

Looking north at **Laurencekirk Station** on 18 September 2015.

LAURISTON 12 A1
Opened 1 November 1865 by the Montrose & Bervie Railway and closed by BR 1 October 1951.
Line lifted – Demolished – Station site part of a caravan park. **NO76018 65716**

KINCARDINESHIRE 27.16 (1901)

LAW JUNCTION 6 D2
Opened in December 1879 by the CR and closed by BR 4 January 1965.
Line Operational – Demolished – No access. **NS82331 53015**

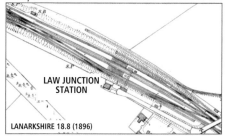
LANARKSHIRE 18.8 (1896)

LAWHEAD SIDINGS 7 A2
LEADBURN 7 B2
Opened 4 July 1855 by the Peebles Railway and closed by BR 7 March 1955.
Line lifted – Demolished - Platforms partially extant - Station site occupied by car park and picnic area. **NT23574 55499**

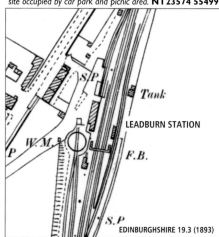
EDINBURGHSHIRE 19.3 (1893)

LEADHILLS 6 D3/6A D3
Opened 1 October 1901 by the Leadhills & Wanlockhead Light Railway and closed by the LM&SR 2 January 1939. It was reopened in 1986 by the **Leadhills & Wanlockhead Railway**, a heritage 2ft gauge system.

LEA END JUNCTION 6 D1
LECH-A-VUIE PLATFORM*13A B4
Opened 1 April 1901 by the NBR "for the purpose of enabling sporting parties visiting Mrs Head of Kinlochailort to leave or join the trains"[1]. It was used by the military during the Second World War and sporting activities continued until closed by BR during the late 1970s.
Line Operational - No access – Platform partially extant.
NM86160 81359

INVERNESS-MAINLAND 137 (1899)

LEITH CENTRAL 22A C1
Opened 1 July 1903 by the NBR, closed by BR 7 April 1952 and adapted as a DMU depot, in which form it lasted until 1972.
Line lifted – Partially demolished – Part of building survives, remainder of station site occupied by a Tesco supermarket.
NT27029 75824

NT2775 (1944)

LEITH NORTH 7 B1/22A C1
Opened 1 August 1879 by the CR as *Leith*, renamed 1 August 1903 as *Leith North*, by BR 7 April 1952 as *North Leith* and closed 30 April 1962.
Line lifted – Demolished – Station site occupied by flats.
NT26362 76818

EDINBURGHSHIRE 1.16 (1894)

LEITH WALK 22A C1
Opened 22 May 1868 by the NBR, closed 1 January 1917, reopened 1 February 1919 and closed by the L&NER 31 March 1930.
Line Out of Use – Demolished – Platforms extant – Station site unused. **NT26389 74954**

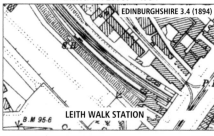
EDINBURGHSHIRE 3.4 (1894)

LENNOXTOWN 6 C1
Opened 1 July 1867 by the Blane Valley Railway as *Lennox-town Blane Valley*, renamed by the NBR 1 October 1881 as *Lennoxtown* and closed by BR 1 October 1951.
Line lifted – Demolished – The Paisley and Clyde Cyclepath passes through the station site. **NS62584 77674**

STIRLINGSHIRE 27.12 (1896)

[1] Dr John McGregor. *NBRSG Journal No.128*

LENTRAN 14 B1
Opened 11 June 1860 by the Inverness & Ross-shire Railway and although closed by BR 13 June 1960 it reopened as a temporary terminus 27 to 29 March 1982 whilst repairs were effected on the Clachnaharry swing bridge.
Line Operational – Demolished – No access. **NH58461 45812**

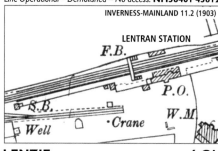
INVERNESS-MAINLAND 11.2 (1903)

LENZIE 6 C1
Opened by the Edinburgh & Glasgow Railway 5 July 1848 as *Kirkintil-loch Junction*, renamed in 1849 as *Campsie Junction*, as *Lenzie Junction* by the NBR in November 1867 and as *Lenzie* in 1890.

Lenzie Station on 13 May 2017.

LESLIE 11 B4
Opened 1 February 1861 by the NBR and closed by the L&NER 4 January 1932.
Line lifted – Demolished – Station site occupied by housing in Valley Gardens. **NO24511 01253**

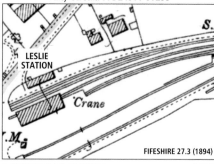
FIFESHIRE 27.3 (1894)

LESMAHAGOW 6 D2
Opened 1 July 1905 by the CR and closed by BR 4 October 1965.
Line lifted – Demolished – Station site occupied by Lesmahagow Fire Station and housing in Station Road.
NS81327 40580

LANARKSHIRE 31.8 (1941)

LETHAM GRANGE 11 D2
Opened 1 May 1883 by the NBR and closed by the L&NER 22 September 1930.
Line Operational – Demolished – Part of station site in commercial use. **NO63455 45383**

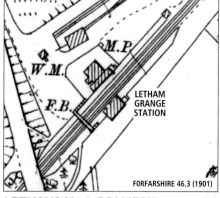
FORFARSHIRE 46.3 (1901)

LETHANS No.1 COLLIERY 11 A4
LETHANS No.2 COLLIERY 11 A4

LETHENTY
16 A2

Opened 1 October 1856 by the Inverness & Oldmeldrum Railway and closed by the L&NER 2 November 1931.
Line lifted – Platform extant – Station site unused.
NJ76955 24627

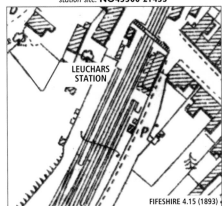

ABERDEENSHIRE 45.16 (1899)

LEUCHARS
11 C3

Opened 18 May 1848 by the Edinburgh, Perth & Dundee Railway as *Leuchers*, renamed 1 July 1852 as *Leuchers Junction* closed by the NBR 1 June 1878, reopened 1 December 1878 as *Leuchars Old* and closed 3 October 1921.
Line lifted – Demolished – Station Road passes through the station site. **NO45300 21433**

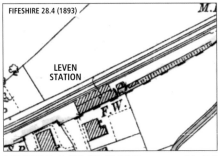

FIFESHIRE 4.15 (1893)

LEUCHARS JUNCTION
11 C3

Opened by the NBR 1 June 1878 as *Leuchars Junction* and renamed by BR c1970 as *Leuchars (for St Andrews)*.

Looking west at Leuchars Station on 18 September 2015.

LEVEN
11 C4

Opened 11 August 1857 by the Edinburgh, Perth & Dundee Railway and closed by BR 6 October 1969.
Line lifted – Demolished – Station site occupied by housing in Station Court. **NO37888 01047**

FIFESHIRE 28.4 (1893)

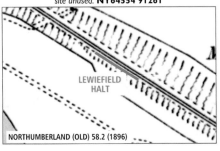

LEVEN DOCK BRANCH
11 C4

LEWIEFIELD HALT
8A A4

Opened 3 July 1933 by the L&NER and closed by BR 15 October 1956.
Line lifted – Demolished - Platform partially extant – Station site unused. **NY64554 91261**

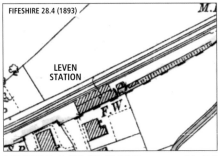

NORTHUMBERLAND (OLD) 58.2 (1896)

LEYSMILL
11 D1

Opened 24 November 1838 by the Arbroath & Forfar Railway and closed by BR 5 December 1955.
Line lifted – Station building in private use – Platform demolished. **NO60644 47690**

FORFARSHIRE 40.10 (1901)

LHANBRYDE
15 B1

Opened 18 August 1858 by the Inverness & Aberdeen Junction Railway and closed by BR 7 December 1964.
Line Operational – Demolished - Station House in private use.
NJ27075 61028

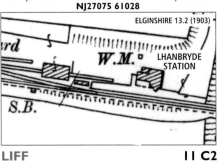

ELGINSHIRE 13.2 (1903)

LIFF
11 C2

Opened 10 June 1861 by the CR and closed by BR 10 January 1955.
Line lifted – Demolished - Station site in use as a pathway and car park for "Lynch Sports Centre". **NO35456 31519**

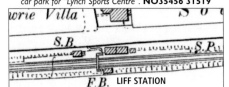

PERTH & CLACKMANNANSHIRE 88.3 (1898)

LILLIEHILL JUNCTION
11 B4

LINDEAN
7 D3

Opened 5 April 1856 by the Selkirk & Galashiels Railway and closed by BR 10 September 1951.
Line lifted - Station House in private use - The re-aligned A7 passes through the station site. **NT48539 31374**

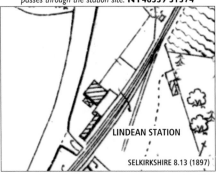

SELKIRKSHIRE 8.13 (1897)

LINDORES
11 B3

Opened 25 January 1909 by the Newburgh & North Fife Railway and closed by BR 12 February 1951.
Line lifted – Station building in private use – Platform demolished. **NO27071 17100**

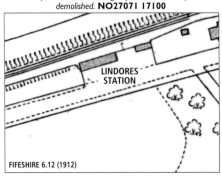

FIFESHIRE 6.12 (1912)

LINLITHGOW
7 A1

Opened by the Edinburgh & Glasgow Railway 21 February 1842.

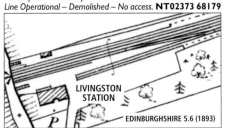

Looking west at Linlithgow Station on 13 May 2017.

LINTMILL
5 B3

Opened 18 August 1906 by the Campbeltown and Machrihanish Light Railway and closed by May 1932.

LINWOOD GOODS
6 B1

LISSENS GOODS
6 A2

LITTLEGILL COLLIERY BRANCH
6 D2

LIVINGSTON
7 A1

Opened 12 November 1849 by the Edinburgh & Bathgate Railway and closed by BR 1 November 1948.
Line Operational – Demolished – No access. **NT02373 68179**

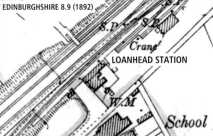

EDINBURGHSHIRE 5.6 (1893)

LIVINGSTON NORTH
7A A1

Opened 24 March 1986.

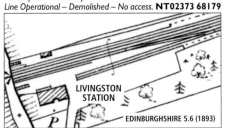

Livingston North Station on 12 May 2017.

LIVINGSTON SOUTH
7A A1

Opened 6 October 1984.

Livingston South Station on 12 May 2017.

LOANHEAD
7 C1/22A D3

Opened 23 July 1874 by the Edinburgh, Loanhead & Roslin Railway and closed by the L&NER 1 May 1933.
Line lifted - Station buildings partially extant in private use – A cycle/walkway passes through the station site.
NT28350 65664

EDINBURGHSHIRE 8.9 (1892)

LOCHAILORT
13 B4

Opened by the NBR 1 April 1901.

Lochailort Station on 14 September 2015.

LOCHANHEAD
3 A1

Opened 7 November 1859 by the Castle Douglas & Dumfries Railway and closed by the LM&SR 25 September 1939.
Line lifted – Station building in private use – Station site unused. **NX91561 71651**

KIRKCUDBRIGHTSHIRE 29.14 (1893)

LOCHARBRIGGS 3 A1

Opened 1 September 1863 by the Dumfries, Lochmaben & Lockerbie Junction Railway and closed by BR 19 May 1952.
Line lifted – Demolished – Station site occupied by housing in Station Road. **NX99256 80394**

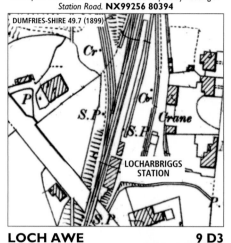

DUMFRIES-SHIRE 49.7 (1899)

LOCH AWE 9 D3

Opened 1 July 1880 by the Callander and Oban Railway, closed by BR 1 November 1965 and reopened 1 May 1985.

Looking west at **Loch Awe Station** on 14 September 2015.

LOCHEARNHEAD 10 C3

Opened 1 July 1904 by the Callander & Oban Railway, closed by the CR 1 January 1917, reopened 6 January 1919 and closed by BR 1 October 1951.
Line lifted – Station building and platforms in private use as the "Lochearnhead Scout Station". **NN58764 23837**

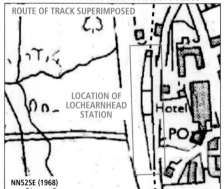

ROUTE OF TRACK SUPERIMPOSED

LOCATION OF LOCHEARNHEAD STATION

NN52SE (1968)

LOCHEE 11 C2

Opened 10 June 1861 by the CR and closed by BR 10 January 1955.
Line lifted – Category B listed station building in use as "Lochee Burns Club"- Platforms demolished. **NO38110 31309**

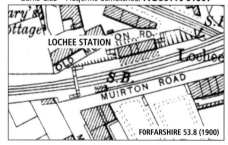

FORFARSHIRE 53.8 (1900)

LOCHEE WEST 11 C2

Opened 10 June 1861 by the CR as *Victoria*, renamed 1 May 1862 as *Camperdown*, 1 February 1896 as *Lochee West*, closed to passengers 1 January 1917 and to goods by BR 24 February 1964.
Line lifted – Demolished – Station site occupied by housing in Elmwood Road and Overton Gardens. **NO37015 31500**

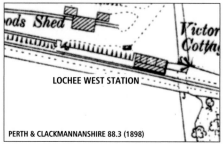

PERTH & CLACKMANNANSHIRE 88.3 (1898)

LOCH EIL OUTWARD BOUND 13A C4

Opened 6 May 1985.

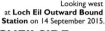

Looking west at **Loch Eil Outward Bound Station** on 14 September 2015.

LOCHEILSIDE 13 C4

Opened by the NBR 1 April 1901.

Looking west at **Locheilside Station** on 14 September 2015.

LOCHGELLY 11 B4

Opened by the NBR 4 September 1848.

Lochgelly Station on 18 September 2015.

LOCH LEVEN 11 B4

Opened shortly after 20 September 1860 by the Fife & Kinross Railway as *Kinross*, renamed by the NBR 16 October 1871 as *Loch Leven* and closed 1 September 1921.
Line lifted – Demolished – Station site partially unused and partially occupied by housing in Queich Place. **NO11746 01495**

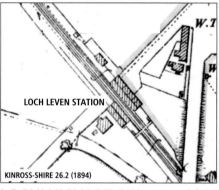

LOCH LEVEN STATION

KINROSS-SHIRE 26.2 (1894)

LOCHLUICHART (HR) 14 A1

Opened on 1 July 1871 by the Dingwall and Skye Railway as *Lochluichart High* and closed by BR 3 May 1954.
Line lifted – Demolished – Station site unused. **NH32335 62529**

PERTH & CLACKMANNANSHIRE 74 (1902)

LOCHLUICHART (BR) 14A A1

Opened 3 May 1954 as the result of a hydroelectric scheme raising the level of Loch Luichart and necessitating realignment of the line and closure of the original station *(qv)*.

Lochluichart Station on 17 September 2015

LOCHMABEN 3 B1

Opened 1 September 1863 by the Dumfries, Lochmaben & Lockerbie Junction Railway and closed by BR 19 May 1952.
Line lifted – Demolished – Station site occupied by Station Court and housing. **NY08181 83164**

DUMFRIES-SHIRE 42.15 (1898)

LOCHMABEN STATION

LOCHMILL GOODS 7 A1

LOCHSIDE (See LOCHWINNOCH)

LOCH SKERROW 2A C2

Opened prior to 1871 by the Portpatrick Railway, initially for private and railway staff use, and closed by BR in 1964/5.
Line lifted – Demolished – Degraded platforms extant – A pathway passes through the station site. **NX60956 68274**

KIRKCUDBRIGHTSHIRE 34SW (1894)

LOCH TAY 10 C2

Opened 1 April 1886 by the Killin Railway as *Loch Tay Killin Pier*, renamed by the CR 1 October 1895 as *Loch Tay*, closed in June 1921, reopened in March 1922 and closed by the LM&SR 9 September 1931.
Line lifted – Station building in private use - The Rob Roy Way passes through the station site. **NN58348 34417**

PERTH & CLACKMANNANSHIRE 68.15 (1899)

LOCHTY GOODS 11 D3

LOCHWINNOCH 6 A2

Opened 12 August 1840 by the Glasgow, Paisley, Kilmarnock and Ayr Railway as *Lochwinnoch*, renamed 1 June 1905 as *Lochside*, closed by BR 4 July 1955, reopened 27 June 1966 and renamed *Lochwinnoch* 13 May 1985.

Lochwinnoch Station on 17 March 2017.

LOCHWINNOCH 6 A2

Opened 1 June 1905 by the G&SWR and closed by BR 27 June 1966.
Line lifted – Demolished – Station site occupied by housing in Station Rise - A cycle/walkway passes through the station site. **NS35494 58852**

LOCHWINNOCH STATION

NS3558 (1965)

LOCKERBIE 3 B1

Opened by the CR 10 September 1847.

Looking north at **Lockerbie Station** on 13 September 2015.

LOGIERIEVE 16 B2

Opened 18 July 1861 by the Formartine & Buchan Railway as *Newburgh Road*, renamed in 1862 as *Logierieve* and closed by BR 4 October 1965.
Line lifted - Station house and platform in private use - The Formartine and Buchan Way passes through the station site. **NJ92146 26933**

LOGIERIEVE STATION

ABERDEENSHIRE 47.6 (1899)

LONGFORGAN 11 C2

Opened in May 1848 by the Dundee & Perth Railway and closed by BR 11 June 1956.

Line Operational – Grade II listed station building extant - Platforms demolished. **NO31978 28601**

PERTH & CLACKMANNANSHIRE 88.5 (1898)

LONGHAVEN 16 C1

Opened 2 August 1897 by the GNofSR and closed by the L&NER 31 October 1932.

Line lifted - Demolished - Station site unused.

NK11488 40065

ABERDEENSHIRE 32.6 (1899)

LONGMORN 15 B1

Opened 1 March 1862 by the Morayshire Railway and closed by BR 6 May 1968.

Line lifted – Station building and one platform extant in private use. **NJ23491 58470**

ELGINSHIRE 12.8 (1904)

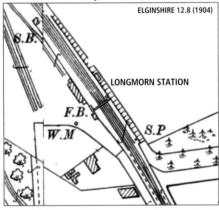

LONGNIDDRY 7 C1

Opened 22 June 1846 by the NBR as *Longniddry Junction* and renamed as *Longniddry* in 1890.

Longniddry Station on 19 September 2015.

LONGRIGGEND 6 D1

Opened in November 1862 by the Slamannan Railway and closed by the L&NER 1 May 1930.

Line lifted – Demolished – Station site partially occupied by a dwelling – A rough track passes through the station site. **NS82030 70086**

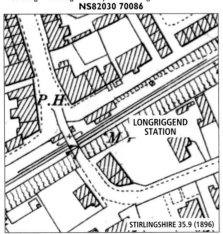

STIRLINGSHIRE 35.9 (1896)

LONGSIDE 16 B1

Opened 3 July 1862 by the Formartine & Buchan Railway and closed by BR 3 May 1965.

Line lifted - Demolished - Platforms extant - The Formartine and Buchan Way passes through the station site. **NK03930 47938**

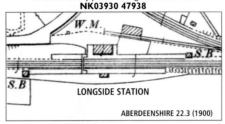

ABERDEENSHIRE 22.3 (1900)

LONGTOWN 3 C1

Opened 29 October 1861 by the Border Union Railway and closed by BR 6 January 1969.

Line lifted – Demolished – Station site occupied by commercial premises. **NY37629 68995**

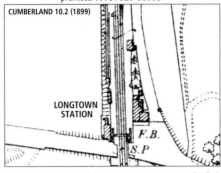

CUMBERLAND 10.2 (1899)

LONGWITTON 8 C4

Opened 1 November 1870 by the NBR as *Rothley*, initially as a private station for the Trevelyan Estate, renamed April 1875 as *Longwitton* and closed by BR 15 September 1952.

Line lifted – Demolished - Platform partially extant – Station site unused. **NZ04499 90762**

NORTHUMBERLAND (OLD) 62.3 (1896)

LONMAY 16 B1

Opened 24 August 1865 by the Formartine & Buchan Railway and closed by BR 4 October 1965.

Line lifted - Demolished - Platforms extant - The Formartine and Buchan Way passes through the station site. **NK01393 58729**

ABERDEENSHIRE 8.6 (1901)

LOSSIEMOUTH 18 B4

Opened 10 August 1852 by the Morayshire Railway and closed by BR 6 April 1964.

Line lifted – Platform partially extant – Station site occupied by a car park, small park and playground. **NJ23841 70858**

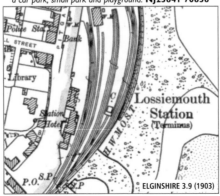

ELGINSHIRE 3.9 (1903)

LOTH 17 D3

Opened 1 November 1870 by the Duke of Sutherland's Railway and closed by BR 13 June 1960.

Line Operational – Station building in private use – Platforms partially extant. **NC95746 10084**

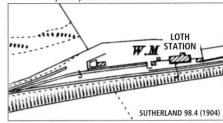

SUTHERLAND 98.4 (1904)

LOUDOUNHILL 6 C2

Opened 1 May 1905 by the G&SWR, closed 1 July 1909, reopened 1 November 1909, closed 1 January 1917, reopened 4 December 1922 and closed by the LM&SR 11 September 1939.

Line lifted – Demolished – Station site in agricultural use. **NS60268 37191**

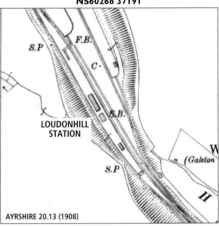

AYRSHIRE 20.13 (1908)

LUFFNESS HALT* 11A D4

Opened 1 September 1903 by the NBR and closed by the L&NER 1 June 1931.

Line lifted – Demolished – Station site absorbed into Luffness Links. **NT48372 81475**

HADDINGTONSHIRE 5.1 (1906)

LUGAR 6 C3

Opened in January 1860 by the Glasgow, Paisley, Kilmarnock and Ayr Railway and closed by BR 3 July 1950.

Line lifted – Demolished – Station site unused. **NS58999 22247**

AYRSHIRE 35.4 (1895)

LUGTON (G&SWR) 6 B1

Opened 27 March 1871 by the Glasgow, Barrhead & Kilmarnock Joint Railway and closed by BR 7 November 1966.

Line Operational – Demolished – No access. **NS41455 52938**

NS4152 (1966)

LUGTON HIGH (CR)   6 B1

Opened 1 May 1903 by the Lanarkshire & Ayrshire Railway as *Lugton*, closed by the CR 1 January 1917, reopened 1 February 1919, renamed by the LM&SR 2 June 1924 as *Lugton High* and closed 4 July 1932.
Line lifted – Demolished – Station site in commercial use.
NS41507 52722

NS4152 (1966)

LUIB   10 B3

Opened 1 August 1873 by the Callander & Oban Railway and closed by BR 28 September 1964.
Line lifted – Demolished – Platforms partially extant – Station site now part of the "Glen Dochart Caravan Park".
NN47864 27970

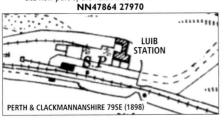

PERTH & CLACKMANNANSHIRE 79SE (1898)

LUIB HOUSES*   13A D1

Opened (or possibly reopened) 3 December 1951 by BR for use by railwaymen's wives and closed c1972.
Line Operational – Demolished – No access.
NH13245 54716 (a)

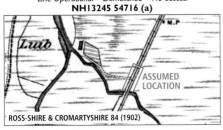

ROSS-SHIRE & CROMARTYSHIRE 84 (1902)

LUMPHANAN   15 D3

Opened 2 December 1859 by the Deeside Extension Railway and closed by BR 28 February 1966.
Line lifted – Demolished – Station site occupied by housing in Station Square and Macbeth Place. **NJ58495 04316**

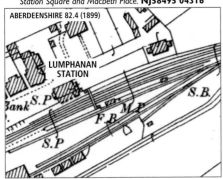

ABERDEENSHIRE 82.4 (1899)

LUNAN BAY   12 A1

Opened 1 May 1883 by the NBR and closed by the L&NER 22 September 1930.
Line Operational - Demolished – No access. **NO69050 52326**

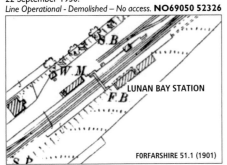

FORFARSHIRE 51.1 (1901)

LUNCARTY   11 A2

Opened 2 August 1848 by the Scottish Midland Junction Railway and closed by BR 18 June 1951.
Line Operational – Demolished – No access. **NO09387 29444**

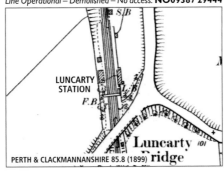

PERTH & CLACKMANNANSHIRE 85.8 (1899)

LUNDIN LINKS   11 C4

Opened 11 August 1857 by the East of Fife Railway and closed by BR 6 September 1965.
Line lifted – Demolished – Station site in use as part of Lundin Golf Club golf course. **NO40451 02432**

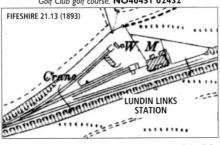

FIFESHIRE 21.13 (1893)

LUTHRIE   11 C3

Opened 25 January 1909 by the Newburgh & North Fife Railway and closed by BR 12 February 1951.
Line lifted – Demolished – Station site occupied by housing.
NO33436 18625

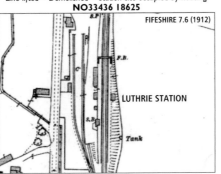

FIFESHIRE 7.6 (1912)

LYBSTER   18 B1

Opened 1 July 1903 by the Wick & Lybster Light Railway and closed by the LM&SR 3 April 1944.
Line lifted – Station building in use as the clubhouse for the "Lybster Golf Club" – Remainder of station site landscaped.
ND24830 35806

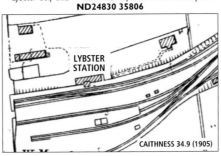

CAITHNESS 34.9 (1905)

LYNE   7 B2

Opened 1 February 1864 by the Symington, Biggar & Broughton Railway and closed by BR 5 June 1950.
Line lifted – Station building and platform in private use.
NT20885 39972

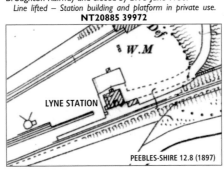

PEEBLES-SHIRE 12.8 (1897)

LYNEDOCH GREENOCK   6 A1

Opened 23 December 1869 by the Greenock & Ayrshire Railway as *Lynedoch*, renamed by the G&SWR in 1898 as *Lynedoch Greenock* and closed by BR 2 February 1959.
Line lifted – Demolished – Station site unused.
NS28034 75496

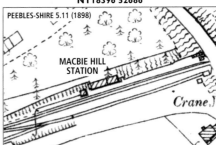

RENFREWSHIRE 2.6 (1896)

LYNESIDE   3 C2

Opened 29 October 1861 by the Leadburn, Linton & Dolphinton Railway as *West Linton*, renamed by the NBR 10 June 1870 as *Lineside*, in 1871 as *Lyneside* and closed by the L&NER 1 November 1929.
Line lifted - Station building and platform in private use.
NY38759 64402

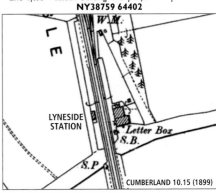

CUMBERLAND 10.15 (1899)

MACBIE HILL   7 B2

Opened 4 July 1864 by the Leadburn, Linton & Dolphinton Railway as *Coalyburn*, renamed by the NBR 25 May 1874 as *Macbie Hill* and closed by the L&NER 1 April 1933.
Line lifted – Demolished – Station site unused.
NT18396 52686

PEEBLES-SHIRE 5.11 (1898)

MACBIE HILL STATION

Crane.

MACDUFF   19 A4

Opened 1 July 1872 by the Banff, Macduff & Turriff Extension Railway and closed by BR 1 October 1951.
Line lifted – Partially demolished - Station site in commercial use by "Seaway Marine Boatbuilders and Chandlery".
NJ70008 64215

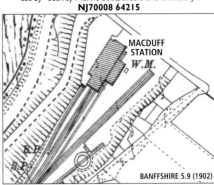

BANFFSHIRE 5.9 (1902)

MACHRIHANISH   5 A3

Opened 18 August 1906 by the Campbeltown and Machrihanish Light Railway and closed by May 1932.

MACHRIHANISH FARM   5A B3

Opened in September 1907 by the Campbeltown and Machrihanish Light Railway and closed by May 1932.

MACMERRY 7 C1

Opened 1 May 1872 by the NBR and closed by the L&NER 1 July 1925.

Line lifted – Demolished – Station site occupied by a field.
NT43100 72343

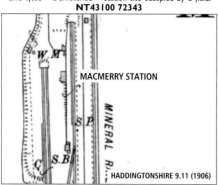

HADDINGTONSHIRE 9.11 (1906)

MADDERTY 11 A3

Opened 21 May 1866 by the Crieff & Methven Junction Railway and closed by BR 1 October 1951.

Line lifted – Station building and platforms in private use.
NN95479 22368

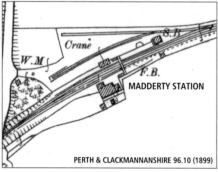

PERTH & CLACKMANNANSHIRE 96.10 (1899)

MAGDALEN GREEN 11 C2

Opened by the Dundee & Perth Railway in June 1878 as *Magdalene Green*, renamed by the CR in 1904 as *Magdalen Green* and although closed by BR 11 June 1956 it was used for a few days in 1957 for the Highland Agricultural Show.

Line Operational – Demolished – Part of station site absorbed into Magdalen Green parkland. **NO38647 29434**

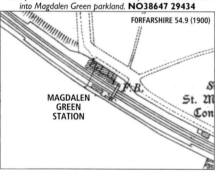

FORFARSHIRE 54.9 (1900)

MAIDENS 6 A4

Opened 17 May 1906 by the Maidens & Dunure Light Railway and closed by the LM&SR 1 December 1930.

Line lifted – Demolished – Station site occupied by a caravan park. **NS22010 07633**

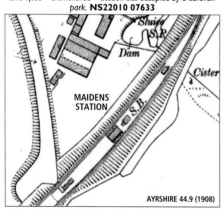

AYRSHIRE 44.9 (1908)

MALLAIG 13 A3

Opened by the NBR 1 April 1901.

Class 156 Unit No.156445 at **Mallaig Station** on 14 September 2015.

MANUEL 7 A1

Opened 21 February 1842 by the Edinburgh & Glasgow Railway as *Bo'ness Junction*, renamed 1 January 1866 as *Manuel*, at an unknown date as *Manuel High Level* and closed by BR 6 March 1967.

Line Operational – Demolished – No access. **NS96972 77207**

MANUEL LOW LEVEL 7A A1

Opened 10 June 1856 by the Monkland Railway, renamed at an unknown date as *Manuel Low Level* and closed by the L&NER 1 May 1933.

Line lifted – Demolished – Station site unused.
NS97021 77221

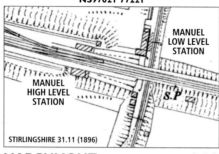

STIRLINGSHIRE 31.11 (1896)

MARCHMONT 8 A2

Opened 16 November 1863 by the Berwickshire Railway and closed by BR 13 August 1948.

Line lifted – Station building and platform in private use.
NT75280 48936

BERWICKSHIRE 22.2 (1898)

MARKINCH 11 C4

Opened by the Edinburgh & Northern Railway 20 September 1847 as *Markinch*, renamed as *Markinch Junction* by the NBR in 1862 and as *Markinch* c1904.

Looking north at **Markinch Station** on 18 September 2015.

MARYFIELD BRANCH 11 C2
MARYHILL 6 C1/21A C1

Opened by the Glasgow, Dumbarton & Helensburgh Railway 31 May 1858, closed by BR 2 April 1951, reopened as *Maryhill Park* 19 December 1960, closed to public 2 October 1961, totally on 29 February 1964 and reopened as *Maryhill* 3 December 1993.

Maryhill Station on 13 May 2017.

MARYHILL CENTRAL 21A C2

Opened 10 August 1896 by the CR as *Maryhill*, renamed by BR 15 September 1952 as *Maryhill Central* and closed 5 October 1964.

Line lifted – Demolished – Station site occupied by part of "Maryhill Shopping Centre". **NS57088 68377**

LANARKSHIRE 6.2 (1909)

MARYKIRK 12 A1

Opened 1 October 1849 by the Aberdeen Railway and closed by BR 11 June 1956.

Line Operational – Demolished – No access. **NO68812 67596**

KINCARDINESHIRE 27.9 (1922)

MARYPORT 3 A3

Opened 4 June 1860 by the Maryport & Carlisle Railway.

Looking north at **Maryport Station** on 30 May 2015.

MARYPORT JUNCTION 3 A3
MAUCHLINE 6 B3

Opened 9 August 1848 by the Glasgow, Paisley, Kilmarnock and Ayr Railway as *Mauchline*, renamed by the G&SWR in 1877 as *Mauchline for Catrine*, in 1903 as *Mauchline* and closed by BR 6 December 1965.

Line Operational – Station building in private use – Platforms demolished. **NS49710 26505**

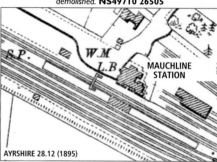

AYRSHIRE 28.12 (1895)

MAUD 16 B1

Opened 18 July 1861 by the Formartine & Buchan Railway as *Brucklay*, renamed 24 April 1865 as *New Maud Junction*, in 1866 as *Maud Junction*, 21 September 1925 by the L&NER as *Maud* and closed by BR 4 October 1965.

Line lifted - Part of station building in use as the "Maud Railway Museum" - Platforms extant - The Formartine and Buchan Way passes through the station site. **NJ92576 47883**

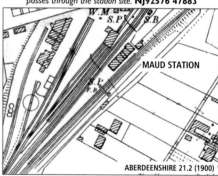

ABERDEENSHIRE 21.2 (1900)

MAWCARSE 11 B3

Opened 15 March 1858 by the Fife & Kinross Railway as *Mawcarse Junction*, renamed by BR in c1959 as *Mawcarse* and closed 15 June 1964.

Line lifted – Demolished – Station site unused.
NO15263 06023

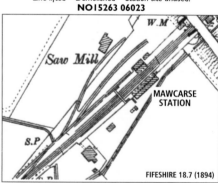

FIFESHIRE 18.7 (1894)

MAXTON 7 D3

Opened in June 1851 by the NBR and closed by BR 15 June 1964.

Line lifted – Station building in private use – Platforms demolished. **NT61682 29959**

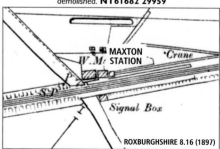

ROXBURGHSHIRE 8.16 (1897)

MAXWELL PARK
21A C3

Opened by the Cathcart District Railway 2 April 1894.

Maxwell Park Station on 18 March 2017.

MAXWELLTOWN
3 A1

Opened 7 November 1859 by the Castle Douglas & Dumfries Railway and although closed by the LM&SR 1 March 1939 was used sporadically for (Queen of the South FC) football trains until 1963.

Line lifted – Station building in private use – The Maxwelltown Railway Path passes through the station site.
NX95604 76398

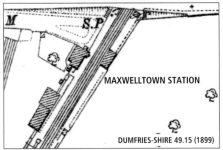

MAYBOLE
6 A4

Opened by the G&SWR 24 May 1860.

Maybole Station on 16 March 2017.

MAYFIELD BRANCH
6 B2
MEADOWBANK STADIUM
22A D2

Opened 14 June 1986 and closed 20 March 1988.
Line Out of Use – Degraded platform extant – Station site unused. **NT27798 74495**

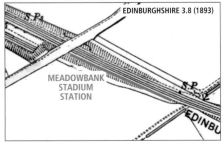

MEIGLE
11 B2

Opened 2 September 1861 by the Alyth Railway as *Fullarton*, renamed by the CR 1 November 1876 as *Meigle* and closed by BR 2 July 1951.
Line lifted – Demolished – Station site in private use.
NO28902 44690

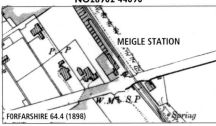

MEIKLE EARNOCK
6 C2

Opened 2 February 1863 by the Hamilton & Strathaven Railway and closed by the LM&SR 12 December 1943.
Line lifted – Demolished – Station site unused.
NS70766 53275

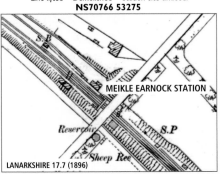

MELDON
4 C1

Opened 23 July 1862 by the Wansbeck Railway and closed by BR 15 September 1952.
Line lifted – Station building and platform in private use.
NZ12154 83392

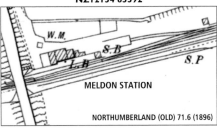

MELROSE
7 D3

Opened 20 February 1849 by the NBR and closed by BR 6 January 1969.
Line lifted – Grade A listed station building in use as Restaurant and Craft Centre - One platform extant - The A6091 passes through the station site. **NT54664 33899**

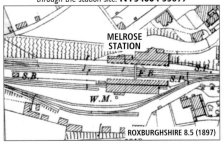

MENSTRIE
10 D4

Opened 3 June 1863 by the Alva Railway and closed by BR 1 November 1954. It was also known as *Menstrie & Glenochil* in some timetables.
Line lifted – Demolished – A footpath passes through the station site. **NS85495 96816**

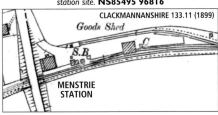

MERCHISTON
7 B1/22A B2

Opened 1 July 1882 by the CR and closed by BR 6 September 1965.
Line lifted – Demolished – Platform partially extant – A service road to Slateford Yard passes through the station site.
NT23328 71968

MERRYTON
6A D2

Opened 12 December 2005.

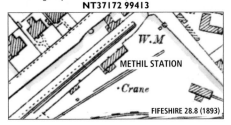

Merryton Station on 19 March 2017.

METHIL
11 C4

Opened 5 May 1887 by the Wemyss & Buckhaven Railway and closed by BR 10 January 1955.
Line lifted - Station building extant in commercial use in a haulage depot – Remainder of station site demolished.
NT37172 99413

METHIL DOCK BRANCH
11 C4
METHVEN
11 A3

Opened 1 January 1858 by the Perth, Almond Valley & Methven Railway and closed by the LM&SR 27 September 1937.
Line lifted – Demolished – Station site in commercial use.
NO02219 25518

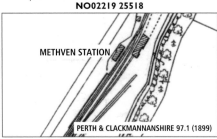

METHVEN JUNCTION
11 A3
METHVEN JUNCTION
11A A3

Opened 21 May 1866 by the CR and was an unadvertised exchange station from 1889 until 27 September 1937 when it took over from the closed branch station (qv). It was closed by BR 1 October 1951.
Line lifted – Demolished – Station site absorbed into farmland.
NO02794 24360

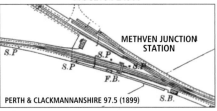

MIDCALDER (See **KIRKNEWTON**)
MIDCALDER JUNCTION
7 A1
MID CLYTH
18 B1

Opened 1 July 1903 by the Wick & Lybster Light Railway and closed by the LM&SR 3 April 1944.
Line lifted – Station House in private use as the "Station House B&B" – A driveway passes through the station site.
ND29926 38325

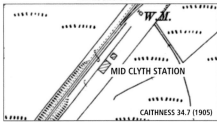

MIDDLETON
4 C1

Opened 23 July 1862 by the Wansbeck Railway as *Middleton*, renamed by the L&NER 1 July 1923 as *Middleton North* and closed by BR 15 September 1952.
Line lifted – Demolished – A cycle/walkway passes through the station site. **NZ06360 85199**

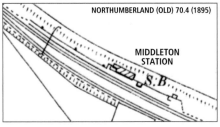

MILLERHILL
7 C1

Opened 1 September 1847 by the NBR and closed by BR 7 November 1955.
Line Operational - Demolished - Station building in private use.
NT32658 69624

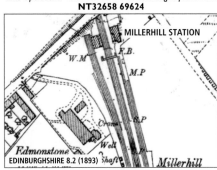

MILLIKEN PARK   6 B1

Opened in March 1846 by the Glasgow, Paisley, Kilmarnock and Ayr Railway as *Cochrane Mill*, renamed as *Milliken Park* 1 March 1853 and closed by BR 18 April 1966.
Line Operational – Demolished. **NS41435 62038**

RENFREWSHIRE 11.11 (1895)

MILLIKEN PARK   6A B1

Opened 15 May 1989 and sited 200 yards south of the original station (qv).

Milliken Park Station on 17 March 2017.

MILLISLE   2 B2

Opened 1 March 1903 by the Portpatrick & Wigtownshire Joint Railway as *Millisle for Garlieston* and closed by BR 25 September 1950.
Line lifted – Station building in private use – Platform demolished. **NX46395 46373**

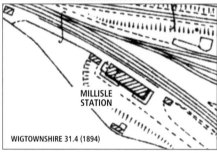

WIGTOWNSHIRE 31.4 (1894)

MILLTIMBER   16 B3

Opened in January 1854 by the Deeside Railway and closed by the L&NER 5 April 1937.
Line lifted – Demolished – One platform extant – The Deeside Way passes through the station site. **NJ85678 01197**

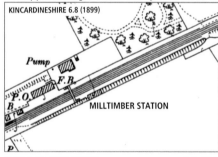

KINCARDINESHIRE 6.8 (1899)

MILNATHORT   11 B3

Opened 15 March 1858 by the Fife & Kinross Railway and closed by BR 15 June 1964.
Line lifted – Demolished – Station site in commercial use.
NO11843 04096

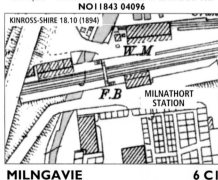

KINROSS-SHIRE 18.10 (1894)

MILNGAVIE   6 C1

Opened by the Glasgow & Milngavie Junction Railway 28 July 1863.

Looking north at Milngavie Station on 13 May 2017.

MILTONISE*   2A A1

Opened by the G&SWR at an unknown date, in use for railwaymen and families in 1926, and closed on an unknown date.
Line Operational – Demolished. **NX18708 73476**

WIGTOWNSHIRE 1SE (1893)

MILTON OF CAMPSIE   6 C1

Opened 5 July 1847 by the NBR as *Miltown*, renamed in 1874 as *Milton*, 1 May 1912 as *Milton of Campsie* and closed by BR 1 October 1951.
Line lifted – Demolished – Platforms extant – The Paisley and Clyde Cycle Path passes through the station site.
NS65197 76599

STIRLINGSHIRE 28.13 (1896)

MILTON OF CRATHES   16A A3

Opened by **The Royal Deeside Railway** in c2010 on a site a few hundred yards from *Crathes* station (qv).

MINTLAW   16 B1

Opened 18 July 1861 by the GNofSR as *Old Deer & Mintlaw*, renamed 1 December 1867 as *Mintlaw* and closed by BR 3 May 1965.
Line lifted - Platforms and building extant - The Formartine and Buchan Way passes through the station site.
NJ98949 48522

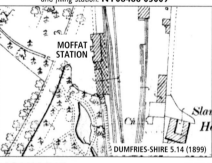

ABERDEENSHIRE 5.16 (1900)

MOFFAT   7 B4

Opened 2 April 1883 by the Moffat Railway and closed by BR 6 December 1954.
Line lifted – Demolished – Station site occupied by a garage and filling station. **NT08488 05009**

DUMFRIES-SHIRE 5.14 (1899)

MONIAIVE   2 D1

Opened 1 March 1905 by the Cairn Valley Light Railway and closed by the LM&SR 3 May 1943.
Line lifted – Platforms demolished - Station building extant.
NX77922 90732

NX79SE (1956)

MONIFIETH   11 D2

Opened by the Dundee & Arbroath Railway 8 October 1838.

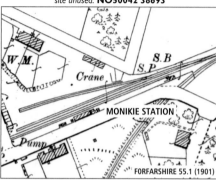

Looking north at Monifieth Station on 18 September 2015.

MONIKIE   11 D2

Opened in July 1871 by the CR and closed by BR 10 January 1955.
Line lifted – Demolished – Degraded platform extant - Station site unused. **NO50042 38693**

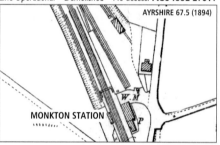

FORFARSHIRE 55.1 (1901)

MONKTON   6 A3

Opened in August 1840 by the Mauchline Railway and closed by the LM&SR 28 October 1940.
Line Operational – Demolished – No access. **NS34882 27617**

AYRSHIRE 67.5 (1894)

MONTGREENAN   6 A2

Opened 1 February 1878 by the Mauchline Railway and closed by BR 7 March 1955.
Line lifted – Station building in private use – Platforms demolished. **NS33974 43385**

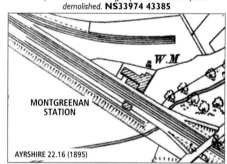

AYRSHIRE 22.16 (1895)

MONTRAVE GOODS   11 C3
MONTROSE (CR)   12 A1

Opened 1 February 1848 by the Aberdeen Railway and closed by the LM&SR 30 April 1934.
Line lifted – Station House in use as a retirement home – Remainder of site occupied by housing. **NO71678 57393**

FORFARSHIRE 37.15 (1900)

MONTROSE (NBR)   12 A1

Opened by the NBR 1 May 1883.

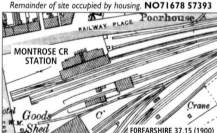

Looking south at Montrose Station on 18 September 2015.

MONTROSE HARBOUR   12 A1
BRANCH

MONYMUSK   16 A3

Opened 21 March 1859 by the Alford Valley Railway and closed by BR 2 January 1950.

Line lifted – Degraded platform extant – Station site unused. **NJ68551 14157**

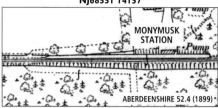

ABERDEENSHIRE 52.4 (1899)

MORAR   13 A4

Opened by the NBR 1 April 1901.

Looking north at **Morar Station** on 14 September 2015.

MORMOND   16 B1

Opened 24 April 1865 by the GNofSR as *Mormond*, re-named by the L&NER 1 June 1939 as *Mormond Halt* and closed by BR 2 October 1965.

Line lifted - Station building in private use - Platforms extant - The Formartine and Buchan Way passes through the station site. **NJ98554 55962**

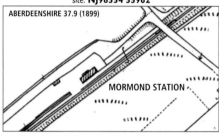

ABERDEENSHIRE 37.9 (1899)

MORNINGSIDE (CR)   6 D2

Opened 15 May 1867 by the CR, closed 1 January 1917, reopened 2 June 1919 and closed by the LM&SR 1 December 1930.

Line lifted – Demolished – Station site unused. **NS83234 55055**

MORNINGSIDE (NBR)   6 D2

Opened 19 September 1864 by the NBR and closed by the L&NER 1 May 1930.

Line lifted – Demolished – Station site unused. **NS83268 55116**

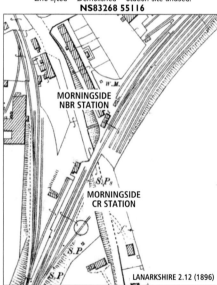

LANARKSHIRE 2.12 (1896)

MORNINGSIDE ROAD   22A B2

Opened 1 December 1884 by the Edinburgh Suburban & Southside Junction Railway as *Morningside*, renamed in 1886 as *Morningside Road* and closed by BR 10 September 1962.

Line Operational – Demolished - One platform extant – No access. **NT24471 70931**

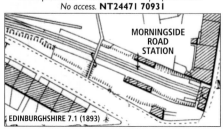

EDINBURGHSHIRE 7.1 (1893)

MORPETH   4 D1

Opened 1 March 1847 by the Newcastle & Berwick Railway.

Morpeth Station on 19 September 2015.

MOSSBAND PLATFORM*   3A C2

Opened in 1914 by the CR as an interchange with the military branch for munitions workers and closed c1922.

Line Operational – Demolished. **NY34923 65059 (e)**

MOSSEND   6 D1

Opened 1 June 1882 by the Wishaw & Coltness Railway and closed by BR 5 November 1962.

Line Operational – Demolished – No access. **NS75027 60420**

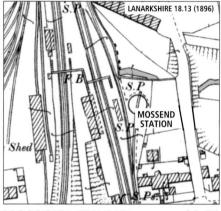

LANARKSHIRE 18.13 (1896)

MOSSGIEL TUNNEL PLATFORM*   6A B3

Opened by the LM&SR and in use for workmen's trains in 1926. Closure date unknown.

Line Operational – Demolished. **NS48096 29079 (a)**

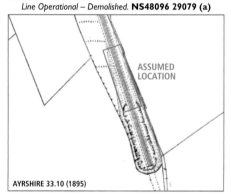

AYRSHIRE 33.10 (1895)

MOSSPARK   21A A3

Opened by the LM&SR 1 March 1934 as *Mosspark West*, renamed by BR as *Mosspark* 3 May 1976, closed 10 January 1983 and reopened 30 July 1990.

Mosspark Station on 18 March 2017.

MOSS ROAD   5A B3

Opened in September 1907 by the Campbeltown & Machrihanish Light Railway and closed by May 1932.

MOSSTOWIE   15 B1

Opened 15 October 1890 by the Inverness & Aberdeen Junction Railway and closed by BR 7 March 1955.

Line lifted – Demolished – No access. **NJ16946 62184**

ELGINSHIRE 15.7 (1904)

MOTHERWELL   6 D2

Opened by the CR 1 August 1885.

Looking south at **Motherwell Station** on 19 March 2017.

MOULDRON WORKS BRANCH   *7 A2*

MOULINEARN CROSSING*   11A A1

Opened by the HR or LM&SR. No other details known.

Line Operational – Crossing Keeper's Cottage in private use. **NN96957 54812**

RENFREWSHIRE 7.6 (1896)

MOUNT FLORIDA   21A C4

Opened by the Cathcart District Railway 1 March 1886.

Mount Florida Station on 18 March 2017.

MOUNT MELVILLE   11 D3

Opened 1 June 1887 by the Anstruther & St Andrews Railway, closed by the NBR 1 January 1917, reopened 1 February 1919 and closed by the L&NER 22 September 1930

Line lifted – Demolished – Station site partially unused – The realigned A915 crosses the south end of the station site. **NO49541 14373**

FIFESHIRE 4.2 (1893)

MOUNT VERNON (CR)   6 C1

Opened by the Rutherglen & Coatbridge Railway 8 January 1866, closed by the LM&SR 16 August 1943 and reopened by BR 4 October 1993.

Mount Vernon Station on 12 May 2017.

MOUNT VERNON (NBR)   6 C1

Opened 1 April 1878 by the NBR as *Mount Vernon*, closed 1 January 1917, reopened 2 June 1919, renamed by BR in 1952 as *Mount Vernon North* and closed 4 July 1955.

Line lifted - Demolished – Central Path passes through the station site. **NS66049 63432**

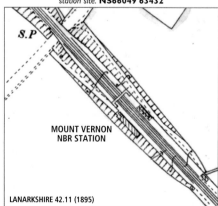

LANARKSHIRE 42.11 (1895)

MOY
14 C2

Opened 19 July 1897 by the HR and closed by BR 3 May 1965.

Line Operational – Station building in private use.
NH76418 34499

INVERNESS-MAINLAND 21 (1900)

MOY PARK
5A B3

Opened 1 May 1912 by the Campbeltown & Machrihanish Light Railway and possibly lasted until 1919.

MUCHALLS
16 B4

Opened in 1850 by the Aberdeen Railway and closed by BR 4 December 1950.

Line Operational – Demolished – No access. **NO90178 91910**

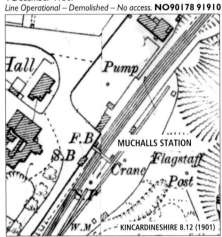

KINCARDINESHIRE 8.12 (1901)

MUIREDGE COLLIERY BRANCH
11 C4

MUIREND
6 C2/21A C4

Opened by the Lanarkshire & Ayrshire Railway 1 May 1903.

Muirend Station on 18 March 2017.

MUIRKIRK
6 C3

Opened in 1896 by the G&SWR and closed by BR 5 October 1964. This replaced an earlier station opened 9 August 1848 by the Glasgow, Paisley, Kilmarnock and Ayr Railway and sited about 0.25 miles to the west.

Line lifted – Station House in private use – Station site in use as a car park for the "Kames Motorsport Complex".
NS69532 26529

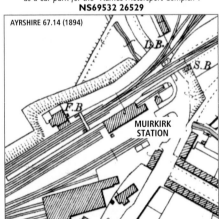

AYRSHIRE 67.14 (1894)

MUIRKIRK STATION

MUIRKIRK JUNCTION
6 C3

MUIR OF ORD
14 B1

Opened by the Inverness & Ross-shire Railway 11 June 1862, closed by BR 13 June 1960 and reopened 4 October 1976

Class 158 Unit No.158717 at **Muir of Ord** Station on 17 September 2015.

MUIRTON HALT*
11A A3

Opened 31 October 1936 by the LM&SR, possibly mainly for travelling football fans to the nearby Muirton Park (St Johnstone FC), and closed by BR 21 November 1959.

Line Operational – Demolished. **NO10756 24485**

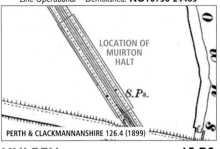

LOCATION OF MUIRTON HALT

S.Ps.

PERTH & CLACKMANNANSHIRE 126.4 (1899)

MULBEN
15 B2

Opened 18 August 1858 by the Inverness & Aberdeen Junction Railway and closed by BR 7 December 1964.

Line Operational - Station building and platform in private use.
NJ35614 50860

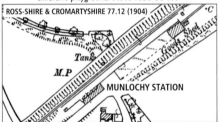

MULBEN STATION

BANFFSHIRE 22.15 (1900)

MUNLOCHY
14 C1

Opened 1 February 1894 by the HR and closed by BR 1 October 1951.

Line lifted – Demolished – Station site partially occupied by a children's playground. **NH64633 53403**

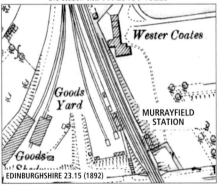

ROSS-SHIRE & CROMARTYSHIRE 77.12 (1904)

MUNLOCHY STATION

MURRAYFIELD
22A B2

Opened 1 August 1879 by the CR and closed by BR 30 April 1962.

Line lifted – Demolished – The Roseburn Path passes through the station site. **NT23136 73223**

Wester Coates

Goods Yard

MURRAYFIELD STATION

EDINBURGHSHIRE 23.15 (1892)

MURTHLY
11 A2

Opened in 1856 by the Perth & Dunkeld Railway and closed by BR 3 May 1965.

Line Operational – Demolished – Southbound platform extant.
NO10095 38361

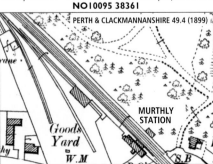

PERTH & CLACKMANNANSHIRE 49.4 (1899)

MURTHLY STATION

Goods Yard

MURTLE
16 B3

Opened 8 September 1853 by the Deeside Railway as *Murtle*, renamed by the L&NER in 1931 as *Murtle Halt* and closed 5 April 1937.

Line lifted - Station building and platform in private use - The Deeside Way passes through the station site.
NJ87249 01866

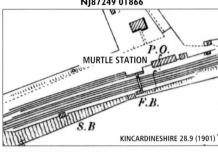

MURTLE STATION

KINCARDINESHIRE 28.9 (1901)

MUSSELBURGH
7 C1

Opened 14 July 1847 by the NBR and closed by BR 7 September 1964.

Line lifted – Demolished – Station site occupied by a car park.
NT34067 72479

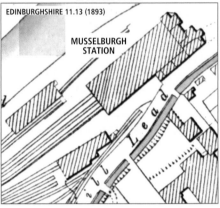

EDINBURGHSHIRE 11.13 (1893)

MUSSELBURGH STATION

MUSSELBURGH
7A C1

Opened 3 October 1988.

Musselburgh Station on 19 September 2015.

MUTHILL
10 D3

Opened in July 1856 by the Crieff Junction Railway and closed by BR 6 July 1964.

Line lifted – Demolished – Station site situated within farm premises. **NN89351 16631**

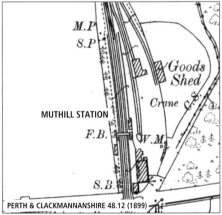

MUTHILL STATION

PERTH & CLACKMANNANSHIRE 48.12 (1899)

NAIRN
14 D1

Opened by the Inverness & Nairn Railway 7 November 1855.

Nairn Station on 17 September 2015.

NEILSTON (CR)
6 B2

Opened by the Lanarkshire & Ayrshire Railway 1 May 1903 as *Neilston*, closed by the CR 1 January 1917, reopened 1 February 1919, renamed 2 June 1924 as *Neilston High* and by BR 18 June 1962 as *Neilston*.

Class 314 Unit No.314215 at **Neilston Station** on 18 March 2017.

NEILSTON (GB&KR)   6 B2

Opened 27 March 1871 by the Glasgow, Barrhead & Kilmarnock Joint Railway as *Neilston*, renamed by BR 15 September 1952 as *Neilston Low* and closed 7 November 1966.
Line Operational – Demolished – No access. **NS47156 57477**

RENFREWSHIRE 8.15 (1895)

NEILSTON GB&KR STATION

NETHERBURN   6 D2

Opened 1 December 1866 by the Lesmahagow Railway as *Bents*, renamed 1 May 1868 as *Netherburn* and closed by BR 1 October 1951.
Line lifted – Demolished – Station site occupied by housing in Draffan Road. **NS80020 47586**

LANARKSHIRE 25.10 (1900)

NETHERBURN STATION

NETHERCLEUGH   3 B1

Opened 10 September 1847 by the CR and closed by BR 13 June 1960.
Line Operational – Demolished. **NY12039 86043**

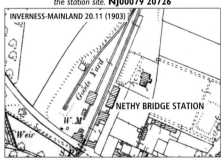

DUMFRIES-SHIRE 9.15 (1898)

NETHERCLEUGH STATION

NETHERTON GOODS   6 B2

NETHY BRIDGE   15 A2

Opened 1 July 1863 by the Strathspey Railway as *Abernethy*, renamed by the GNofSR 1 November 1867 as *Nethy Bridge*, by BR 6 November 1961 as *Nethy Bridge Halt* and closed 18 October 1965.
Line lifted - Station building and platform in use as the "Abernethy Bunkhouse" – The Speyside Way passes through the station site. **NJ00079 20726**

INVERNESS-MAINLAND 20.11 (1903)

NETHY BRIDGE STATION

NEWARTHILL   6 D2

Opened 15 May 1867 by the CR, closed to passengers 1 June 1880 and to goods by BR 6 April 1964.
Line Operational – Demolished – Current CARFIN STATION *occupies the site.* **NS77507 58870**

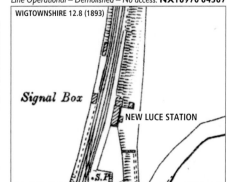

LANARKSHIRE 8.11 (1897)

C.R. EDINBURGH & GLASGOW

Goods Depôt

NEWBIGGING   7 A2

Opened 1 March 1867 by the CR, closed by the LM&SR 12 September 1932, reopened 17 July 1933 and closed 4 June 1945.
Line lifted – Demolished – Station site unused. **NT02055 44988**

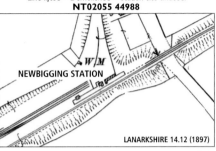

NEWBIGGING STATION

LANARKSHIRE 14.12 (1897)

NEWBURGH   11 B3

Opened in 1906 by the NBR and closed by BR 19 September 1955.
Line Operational – Demolished – No access. **NO22822 18014**

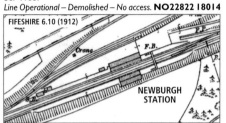

FIFESHIRE 6.10 (1912)

NEWBURGH STATION

NEWCASTLETON   3 D1

Opened 1 March 1862 by the Border Union Railway and closed by BR 6 January 1969.
Line lifted – Demolished – A short roadway passes through the station site - Station site occupied by housing in Frank Coutts Court. **NY48154 87706**

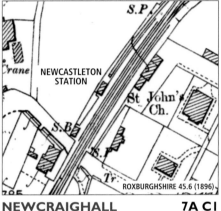

NEWCASTLETON STATION

ROXBURGHSHIRE 45.6 (1896)

NEWCRAIGHALL   7 A C1

Opened 3 June 2002

Newcraighall Station on 19 September 2015.

NEW CUMNOCK   6 C4

Opened by the Glasgow, Paisley, Kilmarnock and Ayr Railway 20 May 1850, closed by BR 6 December 1965 and reopened 27 May 1991.

New Cumnock Station on 20 March 2017.

NEW GALLOWAY   2 C1

Opened 12 March 1861 by the Portpatrick Railway and closed by BR 14 June 1965.
Line lifted – Demolished – Station site landscaped as part of garden for adjacent former Station Master's House. **NX66115 70494**

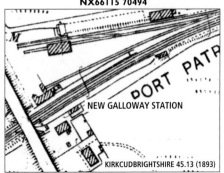

NEW GALLOWAY STATION

PORT PATR

KIRKCUDBRIGHTSHIRE 45.13 (1893)

NEWHAILES   7 C1

Opened 16 May 1859 by the NBR as *New Hailes*, renamed by the L&NER 26 September 1938 as *Newhailes* and closed by BR 6 February 1950.
Line Operational – Demolished – No access. **NT32441 72180**

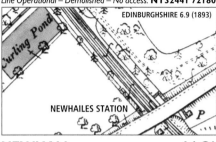

EDINBURGHSHIRE 6.9 (1893)

Curling Pond

NEWHAILES STATION

NEWHALL   14 C1

Planned by the Cromarty & Dingwall Railway but never opened.

NEWHAVEN   22A C1

Opened 1 August 1879 by the CR and closed by BR 30 April 1962.
Line lifted – Demolished - Platforms extant – The Hawthornvale Path passes through the station site. **NT25430 76588**

Smithy

NEWHAVEN STATION

School

EDINBURGHSHIRE 21.13 (1892)

NEWHOUSE   6 D1

Opened 2 July 1888 by the CR and although closed by the LM&SR 1 December 1930 a non-timetabled service ran from 1937 until 31 July 1941.
Line lifted – Demolished – Site unused. **NS79555 61514**

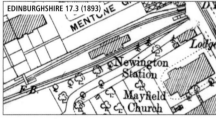

LANARKSHIRE 31.9 (1896)

NEWHOUSE STATION

NEWINGTON   22A C2

Opened 1 December 1884 by the Edinburgh Suburban & Southside Junction Railway and closed by BR 10 September 1962.
Line Operational – Demolished – No access. **NT26809 71493**

EDINBURGHSHIRE 17.3 (1893)

MENTONE

Newington Station

Mayfield Church

NEW LUCE   1 D2

Opened 19 September 1877 by the Girvan & Portpatrick Joint Railway, closed 7 February 1882, reopened 16 February 1882, closed 12 April 1886, reopened 14 June 1886 and closed by BR 6 September 1965.
Line Operational – Demolished – No access. **NX16970 64567**

WIGTOWNSHIRE 12.8 (1893)

Signal Box

NEW LUCE STATION

NEWMACHAR 16 B2

Opened 18 July 1861 by the Formartine & Buchan Railway and closed by BR 4 October 1965.
Line lifted - Station House in private use - Platforms demolished - The Formartine and Buchan Way passes through the station site. **NJ88926 20167**

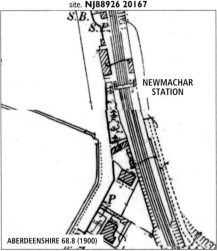

ABERDEENSHIRE 68.8 (1900)

NEWMAINS 6 D2

Opened 15 May 1867 by the CR, closed 1 January 1917, reopened 2 June 1919 and closed by the LM&SR 1 December 1930.
Line lifted – Demolished – Station site partially occupied by housing in McShane Court – A rough pathway passes through the station site. **NS82537 56220**

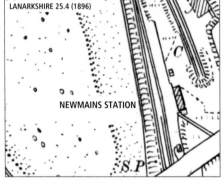

LANARKSHIRE 25.4 (1896)

NEWMILNS 6 B3

Opened 20 May 1850 by the Mauchline Railway and closed by BR 6 April 1964.
Line lifted – Demolished – Station site in commercial use. **NS53288 37024**

AYRSHIRE 42.12 (1894)

NEWPARK 7 A1

Opened 11 October 1869 by the Cleland & Midcalder Railway and closed by BR 14 September 1959.
Line Operational - Demolished – No access. **NT04919 64521**

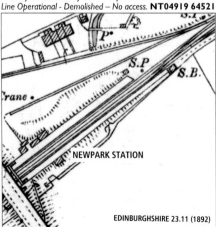

EDINBURGHSHIRE 23.11 (1892)

NEWSEAT 16 C1

Opened 3 July 1862 by the Formartine & Buchan Railway as *New Seat*, renamed by the GNofSR in 1884 as *Newseat*, by the L&NER 22 September 1930 as *Newseat Halt* and closed by BR 3 May 1965.
Line lifted - Station building in private use - Platforms extant - The Formartine and Buchan Way passes through the station site. **NK07796 48052**

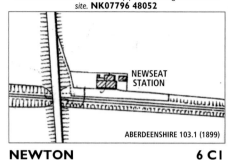

ABERDEENSHIRE 103.1 (1899)

NEWTON 6 C1

Opened by the CR 19 December 1873

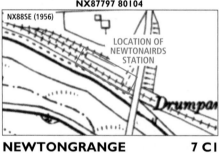

Looking east at **Newton Station** on 18 March 2017.

NEWTONAIRDS 2 D1

Opened 1 March 1905 by the Cairn Valley Light Railway and closed by the LM&SR 3 May 1943.
Line lifted – Demolished – Station site unused. **NX87797 80104**

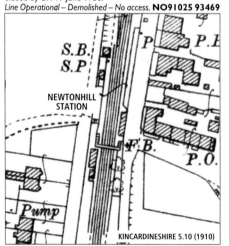

KINCARDINESHIRE 5.10 (1910)

NEWTONGRANGE 7 C1

Opened by the NBR 1 August 1908, closed by BR 6 January 1969 and rebuilt and reopened 6 September 2015.

Looking south at **Newtongrange Station** on 12 May 2017.

NEWTONHILL 16 B3

Opened in November 1850 by the Aberdeen Railway and closed by BR 11 June 1956.
Line Operational – Demolished – No access. **NO91025 93469**

NEWTONMORE 14 C3

Opened by the Inverness & Perth Junction Railway 9 September 1863.

Looking north at **Newtonmore Station** on 15 September 2015.

NEWTON ON AYR 6 A3

Opened by the Glasgow, Paisley, Kilmarnock & Ayr Railway 1 November 1886.

Looking south at **Newton on Ayr Station** on 16 March 2017.

NEWTON STEWART 2 B2

Opened 12 March 1861 by the Portpatrick Railway and closed by BR 14 June 1965.
Line lifted – Demolished – Station site in commercial use as the "Station Industrial Estate". **NX40574 64958**

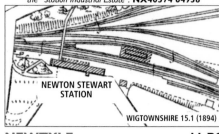

WIGTOWNSHIRE 15.1 (1894)

NEWTYLE 11 B2

Opened 31 August 1868 by the CR and closed by BR 10 January 1955.
Line lifted – Demolished - Station site in private use. **NO29542 41458**

FORFARSHIRE 28.6 (1901)

NIGG 17 C4

Opened 1 June 1864 by the Inverness & Aberdeen Junction Railway and closed by BR 13 June 1960.
Line Operational – Station building in private use – Platforms demolished. **NH80165 76387**

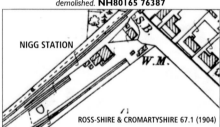

ROSS-SHIRE & CROMARTYSHIRE 67.1 (1904)

NISBET 8 A3

Opened 18 July 1856 by the Jedburgh Railway and closed by BR 13 August 1948.
Line lifted – Station building in private use – Platform demolished. **NT67400 25504**

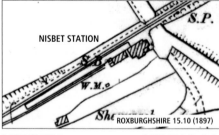

ROXBURGHSHIRE 15.10 (1897)

NITSHILL 6 B1/21A A4

Opened by the Glasgow, Barrhead & Neilston Direct Railway 27 September 1848.

Nitshill Station on 18 March 2017.

NORHAM 8 B2

Opened in July 1851 by the York, Newcastle & Berwick Railway and closed by BR 15 June 1964.
Line lifted - Station and buildings privately preserved as a museum. **NT90748 46787**

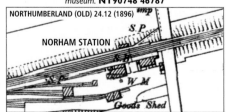

NORTHUMBERLAND (OLD) 24.12 (1896)

NORTH BERWICK 11 D4

Opened by the NBR 17 June 1850.

Looking south at **North Berwick Station** on 19 September 2015.

NORTH CONNEL 9 C2

Opened 7 March 1904 by the Callander & Oban Railway and closed by BR 28 March 1966. It was also known as *North Connel Halt* in some timetables.
Line lifted – Demolished – The A828, Argyll Coastal Road, passes through the station site. **NM91086 34703**

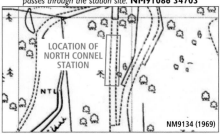

NORTH JOHNSTONE 6 B1

Opened 1 June 1905 by the G&SWR and closed by BR 7 March 1955.
Line lifted – Demolished – Part of station site unused, south edge is car park for Morrisons store – A cycle/walkway passes through the station site. **NS42523 63541**

NORTH LEITH 7 B1/22A C1

Opened 20 May 1846 by the Edinburgh, Leith & Newhaven Railway as *Leith*, renamed by the NBR in 1868 as *North Leith*, closed 1 January 1917, reopened 1 April 1919 and closed by the L&NER 16 June 1947.
Line lifted – Demolished – Station frontage intact - Station site in commercial use. **NT26704 76639**

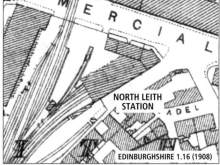

NORTH QUEENSFERRY 7 B1

Opened by the Forth Bridge Railway 2 June 1890.

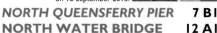

Class 158 Unit No.158725 at **North Queensferry Station** on 18 September 2015.

NORTH QUEENSFERRY PIER 7 B1
NORTH WATER BRIDGE 12 A1

Opened in July 1866 by the Montrose & Bervie Railway and closed by BR 1 October 1951.
Line lifted – Demolished – Station site unused. **NO72491 62517**

NOVAR 17 B4

Opened 23 March 1863 by the Inverness & Ross-shire Railway as *Novar*, renamed by the LM&SR 1 June 1937 as *Evanton* and closed by BR 13 June 1960.
Line Operational – Demolished – No access. **NH61284 66531**

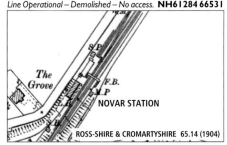

OAKLEY 11 A4

Opened 28 August 1850 by the Stirling & Dunfermline Railway as *Oakley*, renamed by the L&NER 9 March 1925 as *Oakley Fife* and closed by BR 7 October 1968.
Line lifted – One platform partially extant - The West Fife Cycleway passes through the station site. **NT02494 88732**

OAKLEY COLLIERY BRANCH 11 A4
OBAN 9 B3

Opened by the Callander & Oban Railway 1 July 1880.

Looking north at **Oban Station** on 14 September 2015.

OCCUMSTER 18 B1

Opened 1 July 1903 by the Wick & Lybster Light Railway and closed by the LM&SR 3 April 1944.
Line lifted – Demolished – Station site in agricultural use. **ND26488 36153**

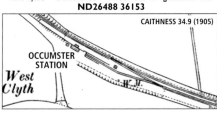

OCHILTREE 6 B3

Opened 1 July 1872 by the G&SWR and closed by BR 10 September 1951.
Line lifted – Station building in private use – Platform demolished. **NS51037 19030**

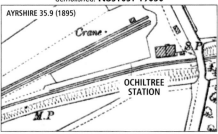

OLD CUMNOCK 6 C3

Opened 20 May 1850 by the Glasgow, Paisley, Kilmarnock & Ayr Railway as *Old Cumnock*, renamed by BR 10 January 1955 as *Cumnock* and closed 6 December 1965.
Line Operational – Station site occupied by the "Bute House Nursing Home" – Platforms demolished. **NS57736 20400**

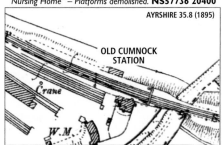

OLD KILPATRICK 6 B1

Opened 1 October 1896 by the Lanarkshire & Dumbarton-shire Railway and closed by BR 5 October 1964.
Line lifted – Demolished – Platform extant. **NS46599 72483**

OLDMELDRUM 16 A2

Opened 1 July 1856 by the Inverurie & Oldmeldrum Railway and closed by the L&NER 2 November 1931.
Line lifted – Partially demolished – Station site in commercial use. **NJ80365 27097**

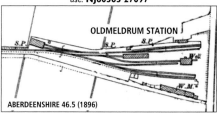

OMOA (See CLELAND)
ORBLISTON 15 B1

Opened 18 August 1858 by the Inverness & Aberdeen Junction Railway as *Fochabers*, renamed by the HR 21 October 1893 as *Orbliston Junction*, by BR 18 June 1962 as *Orbliston* and closed 7 December 1964.
Line Operational – Station house in private use – Platform partially extant. **NJ30430 58244**

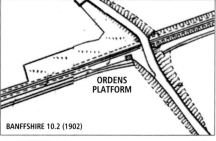

ORDENS PLATFORM 15 D1

Opened 1 October 1859 by the Banff, Portsoy & Strathisla Railway and had intermittent use until closed by BR 6 July 1964.
Line lifted – Station hut and platform extant. **NJ62251 62163**

ORMISTON 7 C1

Opened 1 May 1872 by the NBR and closed by the L&NER 3 April 1933.
Line lifted – Demolished – Platform partially extant - The Pencaitland Railway Walk passes through the station site. **NT41626 69723**

ORTON   15 B1
Opened 18 August 1858 by the Inverness & Aberdeen
Junction Railway and closed by BR 7 December 1964.
Line Operational – Station building in private use.
NJ31189 52969

BANFFSHIRE 13.9 (1902)

OVERTON BRANCH   6 A1
OVERTOWN   6 D2
Opened in January 1881 by the Wishaw & Coltness Railway
as *Overtown Waterloo*, renamed in 1866 as *Overtown*, closed
by the CR 1 January 1917, reopened 1 January 1919 and
closed by the LM&SR 5 October 1942.
Line Operational – Demolished. **NS80770 53566**

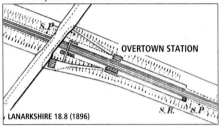

LANARKSHIRE 18.8 (1896)

OXTON   7 D2
Opened 2 July 1901 by the Lauder Light Railway and closed
by the L&NER 12 September 1932.
*Line lifted – Station House and station site in private use -
Demolished.* **NT49943 53614**

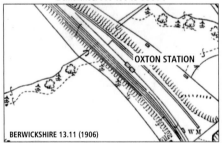

BERWICKSHIRE 13.11 (1906)

OYNE   15 D2
Opened 20 September 1854 by the GNofSR and closed by
BR 6 May 1968.
Line Operational – Demolished. **NJ67279 25879**

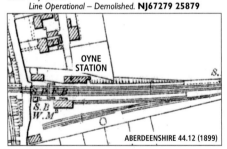

ABERDEENSHIRE 44.12 (1899)

PAISLEY ABERCORN   6 B1
Opened 1 May 1866 by the G&SWR as *Paisley*, renamed in
1888 as *Paisley Abercorn* and closed by BR 5 June 1967.
Line lifted – Demolished – Station site unused.
NS48668 64728

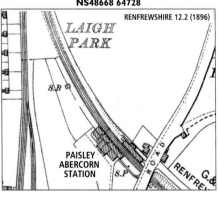

RENFREWSHIRE 12.2 (1896)

PAISLEY CANAL (G&SWR)   6 B1
Opened by the G&SWR 1 July 1885 and closed by BR 10
January 1983.
*Line lifted – Platforms demolished – Station building in private
use as the "Canal Station Bar Diner" – A cycle/walkway passes
through the station site.* **NS48184 63429**

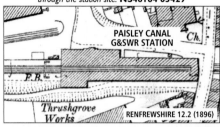

RENFREWSHIRE 12.2 (1896)

PAISLEY CANAL (BR)   6A B1
Opened 28 July 1990 as a termi-
nus, sited to the east of the original station *(qv)*.

Class 156 Unit No.156511 at **Paisley
Canal Station** on 7 June 2011.

PAISLEY GILMOUR STREET   6 B1
Opened by the Glasgow, Paisley,
Kilmarnock & Ayr Railway 14 July
1840.

Looking east at **Paisley Gilmour
Street Station** on 17 March 2017.

PAISLEY ST JAMES   6 B1
Opened by the Glasgow, Paisley &
Greenock Railway 29 March 1841.

Looking south at **Paisley
St James Station** on 17 March 2017.

PAISLEY WEST   6 B1
Opened 1 June 1897 by the G&SWR and closed by BR 14
February 1966.
*Line lifted – Demolished – A cycle/walkway passes through the
station site.* **NS47256 63397**

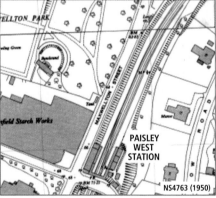

NS4763 (1950)

PALNURE   2 B2
Opened 1 July 1861 by the Portpatrick Railway and closed
by BR 7 May 1951.
*Line lifted – Station building in private use – Platform
demolished.* **NX45099 63408**

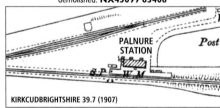

KIRKCUDBRIGHTSHIRE 39.7 (1907)

PARADISE SIDING*   16A A2
Opened c1884 by the GNofSR for workmen's trains and
closed by the L&NER c1938.
*Line lifted – Demolished – Aquithie Road passes through the
station site.* **NJ73568 17135**

ABERDEENSHIRE 54.14 (1899)

PARK   16 A3
Opened 8 September 1853 by the Deeside Railway and
closed by BR 28 February 1966.
Line lifted – Station building in private use as an office building.
NO79283 98773

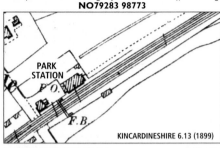

KINCARDINESHIRE 6.13 (1899)

PARKHEAD FOR   6A C1
CELTIC PARK
Opened 1 February 1897 by the CR as *Parkhead*, renamed
in 1899 as *Parkhead for Celtic Park*, by BR 3 March 1952 as
Parkhead Stadium and closed 5 October 1964.
Line lifted – Demolished – Station site unused.
NS62400 63901

NS6263 (1953)

PARKHEAD NORTH   6A C1
Opened 23 November 1870 by the NBR as *Parkhead*,
renamed by BR 30 June 1952 as *Parkhead North* and closed
19 September 1955.
Line Operational – Demolished – No access. **NS62553 64678**

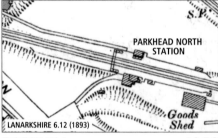

LANARKSHIRE 6.12 (1893)

PARKHILL   16 B3
Opened 18 July 1861 by the Formartine & Buchan Railway
and closed by BR 3 April 1950.
*Line lifted - Demolished - Platform extant - The Formartine and
Buchan Way passes through the station site.* **NJ88979 14453**

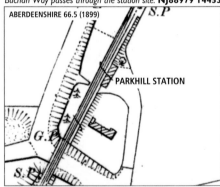

ABERDEENSHIRE 66.5 (1899)

PARKHOUSE HALT*   3A C2
Opened 7 July 1941 by the L&NER as a non-timetabled halt
and closed by BR 6 January 1969.
Line lifted – Demolished – Platform partially extant.
NY38564 60311

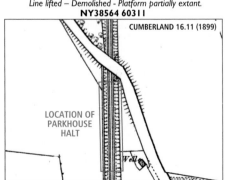

CUMBERLAND 16.11 (1899)

PARKSIDE HALT   18A B1

Opened 27 January 1936 by the LM&SR and closed 3 April 1944.

Line lifted – Demolished – Station site unused.
ND25123 36421

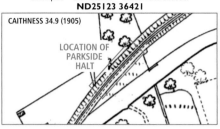

CAITHNESS 34.9 (1905)

LOCATION OF PARKSIDE HALT

PARSONS PLATFORM*   4A C1

Possibly opened by the NBR as a private station for Sir C Parsons and in use in 1937. Closure date unrecorded but it was also known as *Ray House Halt*.

Line lifted – Demolished – A roadway passes through the station site. **NY96833 85649**

Ray Cottage

LOCATION OF PARSONS PLATFORM

NORTHUMBERLAND (OLD) 61.16 (1896)

PARTICK   21A B2

Opened 17 December 1979, re-placing the original station opened 1 December 1882 by the NBR and sited a short distance to the west.

Looking east at **Partick Station** on 13 May 2017.

PARTICK CENTRAL   21A C2

Opened 1 October 1896 by the Lanarkshire & Dumbarton-shire Railway as *Partick Central*, renamed by BR 15 June 1959 as *Kelvin Hall* and closed 5 October 1964.

Line lifted – Demolished – Station site in commercial use.
NS56109 66369

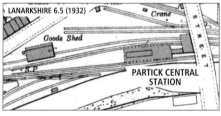

LANARKSHIRE 6.5 (1932)

Crane

Goods Shed

S.P.

PARTICK CENTRAL STATION

STREET

PARTICK WEST   21A B2

Opened 1 October 1896 by the Lanarkshire & Dumbarton-shire Railway and closed by BR 5 October 1964.

Line lifted – Demolished – The Clyde and Loch Lomond Cycleway passes through the station site. **NS55095 66481**

NS5566 (1949)

MEADOW ROAD

PARTICK WEST STATION

SOUTH STREET

PARTON   2 C1

Opened 12 March 1861 by the Portpatrick Railway and closed by BR 14 June 1965.

Line lifted – Station building and platform in private use.
NX69155 70098

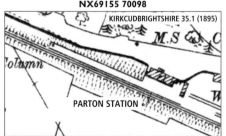

KIRKCUDBRIGHTSHIRE 35.1 (1895)

M.S.C

Column

PARTON STATION

PATNA   6 B4

Opened in 1897 by the G&SWR and closed by BR 6 April 1964.

Line Operational for Freight – Demolished. **NS41685 10931**

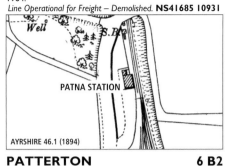

Well   S.B.

PATNA STATION

AYRSHIRE 46.1 (1894)

PATTERTON   6 B2

Opened by the Lanarkshire & Ayr-shire Railway 1 May 1903, closed by CR 1 January 1917, reopened 1 February 1919 as *Patterton for Darnley Rifle Range* and renamed by BR in 1955 as *Patterton*.

Patterton Station on 18 March 2017.

PEACETON BRANCH   6 A2

PEACOCK CROSS   6 C2

Opened in December 1878 by the Glasgow, Bothwell, Hamilton & Coatbridge Railway as *Hamilton Peacock Cross*, renamed in 1882 as *Peacock Cross* and closed by the NBR 1 January 1917.

Line lifted – Demolished – Station site in commercial use.
NS71091 55655

PEACOCK CROSS STATION

LANARKSHIRE 17.4 (1896)

PEEBLES (CR)   7 B2

Opened 1 February 1864 by the Peebles Railway and closed by BR 5 June 1950.

Line lifted – Demolished – Station site occupied by housing.
NT24930 40249

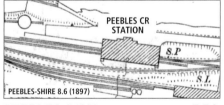

PEEBLES CR STATION

S.P.

PEEBLES-SHIRE 8.6 (1897)

S.L.

PEEBLES (NBR)   7 B2

Opened 1 October 1864 by the Symington, Biggar & Broughton Railway as *Peebles*, renamed by BR 25 September 1950 as *Peebles East*, in 1958 as *Peebles* and closed 5 February 1962.

Line lifted - Demolished - The A703, Edinburgh Road, passes through the station site. **NT25350 40751**

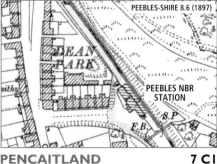

PEEBLES-SHIRE 8.6 (1897)

DEAN PARK

PEEBLES NBR STATION

S.P.

F.B.

PENCAITLAND   7 C1

Opened 14 October 1901 by the Gifford & Garvald Light Railway and closed by the L&NER 3 April 1933.

Line lifted – Demolished - The Pencaitland Railway Walk passes through the station site. **NT43721 68602**

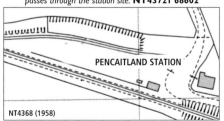

PENCAITLAND STATION

NT4368 (1958)

PENICUIK   7 B1

Opened 2 September 1872 by the Penicuik Railway and closed by BR 10 September 1951.

Line lifted – Demolished - Station site occupied by houses in Bankmill View. **NT23666 59655**

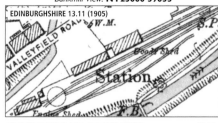

EDINBURGHSHIRE 13.11 (1905)

VALLEYFIELD ROAD   W.M.   S.P.

Station

F.B.

PENICUIK GAS WORKS BRANCH   7 B1

PENTON   3 D1

Opened 1 March 1862 by the Border Union Railway and closed by BR 6 January 1969.

Line lifted - Station building in private use - Platforms partially extant. **NY43944 77330**

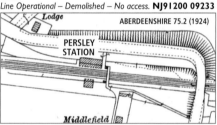

CUMBERLAND 3.13 (1899)

S.P.

PENTON STATION

S.P.

PERSLEY   16 B3

Opened 1 June 1903 by the GNofSR as *Persley*, renamed by the L&NER 16 July 1926 as *Persley Halt* and closed 5 April 1937.

Line Operational – Demolished – No access. **NJ91200 09233**

Lodge

ABERDEENSHIRE 75.2 (1924)

PERSLEY STATION

Middlefield

PERTH   11 A3

Opened by the Scottish Midland Junction Railway 2 August 1848 as *Perth General* and renamed by BR 30 June 1952 as *Perth*.

Class 158 Unit No.158701 at **Perth Station** on 18 September 2015.

PERTH (NBR) GOODS   11 A3

PERTH HARBOUR BRANCH   11 B3

PERTH PRINCES STREET   11 B3

Opened 1 March 1849 by the Dundee & Perth Railway, closed 1 January 1917, reopened 2 June 1919 and closed by BR 28 February 1966.

Line Operational – Demolished – One platform extant – No access. **NO11962 23165**

PERTH & CLACKMANNANSHIRE 98.5 (1900)

WILLIAM STREET   Hotel

NELSON STREET   Timber Yd   W.M.

Princes St. Sta.

Goods Yd   Crane   W.M.

PLACE

PETERHEAD   16 C1

Opened 3 July 1862 by the Formartine & Buchan Railway and closed by BR 3 May 1965.

Line lifted – Demolished – Station site occupied by the "Peterhead Academy". **NK12855 46615**

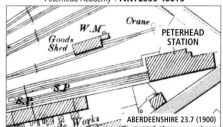

W.M.   Crane

Goods Shed   PETERHEAD STATION

S.P.

S.P.   Works   ABERDEENSHIRE 23.7 (1900)

PETERHEAD HARBOUR BRANCH   **16 C1**

PETTERIL JUNCTION   **3 C2**

PETTYCUR BRANCH   **11 B4**

PHILORTH (PRIVATE)   **19 B4**

Opened 24 April 1865 by the Formartine & Buchan Railway as *Philorth*, a private halt for Philorth House. It was opened to the public by the L&NER 26 July 1926 as *Philorth Halt* and closed by BR 4 October 1965.

Line lifted - Station building in private use - Platform extant - The Formartine and Buchan Way passes through the station site. **NK00693 64623**

PHILORTH STATION

ABERDEENSHIRE 3.9 (1901)

PHILORTH BRIDGE HALT 19A B4

Opened 1 July 1903 by the GNofSR and closed by BR 3 May 1965.

Line lifted - Demolished – A short access road passes through the station site. **NK02176 64443**

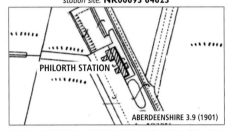

ABERDEENSHIRE 3.10 (1924)

PHILORTH BRIDGE HALT

Well

PHILPSTOUN   **7 A1**

Opened 12 October 1865 by the Edinburgh & Glasgow Railway and closed by BR 18 June 1951.

Line Operational – Demolished – No access. **NT05466 77099**

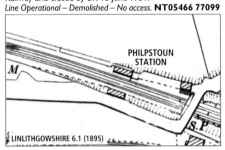

PHILPSTOUN STATION

LINLITHGOWSHIRE 6.1 (1895)

PIERSHILL   **7 C1/22A D2**

Opened 1 May 1891 by the NBR, closed 1 January 1917, reopened 1 April 1919 and closed by BR 7 September 1964.

Line Out of Use – Demolished – Station site unused. **NT28271 74351**

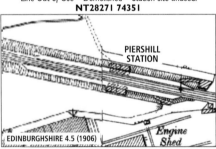

PIERSHILL STATION

EDINBURGHSHIRE 4.5 (1906)

Engine Shed

PILRIG   **22A C1**

Opened c1904 by the CR and closed by the LM&SR c1927.

Line lifted – Demolished – Station site in commercial use. **NT26256 75761 (a)**

NT2675 (1948)

ASSUMED LOCATION

PINKHILL   **22A A2**

Opened 1 February 1902 by the NBR, closed 1 January 1917, reopened 1 February 1919 and closed by BR 1 January 1968.

Line lifted – Demolished – Platforms extant - The Corstorphine Branch Railway Route passes through the station site. **NT21122 72790**

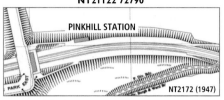

PINKHILL STATION

PARK ST.

NT2172 (1947)

PINMORE   **2 A1**

Opened 19 September 1877 by the Girvan & Portpatrick Junction Railway, closed 7 February 1882, reopened 16 February 1882, closed 12 April 1886, reopened 14 June 1886 and closed by BR 6 September 1965.

Line Operational – Station building in private use – Platforms demolished – No access. **NX20322 91995**

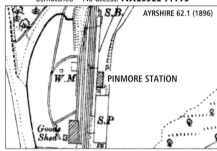

S.B.

AYRSHIRE 62.1 (1896)

W.M.

PINMORE STATION

S.P.

Goods Shed

PINWHERRY   **2 A1**

Opened 19 September 1877 by the Girvan & Portpatrick Junction Railway, closed 7 February 1882, reopened 16 February 1882, closed 12 April 1886, reopened 14 June 1886 and closed by BR 6 September 1965.

Line Operational – Station building in private use – Platforms demolished – No access. **NX19417 87248**

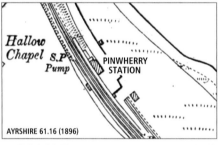

Hallow Chapel

S.P. Pump

PINWHERRY STATION

AYRSHIRE 61.16 (1896)

PITCAPLE   **16 A2**

Opened 20 September 1854 by the GNofSR and closed by BR 6 May 1968.

Line Operational – Demolished – No access. **NJ7231725670**

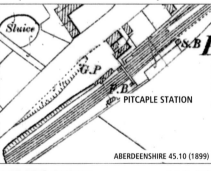

Sluice

G.P.

F.B.

PITCAPLE STATION

ABERDEENSHIRE 45.10 (1899)

PITCROCKNIE   **11A B2**

Opened in June 1912 by the CR as *Porterochney*, renamed in 1912 as *Pitcrocknie* and enjoyed only erratic use until closed by the LM&SR in c1947.

Line lifted – Demolished – Station site in use as part of car park and walkway at Alyth Golf Club. **NO26056 48328**

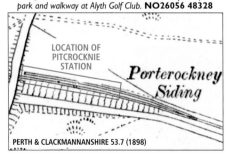

LOCATION OF PITCROCKNIE STATION

Porterockney Siding

PERTH & CLACKMANNANSHIRE 53.7 (1898)

PITFODELS   **16 B3**

Opened 2 July 1894 by the GNofSR as *Pitfodels*, renamed by the L&NER 16 July 1926 as *Pitfodels Halt* and closed 5 April 1937.

Line lifted - Platforms and station building extant - The Deeside Way passes through the station site. **NJ90650 03304**

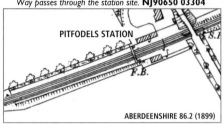

PITFODELS STATION

F.B.

ABERDEENSHIRE 86.2 (1899)

PITLOCHRY   **10 D1**

Opened 1 June 1863 by the Inverness & Perth Junction Railway as *Pitlochry*, renamed by the LM&SR in 1930 as *Pitlochry for Kinloch-Rannoch* and reverted to *Pitlochry* by BR in 1955.

Pitlochry Station on 15 September 2015.

PITLURG   **16 B2**

Opened 2 August 1897 by the GNofSR and closed by the L&NER 31 October 1932.

Line lifted – Demolished – Platforms partially extant – Station site unused. **NK02091 34343**

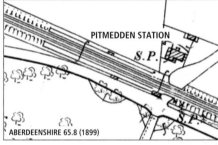

ABERDEENSHIRE 39.6 (1899)

S.B.

F.B.

PITLURG STATION

PITMEDDEN   **16 B3**

Opened in November 1873 by the GNofSR and closed by BR 7 December 1964.

Line Operational – Demolished. **NJ8637915003**

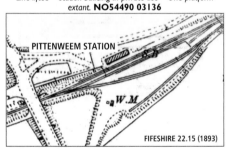

PITMEDDEN STATION

S.P.

ABERDEENSHIRE 65.8 (1899)

PITTENWEEM   **11 D3**

Opened 1 September 1863 by the Leven & East of Fife Railway, closed by the NBR 1 January 1917, reopened 1 February 1919 and closed by BR 6 September 1965.

Line lifted – Station building in private use – One platform extant. **NO54490 03136**

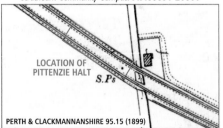

PITTENWEEM STATION

W.M.

FIFESHIRE 22.15 (1893)

PITTENZIE HALT   **10A D3**

Opened 15 September 1958 by BR and closed 6 July 1964.

Line lifted – Demolished – Station site occupied by part of Strathearn Community Campus. **NN86831 20800**

LOCATION OF PITTENZIE HALT

S.Ps

PERTH & CLACKMANNANSHIRE 95.15 (1899)

PLAIDY 16 A1

Opened 4 June 1860 by the Banff, Macduff & Turriff Extension Railway and closed by the L&NER 22 May 1944.

Line lifted – Demolished – Station site occupied by a dwelling.
NJ72899 54859

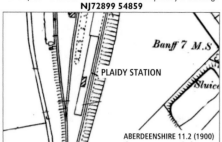
ABERDEENSHIRE 11.2 (1900)

PLAINS 6 D1

Opened in May 1882 by the Bathgate & Coatbridge Railway and closed by BR 18 June 1951.

Line Operational – Demolished – No access. **NS79742 66763**

LANARKSHIRE 8.7 (1897)

PLASHETTS 8 A4

Opened 1 January 1862 by the Border Counties Railway and closed by BR 15 October 1956.

Line lifted – Demolished – Station site under Kielder Water.
NY66596 90156

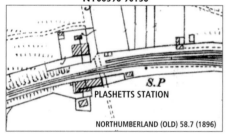
NORTHUMBERLAND (OLD) 58.7 (1896)

PLEAN 10 D4

Opened 1 March 1904 by the CR and closed by BR 11 June 1956.

Line Operational – Demolished – No access. **NS83641 88318**

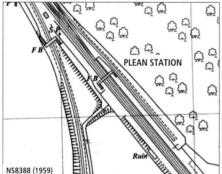
NS8388 (1959)

PLEAN PITS BRANCH 10 D4

PLOCKTON 13 B2

Opened by the HR 2 November 1897.

Looking east at **Plockton Station** on 17 September 2015.

POLKEMMET WEIGHS SIDINGS 7 A1

POLLOCKSHAWS EAST 6 C1/21A C4

Opened by the Cathcart District Railway 2 April 1894 as *Pollockshaws* and renamed by BR 5 May 1952 as *Pollockshaws East*.

Pollockshaws East Station on 18 March 2017.

POLLOCKSHAWS WEST 6 C1/21A C4

Opened by the Glasgow, Barrhead & Neilston Direct Railway 27 September 1848 as *Pollockshaws* and renamed by BR 5 May 1952 as *Pollockshaws West*.

Pollockshaws West Station on 18 March 2017.

POLLOKSHIELDS 21A C3

Opened in September 1862 by the Glasgow, Paisley, Kilmarnock & Ayr Railway, it was amalgamated with *Shields (G&SWR)* and *Shields Road (City of Glasgow Union Railway)* stations by the LM&SR 1 April 1925 and designated as *Shields Road (qv)*.

Line Operational – Demolished – No access. **NS57636 63974**

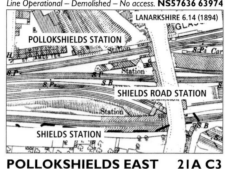
LANARKSHIRE 6.14 (1894)

POLLOKSHIELDS EAST 21A C3

Opened by the Cathcart District Railway 1 March 1886, closed 1 January 1917 and reopened 1 April 1919.

Pollockshields East Station on 18 March 2017.

POLLOKSHIELDS WEST 21A C3

Opened 2 April 1894 by the Cathcart District Railway.

Pollockshields West Station on 18 March 2017.

POLMONT 7 A1

Opened 21 February 1842 by the Edinburgh & Glasgow Railway.

Class 170 Unit No.170458 at **Polmont Station** on 13 May 2017.

POLTON 7 C1/22A D4

Opened 15 April 1867 by the Esk Valley Railway and closed by BR 10 September 1951.

Line lifted – Demolished - Station site occupied by housing in Stevenson Place. **NT28885 64830**

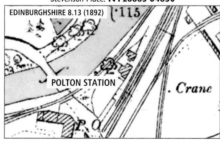
EDINBURGHSHIRE 8.13 (1892)

POMATHORN 7 B1

Opened 4 July 1855 by the Peebles Railway as *Penicuik*, renamed by the NBR 2 September 1872 as *Pomathorn*, by the L&NER 7 July 1947 as *Pomathorn Halt* and closed by BR 5 February 1962.

Line lifted – Platform partially extant – Station site unused.
NT24240 59270

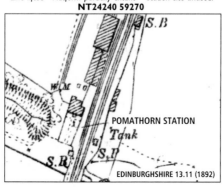
EDINBURGHSHIRE 13.11 (1892)

PONFEIGH 6 D3

Opened in December 1865 by the CR and closed by BR 5 October 1964.

Line lifted – Demolished – Station site in commercial use.
NS87345 36564

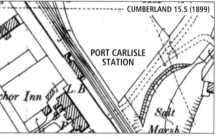
LANARKSHIRE 32.15 (1896)

POOL COLLIERY 7 A2
PORT CARLISLE 3 C2

Opened 22 June 1854 by the Port Carlisle Railway, closed by the NBR 1 January 1917, reopened 1 February 1919 and closed by the L&NER 1 June 1932.

Line lifted – Demolished – Platform partially extant – Station site in use as car park for the "Port Carlisle Bowling Club".
NY24041 62222

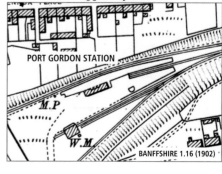
CUMBERLAND 15.5 (1899)

PORT CARLISLE DOCK BRANCH 3 C2
PORT ELPHINSTONE 16 A2
PORTESSIE (GNofSR) 18 C4

Opened 1 May 1866 by the GNofSR and closed by BR 6 May 1968.

PORTESSIE (HR) 18 C4

Opened 1 August 1884 by the HR and closed 9 August 1915.

It can only be assumed that its reference on the map was in anticipation of reopening at a later date.

Lines lifted – Demolished – The Moray Coast Trail passes through the station site. **NJ44611 66578**

BANFFSHIRE 2.6 (1902)

PORTESSIE JUNCTION 18 C4
PORT GLASGOW 6 A1

Opened by the Glasgow, Paisley & Greenock Railway 31 March 1841.

Port Glasgow Station on 17 March 2017.

PORT GORDON 18 C4

Opened 1 May 1886 by the GNofSR and closed by BR 6 May 1968.

Line lifted – Demolished – Station site occupied by a small park and bowling green. **NJ39418 64068**

BANFFSHIRE 1.16 (1902)

PORTKNOCKIE 18 C4
Opened 1 May 1886 by the GNofSR and closed by BR 6 May 1968.
Line lifted – Demolished – Station site occupied by housing in Station Court. **NJ48629 68326**

BANFFSHIRE 2.4 (1902)

PORTLETHEN 16 B3
Opened by the Aberdeen Railway 1 February 1850, closed by BR 11 June 1956 and reopened 17 May 1985.

Class 170 Unit No.170413 at **Portlethen** Station on 18 September 2015.

PORTOBELLO 7 C1/22A D2
Opened 22 June 1846 by the Edinburgh & Dalkeith Railway and closed by BR 7 September 1964.
Line Operational – Demolished – No access. **NT30326 73503**

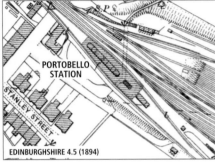
EDINBURGHSHIRE 4.5 (1894)

PORT OF MENTEITH 10 C4
Opened 26 May 1856 by the Forth & Clyde Junction Railway as *Cardross*, renamed in 1858 as *Port of Monteith*, in 1880 as *Port of Menteith* and closed by the L&NER 1 October 1934.
Line lifted – Station House in private use – Demolished. **NS60331 96092**

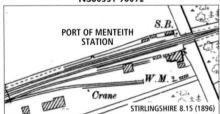
STIRLINGSHIRE 8.15 (1896)

PORTPATRICK 1 D2
Opened 28 August 1862 by the Portpatrick Railway and closed by BR 6 February 1950.
Line lifted – Demolished – Station site occupied by housing in Old Station Court. **NX00281 54450**

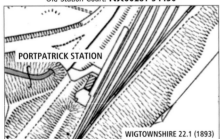
WIGTOWNSHIRE 22.1 (1893)

PORTSOY 18 D4
Opened 1 April 1884 by the GNofSR and closed by BR 6 May 1968.
Line lifted – Station building in use as "Portsoy Scout Hall". **NJ58927 65692**

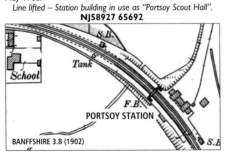
BANFFSHIRE 3.8 (1902)

POSSIL 21A C1
Opened 1 February 1897 by the Lanarkshire & Dumbartonshire Railway for workmen's trains, opened to the public 1 October 1897, closed 1 May 1908, reopened by the LM&SR 8 January 1934 and closed by BR 5 October 1964.
Line lifted – Demolished – Station site occupied by demolition contractors. **NS58732 68853**

NS5868 (1950)

POSSILPARK & PARKHOUSE 21A D2
Opened 3 December 1993 on the opposite side of the roadbridge to the original *Possilpark* station which was opened by the NBR in February 1885 and closed 1 January 1917.

Possilpark & Parkhouse Station on 13 May 2017.

POTTERHILL 6 B1
Opened 1 June 1886 by the G&SWR, closed to passengers 1 January 1917 and to goods by BR 9 June 1959.
Line lifted – Demolished – Station building in private use – Remainder of site occupied by housing in Lapsley Avenue. **NS48339 61909**

RENFREWSHIRE 12.6 (1895)

POWFOOT HALT* 3A B2
Opened in May 1941 by the LM&SR for ICI explosives factory workers. Closure date unknown.
Line Operational – Demolished. **NY16390 66393**

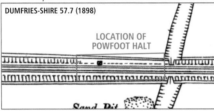
DUMFRIES-SHIRE 57.7 (1898)
LOCATION OF POWFOOT HALT

PRESTONPANS 7 C1
Opened by the NBR 22 June 1846 as *Tranent* and renamed 1 July 1858 as *Prestonpans*.

Looking west at **Prestonpans** Station on 19 September 2015.

PRESTWICK 6 A3
Opened 5 August 1839 by the Glasgow, Paisley, Kilmarnock & Ayr Railway as *Prestwick*, closed 10 October 1839, reopened in June 1841, closed 29 November 1841, reopened in March 1846 and renamed by BR 28 May 1995 as *Prestwick Town*.

Prestwick Town Station on 16 March 2017.

PRESTWICK INTERNATIONAL AIRPORT 6A A3
Opened 5 September 1994 as *Glasgow Prestwick Airport* and subsequently renamed as *Prestwick International Airport*.

Looking north at **Prestwick International Airport** Station on 16 March 2017.

PRIESTHILL & DARNLEY 21A B4
Opened 23 April 1990.

Class 156 Unit No.156503 at **Priestfield & Darnley** Station on 18 March 2017.

PRINCES PIER (See GREENOCK)
PRINT WORKS BRANCH 6 C2

QUARTER 6 C2
Opened 2 February 1863 by the Hamilton & Strathaven Railway as *Quarter Road*, renamed by the CR 1 May 1909 as *Quarter* and closed by the LM&SR 1 October 1945.
Line lifted – Demolished – Station site landscaped as part of a garden. **NS71852 51064**

LANARKSHIRE 17.16 (1896)

QUEENS PARK (GLASGOW) 21A C3
Opened 1 March 1886 by the Cathcart District Railway.

Queens Park (Glasgow) Station on 18 March 2017.

RACKS 3 A1
Opened in 1851 by the Glasgow, Dumfries and Carlisle Railway and closed by BR 6 December 1965.
Line Operational – Station building in private use – Platforms demolished. **NY03319 74329**

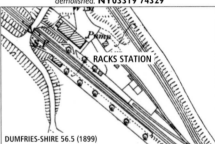
DUMFRIES-SHIRE 56.5 (1899)

RANKINSTON 6 B4
Opened 1 January 1884 by the G&SWR and closed by BR 3 April 1950.
Line lifted – Demolished – Station site landscaped. **NS45122 14432**

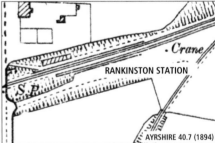
AYRSHIRE 40.7 (1894)

RANNOCH 10 B1
Opened 7 August 1894 by the NBR as *Rannoch for Kinloch-Rannoch* and renamed by BR c1987 as *Rannoch*.

Looking north at **Rannoch** Station on 15 September 2015.

RATCHILL SIDING* 16A A2
Opened c1903 by GNofSR for workmen's trains and closed by the LN&ER c1938.
Line lifted – Demolished – A service road for a quarry passes through the station site. **NJ76793 17292**

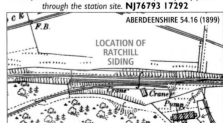
ABERDEENSHIRE 54.16 (1899)
LOCATION OF RATCHILL SIDING

RATHEN 19 B4
Opened 24 April 1865 by the Formartine & Buchan Railway and closed by BR 4 October 1965.
Line lifted - Station building in private use - Platform extant - The Formartine and Buchan Way passes through the station site. **NK01598 62412**

ABERDEENSHIRE 3.14 (1900)

RATHO 7 B1
Opened 21 February 1842 by the Edinburgh & Glasgow Railway and closed by BR 18 June 1951.
Line Operational – Demolished – Platforms partially extant – No access. **NT13268 72181**

RATHO (LOW LEVEL) 7 B1
Opened 1 March 1866 by the Edinburgh & Glasgow Railway and closed by the L&NER 22 September 1930.
Line lifted – Demolished – Station site unused. **NT13283 72233**

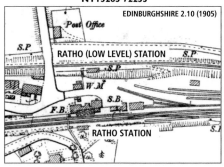
EDINBURGHSHIRE 2.10 (1905)

RATHVEN 18 C4
Opened 1 August 1884 by the HR and closed 9 August 1915. *It can only be assumed that its appearance on the map was in anticipation of reopening at a later date.*
Line lifted – Demolished – Station site unused. **NJ44145 64524**

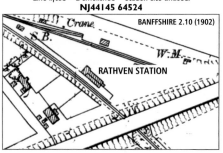
BANFFSHIRE 2.10 (1902)

RAVELRIG 7 B1
Opened 4 April 1884 by the CR, closed in June 1920, reopened by the LM&SR in 1927 and closed in January 1945. It was also known as *Ravelrig Junction, Ravelrig Platform, Ravelrig Halt* and *Ravelrig Junction Platform* in various timetables.
Line Operational – Demolished. **NT14345 67611**

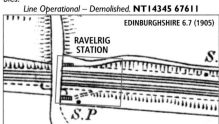
EDINBURGHSHIRE 6.7 (1905)

RAVENSCRAIG 6 A1
Opened 15 May 1865 by the Greenock & Wemyss Bay Railway, closed 1 January 1917, reopened 2 June 1919 and closed by the LM&SR 1 February 1944.
Line Operational – Demolished – No access. **NS24390 75082**

RENFREWSHIRE 1.12 (1896)

RAVENSWOOD JUNCTION 7 D3
RAWYARDS 6 D1
Opened prior to March 1845 by the Ballochney Railway and closed by the L&NER 1 May 1930.
Line lifted – Demolished – Station site occupied by housing and the west end of Northburn Avenue. **NS76737 66410**

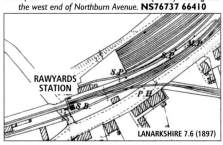
LANARKSHIRE 7.6 (1897)

REDCASTLE 14 B1
Opened 1 February 1894 by the HR and closed by BR 1 October 1951.
Line lifted – Station building and platform in private use. **NH58240 51104**

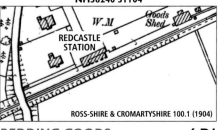
ROSS-SHIRE & CROMARTYSHIRE 100.1 (1904)

REDDING GOODS 6 D1
REEDSMOUTH 4 B1
Opened 1 November 1864 by the Border Counties Railway and closed by BR 15 October 1956.
Line lifted - Station building and platforms in private use. **NY86517 82006**

NORTHUMBERLAND (OLD) 68.11 (1895)

RENFREW FULBAR STREET 6 B1/21A A2
Opened 1 May 1866 by the Paisley & Renfrew Railway as *Renfrew*, renamed in September 1867 as *Renfrew Fulbar Street* and closed by BR 5 June 1967.
Line lifted – Demolished – Station House in private use. **NS50530 67931**

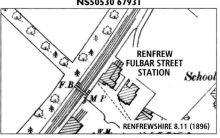
RENFREWSHIRE 8.11 (1896)

RENFREW PORTERFIELD 6A B1
Opened 1 June 1903 by the Glasgow & Renfrew District Railway, closed by the LM&SR 5 June 1926, reopened 14 June 1926 and closed 19 July 1926.
Line lifted – Demolished – Station site occupied by housing in Nethergreen Crescent. **NS49759 67155**

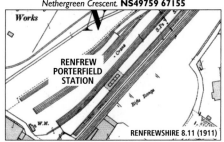
RENFREWSHIRE 8.11 (1911)

RENFREW WHARF 6 B1/21A A2
Opened 3 April 1837 by the Paisley & Renfrew Railway, closed 1 February 1866, reopened in September 1867 and closed by BR 5 June 1967.
Line lifted – Demolished – Station site unused. **NS50874 68490**

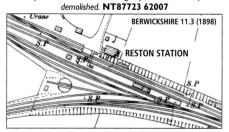
RENFREWSHIRE 8.7 (1895)

RENTON 6 B1
Opened 15 July 1850 by the Caledonian & Dumbartonshire Railway.

Class 320 Unit No.320304 at **Renton Station** on 13 September 2015.

RESTON 8 B1
Opened 22 June 1846 by the NBR and closed by BR 4 May 1964. It was also known as *Reston Junction, Reston for Coldingham & St Abbs* and *Reston for St Abbs* in various timetables.
Line Operational – Station building in private use – Platforms demolished. **NT87723 62007**

BERWICKSHIRE 11.3 (1898)

RHU 10 A4
Opened 7 August 1894 by the West Highland Railway as *Row*, renamed by the L&NER 24 February 1927 as *Rhu* closed by BR 9 January 1956, reopened 4 April 1960 as *Rhu Halt* and closed 15 June 1964.
Line Operational – Demolished - Degraded platforms extant. **NS27294 84461**

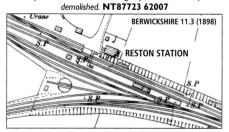
DUMBARTONSHIRE 16.4 (1897)

RICCARTON & CRAIGIE 6 B3
Opened in 1902 by the G&SWR but was never provided with a passenger service and closed to goods by BR 5 July 1965.
Line lifted – Demolished – The A71 passes through the station site. **NS42565 36463**

AYRSHIRE 23.1 (1906)

RICCARTON JUNCTION 7 D4
Opened 2 June 1862 by the Border Union Railway as *Riccarton*, renamed by the NBR 1 January 1905 as *Riccarton Junction* and closed by BR 6 January 1969.
Line lifted – Demolished - Platforms partially extant. **NY53947 97704**

ROXBURGHSHIRE 39.13 (1896)

RIDDINGS　　　　　　　　3 C1

Opened 1 March 1862 by the Border Union Railway as *Riddings Junction* and closed by BR 15 June 1964.
Line lifted - Station building in commercial use – Station site part of Riddings Farm. **NY40767 75152**

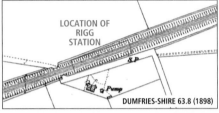

RIGG　　　　　　　　　　3 C2

Opened 1 June 1901 by the Glasgow, Dumfries and Carlisle Railway and although closed by the LM&SR 1 November 1942 it continued to be used by workmen's trains for a time.
Line Operational – Demolished – No access. **NY28702 66969**

ROBROYSTON　　　　　　6A C1

Opened 1 November 1898 by the CR, closed 1 January 1917, reopened 2 June 1919, closed by BR 11 July 1956 and reopened on a site slightly to the east on 15 December 2019.

Robroyston Station on 13 September 2020.

ROCKCLIFFE*　　　　　　3 C2

Opened 10 September 1847 by the CR, closed 1 January 1917, reopened 2 December 1919 and although closed by BR 17 July 1950 workmen's trains continued to use it until 6 December 1965.
Line Operational – Station Master's House in private use – Demolished. **NY36998 61160**

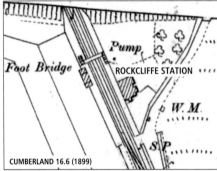

ROGART　　　　　　　　17 C3

Opened 13 April 1868 by the Sutherland Railway, closed by BR 13 June 1960, reopened 6 March 1961, renamed as *Rogart Halt* 12 June 1961 and as *Rogart* 17 May 1982. Looking west at **Rogart Station** on 16 September 2015.

ROME STREET JUNCTION　　3 C2

ROSEHAUGH*　　　　　　14A C1

Opened by the HR as a private station for Rosehaugh House. Opening and closure dates unknown.
Line lifted – Demolished – Station site in use as part of a field.
NH68316 54987

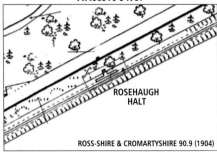

ROSEMILL　　　　　　　11 C2

Opened in 1862 by the CR, closed to passengers in 1904 and to goods by BR 10 August 1964.
Line lifted – Station building and platform in private use – The Railway Path passes through the station site.
NO36420 35431

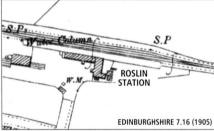

ROSEMOUNT　　　　　　11 B2

Opened in September 1857 by the Scottish Midland Junction Railway and closed by BR 10 January 1955.
Line lifted – Station House in private use – Platforms extant.
NO19052 43209

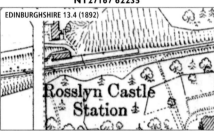

ROSLIN　　　　　　7 B1/22A C4

Opened 23 July 1874 by the Edinburgh, Loanhead & Roslin Railway and closed by the L&NER 1 May 1933.
Line lifted – Demolished - Station site occupied by housing in Station Road. **NT27212 63577**

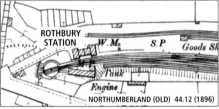

ROSSLYN CASTLE　　　7 B1/22A C4

Opened 2 September 1872 by the Penicuik Railway as *Rosslyn*, renamed 16 February 1874 as *Rosslyn Castle* and closed by BR 10 September 1951.
Line lifted - Platform extant - The Penicuik to Musselburgh Cycle-Walkway passes through the station site.
NT27167 62235

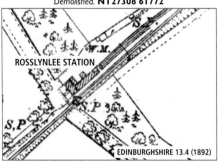

ROSSLYNLEE　　　　　7 C1/22A C4

Opened 4 July 1855 by the Penicuik Railway as *Roslin*, renamed in 1864 as *Rosslyn*, 2 September 1872 as *Rosslynlee*, closed 1 January 1917, reopened 2 June 1919 and closed by BR 5 February 1962.
Line lifted - Station building in private use – Platform Demolished. **NT27308 61772**

ROSSLYNLEE HOSPITAL　　7A B1
HALT

Opened 11 December 1958 by BR and closed 5 February 1962.
Line lifted – Station site unused.
NT2640760906

ROSTER ROAD HALT　　　18A B1

Opened 27 January 1936 by the LM&SR and closed 3 April 1944.
Line lifted – Demolished – A short driveway passes through the station site. **ND29199 37437**

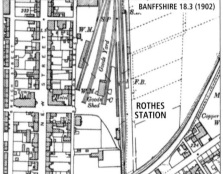

ROSYTH　　　　　　　　11A B4

Opened 28 March 1917 by the NBR as *Rosyth Halt* (unadvertised), opened to the public 1 December 1919 and renamed by BR 16 May 1983 as *Rosyth*.

Rosyth Station on 18 September 2015.

ROTHBURY　　　　　　　8 C4

Opened 1 November 1870 by the Northumberland Central Railway and closed by BR 15 September 1952.
Line lifted – Demolished - Station site occupied by "Rothbury Fire Station". **NU06252 01616**

ROTHES　　　　　　　　15 B1

Opened 23 August 1858 by the Morayshire Railway and closed by BR 6 May 1968.
Line lifted – Demolished – Station site occupied by commercial premises in Station Street. **NJ27862 49409**

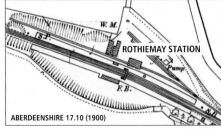

ROTHIEMAY　　　　　　15 D1

Opened 11 October 1856 by the GNofSR and closed by BR 6 May 1968.
Line Operational – Demolished. **NJ53116 46067**

ROTHIE-NORMAN 16 A2

Opened 5 September 1857 by the Banff, Macduff & Turriff Junction Railway as *Rothie*, renamed by the GNofSR 1 March 1870 as *Rothie-Norman* and closed by BR 1 October 1951.

Line lifted – Demolished - Station site occupied by a car park. **NJ72301 35555**

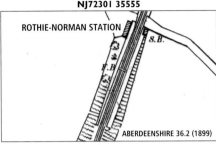

ROTHIE-NORMAN STATION — S.B.

ABERDEENSHIRE 36.2 (1899)

ROUGH CASTLE GOODS 6 D1
ROUGHRIGG COLLIERY (EAST) 6 D1
ROW (See RHU)
ROXBURGH 8 A3

Opened 17 June 1850 by the NBR and closed by BR 15 June 1964.

Line lifted – Station building in private use – Platforms Demolished. **NT69748 30553**

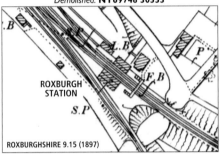

ROXBURGH STATION — S.P.

ROXBURGHSHIRE 9.15 (1897)

ROY BRIDGE 14 A4

Opened 7 August 1894 by the West Highland Railway.

Looking west at **Roy Bridge Station** on 14 September 2015.

RUMBLING BRIDGE 11 A4

Opened 1 October 1870 by the NBR and closed by BR 15 June 1964.

Line lifted – Demolished – One platform extant – A roadway passes through the station site. **NT01826 99341**

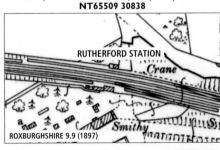

PERTH & CLACKMANNANSHIRE 135.1 (1899)

RUMBLING BRIDGE STATION

RUTHERFORD 8 A3

Opened in June 1851 by the NBR and closed by BR 15 June 1964.

Line lifted – Demolished – Platforms partially extant. **NT65509 30838**

RUTHERFORD STATION — Crane

Smithy

ROXBURGHSHIRE 9.9 (1897)

RUTHERGLEN (BR) 21A D3

Opened 5 November 1979 and replaced the original station (*qv*), on the Dalmarnock line.

Class 320 Unit No.320317 at **Rutherglen Station** on 18 March 2017.

RUTHERGLEN (CR) 6 C1

Opened 31 March 1879 by the CR and closed by BR 5 November 1979.

Lines Operational – Demolished - Platforms on east side of triangle now occupied by **RUTHERGLEN** (BR) *station.* **NS61303 61878**

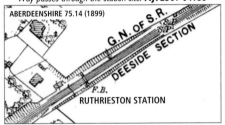

LANARKSHIRE 10.3 (1893)

MIDDLE WARD

RUTHERGLEN STATION

RUTHRIESTON 16 B3

Opened in June 1856 by the Deeside Railway, closed by the GNofSR in April 1867, reopened 1 June 1885 and closed by the L&NER 5 April 1937.

Line lifted – Demolished – One platform extant – The Deeside Way passes through the station site. **NJ92507 04153**

ABERDEENSHIRE 75.14 (1899)

G.N. OF S.R. DEESIDE SECTION

F.B. RUTHRIESTON STATION

RUTHVEN ROAD 11 A3

Opened in May 1859 by the Perth, Almond Valley & Methven Railway and closed by BR 1 October 1951. It was also known as *Ruthven Road Crossing*, *Ruthven Road Siding* and *Ruthven Road Halt* in various timetables.

Line lifted – Station House in private use – An access road passes through the station site. **NO08103 25655**

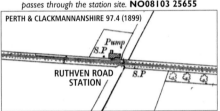

PERTH & CLACKMANNANSHIRE 97.4 (1899)

Pump S.P.

RUTHVEN ROAD STATION — S.P.

RUTHWELL 3 B1

Opened 23 August 1848 by the Glasgow, Dumfries and Carlisle Railway and closed by BR 6 December 1965.

Line Operational – Station building in private use – Platforms demolished. **NY09013 69581**

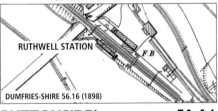

RUTHWELL STATION — F.B.

DUMFRIES-SHIRE 56.16 (1898)

RUTTONSIDE* 7A A4

Opened 3 January 1900 by the CR for railwaymen and families and closed by the LM&SR after 1926.

Line Operational – Demolished. **NT04055 07996 (a)**

DUMFRIES-SHIRE 16.1 (1898)

Sheepfold

Ruttonside

ASSUMED LOCATION

RYELAND 6 C2

Opened 1 May 1905 by the CR, closed 1 July 1909, reopened 1 November 1909, closed 1 January 1917, reopened in August 1919 and closed by the LM&SR 11 September 1939.

Line lifted – Demolished – Station site unused. **NS65537 40344**

Ryeland

RYELAND STATION

NS6540 (1967)

ST ANDREWS 11 D3

Opened 1 June 1887 by the NBR and closed by BR 6 January 1969.

Line lifted – Demolished - Station site occupied by part of Potherham Bridge Car Park. **NO50421 16754**

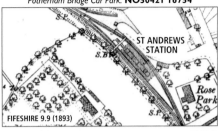

ST ANDREWS STATION

Rose Park

FIFESHIRE 9.9 (1893)

ST BOSWELLS 7 D3

Opened 20 February 1849 by the NBR and closed by BR 6 January 1969.

Line lifted – Demolished – Platforms partially extant. **NT57735 31620**

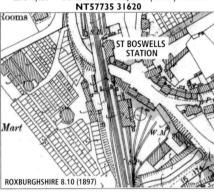

Rooms

Mart

ST BOSWELLS STATION

W.M.

ROXBURGHSHIRE 8.10 (1897)

ST BRIDE'S CROSSING* 10A C3

Opened by the CR at an unknown date and closed by the LM&SR after July 1926.

Line lifted – Demolished – Rob Roy Way passes through the station site. **NN58371 10072**

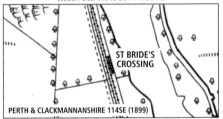

ST BRIDE'S CROSSING

PERTH & CLACKMANNANSHIRE 114SE (1899)

ST COMBS 19 C4

Opened 1 July 1903 by the GNofSR and closed by BR 3 May 1965.

Line lifted - Demolished – Station site in use as a small children's grassed play area. **NK05332 63104**

ST COMBS STATION

W.M.

ABERDEENSHIRE 3.15 (1924)

ST CYRUS 12 A1

Opened 1 November 1865 by the Montrose & Bervie Railway and closed by BR 1 October 1951.

Line lifted – Demolished – Platforms partially extant – Station site partially occupied by housing in Old Station Square. **NO74788 64863**

S.B.

ST CYRUS STATION

W.M.

Goods Shed

Well

KINCARDINESHIRE 30.3 (1901)

ST FILLANS   10 C3
Opened 1 October 1901 by the Comrie, St Fillans & Lochearnhead Railway and closed by BR 1 October 1951. *Line lifted – Demolished – Station buildings extant - Station site in use as a caravan park.* **NN69967 24397**

ROUTE OF TRACK SUPERIMPOSED   NN6924 (1969)

ST FORT   11 C3
Opened 1 June 1878 by the NBR and closed by BR 6 September 1965. *Line Operational – Station building in private use – No access.* **NO41077 24284**

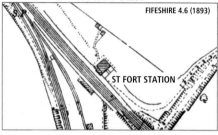

FIFESHIRE 4.6 (1893)

ST JAMES (PAISLEY)
(See **PAISLEY ST JAMES**)

ST MARNOCKS GOODS   6 B3
ST MONANS   11 D4
Opened 1 September 1863 by the Leven & East of Fife Railway as *St Monance*, renamed by the NBR in 1875 as *St Monans*, by the L&NER in 1936 as *St Monance* and closed by BR 6 September 1965. *Line lifted – Station building in use as the "East Neuk Veterinary Practice" – Platforms demolished.* **NO52397 01937**

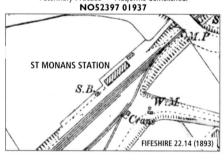

FIFESHIRE 22.14 (1893)

ST ROLLOX   21A D2
Opened 1 August 1883 by the Glasgow, Garnkirk & Coatbridge Railway and closed by BR 5 November 1962. *Line lifted – Demolished – A service road passes through the landscaped station site.* **NS60445 66783**

LANARKSHIRE 6.7 (1894)

SALTCOATS (CR)   6 A2
Opened 4 September 1888 by the Lanarkshire & Ayrshire Railway as *Saltcoats*, closed 1 January 1917, reopened 1 February 1919, renamed by the LM&SR 2 June 1924 as *Saltcoats North* and closed 4 July 1932. *Line lifted – Demolished – Station site occupied by housing in Argyle Place.* **NS24540 41941**

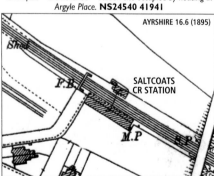

AYRSHIRE 16.6 (1895)

SALTCOATS (G&SWR)   6 A2
Opened by the G&SWR in 1882 as *Saltcoats*, renamed by BR 30 June 1952 as *Saltcoats Central*, and reverted back to *Saltcoats* 4 February 1965,

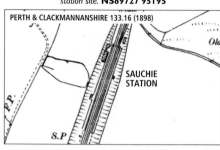

Saltcoats Station on 16 March 2017.

SALTOUN   7 D1
Opened 14 October 1901 by the Gifford & Garvald Light Railway and closed by the L&NER 3 April 1933. *Line lifted – Demolished – Station site unused.* **NT45446 66567**

HADDINGTONSHIRE 14.8 (1906)

SALZCRAGGIE   17A D2
Opened 28 July 1874 by the HR for a private shooting estate, and made available to the public from July 1907. It was closed by BR 29 November 1965 and was also known as *Salzcraggie Halt* and *Salzcraggie Platform*. *Line Operational – Demolished – No access.* **NC99531 18144**

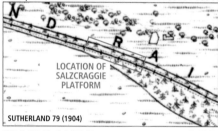

SUTHERLAND 79 (1904)

SANDILANDS   6 C2
Opened 1 April 1864 by the CR and closed by BR 5 October 1964. *Line lifted – Demolished – Station site unused.* **NS89183 38673**

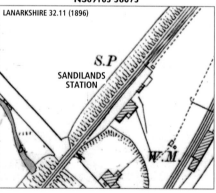

LANARKSHIRE 32.11 (1896)

SANDYFORD PLATFORM   6A B1
Opened in June 1914 by the G&SWR for workmen's trains as *Sandyford Platform*, renamed by the LM&SR in 1941 as *Sandyford Halt*, opened to the public by BR 18 April 1966 and closed 5 June 1967. *Line lifted – Demolished – Station site unused.* **NS48946 66284**

NS4866 (1949)

SANQUHAR   6 D4
Opened 28 October 1850 by the Glasgow, Paisley, Kilmarnock and Ayr Railway, closed by BR 6 December 1965 and reopened 27 June 1994.

Sanquhar Station on 20 March 2017.

SAUCHIE   10 D4
Opened in October 1873 by the Stirling & Dunfermline Railway, closed by the NBR 1 January 1917, reopened 2 June 1919 and closed by the L&NER 22 September 1930. *Line lifted – Demolished - The Devon Way passes through the station site.* **NS89727 95195**

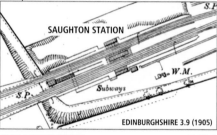

PERTH & CLACKMANNANSHIRE 133.16 (1898)

SAUGHTON   7 B1/22A A2
Opened 21 February 1842 by the Edinburgh & Glasgow Railway as *Corstorphine*, renamed by the NBR 1 February 1902 as *Saughtree*, closed 1 January 1917, reopened 1 February 1919 and closed 1 March 1921. *Line Operational – Demolished – No access.* **NT20503 71843**

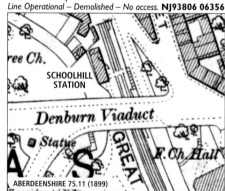

EDINBURGHSHIRE 3.9 (1905)

SAUGHTREE   7 D4
Opened 1 July 1862 by the Border Counties Railway, closed by the L&NER 1 December 1944, reopened by BR 23 August 1948 and closed 15 October 1956. *Line lifted - Station building in private use as "Saughtree Station B&B" – Platform restored with a short length of relaid track.* **NY56466 98080**

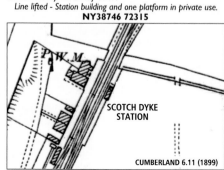

ROXBURGHSHIRE 39.14 (1896)

SCHOOLHILL   16 B3
Opened 1 September 1893 by the GNofSR and closed by the L&NER 5 April 1937. *Line Operational – Demolished – No access.* **NJ93806 06356**

ABERDEENSHIRE 75.11 (1899)

SCOTCH DYKE   3 C1
Opened 29 October 1861 by the Border Union Railway and closed by BR 2 May 1949. *Line lifted - Station building and one platform in private use.* **NY38746 72315**

CUMBERLAND 6.11 (1899)

SCOTSCALDER 20 A4

Opened 28 July 1874 by the Sutherland & Caithness Railway.

Looking south at **Scotscalder Station** on 16 September 2015.

SCOTSGAP 4 C1

Opened 23 July 1862 by the Wansbeck Railway as *Scots Gap Junction*, renamed by the NBR in 1901 as *Scotsgap* and closed by BR 15 September 1952. It was also known as *Scots Gap for Cambo* and *Scotsgap for Cambo* in some timetables.
Line lifted - Station building in private use - Platform extant – Remainder of station site in commercial use.
NZ03865 86402

SCOTSTOUN 21A A2

Opened 1 October 1896 by the Lanarkshire & Dumbartonshire Railway as *Victoria Park*, renamed by the CR 1 October 1901 as *Scotstoun*, by BR 30 June 1952 as *Scotstoun East* and closed 5 October 1964.
Line lifted – Demolished – Platform extant - The Clyde and Loch Lomond Cycleway passes through the station site.
NS53380 67171

SCOTSTOUNHILL 21A B2

Opened 1 December 1882 by the Glasgow, Yoker & Clydebank Railway.

Looking north at **Scotstounhill Station** on 13 September 2015.

SCOTSTOUN SHOWYARD* 21A B2

Opened c1904 by the NBR and closed by BR in May 1948.
Line Operational – Demolished. **NS53491 68019**

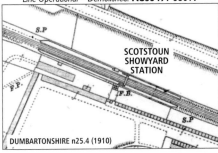

SCOTSTOUN WEST 21A A2

Opened 1 October 1896 by the Lanarkshire & Dumbartonshire Railway as *Scotstoun*, renamed by the CR 1 October 1901 as *Scotstoun West* and closed by BR 5 October 1964.
Line lifted – Demolished – Platform extant – Station site unused. **NS52244 67948**

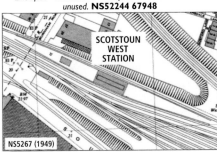

SEAFIELD OIL WORKS 7 A1

SELKIRK 7 D3

Opened 5 April 1856 by the Selkirk & Galashiels Railway and closed by BR 10 September 1951.
Line lifted – Demolished - Station site occupied by dwellings and car park in Whinfield Road. **NT46631 28872**

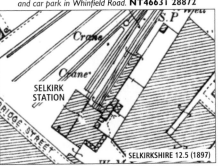

SETON MAINS HALT 22A C1

Opened 1 May 1914 by the NBR and closed by the L&NER 22 September 1930.
Line Operational – Demolished – No access. **NT42371 75003**

SHANDON 10 A4

Opened 7 August 1894 by the West Highland Railway and closed by BR 15 June 1964.
Line Operational – Demolished. **NS2507988144**

SHANKEND 7 D4

Opened 1 July 1862 by the Border Union Railway and closed by BR 6 January 1969.
Line lifted - Station building and platform in private use.
NT52386 05714

(see map below)

SHAWFAIR 7A C1

Opened 6 September 2015.

Shawfair Station on 12 May 2017.

SHAWFIELD BRANCH 6 D2

SHAWLANDS 21A C3

Opened 2 April 1894 by the Cathcart District Railway.

Shawlands Station on 18 March 2017.

SHETTLESTON 6 C1

Opened 23 November 1870 by the NBR

Shettleston Station on 12 May 2017.

SHIELDHILL 3 A1

Opened 1 September 1863 by the Dumfries, Lochmaben & Lockerbie Junction Railway and closed by BR 19 May 1952.
Line lifted - Station site occupied by a dwelling.
NY02983 85139

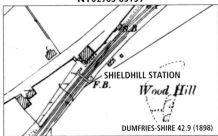

SHIELDHILL COLLIERY BRANCH 6 D1

SHIELDMUIR 6A D2

Opened 14 May 1990.

Shieldmuir Station on 19 March 2017.

SHIELDS 21A C3

Opened 1 July 1885 by the G&SWR, closed 1 January 1917, reopened in April 1920 and closed by the LM&SR 1 November 1924. It was amalgamated with *Pollokshields (G&SWR)* and *Shields Road (City of Glasgow Union Railway)* stations by the LM&SR and reopened 1 April 1925 as *Shields Road (qv)*.
Line lifted – Demolished – Station site unused.
NS57594 63890
FOR MAP SEE POLLOKSHIELDS (PAGE 117)

SHIELDS ROAD 21A C3

Opened 12 December 1870 by the City of Glasgow Union Railway and closed by the G&SWR 1 January 1917 (except for workmen's trains). It was amalgamated with *Shields (G&SWR)* and *Pollokshields (G&SWR)* stations by the LM&SR, reopened 1 April 1925 and closed by BR 14 February 1966.
Line Operational – Demolished – No access.
NS57631 63942
FOR MAP SEE POLLOKSHIELDS (PAGE 117)

SHOTTS 6 D1

Opened 9 July 1869 by the Cleland & Midcalder Railway.

Shotts Station on 19 March 2017.

SILLOTH 3 B2

Opened 4 September 1856 by the Carlisle & Silloth Bay Railway and closed by BR 7 September 1964.
Line lifted - Demolished - Station site occupied by housing in Station Mews – Platform partially incorporated into a new building. **NY10939 53422**

(see map below)

SINCLAIRTOWN 11 C4

Opened in May 1848 by the Edinburgh & Northern Railway, closed by the NBR 1 January 1917 (except for workmen's trains), reopened 1 February 1919 and closed by BR 6 October 1969.
Line Operational - Demolished – No access. **NT29062 92937**

(see map below)

SINGER　　　　　　　6 B1/21A A1

Opened 4 November 1907 by the NBR.

*Looking west at **Singer Station** on 13 September 2015.*

SINGER WORKERS PLATFORM*　　21A A1

Opened after 1942 by the L&NER and closed by BR 1 May 1967.

Line lifted – Demolished – Station site occupied by the "Clyde Shopping Centre". **NS49889 70639**

SINGER WORKERS PLATFORM

NS4970 (1948)

SKARES　　　　　　　6 B3

Opened 1 July 1901 by the G&SWR and closed by BR 10 September 1951.

Line lifted – Demolished – Station site partially occupied by two dwellings. **NS52922 19020**

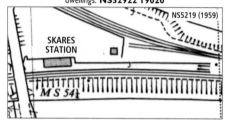

NS5219 (1959)

SKARES STATION

SKELBO　　　　　　　17 C3

Opened 2 June 1902 by the Dornoch Light Railway and closed by BR 13 June 1960.

Line lifted – Demolished – Platform extant – Station site unused. **NH80049 94827**

SUTHERLAND 110.6 (1904)

SKELBO STATION

SLAMANNAN　　　　　　6 D1

Opened 5 August 1840 by the Slamannan Railway and closed by the L&NER 1 May 1930.

Line lifted – Demolished – A short access road passes through the station site. **NS85829 72391**

SLAMANNAN STATION

STIRLINGSHIRE 35.6 (1896)

SLATEFORD　　　　7 B1/22A B2

Opened in 1871 by the CR.

*Looking west at **Slateford Station** on 12 May 2017.*

SLOCHD CROSSING*　　14A D2

Opened prior to 1922 by the HR for railwaymen's families and closed by the LM&SR c1935.

Line Operational – Demolished. **NH83440 25651**

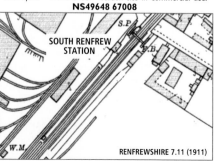

INVERNESS–MAINLAND 45 (1900)

SMEATON　　　　　　　7 C1

Opened 1 May 1872 by the NBR and closed by the L&NER 22 September 1930.

Line lifted – Demolished – The Pencaitland Railway Walk passes through the station site. **NT35381 69330**

SMEATON STATION

EDINBURGHSHIRE 8.4 (1893)

SORBIE　　　　　　　2 B2

Opened 2 August 1875 by the Wigtownshire Railway and closed by BR 25 September 1950.

Line lifted – Station building in private use – Platform demolished. **NX43515 47569**

WIGTOWNSHIRE 26.15 (1894)

SORBIE STATION

SOUTH COBBINSHAW BRANCH　　7 A2

SOUTH LEITH　　　　　7 C1

Opened in July 1832 by the Edinburgh & Dalkeith Railway as *Leith*, closed in 1846, reopened by the NBR 1 October 1859 as *South Leith* and closed 1 July 1903.

Line lifted – Demolished – Tower Street passes through the station site. **NT27354 76586**

EDINBURGHSHIRE 1.16 (1894)

SOUTH LEITH STATION

SOUTH GYLE　　　　　7A B1

Opened 9 May 1985.

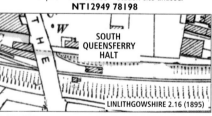

South Gyle Station on 12 May 2017.

SOUTH QUEENSFERRY GOODS 7 B1
SOUTH QUEENSFERRY HALT　　7A B1

Opened 1 December 1919 by the NBR and closed by the L&NER 14 January 1929.

Line lifted – Demolished – Station site unused. **NT12949 78198**

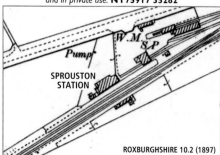

SOUTH QUEENSFERRY HALT

LINLITHGOWSHIRE 2.16 (1895)

SOUTH RENFREW　　　　6A B1

Opened 19 April 1897 by the G&SWR and closed by BR 5 June 1967.

Line lifted – Demolished – Station site in commercial use. **NS49648 67008**

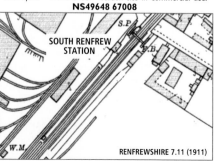

SOUTH RENFREW STATION

RENFREWSHIRE 7.11 (1911)

SOUTHWICK　　　　　　2 D2

Opened in September 1860 by the Castle Douglas & Dumfries Railway, closed by the LM&SR 25 September 1939, reopened 3 February 1941 and closed by BR 3 May 1965.

Line lifted – Demolished – Degraded platforms partially extant - Station site unused. **NX85566 63422**

SOUTHWICK STATION

KIRKCUDBRIGHTSHIRE 43.4 (1893)

SPEAN BRIDGE　　　　13 D4

Opened 7 August 1894 by the West Highland Railway.

*Looking west at **Spean Bridge Station** on 14 September 2015.*

SPEY BAY　　　　　　18 C4

Opened 1 May 1866 by the GNofSR as *Fochabers-on-Spey*, renamed by the GNofSR in 1893 as *Fochabers*, 1 January 1916 as *Fochabers & Spey Bay*, 1 January 1919 as *Spey Bay* and closed by BR 6 May 1968.

Line lifted – Station building in private use – Remainder demolished. **NJ35484 64170**

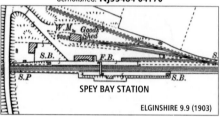

SPEY BAY STATION

ELGINSHIRE 9.9 (1903)

SPIRESLACK PIT BRANCH　　6 D3
SPRINGBURN　　　　　21A D2

Opened 1 January 1887 by the City of Glasgow Union Railway, closed 1 January 1917 by the NBR (except for workmen's trains) and reopened to the public 2 June 1919.

*Class 334 Unit No.334037 at **Springburn Station** on 13 May 2017.*

SPRINGFIELD　　　　　11 C3

Opened 20 September 1847 by the Edinburgh & Northern Railway.

***Springfield Station** on 18 September 2015.*

SPRINGSIDE　　　　　6 A2

Opened 2 June 1890 by the G&SWR and closed by BR 6 April 1964.

Line lifted – Demolished – A cycle/walkway passes through the station site. **NS36901 39105**

AYRSHIRE 17.11 (1895)

SPRINGSIDE STATION

SPROUSTON　　　　　　8 A2

Opened 27 July 1849 by the York, Newcastle & Berwick Railway and closed by BR 4 July 1955.

Line lifted - Platforms demolished – Station building extended and in private use. **NT75917 35282**

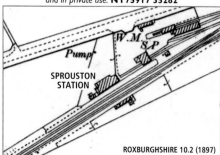

SPROUSTON STATION

ROXBURGHSHIRE 10.2 (1897)

SPROUSTON JUNCTION 8 A2
STANLEY 11 A2

Opened in 1856 by the Scottish Midland Junction Railway and closed by BR 11 June 1956. It was also known as *Stanley Junction* in some timetables.

Line Operational – Demolished – No access. **NO11121 33658**

PERTH & CLACKMANNANSHIRE 74.13 (1899)

STANNERGATE GOODS 11 C2

Opened 1 February 1901 by the Dundee & Arbroath Joint Railway and closed to passengers 1 May 1916.

Line Operational – Demolished – No access. **NO43851 31041**

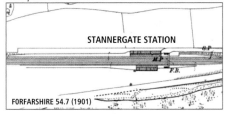

FORFARSHIRE 54.7 (1901)

STANLEY JUNCTION 11 A2
STEELE ROAD 7 D4

Opened 2 June 1862 by the Border Union Railway and closed by BR 6 January 1969.

Line lifted - Station building and platform in private use. **NY52203 93050**

ROXBURGHSHIRE 42.12 (1896)

STEELEND GOODS 11 A4
STEPFORD 2 D1

Opened 1 March 1905 by the Culm Valley Light Railway and closed by the LM&SR 3 May 1943.

Line lifted – Demolished – Station site landscaped as part of garden for adjacent former Station Master's house. **NX86372 81686**

NX88SE

STEPPS ROAD 6 C1

Opened in 1832 by the Wishaw & Coltness Railway as *Cumbernauld Road*, renamed by the CR 1 August 1883 as *Stepps Road*, by the LM&SR 1 September 1924 as *Stepps* and closed by BR 5 November 1962. Prior to 1883 it was also known as *Steps* or *Steps Road*.

Line Operational – Demolished. **NS65772 68382**

LANARKSHIRE 7.1 (1897)

STEPPS 6A C1

Opened 15 May 1989 and sited about 1.5 miles east of the original station (qv).

Stepps Station on 13 May 2017.

STEVENSTON (CR) 6 A2

Opened 4 September 1888 by the Lanarkshire & Ayrshire Railway as *Stevenston*, closed 1 January 1917, reopened 1 February 1919, renamed by the LM&SR 2 June 1924 as *Stevenston Moor Park* and closed 4 July 1932.

Line lifted – Demolished – Station site occupied by "Thistle Day Services". **NS26685 41455**

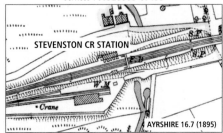

AYRSHIRE 16.7 (1895)

STEVENSTON (G&SWR) 6 A2

Opened in March 1850 by the Ardrossan Railway.

Class 380 Unit No.380004 at **Stevenston Station** on 16 March 2017.

STEWARTON 6 B1

Opened 27 March 1871 by the Glasgow, Barrhead & Kilmarnock Joint Railway, closed by BR 7 November 1966 and reopened 5 June 1967

Stewarton Station on 19 March 2017.

STEWARTON PLANTATION 5 B3

Opened 18 August 1906 by the Campbeltown & Machrihanish Light Railway and closed by May 1932.

STIRLING 10 D4

Opened 1 March 1848 by the Scottish Central Railway.

Looking south at **Stirling Station** on 13 May 2017.

STIRLING SHORE RD GOODS 10 D4
STOBO 7 B2

Opened 1 February 1864 by the Symington, Biggar and Broughton Railway and closed by BR 5 June 1950.

Line lifted – Station building and platform in private use. **NT17303 36219**

PEEBLES-SHIRE 16.3 (1897)

STOBS 7 D4

Opened 1 July 1862 by the Border Union Railway as *Barnes*, renamed by the NBR in 1862 as *Stobs* and closed by BR 6 January 1969.

Line lifted - Station building and platform in private use. **NT50486 09745**

ROXBURGHSHIRE 32.3 (1897)

STOBS CAMP* 7A D4

Opened prior to 25 August 1903 by the NBR and closed at an unknown date.

Line lifted – Demolished - Station site unused. **NT50445 10722**

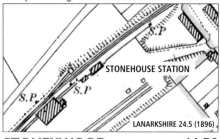

NT51SW

STONEHAVEN 16 B4

Opened 1 November 1849 by the Aberdeen Railway.

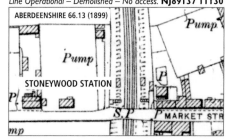

Stonehaven Station on 18 September 2015.

STONEHOUSE 6 D2

Opened 1 July 1905 by the CR and closed by BR 4 October 1965.

Line lifted – Demolished – The A71, Stonehouse By-pass, passes through the station site. **NS75317 46993**

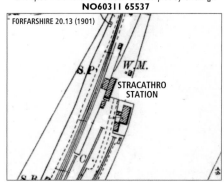

LANARKSHIRE 24.5 (1896)

STONEYWOOD 16 B3

Opened 1 July 1887 by the GNofSR and closed by the L&NER 5 April 1937.

Line Operational – Demolished – No access. **NJ89137 11130**

ABERDEENSHIRE 66.13 (1899)

STONEYWOOD GOODS BRANCH 10 D4
STOW 7 D2

Opened 1 November 1848 by the NBR, closed by BR 6 January 1969 and reopened 6 September 2015.

Stow Station on 12 May 2017.

STRACATHRO 11 D1

Opened 8 June 1896 by the Brechin & Edzell Railway as *Inchbare*, renamed by the CR 1 October 1912 as *Dunlappie*, 1 November 1912 as *Stracathro*, closed by the LM&SR 27 April 1931, reopened 4 July 1938 and closed 26 September 1938.

Line lifted – Demolished - Station site occupied by dwellings. **NO60311 65537**

FORFARSHIRE 20.13 (1901)

STRAGEATH HALT 10A D3
Opened 15 September 1958 by BR and closed 6 July 1964.
Line lifted – Demolished – Station site in use as a field.
NN88103 17885

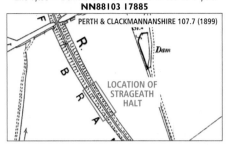

PERTH & CLACKMANNANSHIRE 107.7 (1899)

LOCATION OF STRAGEATH HALT

STRANRAER HARBOUR 1 D2
Opened 1 October 1862 by the Portpatrick Railway as *Stranraer Harbour* and renamed by BR 17 May 1993 as *Stranraer*.

Stranraer Station on 16 March 2017.

STRANRAER TOWN 1 D2
Opened 12 March 1861 by the Portpatrick Railway as *Stranraer*, renamed by BR 2 March 1953 as *Stranraer Town* and closed 7 March 1966.
Line Out of Use – Demolished – Platforms partially extant – Station site in use as a yard for "James King Bus & Coach Hire" and Network Rail. **NX06683 60384**

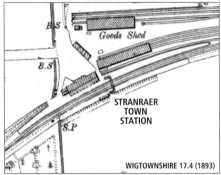

Goods Shed

STRANRAER TOWN STATION

WIGTOWNSHIRE 17.4 (1893)

STRATHAVEN CENTRAL 6 C2
Opened 1 October 1904 by the CR as *Strathaven Central*, renamed by BR 14 June 1965 as *Strathaven* and closed 4 October 1965.
Line lifted – Demolished - Platform extant – Station site unused.
NS70233 44227

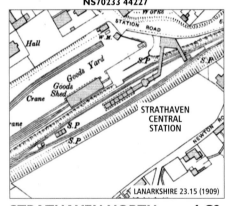

STRATHAVEN CENTRAL STATION

LANARKSHIRE 23.15 (1909)

STRATHAVEN NORTH 6 C2
Opened 1 October 1904 by the Hamilton & Strathaven Railway, closed by the CR 1 January 1917, reopened 1 February 1919 and closed by the LM&SR 1 October 1945.
Line lifted – Demolished – Station site unused.
NS70932 45077

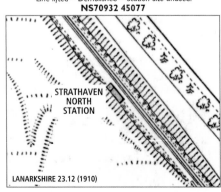

STRATHAVEN NORTH STATION

LANARKSHIRE 23.12 (1910)

STRATHAVON COLLIERY 6 D1

STRATHBLANE 6 C1
Opened 1 July 1867 by the Blane Valley Railway and closed by BR 1 October 1951.
Line lifted – Station site unused.
NS56385 79247

Crane

STRATHBLANE STATION

STIRLINGSHIRE 27.6 (1914)

STRATHBUNGO 6 C1/21A C3
Opened 1 December 1877 by the Glasgow, Barrhead and Kilmarnock Joint Railway and closed by BR 28 May 1962.
Line Operational – Platforms demolished – Street-level station building in use as a retail shop. **NS57726 62838**

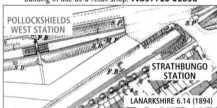

POLLOCKSHIELDS WEST STATION

STRATHBUNGO STATION

LANARKSHIRE 6.14 (1894)

STRATHCARRON 13 C2
Opened 19 August 1870 by the Dingwall & Skye Railway.

Looking north at **Strathcarron Station** on 17 September 2015.

STRATHMIGLO 11 B3
Opened 8 June 1857 by the Fife & Kinross Railway and closed by BR 5 June 1950.
Line lifted - Station building in private use - Platform extant and remodelled. **NO2120510262**

FIFESHIRE 12.9 (1893)

STRATHMIGLO STATION

Stedmore La

STRATHORD 11 A2
Opened in June 1849 by the Scottish Midland Junction Railway as *Dunkeld Road*, renamed by the Scottish North Eastern Railway 1 February 1857 as *Strathord Siding*, by the CR in August 1866 as *Strathord* and closed by the LM&SR 13 April 1931.
Line Operational – Demolished – Platform partially extant – No access. **NO09304 30961**

STRATHORD STATION

PERTH & CLACKMANNANSHIRE 85.4 (1899)

STRATHPEFFER 14 B1
Opened 3 June 1885 by the HR and closed by the LM&SR 23 February 1946.
Line lifted – Station building in use as "The Highland Museum of Childhood" and retail shops. **NH48591 58390**

Goods W.M. Shed

Tank

STRATHPEFFER STATION

ROSS-SHIRE & CROMARTYSHIRE 88.1 (1876)

STRATHYRE 10 B3
Opened 1 June 1870 by the Callander & Oban Railway and closed by BR 28 September 1965.
Line lifted – Demolished – Station site occupied by housing in Old Station Court. **NN56025 17049**

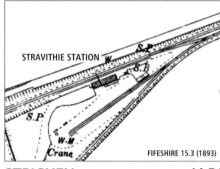

Hot P.O.

STRATHYRE STATION

S.P.

NN51

STRAVITHIE 11 D3
Opened 1 June 1887 by the Anstruther & St Andrews Railway and closed by the L&NER 22 September 1930.
Line lifted – Station House and platform in private use as the "Old Station Guest House" – An ex-BR railway carriage is parked alongside the platform as accommodation.
NO53198 13431

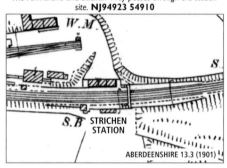

STRAVITHIE STATION

S.P.

W.M. Crane

FIFESHIRE 15.3 (1893)

STRICHEN 16 B1
Opened 24 April 1865 by the Formartine & Buchan Railway and closed by BR 4 October 1965.
Line lifted - Station building in private use - Platforms extant - The Formartine and Buchan Way passes through the station site. **NJ94923 54910**

W.M.

S.B. STRICHEN STATION

ABERDEENSHIRE 13.3 (1901)

STROME FERRY 13 B2
Opened by the Dingwall & Skye Railway 19 August 1870 as *Strome Ferry* and renamed by BR in 1962 as *Stromeferry*.

Looking west at **Stromeferry Station** on 17 September 2015.

STRUAN 10 D1
Opened 9 September 1863 by the Inverness & Perth Junction Railway and closed by BR 3 May 1965.
Line Operational – Demolished – Platforms extant.
NN79960 65705

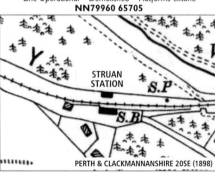

STRUAN STATION

S.P.

S.B.

PERTH & CLACKMANNANSHIRE 20SE (1898)

SUMMERSTON 21A C1
Opened 3 December 1993.

Summerston Station on 13 May 2017.

SUMMERSTON   6 C1/21A C1

Opened 1 October 1879 by the Kelvin Valley Railway and closed by BR 2 April 1951.

Line lifted – Demolished – House erected on station site.
NS57878 71954

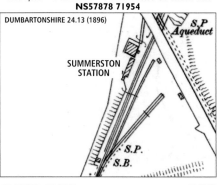

DUMBARTONSHIRE 24.13 (1896)

SUNILAWS   8 B2

Opened in July 1859 by the York, Newcastle & Berwick Railway as *Wark*, renamed by the NER 1 October 1871 as *Sunilaws* and closed by BR 4 July 1955.

Line lifted - Station building in private use – Platforms extant.
NT82593 37455

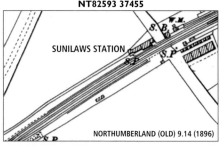

NORTHUMBERLAND (OLD) 9.14 (1896)

SWINLEES BRANCH   6 A2
SYMINGTON   7 A2

Opened 30 November 1863 by the CR and closed by BR 4 January 1965.

Line Operational - Demolished – No access. **NS99051 36119**

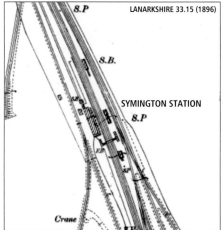

LANARKSHIRE 33.15 (1896)

TAIN   17 C4

Opened by the Inverness & Aberdeen Junction Railway 1 June 1864.

Tain Station on 16 September 2015.

TANNADICE   11 C1

Opened 1 June 1895 by the CR and closed by BR 4 August 1952.

Line lifted – Demolished – Station site occupied by a dwelling – Platform partially extant. **NO48665 58346**

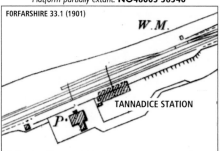

FORFARSHIRE 33.1 (1901)

TARBOLTON   6 B3

Opened 1 September 1870 by the G&SWR and closed by the LM&SR 4 January 1943.

Line Operational – Station building in commercial use as "Countryfresh Meats" – Platforms demolished.
NS43992 25007

AYRSHIRE 28.4 (1895)

TARBRAX BRANCH   7 A2
TARFF   2 C2

Opened 7 March 1864 by the Kirkcudbright Railway as *Tarff for Gatehouse*, renamed 1 September 1865 as *Gatehouse*, 1 August 1871 as *Tarff* and closed by BR 3 May 1965.

Line lifted – Station building in private use – Station site in commercial use. **NX68567 56451**

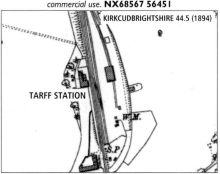

KIRKCUDBRIGHTSHIRE 44.5 (1894)

TARSET   4 B1

Opened 1 February 1861 by the Border Counties Railway as *Tarset*, renamed by BR 9 September 1955 as *Tarset Halt* and closed 15 October 1956.

Line lifted - Station building and platform in private use.
NY78971 85277

NORTHUMBERLAND (OLD) 67.4 (1895)

TAUCHERS HALT   15A C1

Opened in July 1922 by the HR as a private platform, opened to the public by BR 13 June 1955 and closed 7 December 1964.

Line Operational – Demolished. **NJ37145 50057**

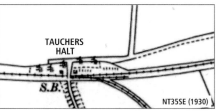

NT35SE (1930)

TAYNUILT   9 C2

Opened by the Callander & Oban Railway 1 July 1880.

Looking west at **Taynuilt Station** on 14 September 2015.

TAYPORT   11 C2

Opened 12 May 1879 by the NBR and closed by BR 22 May 1966.

Line lifted – Demolished – Station site occupied by housing in Tay Street. **NO45813 29067**

FIFESHIRE 1.11 (1893)

THANKERTON   7 A2

Opened 15 February 1848 by the CR and closed by BR 4 January 1965.

Line Operational – Station building in private use – Platforms demolished. **NS97283 38063**

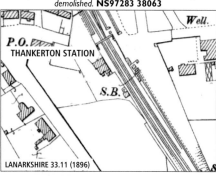

LANARKSHIRE 33.11 (1896)

THE MOUND   17 C3

Opened 13 August 1868 by the Sutherland Railway and closed by BR 13 June 1960. It was also known as *The Mound Junction*.

Main Line Operational – Station building in private use – Platforms extant. **NH77527 98351**

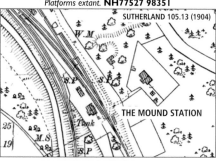

SUTHERLAND 105.13 (1904)

THORNBRIDGE HALT*   6A D1

Opened 1 December 1899 by the CR for workmen's trains and closed by the LM&SR 1 August 1938.

Line Operational for Freight – Demolished – No access.
NS91311 80661 (a)

NS9180 (1951)

THORNEYBURN   4 A1

Opened 1 February 1861 by the Border Counties Railway and closed by BR 15 October 1956.

Line lifted - Station building and partially extant platform in private use. **NY77379 86356**

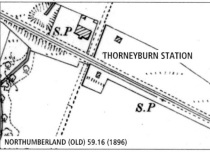

NORTHUMBERLAND (OLD) 59.16 (1896)

THORNHILL   6 D4

Opened 28 October 1850 by the Glasgow, Dumfries and Carlisle Railway and closed by BR 6 December 1965.

Line Operational - Station building in private use - Platforms extant. **NX88968 96488**

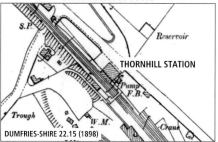

DUMFRIES-SHIRE 22.15 (1898)

THORNIELEE 7 C2

Opened 18 June 1866 by the Innerleithen & Galashiels Railway and closed by BR 6 November.
Line lifted - Station building and platform in private use.
NT41211 36170

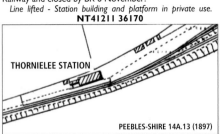

THORNIELEE STATION

PEEBLES-SHIRE 14A.13 (1897)

THORNLIEBANK 6 B1/21A B4

Opened by the Busby Railway 1 October 1881.

Thornliebank Station
on 18 March 2017.

THORNLIEBANK GOODS 6 B1
THORNTON 11 C4

Opened 4 September 1848 by the Edinburgh & Northern Railway and closed by BR 6 October 1969. It was also known as *Thornton Junction*.
Line Operational – Demolished – No access. **NT29933 97701**

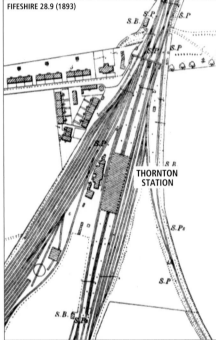

FIFESHIRE 28.9 (1893)

THORNTON STATION

THORNTONHALL 6 C2

Opened by the Busby Railway 1 September 1868 as *Eaglesham Road*, renamed 1 June 1877 as *Thornton Hall* and by the LM&SR in 1943 as *Thorntonhall*.

Thorntonhall Station
on 18 March 2017.

THROSK PLATFORM 10 D4

Opened in December 1890 by the Alloa Railway and closed by BR 18 April 1966.
Line lifted – Demolished – Station site unused.
NS86182 90923

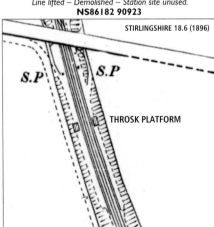

STIRLINGSHIRE 18.6 (1896)

THROSK PLATFORM

THRUMSTER 18 B1

Opened 1 July 1903 by the Wick & Lybster Light Railway and closed by the LM&SR 3 April 1944.
Line lifted – Station building restored and preserved as part of "Thrumster Station Garden Park". **ND33673 45205**

THRUMSTER STATION

CAITHNESS 29.4 (1905)

THURSO 20 A3

Opened by the Sutherland & Caithness Railway 28 July 1874.

Thurso Station
on 16 September 2015.

TIBBERMUIR 11 A3

Opened in February 1859 by the Perth, Almond Valley & Methven Railway and closed by BR 1 October 1951. It was also known as *Tibbermuir Crossing, Tibbermuir & Powfoot Siding, Tibbermuir & Powbridge* and *Tibbermuir Halt* in various timetables.
Line lifted – Demolished – Station site occupied by bungalows – An access road passes through the station site.
NO04914 24548

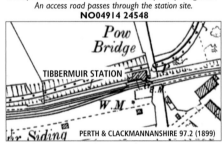

Pow Bridge

TIBBERMUIR STATION

PERTH & CLACKMANNANSHIRE 97.2 (1899)

TILLICOULTRY 10 D4

Opened in January 1852 by the Stirling & Dunfermline Railway and closed by BR 15 June 1964.
Line lifted – Demolished – Station site occupied by a small park – The Devon Way passes through the station site.
NS92012 96661

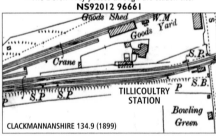

TILLICOULTRY STATION

CLACKMANNANSHIRE 134.9 (1899)

TILLIETUDLEM 6 D2

Opened in May 1877 by the CR and closed by BR 1 October 1951.
Line lifted – Degraded platforms extant – Station site unused.
NS80830 45851

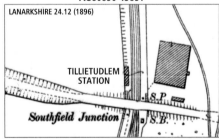

LANARKSHIRE 24.12 (1896)

TILLIETUDLEM STATION

Southfield Junction

TILLYFOURIE 15 D3

Opened 2 June 1860 by the Alford Valley Railway and closed by BR 2 January 1950.
Line lifted – Demolished – Degraded platform partially extant – A pathway passes through the station site. **NJ64543 12349**

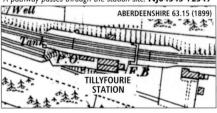

ABERDEENSHIRE 63.15 (1899)

TILLYFOURIE STATION

TILLYNAUGHT 15 D1

Opened 1 September 1859 by the Banff, Portsoy and Strathisla Railway and closed by BR 6 May 1968. It was also known as *Tillynaught Junction* in some timetables.
Line lifted – Demolished – Platforms infilled – Station site in commercial use. **NJ60086 61784**

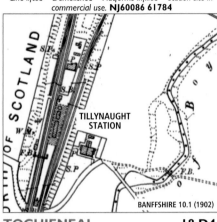

OF SCOTLAND

TILLYNAUGHT STATION

BANFFSHIRE 10.1 (1902)

TOCHIENEAL 18 D4

Opened 1 April 1884 by the GNofSR and closed by BR 1 October 1951.
Line lifted – Demolished – Station site unused. **NJ52323 65666**

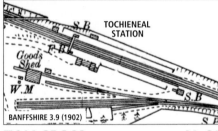

TOCHIENEAL STATION

BANFFSHIRE 3.9 (1902)

TOLLCROSS 6A C1

Opened 1 February 1897 by the CR and closed by BR 5 October 1964.
Line lifted – Demolished – Station site unused.
NS63864 63011

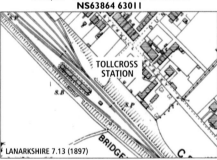

TOLLCROSS STATION

LANARKSHIRE 7.13 (1897)

TOMATIN 14 C2

Opened 19 July 1897 by the HR and closed by BR 3 May 1965.
Line Operational – Demolished – Platform extant.
NH79535 29360

Tomatin Sta.

INVERNESS-MAINLAND 32 (1900)

TORPHINS 15 D3

Opened 2 December 1859 by the Deeside Extension Railway and closed by BR 28 February 1966.
Line lifted – Demolished – Station site occupied by housing in Station Road. **NJ62416 01834**

TORPHINS STATION

ABERDEENSHIRE 82.6 (1899)

TORRANCE 6 C1

Opened 1 October 1879 by the Kelvin Valley Railway and closed by BR 2 April 1951.

Line lifted – Demolished – Station site partially occupied by housing in Michael McParland Drive - A cycle/walkway passes through the station site. **NS6193874088**

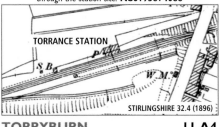

STIRLINGSHIRE 32.4 (1896)

TORRYBURN 11 A4

Opened 2 July 1906 by the Keith & Dufftown Railway and closed by the L&NER 7 July 1930.

Line Operational – Demolished – No access. **NT02233 86239**

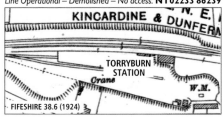

FIFESHIRE 38.6 (1924)

TOWIEMORE GOODS 15 C1
TOWIEMORE HALT 15A C1

Opened in 1924 by the L&NER for distillery workers and closed by BR 6 May 1968.

Line Operated by the Keith & Dufftown Railway – Demolished – Platforms partially extant. **NJ39473 45581**

BANFFSHIRE 19.12 (1903)

TOWNHILL JUNCTION 11 B4
TRABBOCH 6 B3

Opened 1 July 1896 by the G&SWR and closed by BR 10 September 1951.

Line Operational for Freight – Demolished. **NS43446 21102**

AYRSHIRE 34.6 (1908)

TRANENT BRANCH 7 C1
TRINITY & NEWHAVEN 22A B1

Opened 19 February 1846 by the Edinburgh, Leith & Newhaven Railway, closed by the NBR 1 January 1917, reopened 1 February 1919 and closed by the L&NER 2 November 1925.

Line lifted – Station building and platforms extant – The Trinity Path passes through the station site. **NT24915 76894**

EDINBURGHSHIRE 1.15 (1931)

TRODIGAL 5A A3

Opened 18 August 1906 by the Campbeltown & Machrihanish Light Railway and closed by May 1932.

TROON 6 A3

Opened by the G&SWR 2 May 1892.

*Looking north at **Troon** Station on 16 March 2017.*

TROON HARBOUR BRANCH 6 A3
TULLIBARDINE 10 D3

Opened in May 1857 by the Crieff Junction Railway and closed by BR 6 July 1964.

Line lifted - Station building and platform in private use. **NN91797 13587**

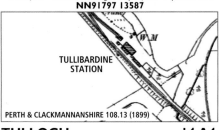

PERTH & CLACKMANNANSHIRE 108.13 (1899)

TULLOCH 14 A4

Opened by the West Highland Railway 7 August 1894 as *Inverlair*, renamed by the NBR 1 January 1895 as *Tulloch for Loch Laggan & Kingussie* and by BR c1948 as *Tulloch*.

*Looking west at **Tulloch** Station on 15 September 2015.*

TURNBERRY 6 A4

Opened 17 May 1906 by the Maidens & Dunure Light Railway and although closed by the LM&SR 2 March 1942 continued to be used for a period for workmen's trains.

Line lifted – Demolished – Station site occupied by a car park for the Turnberry Hotel. **NS20654 05787**

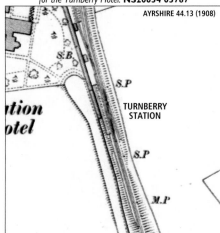

AYRSHIRE 44.13 (1908)

TURNHOUSE 7 B1

Opened in September 1897 by the NBR and closed by the L&NER 22 September 1930.

Line Operational – Demolished – No access. **NT16313 73931**

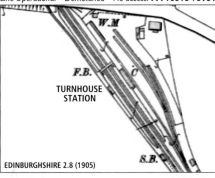

EDINBURGHSHIRE 2.8 (1905)

TURRIFF 16 A1

Opened 5 September 1857 by the Banff, Macduff & Turriff Junction Railway and closed by BR 1 October 1951.

Line lifted – Demolished – Station site occupied by Bridgend Terrace and the A647. **NJ72450 49349**

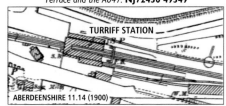

ABERDEENSHIRE 11.14 (1900)

TWEEDBANK 7A D2

Opened 6 September 2015.

*Class 158 Unit No.158867 at **Tweedbank** Station on 12 May 2017.*

TWEEDMOUTH 8 C2

Opened 29 March 1847 by the Newcastle & Berwick Railway and closed by BR 15 June 1964.

Line Operational – Station site partially in commercial use. **NT99624 51891**

NT9951 (1961)

TWIZELL 8 B2

Opened in August 1861 by the York, Newcastle & Berwick Railway and closed by BR 4 July 1955.

Line lifted - Platforms partially extant - Station Master's House in private use - A roadway passes through the station site. **NT87648 43726**

NORTHUMBERLAND (NEW) 6.5 (1922)

TYNDRUM LOWER 10 A2

Opened by the CR 1 May 1877 as *Tyndrum* and renamed by BR 28 February 1953 as *Tyndrum Lower*.

*Looking south at **Tyndrum Lower** Station on 17 September 2015.*

TYNDRUM UPPER 10 A2

Opened by the West Highland Railway 7 August 1894 as *Tyndrum*, renamed by BR 21 September 1953 as *Tyndrum Upper* and 17 May 1993 as *Upper Tyndrum*.

*Looking north at **Upper Tyndrum** Station on 13 September 2015.*

TYNEHEAD 7 C1

Opened 1 August 1848 by the NBR and closed by BR 6 January 1969.

Line Operational - Station building in private use - Platforms demolished. **NT39365 59162**

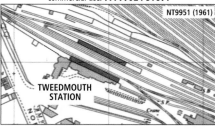

EDINBURGHSHIRE 15.9 (1906)

UDDINGSTON 6 C1

Opened by the Clydesdale Junction Railway 1 June 1849 as *Uddingston*, renamed by BR 3 March 1952 as *Uddingston Central* and c1961 reverted back to *Uddingston*.

Uddingston Station on 19 March 2017.

UDDINGSTON EAST   6A C2

Opened 1 April 1878 by the Glasgow, Bothwell, Hamilton & Coatbridge Railway as *Uddingston*, closed by the NBR 1 January 1917, reopened 2 June 1919, renamed by BR 28 February 1953 as *Uddingston East* and closed 4 July 1955.
Line lifted – Demolished – Mansfield Drive and a walkway pass through the station site. **NS69995 60722**

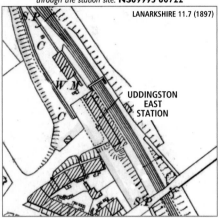

LANARKSHIRE 11.7 (1897)

UDDINGSTON WEST   6A C1

Opened in June 1888 by the NBR, closed 1 January 1917, reopened 2 June 1919 and closed by BR 4 July 1955.
Line lifted – Demolished – Station site unused.
NS69365 61381

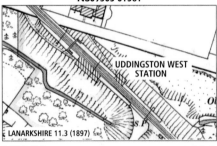

LANARKSHIRE 11.3 (1897)

UDNY   16 B2

Opened 18 July 1861 by the Formartine & Buchan Railway and closed by BR 4 October 1965.
Line lifted - Demolished - Platforms extant - The Formartine and Buchan Way passes through the station site.
NJ90697 24383

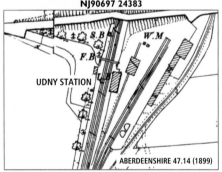

ABERDEENSHIRE 47.14 (1899)

ULBSTER   18 B1

Opened 1 July 1903 by the Wick & Lybster Light Railway and closed by the LM&SR 3 April 1944.
Line lifted – Station building in private use – Platform extant.
ND31801 40699

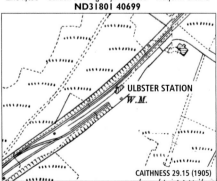

CAITHNESS 29.15 (1905)

UPHALL   7 A1

Opened by the Edinburgh & Bath-gate Railway 12 November 1849 as *Houston*, renamed as *Uphall* by NBR 1 August 1865, closed by BR 9 January 1956 and reopened 24 March 1986.

Uphall Station on 12 May 2017.

UPLAWMOOR   6 B2

Opened 1 May 1903 by the Lanarkshire & Ayrshire Railway, closed by the CR 1 January 1917, reopened 1 February 1919 and closed by BR 2 April 1962.
Line lifted – Demolished – Station site unused.
NS43792 55060

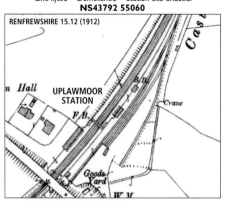

RENFREWSHIRE 15.12 (1912)

UPPER GREENOCK   6 A1

Opened 15 May 1865 by the Greenock & Wemyss Bay Railway and closed by BR 5 June.
Line Operational – Demolished – No access. **NS27797 75352**

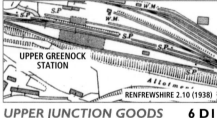

RENFREWSHIRE 2.10 (1938)

UPPER JUNCTION GOODS   6 D1
UPPER PORT GLASGOW   6 A1
GOODS

UPPER TYNDRUM (See TYNDRUM UPPER)
URQUHART   15 B1

Opened 12 August 1884 by the GNofSR and closed by BR 6 May 1968.
Line lifted – Demolished – Station site occupied by a private dwelling and garden. **NJ28741 63072**

ELGINSHIRE 8.11 (1903)

VELVET HALL   8 B2

Opened in July 1851 by the York, Newcastle & Berwick Railway and closed by BR 4 July 1955.
Line lifted - Station building in residential use - Platforms partially extant in garden. **NT94198 48939**

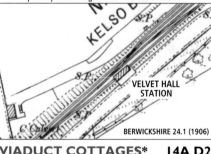

BERWICKSHIRE 24.1 (1906)

VIADUCT COTTAGES*   14A D2

Opened at an unknown date for railwaymen's families and closed by BR post 1960.
Line Operational – Demolished. **NH84785 23762 (a)**

INVERNESS-MAINLAND 45 (1900)

VICTORIA PARK WHITEINCH   21A B2

Opened 14 December 1896 by the Glasgow City & District Railway as *Victoria Park Whiteinch*, closed by the NBR 1 January 1917, reopened 2 June 1919, renamed by the L&NER 13 July 1925 as *Whiteinch Victoria Park* and closed by BR 2 April 1951.
Line lifted – Demolished – Station site part of Victoria Park Nature Walk. **NS53635 67404**

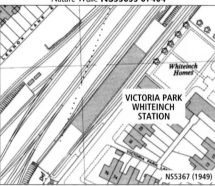

NS5367 (1949)

WALKERBURN   7 C2

Opened 15 January 1867 by the Innerleithen & Galashiels Railway and closed by BR 5 February 1962.
Line lifted - Station building and platform extant - Station site in commercial use. **NT36069 36826**

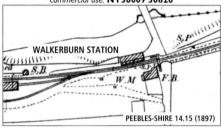

PEEBLES-SHIRE 14.15 (1897)

WALL   4 B1

Opened 5 April 1858 by the Border Counties Railway and closed by BR 19 September 1955.
Line lifted - Rebuilt station building and platform in private use – A track passes through the station site. **NY91653 68405**

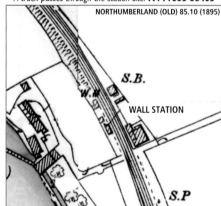

NORTHUMBERLAND (OLD) 85.10 (1895)

WALLYFORD   7A C1

Opened 13 June 1994.

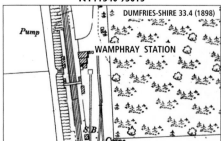

Looking west at **Wallyford Station** on 19 September 2015.

WAMPHRAY   7 B4

Opened 10 September 1847 by the CR and closed by BR 13 June 1960.
Line Operational – Demolished – Station House in private use.
NY11340 95015

DUMFRIES-SHIRE 33.4 (1898)

WANLOCKHEAD 6 D4

Opened 1 October 1902 by the Leadhills & Wanlockhead Light Railway and closed by the LM&SR 2 January 1939. At 1,498ft above sea level it was the highest standard gauge station in Britain.

Line lifted – Demolished – Station site in commercial use.
NS87420 12626

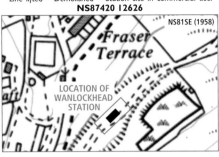

WARDHOUSE 15 D2

Opened 1 December 1854 by the GNofSR and closed by BR 5 June 1961.

Line Operational – Derelict station building and degraded platform extant. **NJ57881 29620**

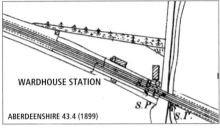

WARK 4 B1

Opened in April 1860 by the Border Counties Railway and closed by BR 15 October 1956.

Line lifted - Station building and platform in private use.
NY87150 76812

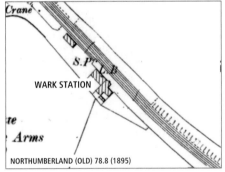

WARTLE 16 A2

Opened 5 September 1857 by the Banff, Macduff & Turriff Junction Railway and closed by BR 1 October 1951.

Line lifted – Station building in private use – Platform demolished. **NJ72026 30133**

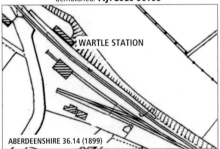

WATERLOO GOODS BRANCH 16 B3

WATERSIDE 6 B4

Opened 7 August 1856 by the Ayr & Dalmellington Railway and closed by BR 6 April 1964.

Line Operational for Freight – Demolished. **NS43748 08619**

WATTEN 20 B4

Opened 28 July 1874 by the Sutherland & Caithness Railway and closed by BR 13 June 1960.

Line Operational – Station House in private use – Platforms extant and preserved. **ND25052 55768**

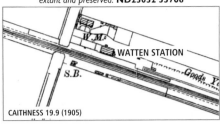

WELSH'S CROSSING HALT 18A B1

Opened 27 January 1936 by the LM&SR and closed 3 April 1944.

Line lifted – Demolished – Station site unused.
ND32488 43433

WEMYSS BAY 5 D1

Opened by the Greenock & Wemyss Bay Railway 15 May 1865.

Class 385 Unit No.385001 at **Wemyss Bay Station** on 17 March 2017.

WEMYSS CASTLE 11 C4

Opened 8 August 1881 by the Wemyss & Buckhaven Railway and closed by BR 10 January 1955.

Line lifted – Station building extant as part of "Alistair Buchan Ltd" garage premises – Remainder demolished.
NT33783 96903

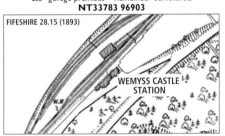

WEST CALDER 7 A1

Opened by the Cleland & Midcalder Railway 9 July 1869.

West Calder Station on 19 March 2017.

WESTCRAIGS 6 D1

Opened 11 August 1862 by the Bathgate & Coatbridge Railway and closed by BR 9 January 1956.

Line Operational – Demolished. **NS89818 66772**

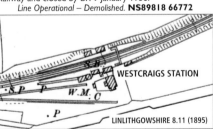

WEST CULTS 16 B3

Opened 1 August 1894 by the GNofSR and closed by the L&NER 5 April 1937.

Line lifted – Demolished – One platform extant – The Deeside Way passes through the station site. **NJ88986 02621**

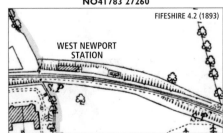

WESTER HAYLES 7A B1

Opened 11 May 1987.

Wester Hayles Station on 12 May 2017.

WESTERTON 6 B1/21A B1

Opened by the NBR 1 August 1913.

Looking south at **Westerton Station** on 13 May 2017.

WEST FEARN PLATFORM* 17 B3

Opened 1 October 1864 by the Inverness & Aberdeen Junction Railway as *Mid Fearn*, closed 1 September 1865 and reopened by the LM&SR after 1926 as *Mid Fearn Platform*. It was subsequently renamed as *West Fearn Platform* and closed after 1928.

Line Operational – Demolished. **NH63084 87764**

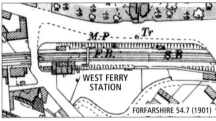

WEST FERRY 11 C2

Opened in May 1848 by the Dundee & Arbroath Joint Railway, closed 1 January 1917, reopened 1 February 1919 and closed by BR 4 September 1967.

Line Operational – Station building in private use – Platforms demolished. **NO45498 31108**

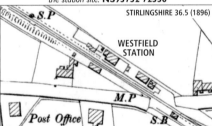

WESTFIELD 7 A1

Opened in June 1864 by the Monkland Railway and closed by the L&NER 1 May 1930.

Line lifted - Demolished – A short access road passes through the station site. **NS93752 72356**

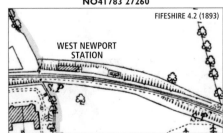

WEST KILBRIDE 6 A2

Opened by the G&SWR 1 May 1878.

West Kilbride Station on 17 March 2017.

WEST NEWPORT 11 C2

Opened 12 May 1879 by the Newport Railway as *West Newport*, closed by the NBR 12 January 1880, reopened 20 June 1887, renamed by BR in June 1956 as *Newport-on-Tay West* and closed 5 May 1969.

Line lifted – Demolished – Station site absorbed into parkland – A nature trail passes through the station site.
NO41783 27260

WESTON BRIDGE HALT*　　6A B3
Opened prior to 1920 by the G&SWR for workmen's trains and closed by the LM&SR prior to 1939.
Line Operational for Freight – Demolished. **NS41021 23693**

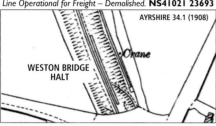

AYRSHIRE 34.1 (1908)

WEST WEMYSS　　11 C4
Opened 8 August 1881 by the Wemyss & Buckhaven Railway, closed by the NBR 1 January 1917, reopened 2 June 1919 and closed by BR 7 November 1949.
Line lifted – Demolished – Degraded platforms extant – Station site unused. **NT31397 96716**

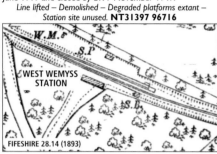

FIFESHIRE 28.14 (1893)

WHAUPHILL　　2 B2
Opened 2 August 1875 by the Wigtownshire Railway and closed by BR 25 September 1950.
Line lifted – Demolished – Station site in commercial use by "Tarff Valley Ltd". **NX40484 49871**

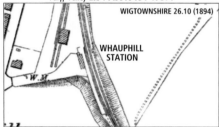

WIGTOWNSHIRE 26.10 (1894)

WHIFFLET (HIGH LEVEL) (CR)　　6 C1
Opened 1 June 1886 by the CR as *Whifflet High Level*, closed 1 January 1917, reopened 1 March 1919, renamed by BR 7 November 1953 as *Whifflet Upper* and closed 5 October 1964.
Line lifted – Demolished – Station site unused.
NS73554 64388

WHIFFLET (LOW LEVEL) (CR)　　6 C1
Opened 1 June 1886 by the CR as *Whifflet Low Level*, renamed by BR 7 November 1953 as *Whifflet Lower* and closed 5 November 1962.
Line Operational – Demolished – No access. **NS73506 64365**

WHIFFLET (NBR)　　6 D1
Opened 26 August 1895 by the NBR, closed 1 January 1917 (except for workmen's trains), reopened 2 June 1919 and closed by the L&NER 22 September 1930.
Line Operational – Demolished – No access. **NS73608 64314**

LANARKSHIRE 8.9 (1897)

WHIFFLET　　6A C1
Opened 21 December 1992 and sited to the south of *Whifflet Lower* (qv).

Whifflet Station on 12 May 2017.

WHINHILL　　6A A1
Opened 14 May 1990.

Whinhill Station on 17 March 2017.

WHISTLEFIELD　　10 A4
Opened 21 October 1896 by the West Highland Railway as *Whistlefield*, renamed by BR 13 June 1960 as *Whistlefield Halt* and closed 15 June 1964.
Line Operational – Demolished. **NS23532 93106**

DUMBARTONSHIRE 9SE (1896)

WHITBURN　　7 A1
Opened in 1850 by the Edinburgh & Glasgow Railway, closed in December 1852, reopened by the NBR 19 September 1864 and closed by the L&NER 1 May 1930.
Line lifted – Demolished – Station site unused – A pathway passes through the station site. **NS96292 65210**

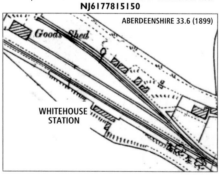

LINLITHGOWSHIRE 9.14 (1895)

WHITECRAIGS　　6 B2
Opened by the Lanarkshire & Ayrshire Railway 1 May 1903.

Whitecraigs Station on 18 March 2017.

WHITEHOUSE　　15 D3
Opened 21 March 1859 by the Alford Valley Railway and closed by BR 2 January 1950.
Line lifted – Demolished – Station site in commercial use.
NJ6177815150

ABERDEENSHIRE 33.6 (1899)

WHITEINCH　　6 B1/21A B2
Opened 1 October 1896 by the Lanarkshire & Dumbartonshire Railway as *Whiteinch*, renamed by BR 28 February 1953 as *Whiteinch Riverside* and closed 5 October 1964.
Line lifted – Demolished – Station site occupied by housing in Curle Street and a car dealership. **NS54279 66663**

NS5466 (1949)

WHITERIGG　　6 D1
Opened in 1836 by the Slamannan Railway and closed by the L&NER 1 May 1930.
Line lifted – Demolished – Station site unused. **NS77972 67574**

LANARKSHIRE 8.2 (1910)

WHITEWARE JUNCTION　　11 A4
WHITHORN　　2 B2
Opened 9 July 1877 by the Wigtownshire Railway and closed by BR 25 September 1952.
Line lifted – Demolished – Station site landscaped.
NX44588 40860

WIGTOWNSHIRE 31.16 (1895)

WHITRIGG　　3 B2
Opened 1 October 1870 by the Solway Junction Railway and closed by the LM&SR in May 1921.
Line lifted – Demolished – Station site occupied by a private dwelling. **NY22371 57736**

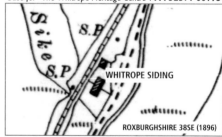

CUMBERLAND 14.16 (1899)

WHITROPE SIDING*　　7A D4
Opened 1 April 1914 by the NBR for railway staff and closed by BR 6 November 1967.
Line lifted – Demolished – Track relaid and station site now base for "The Whitrope Heritage Centre". **NT52571 00195**

ROXBURGHSHIRE 38SE (1896)

WICK　　18 B1
Opened by the Sutherland & Caithness Railway 28 July 1874.

Wick Station on 16 September 2015.

WIGTON　　3 C2
Opened 10 May 1843 by the Maryport & Carlisle Railway.

Looking north at **Wigton Station** on 30 May 2015.

WIGTOWN   2 B2
Opened 7 April 1875 by the Wigtownshire Railway and closed by BR 25 September 1950.
Line lifted – Station House in private use – Platforms partially extant – Station site unused. **NX43439 54807**

WIGTOWNSHIRE 21.11 (1894)

WILLIAMWOOD   6A C2
Opened by the LM&SR 8 July 1929.

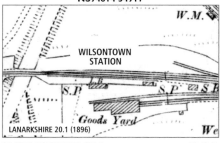
Looking north at **Williamwood Station** on 18 March 2017.

WILSONTOWN   7 A1
Opened 1 March 1867 by the CR and closed by BR 10 September 1951.
Line lifted – Demolished – Station site in industrial use. **NS94814 54917**

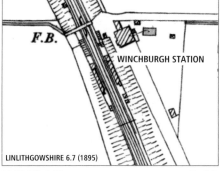
LANARKSHIRE 20.1 (1896)

WINCHBURGH   7 A1
Opened 21 February 1842 by the Edinburgh & Glasgow Railway and closed by the L&NER 22 September 1930.
Line Operational – Demolished – No access. **NT08945 75406**

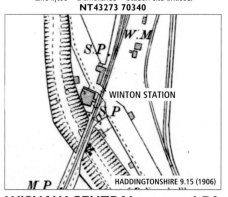
LINLITHGOWSHIRE 6.7 (1895)

WINTON   7 C1
Opened in July 1872 by the NBR and closed by the L&NER 1 July 1925.
Line lifted – Demolished – Station site unused. **NT43273 70340**

HADDINGTONSHIRE 9.15 (1906)

WISHAW CENTRAL   6 D2
Opened by the CR 1 June 1880 as *Wishaw Central* and renamed by BR 4 June 1965 as *Wishaw*.

Wishaw Station on 19 March 2017.

WISHAW SOUTH   6 D2
Opened in May 1845 by the Wishaw & Coltness Railway as *Wishaw*, renamed by the CR 1 June 1880 as *Wishaw South* and closed by BR 15 September 1958.
Line Operational – Demolished – No access. **NS78936 54326**

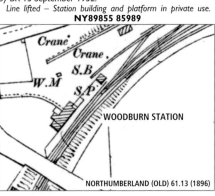
LANARKSHIRE 18.3 (1896)

WOODBURN   4 B1
Opened 1 May 1865 by the Wansbeck Railway and closed by BR 15 September 1952.
Line lifted – Station building and platform in private use. **NY89855 85989**

NORTHUMBERLAND (OLD) 61.13 (1896)

WOODEND COLLIERY   7 A1
WOODHALL   6A A1
Opened by the LM&SR 1 October 1945 as *Woodhall Halt* and renamed by BR 15 April 1966 as *Woodhall*.

Class 380 Unit No.380020 at **Woodhall Station** on 17 March 2017.

WOODMUIR BRANCH   7 A1
WOODSIDE   16 B3
Opened 1 January 1858 by the GNofSR and closed by the L&NER 5 April 1937.
Line Operational – Platforms demolished – Station House in commercial use. **NJ92164 09119**

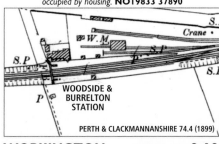
ABERDEENSHIRE 75.2 (1924)

WOODSIDE & BURRELTON   11 B2
Opened 2 August 1848 by the Scottish Midland Junction Railway as *Woodside*, renamed by the CR 1 October 1905 as *Woodside & Burrelton*, by the LM&SR 1 September 1927 as *Burrelton* and closed by BR 11 June 1956.
Line lifted – Station House in private use – Station site occupied by housing. **NO19833 37890**

PERTH & CLACKMANNANSHIRE 74.4 (1899)

WORKINGTON   3 A3
Opened 19 January 1846 by the Whitehaven Junction Railway as *Workington*, renamed by the LM&SR 2 June 1924 as *Workington Main* and by BR 6 May 1968 as *Workington*.

Looking south at **Workington Station** on 30 May 2015.

WORMIT   11 C2
Opened 1 May 1899 by the Newport Railway and closed by BR 5 May 1969.
Line lifted – Station building removed and rebuilt at Bo'ness on the preserved Bo'ness and Kinneil Railway – Station site occupied by housing in Bridgehead Place. **NO39648 26282**

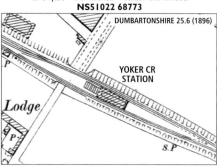
FIFESHIRE 4.1 (1912)

WORMIT GOODS   11 C3

YOKER (CR)   6 B1/21A A2
Opened 1 October 1896 by the Lanarkshire & Dumbartonshire Railway as *Yoker*, renamed by the CR in 1913 as *Yoker for Renfrew*, by BR in 1953 as *Yoker Ferry* and closed by BR 5 October 1964.
Line lifted – Demolished – Station site unused. **NS51022 68773**

DUMBARTONSHIRE 25.6 (1896)

YOKER (NBR)   6 B1/21A A1
Opened by the Glasgow, Yoker & Clydebank Railway 1 December 1882 as *Yoker*, closed 1 January 1917, reopened 1 February 1919, renamed by BR 28 February 1953 as *Yoker High* and 14 June 1965 reverted back to *Yoker*.
Looking west at **Yoker Station** on 13 September 2015.

YORKHILL   21A B2
Opened 2 February 1885 by the Glasgow City & District Railway, closed by the NBR 1 January 1917, reopened 1 February 1919 and closed 1 April 1921.
Line Operational – Demolished – No access. **NS56025 66107**

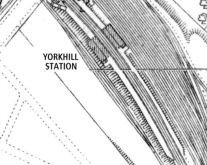
LANARKSHIRE 6.5 (1894)

EARLY BRITISH RAILWAYS' STATION CLOSURES
According to the data utilised in this index the very first closure occurred in May 1948 when the special occasions-only *Scotstoun Showground* was dispensed with, but later that year came the first branchline closure when *Jedburgh, Jedfoot, Kirkbank* and *Nisbet* closed, along with the line, on 13 August 1948. Also on the same day the three stations between Duns and St Boswells, *Marchmont, Greenlaw* and *Gordon* suffered the same fate!

Surprisingly, only two more stations disappeared from the network that year; *Saughtree* on 23 August and *Livingston* on 1 November.

NOTES FOR MAP LEGENDS

NOTES FOR MAP 2
CAIRN VALLEY LIGHT RAILWAY
This line, running from Cairn Valley Junction, about 1.25 miles north of Dumfries, to Moniaive was granted a Light Railway Order on 29 December 1899 but, due to engineering difficulties, it did not open until 1 March 1905. The G&SWR operated the line from the outset with a 1-road engine shed being installed at Moniaive. The initial motive power was provided by a trio of railmotor sets but these proved to be unreliable and loco-hauled stock was introduced in 1909. Revenue did not live up to expectations, the loco shed closed in 1921, the line was closed to passengers by the LM&SR 3 May 1943 and totally closed by BR 4 July 1949.

NOTES FOR MAP 3
SOLWAY VIADUCT
The viaduct was built by the Solway Junction Railway which had been formed on 30 June 1864 with the objective of providing a more direct route for the transportation of iron ore from Cumberland to Ayrshire.

The viaduct, built in trestle style, consisted of 193 spans and 2,892 tonf of cast iron and 1,807 tonf of wrought iron were used in its construction. Freight traffic commenced on 13 September 1869 and passenger services on 8 March 1870.

In the winter of 1874/5 cracks started to appear in the cast iron columns as a result of water seepage and freezing and in January 1881 it was seriously damaged by large sheets of ice attempting to flow past the structure.

It was rebuilt and reopened in 1884 but by 1914 an inspection report noted that it was in need of heavy repair and, although it found additional use with war traffic, this was never undertaken.

The LM&SR finally closed it in 1926 and by November 1935 the viaduct had been demolished.

NOTES FOR MAP 5
CAMPBELTOWN & MACHRIHANISH LIGHT RAILWAY
In 1876 a colliery tramway was built from Kikivan Pit, just east of Machrihanish, to Campbeltown and the owners of the line, wishing to improve receipts by handling the summer tourist traffic arriving by boat, applied for a LRO which was granted on 8 May 1905.

Construction commenced in November 1905 and the route, with an extension to Machrihanish, generally followed that of the former tramway. The 2ft 3in gauge line opened on 18 August 1908 and survived into post-grouping days, closing in 1932 and being dismantled in 1934.

None of the stations or halts had platforms and it was not uncommon for trains to pick up passengers at level crossings.

NOTES FOR MAP 6
MAIDENS & DUNURE LIGHT RAILWAY
A Light Railway Order was granted for the line on 30 September 1899. It was designed to connect communities along the coast which had been by-passed by the line from Girvan and Ayr via Maybole

and eventually opened on 17 May 1906. It was single-line and ran 20 miles from Alloway Junction in the north to Girvan Junction in the south with closure to passengers commencing on 1 December 1930 when the 15 miles between Alloway Junction and Turnberry was used for goods only by the LM&SR. The line from Turnberry to Girvan Junction closed on 2 March 1942 whilst part of the northern section reopened to passengers when Heads of Ayr Holiday Camp station opened for the summer season on 17 May 1947. The line was finally dispensed with by BR on 14 September 1968.

NOTES FOR MAP 11
INCHTURE TRAMWAY
This 2-mile long standard gauge roadside tramway was opened by the Dundee & Perth Railway in 1849. It had a junction with the main line at Inchture station and goods trains were steam hauled whilst passenger services were operated by a horse-drawn tram. It was taken over by the CR in 1865 and lasted until 1 January 1917 when it was closed as a wartime measure. The rails were lifted for use elsewhere and the small tram shed at Crossgates, at the northern end of the line, was subsequently converted into a cottage.

In view of the closure date this line should not have been included on the RCH map.

CARMYLLIE RAILWAY
The 6.5-mile long line was built by Lord Dalhousie and opened in about May 1854, its primary purpose being to carry stone from the quarries at Carmyllie to the Dundee & Arbroath Railway at Elliott Junction. It was ceded to the Scottish North Eastern Railway in 1865 and the CR the following year with passenger services commencing on 1 February 1900 following the granting of a Light Railway Order on 6 August 1898. The passenger service was withdrawn by the LM&SR/L&NER Joint on 2 December 1929 and the line was closed by BR 19 May 1965.

NOTES FOR MAPS 14 & 17
CROMARTY & DINGWALL LIGHT RAILWAY
Authorised by a Light Railway Order on 1 August 1902, construction did not commence immediately and had only extended some six miles to the west of Cromarty when the project was abandoned following the outbreak of the First World War in 1914. The track was subsequently lifted and none of the stations shown on this map were ever constructed.

NOTES FOR MAPS 15 & 18
KEITH TO PORTESSIE BRANCH (HR)
The line was fully opened from Keith to Portessie on 1 May 1886 but, following the arrival of the GNofSR at Portessie, traffic diminished and First World War wartime economies led to the closure of all the stations on 9 August 1915. The branch was requisitioned by the Admiralty in 1917 and sections of the line were removed for use elsewhere. Although it was intended to reopen the stations after the war this never materialised and what sections had been relaid were used for freight only.

It can only be assumed that the appearance of Enzie Rathven, Buckie (HR), Portessie (HR) and Drybridge on this map was in anticipation of them reopening at a later date, however Aultmore continued in use as a goods station until closure by BR on 3 October 1966.

NOTES FOR MAP 17
DORNOCH LIGHT RAILWAY
Running from The Mound to Dornoch this 7.75 mile long line was granted a Light Railway Order on 13 August 1898 and opened on 2 June 1902. A 1-road timber-built dead-ended engine shed was provided at Dornoch and the line was worked from the outset by the HR as an independent concern until becoming part of the LM&SR at grouping. It was closed by BR 13 June 1960.

NOTES FOR MAP 18
WICK & LYBSTER LIGHT RAILWAY
Authorized by a Light Railway Order issued on 27 November 1899, this 13 miles 39 chains long line was financed by a Government grant of £25,000, the HR and local subscriptions of £72,000, the motive for its construction being the development of the fishing port at Lybster.

The line opened on 1 July 1903 with a 1-road timber-built through-road shed being provided at Lybster and was worked by the HR until subsumed into the LM&SR on grouping. The traffic never thoroughly materialised as road improvements were effected in the 1930s and the last train ran on 1 April 1944, with the stations and line closing two days later.

NOTES FOR MAPS 4A & 8A
KIELDER WATER
This, the largest man-made reservoir in the UK with a capacity of 44 billion gallons, was authorized by Parliament in 1974 and built during the period 1975 – 1981. It was flooded in 1982 and, along with a hydro-electric plant, officially opened in the same year.

Part of the construction involved the demolition of Plashetts Station (See Map 8A)

NOTES FOR MAP 8A
PENMANSHIEL DEVIATION
The 267 yard-long Penmanshiel Tunnel opened in 1846 and was undergoing structural repairs and rebuilding to accommodate 8ft 6in high containers when it collapsed on 17 March 1979. Engineers were working in the tunnel at the time and, sadly, two men were killed.

The plan was to repair the tunnel and reopen it but it was found that the ground was not stable enough and the decision was made to realign the route through a cutting. This resulted in the abandonment of 1,100 yards of track, including the tunnel, and the line was closed until 20 August 1979 before the new alignment could be opened.

During this period Dunbar and Berwick-upon-Tweed stations acted as termini with special 'bus services operating a shuttle.

THREE STATIONS CLOSED DURING THE BR ERA

Jedfoot Station viewed on 3 August 1964. It was one of the very first to close, some sixteen years earlier, on 13 August 1948. *Neal Caplan/Online Transport Archive*

The "legendary" **Riccarton Junction Station** viewed from a passing train on 9 October 1963. It had an engine shed and its own small community of railway employees and until BR days, was only accessible by rail. It closed, along with the "Waverley" route on 6 January 1969. *Neal Caplan/Online Transport Archive*

Looking east at **Comrie Station** on 12 April 1965. It was opened by the CR 1 June 1893 and closed by BR 6 July 1964. *Neal Caplan/Online Transport Archive*

GLASGOW SUBWAY

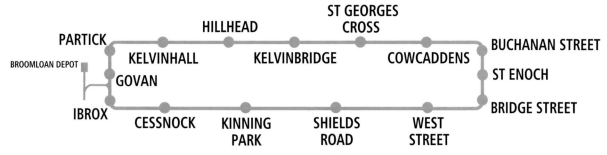

The Glasgow Subway was opened on 14 December 1896 by the Glasgow Subway Company after six years of construction with a track of 4ft gauge, disposed in a loop just short of 6.5 miles long and running entirely through 11ft diameter tunnels. The initial method of traction was by cables but, following the purchase of the line by Glasgow Corporation in 1923, the system was electrified in 1935 with a 600Vdc supply accessed via a third rail.

The fifteen stations were built as island platforms, leading to the provision of carriages that only opened on one side, and the clockwise and anticlockwise tracks were originally independent of each other as the layout was devoid of points, leading to the lines being known as Inner Circle and Outer Circle.

The first depot was sited above ground at **Govan** and to facilitate the maintenance of the carriages trains had to be craned off the tracks and onto the system at the depot. The current maintenance depot, located at **Broomloan Road** (NS55512 65498, [55.860941, -4.3101570]) between Govan and Ibrox stations, is also above ground but trains are now able to access it through the installation of points and a ramp during a modernisation programme commenced in 1977. This programme was badly needed as the whole system was showing severe signs of wear and tear and a large amount of track was replaced and stations refurbished and rebuilt.

The current rolling stock, built by Metro-Cammell Birmingham, was introduced between 1977 and 1992 and comprises of 36 cars in 3-car formations. Seventeen new units in 4-car formation were due to be introduced in 2020 but none were in service by January 2021.

EDINBURGH TRAMS

As proposed in 2001 the system would be composed of three routes: a circular one around the northern suburbs and radial lines to Newbridge in the west and Newcraighall in the south but the cost of building them all was deemed prohibitive.

In the end a route from Edinburgh Airport to Leith was approved in 2003 and costed at £375m but by the time that construction commenced in 2008 it had risen to £528m and the route was truncated again with the eastern end now terminating at York Place.

The 8.7 mile-long standard gauge system opened on 31 May 2014 and is operated by a fleet of 27 Urbos 3 trams with a power system of 750Vdc supplied by overhead lines.

In 2015 it was proposed to extend the line west to Newhaven and this was agreed by Edinburgh Council in March 2019 with it due to open in 2023.

Edinburgh Trams Nos **253** and **252** passing at **Edinburgh Park Tram Stop** on 12 May 2017.

BRITISH RAILWAYS
MOTIVE POWER DEPOTS
& STABLING POINTS
SCOTTISH REGION

One of the earliest BR casualties was the 2TS **Macduff MPD**, viewed here in private use on 21 July 1965. It closed, along with the branch line, on 1 October 1951.

The hybrid codes and list reproduced here are based on the first one which was issued by British Railways in February 1950. Between 1948 and this date two of the depots in this region, Perth (LNER) and Jedburgh, were closed but are included to show those in use when the system was nationalised.

DEPOT	CLOSURE DATE	LOCATION	SITE STATUS
60A Inverness	June 1962	NH67104560	Morrisons Supermarket car park
Dingwall	c1962	NH55235830	Cambrai Court and car park
Fortrose	October 1950	NH72465663	Housing in Station Crescent
Kyle of Lochalsh	18 June 1962	NG76182752	Douglas Row and car park
60B Aviemore	July 1962 (s)	NH89791291	Preserved Strathspey Railway
Boat of Garten	November 1958	NH94471926	Site of Permanent Way depot on SR
60C Helmsdale	July 1961	ND02321554	Site unused
Dornoch	11 June 1960	NH79899002	Site of Commercial building
Tain	18 June 1962	NH78448224	Site unused
60D Wick	July 1962	ND35975082	In use as a supermarket
Thurso	1962	ND11276775	Dwellings
60E Forres	May 1959	NJ02975900	Site part of station car park
61A Kittybrewster	12 June 1961 (s)	NJ93150794	MOT Inspection Centre
Alford	2 January 1959	NJ58301581	Site Unused
Inverurie*	March 1959 (s)	NJ77302210	Commercial Estate
Ballater	April 1958 (s)	NO37119588	Dwellings
Fraserburgh	June 1961(s)	NJ99896666	In commercial use
Macduff	1 October 1951	NJ69916411	In commercial use
Peterhead	June 1961 (s)	NK12674663	Site Unused, grassland

DEPOT	CLOSURE DATE	LOCATION	SITE STATUS
61B Aberdeen Ferryhill	March 1967 (s)	NJ94030455	Housing in Polmuir Gardens
61C Keith	June 1961 (s)	NJ43335178	Site in commercial use
Banff	July 1964	NJ68646461	Site Unused
Elgin	June 1961 (s)	NJ22576245	In use as a Moray Council Depot
62A Thornton Junction	April 1967	NT28309706	Site Unused
Anstruther	December 1960	NO56110347	Dreelside Housing Estate
Burntisland	1958 (s)	NT23678582	Site of car park
Kirkcaldy*	1959	NT27859219	Site Unused, adjacent to running line
Ladybank	1958 (s)	NO30620997	Site Unused, adjacent to running line
Methil*	1958	NO38050015	Site Unused, wasteground
62B Dundee Tay Bridge	1 May 1967	NO39852960	Tesco Extra Car Park
Arbroath	3 January 1959	NO63854161	Site Unused in a small park area
Dundee West	1958 (s)	NO39402945	Site Unused
Montrose	May 1966	NO71275803	Co-Op store and Car Park
St Andrews	September 1960	NO49881731	Site of Old Course Hotel
Tayport	1 October 1951	NO45942887	Housing Estate
62C Dunfermline Upper	1 May 1967	NT10088783	Site Unused
Alloa	January 1967	NS88839314	Housing in Old Brewery Lane
Inverkeithing*	1966	NT13118372	Site Unused, adjacent to running line
Kelty*	1964	NT15019580	Site in agricultural use
Loch Leven	14 April 1951	NO11810142	Site part of Loch Leven Heritage Trail
63A Perth South	1 May 1967 (s)	NO11652180	Commercial Estate
Aberfeldy	1962	NN86064927	Housing in Appin Place
Alyth	July 1951	NO24864828	Housing in Mart Street
Blair Atholl	1962	NN86876528	In Commercial Use
Crieff	13 September 1958	NN86362119	Housing in Duchlage Court
Perth (LNER)	7 January 1950	NO11282285	Network Rail Depot
63B Stirling	13 June 1966	NS80089310	Commercial Use
Killin Loch Tay	27 September 1965	NN58483451	Incorporated in a dwelling as a garage
Stirling Shore Road	16 September 1957	NS79759432(n)	Site of Ambulance Station
(Two buildings on separate sites)		NS79759400(s)	Commercial Use
63C Forfar	18 July 1964	NO46175154	In Commercial Use
Brechin	2 August 1952	NO60736004	In grounds of Andover Primary School
63D Fort William	18 June 1962 (s)	NN10487428	Site used for roadway
Mallaig	18 June 1962	NM67479700	Site used for A830
63E Oban	12 March 1962	NM85632943	Industrial Yard
Ballachulish	12 March 1962	NN08255844	Car Parking in Old Railway Goods Yard
64A St Margarets	1 May 1967	NT28207427	Commercial Development
Dunbar	June 1964	NT68107843	Site Unused, adjacent to running line
Galashiels	April 1962	NT49633600	Site of Asda Superstore
Granton*	c1964	NT23757715	Commercial Development
Hardengreen*	1962	NT32346622	Housing in Westfield Bank
Longniddry	June 1959	NT44827634	Site Unused, adjacent to running line
North Berwick	February 1958	NT54498504	Site Unused, adjacent to running line
North Leith*	c1951	NT26647258	Housing in Dalkeith Road
Peebles	October 1955	NT25104100	Site of Tesco Superstore
Penicuik	10 September 1951	NT23635964	Housing off Bankview Mill
Polton*	10 September 1951	NT28886480	Part of Stevenson Place
Seafield	13 October 1962	NT28417635	Part of Depot on Marine Esplanade
South Leith*	c1960 (s)	NT28447592	Site Unused
64B Haymarket	9 September 1963	NT22957281	Site of Haymarket Depot

DEPOT	CLOSURE DATE	LOCATION	SITE STATUS
64C Dalry Road	3 October 1965	NT23757260	Site Unused
64D Carstairs	December 1966 (s)	NS95324542	Sidings
64E Polmont	May 1964	NS92387827	Site Unused
Kinneil	September 1952	NS98428113	Site Unused, adjacent to running line
64F Bathgate	August 1966	NS97746841	Site of Car Park
64G Hawick	3 January 1966	NT50501531	Site of Teviotdale Leisure Centre
Kelso	July 1955	NT73203323	Commercial Development
Riccarton Junction*	October 1958	NY54109750	Site Unused
Jedburgh	2 April 1949	NT65672153	Site Unused
St Boswells	16 November 1959	NT57753158	In Commercial Use
65A Eastfield	November 1966 (s)	NS60036867	Site of Eastfield Depot
Aberfoyle	1 October 1951	NN52350085	Site Unused
Kilsyth	1 October 1951	NS71137793	Site Unused
Lennoxtown	1 October 1951	NS62707781	Commercial Development
Whiteinch	c1951	NS53686752	Site Unused
65B St Rollox	7 November 1966	NS62206730	Site of Broomfield Court Care Home
65C Parkhead	18 October 1965	NS62806457	Commercial Estate
65D Dawsholm	3 October 1964	NS56456858	Site of St Gregory's Catholic Church
Dumbarton	5 October 1964	NS40537517	Housing in Park Street
Stobcross	October 1950	NS56686572	Site Unused, adjacent to running line
65E Kipps	January 1963	NS73856578	Industrial Development
65F Grangemouth	November 1965 (s)	NS91278076	Warehouse and Distribution centre
65G Yoker	January 1964	NS51696866	Part of Yoker Sports Centre
65H Helensburgh	7 November 1960	NS29788243	Co-op Supermarket Car Park
Arrochar*	October 1959	NN30870434	Site Unused, adjacent to running line
65I Balloch	7 November 1960	NS38948196	Grassland
66A Polmadie	1 May 1967	NS59786266	Site of part of Polmadie Depot
Paisley St James*	3 January 1953	NS47346473	Site Unused
66B Motherwell	1 May 1967 (s)	NS74905795	Depot for Direct Rail Services
Morningside*	November 1954	NS83325517	Site Unused
66C Hamilton	November 1962 (s)	NS71065597	Site of Douglas View Care Centre
66D Greenock Ladyburn	December 1966	NS30157503	Housing in Macgillivary Avenue
Greenock Princes Pier	May 1959	NS27207683	Site Unused
67A Corkerhill	1 May 1967	NS54536278	Site of Corkerhill Depot
67B Hurlford	3 October 1966	NS45473603	Industrial Development
Beith	5 November 1962	NS34555338	Housing in Balfour Avenue
Muirkirk	5 October 1964	NS69532645	Part of Kames Motorsport Circuit
67C Ayr	3 October 1966 (s)	NS34302275	Site Unused, adjacent to running line
67D Ardrossan	15 February 1965	NS23594240	Site Unused, adjacent to running line
68A Carlisle Kingmoor†	1 January 1968	NY38585770	Kingmoor Nature Reserve
Carlisle Durran Hill†	2 November 1959	NY42205490	Site Unused
68B Dumfries	2 May 1966	NX97757638	Site of Divisional Police Headquarters
Kirkcudbright	1955	NX68635125	Housing in St Mary Street
68C Stranraer	October 1966	NX06806050	Still Standing, unused
Newton Stewart	1959	NX40266490	In Industrial Use
68D Beattock	29 April 1967	NT07680248	Site in use for sidings
Lockerbie	5 February 1951	NY13768184	Site of Depot for Nordic Tyres

Notes

(s) indicates that the depot/stabling point ceased servicing steam locomotives from that date but remained open for diesels.

* Stabling Point - usually consisting of at least an engine pit but may also have possessed coaling and watering facilities as well as a turntable.

† In this initial compilation the ex-CR Carlisle Kingmoor, and all the sub sheds, were included in the Scottish Region.

Site Status entries in **RED** indicate that the building is still standing, **PURPLE** that the depot or site is part of a preserved line.

PRESERVED RAILWAY LINES
A BRIEF SUMMARY OF THE HISTORY, ROUTES AND CONTACT DETAILS

ALFORD VALLEY RAILWAY (15A)

Alford Valley Railway, Stewart Road, Alford, Aberdeenshire AB33 8UA,
info@alfordvalleyrailway.org.uk 019755 64332 or 07867 626911
www.alfordvalleyrailway.org.uk

The construction of the Alford Valley Railway started in 1856 and the line
opened in 1859 as a GNofSR branch line from Kintore Station The line was
closed by BR on 31 December 1965 and the 0.84 mile long 2ft gauge line was
opened from *Alford Station* to a platform at *Haughton Park* in 1984.

The platform at Alford is original but the station building is a replacement for
the one demolished when the line was closed.

BO'NESS & KINNEIL RAILWAY (7A)

Bo'ness Station, Union Street, Bo'ness EH51 9AQ
enquiries.railway@srps.org.uk 01506 822298
https://www.bkrailway.co.uk/

The 5 mile long route, effectively from Manuel Low Level Station to Bo'ness
(Borrowstounness), was opened by the Monkland Railway in 1856, became
part of the NBR, then the L&NER and was closed by BR in November 1965.
There are currently four stations on the system, *Bo'ness, Kinneil, Birkhill* and
Manuel, all of which have been constructed from scratch by the Scottish
Railway Preservation Society.

Bo'ness, the northern terminus of the line was built in the 1980s and consists
of a marvellous collection of buildings and structures retrieved from potential
destruction and demolition. The trainshed was rescued from *Haymarket Station*
(Maps 7 B1/22A B2), the station office from *Wormit Station* (Map 11 C2), the
footbridge from *Murthly Station* (Map 11 A2) and the signal box from *Garnqueen
South Junction*. All four, as a collection, are listed by Historic Scotland in
Category A. It is also the site of the maintenance facility for the line.

CALEDONIAN RAILWAY (BRECHIN) (11A)

The Station, Park Road, Brechin DD9 7AF
enquiries@caledonianrailway.com 01356 622992
http://www.caledonianrailway.com/

The four mile long route from Brechin to Bridge of Dun is the west part of
the branch line from Kinnaber Junction that was opened by the Aberdeen
Railway on 1 Feb 1848 and totally closed by BR in 1981. A 1TS engine shed
was opened at the terminus on the same date and replaced in 1894 by a larger
2TS brick built depot on another site. This was closed by BR on 2 August 1952.

The line was taken over by the Brechin Railway Preservation Society who
formed Caledonian Railway (Brechin) Ltd to operate it and services commenced in 1993.

There are currently two stations on the 4-mile long line, *Brechin* and *Bridge
of Dun* both of which have original buildings that have been thoroughly
renovated and restored.

There are plans to extend the line eastwards to the only other station on
the branch, at *Dubton*, giving a total line length of some 7½ miles.

KEITH & DUFFTOWN RAILWAY (15A)

Keith Town Station, Church Road, Old Keith, Keith, Moray AB55 5BR
01340 821181
http://keith-dufftown-railway.co.uk/

The 11 miles long line from Keith Town to Dufftown was opened in 1862 by
the Keith & Dufftown Railway and became a part of the GNofSR route from
Aberdeen to Elgin. By 1968 all the stations had been closed by BR but the line
was retained for freight, serving the distillery in Dufftown, whilst all the track
west of Dufftown was lifted.

At the north end the section to Keith Junction from Keith Town is still intact
although two 60ft long track panels were removed on the orders of Network
Rail to prevent any access between the two systems.

The line was taken over by the Keith & Dufftown Railway Association in 1998

and there are currently three stations open, *Keith Town, Drummuir* and *Dufftown*, and three that have closed: *Drummuir Curlers' Platform,* which technically
predates this atlas and enjoyed a brief existence during GNofSR days, *Towiemore Halt,* the platform of which has degraded but the stone-built station hut
is now a PW store and *Auchindachy* where the platform is overgrown but still
intact and the former station house is now a private residence.

LEADHILLS & WANLOCKHEAD RAILWAY (6A)

The Station, Station Road, Leadhills, South Lanarkshire ML12 6XS
secretary@leadhillsrailway.co.uk
https://www.leadhillsrailway.co.uk/

The 7.2 miles long Leadhills & Wanlockhead Light Railway was opened
throughout from its junction with the Caledonian Railway main line at Elvanfoot to the terminus at Wanlockhead on 1 October 1902. It was primarily
used for the transportation of lead from the mines in the area and was closed
by the LM&SR on 2 January 1939.

The Leadhills and Wanlockhead Railway, which opened in 1986 is a 2ft
narrow gauge system laid on the trackbed of the former standard gauge line
and extending about 0.6 miles west of Leadhills Station to Glengonnar Halt. It
has the distinction of being the highest adhesion-worked line in Britain with a
summit of 1,498ft (Druimuachdar Summit near Blair Atholl [Map 10] is the
highest on Network Rail at 1,484ft). The only former station in use is the single
platform *Leadhills* which has a reconstructed signal box containing the original
lever frame from the Arrochar and Tarbet signal box.

ROYAL DEESIDE RAILWAY (16A)

Milton of Crathes, Banchory, AberdeenshireAB31 5QH
opsdir@deeside-railway.co.uk 01330 844416
http://www.deeside-railway.co.uk/

The 1-mile long railway is part of the Deeside Railway line from Aberdeen
to Banchory which opened on 8 September 1853. This short section of track
was taken over by the Royal Deeside Railway in 1996 with the intention of
reopening the line from *Milton of Crathes* to *Banchory*. Currently the only
station on the line is *Milton of Crathes* which was built by the preservation
group and it terminates at Birkenbaud Crossing.

STRATHSPEY RAILWAY (14A/15A)

Aviemore Station, Dalfaber Road, Aviemore, Inverness-shire PH22 1PY
01479 810725
https://www.strathspeyrailway.co.uk/

The line from Forres to Aviemore was opened by the Inverness & Perth
Junction Railway on 3 August 1863 and was the main route from Perth to
Inverness until, under a perceived threat of competition from the route of the
Invergarry & Fort Augustus Railway, the HR sponsored the thirty miles shorter
(but with much heavier gradients) Inverness to Aviemore Direct Railway line
via Carr Bridge. This was passed through Parliament on 28 July 1884 and
opened throughout on 1 November 1898 (Map 14), thus reducing the impor-
tance of the link to Inverness via Forres and Grantown-on-Spey. The line was
closed by BR on 18 October 1965.

The 10 miles long Strathspey Railway from *Aviemore* to *Broomhill* was opened
in 1978 and there are currently three operational stations: *Aviemore, Boat of
Garten* and *Broomhill*. Until 1998 the southern terminus was at *Aviemore
(Speyside)*, built by the preservation group some three hundred yards north of
the mainline station. Since access was made to Aviemore it is no longer in
regular use but the signal box, formerly at Garve West, continues to be
deployed and the coaling facility occupies part of the station site

Following refurbishment the Strathspey Railway uses Platform 3 at *Aviemore
Station* and its operational headquarters are at the preserved 4TS Aviemore
MPD which was opened in 1898 by the HR, closed to steam by BR in July 1962
and totally in 1966. It was let out for commercial use until taken over by the
Strathspey Railway in 1975.

Boat of Garten station features original buildings dating from 1904 by the
architect William Roberts. It was originally a parallel junction between the HRs
main line from Perth to Forres and the GNofSR branch to Craigellachie. Today
there are two passenger platforms and the yard stores the majority of the SR's
out of use rolling stock.

PRINCIPAL RAILWAY WALKS

A BRIEF SUMMARY OF THE HISTORY, ROUTES AND WEBSITE ADDRESSES

BORDERS ABBEYS WAY (8A)

http://bordersabbeysway.com/

ROXBURGH   KIRKBANK   NISBET

This 64.5 mile walk was developed around the four ruined Border Abbeys and the location of an earlier but short-lived Tironsian Abbey in Selkirk. They are now in ruins but are monuments to the many Cistercian and Augustinian monks who lived here in the twelfth to sixteenth centuries. Part of the walk follows the former North British Railway's Jedburgh branch, closed by BR on 10 August 1964, from south of *Roxburgh* to *Nisbet*.

CLYDE & LOCH LOMOND CYCLE WAY (21A)

http://www.sustrans.org.uk

| | SCOTSTOUN WEST | | WHITEINCH | |
| YOKER FOR RENFREW | | SCOTSTOUN EAST | | PARTICK WEST |

The Clyde & Loch Lomond Cycleway forms one element of the 601 miles-long National Cycleway Route No.7 from Sunderland to Inverness. This section is just 20 miles long and utilises the trackbed of the former Caledonian Railway line between *Partick West* and *Yoker for Renfrew* stations for part of it. The line was opened on 1 October 1896 and closed by BR on 5 October 1964.

DAVA WAY (15A)

http://www.davaway.org.uk/

			HUNTLYS CAVE	GRANTOWN-ON-SPEY
FORRES				
	DUNPHAIL	DAVA	CASTLE GRANT PLATFORM	

Established in 2005 this 24 mile-long walk utilises the trackbed of the former Inverness & Perth Junction Railway line from *Forres* to *Grantown-on-Spey (West)*. The line opened on 3 August 1863 and was closed by BR on 18 October 1965.

DEESIDE WAY (15A/16A)

http://www.deesideway.org/

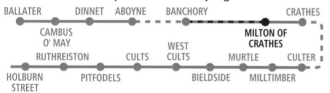

BALLATER	DINNET	ABOYNE	BANCHORY		CRATHES
	CAMBUS O' MAY			MILTON OF CRATHES	
			WEST		
	RUTHREISTON	CULTS	CULTS	MURTLE	CULTER
HOLBURN STREET	PITFODELS			BIELDSIDE	MILLTIMBER

The route of this 41 mile-long walkway follows the River Dee from the outskirts of Aberdeen to Ballater in the Cairngorms and utilises the trackbed of the former Great North of Scotland Railway from Aberdeen to *Culter*, *Crathes* to *Banchory* (where it shares the trackbed with the Royal Deeside Railway) and then *Aboyne* to *Ballater*. The line was opened throughout on 17 October 1866, closed to passengers by BR on 28 February 1966 and totally on 18 July 1966. It is also National Cycle Network Route No.195.

DEVON WAY (10A/11A)

https://www.walkhighlands.co.uk/fife-stirling/dollar-tillicoultry.shtml

TILLICOULTRY   DOLLAR

This 3.25 miles-long walk uses the trackbed of the former North British Railway line between *Dollar* and *Tillicoultry*. The line was opened on 3 May 1869 by the Devon Valley Railway, closed to passengers by BR on 15 June 1964 and totally on 26 June 1973.

ELLIOT NATURE TRAIL (11A)

http://www.walkscotland.com/walk13.htm

ARBIRLOT   ELLIOT

A short 2 mile-long walk between *Elliot* and *Arbirlot* on part of the trackbed of the Carmyllie branch which first opened for freight in February 1855 and closed by BR on 24 May 1965.

FIFE COASTAL PATH (11A)

http://www.fifecoastalpath.co.uk/

| WEMYSS CASTLE | | | LARGO | |
| | BUCKHAVEN | LUNDIN LINKS | | GUARD BRIDGE |

The Fife Coastal Path runs from the Forth Estuary in the south, to the Tay Estuary in the north and stretches for 117 miles. The trackbeds of the *Wemyss Castle* to *Buckhaven* (Opened by the Wemyss & Buckhaven Railway on 8 August 1881 and closed by BR on 10 January 1955), *Lundin Links* to *Largo* (Opened by the East of Fife Railway on 11 August 1857 and closed by BR on 6 September 1965) and *Guard Bridge* to *Leuchars* (Opened by the St Andrews Railway on 1 July 1852 and closed by BR on 6 September 1965) lines form part of the route.

FORMARTINE & BUCHAN WAY (16A/19A)

https://www.walkhighlands.co.uk/aberdeenshire/formartine-buchan-way.shtml

	BRUCKLAY	MORMOND	RATHEN	KIRTON BRIDGE PLATFORM
		STRICHEN	LONMAY	PHILORTH FRASERBURGH
		MINTLAW	NEWSEAT	PETERHEAD
MAUD JUNCTION	ABBEY OF DEER HALT	LONGSIDE	INVERUGIE	
	ARNAGE	ESSLEMONT	NEW MACHAR	DYCE
	AUCHNAGATT	ELLON	LOGIEREVE	PARKHILL

The Buchan Countryside Group began the work of reopening the route as a cycleway and footpath in 1987 and the Formartine and Buchan Way opened in the early 1990s. It runs along the former Great North of Scotland Railway route from *Dyce* on the fringes of Aberdeen north to *Maud Junction* where it splits with branches heading to *Fraserburgh* and *Peterhead*.

The Fraserburgh branch was opened on 24 April 1865 by the Formartine & Buchan Railway and closed to passengers by BR on 4 October 1965, whilst the Peterhead branch was opened by the Formartine & Buchan Railway on 3 July 1862 and closed to passengers by BR on 3 May 1965. Both continued in use for goods until total closure came, for Peterhead on 7 September 1970 and Fraserburgh during 1979.

INNOCENT RAILWAY PATH (22A)

http://www.edinburghguide.com/book/transport/cycling/innocentrailwaypath

ST LEONARD'S

The Innocent Railway Path, which opened in 1981, runs from the Newington/St Leonard's area under Holyrood Park, by means of the 1700 ft long Innocent Railway Tunnel, and through to Brunstane via Duddingston and Craigmillar. It is a section of the John Muir Way *(qv)* and the UK-wide National Cycle Network's Route 1 (NCN1) and follows part of the Edinburgh and Dalkeith Railway which opened in July 1831, originally as a 4ft 6in gauge horse-drawn tramway but converted to a standard gauge steam-hauled line by the North British Railway in 1845. St Leonard's station closed to passengers in 1847 and the branch was closed totally by BR on 22 July 1968.

JOHN MUIR WAY (6A)

http://johnmuirway.org/

| STRATHBLANE | | LENNOXTOWN | | KIRKINTILLOCH |
| | CRAIGEND PLATFORM | CAMPSIE GLEN | | MILTON OF CAMPSIE | |

John Muir (1838-1914) was a Scottish-American naturalist, author, environmental philosopher, glaciologist and an early advocate of preservation of wilderness in the USA. The John Muir Way, completed in 2014, is dedicated to his memory and stretches 134 miles across Scotland's heartland, running between Helensburgh in the west through to Dunbar, Muir's birthplace, on the east coast. Parts of it use former railway trackbeds, namely the Edinburgh St Leonard's line (Innocent Railway Path *[qv]*) and a section of the North British Railway's line from *Strathblane* to *Kirkintilloch* which was opened throughout on 1 July 1867 and closed to passengers by BR on 1 October 1951.

LOCH LEVEN HERITAGE TRAIL (11A)

http://www.lochlevenheritagetrail.co.uk/

LOCH LEVEN ——————————— BLAIRADAM

This 13 mile long trail circumvents the loch and uses a short section of the former trackbed between *Loch Leven* and *Blairadam* which was opened by the Kinross-shire Railway on 20 September 1860 and closed by BR on 4 May 1970.

MORAY COAST TRAIL (18A)

http://www.morayways.org.uk/moray-coast-trail.asp

GARMOUTH — BUCKPOOL BUCKIE — FINDOCHTY — CULLEN
SPEY PORT PORTESSIE PORTKNOCKIE
BAY GORDON

The Moray Coast Trail links the coastline and settlements of Moray by a way-marked coastal trail of approximately 50 miles from Forres to Findhorn and Cullen and most of the trackbed of the former Great North of Scotland Railway line from *Garmouth* to *Cullen* is utilised. This was opened throughout on 1 May 1886 and closed by BR on 6 May 1968.

PAISLEY & CLYDE WALKWAY (6A)

http://www.sustrans.org.uk/

KILMACOLM — HOUSTON
LYNEDOCK BRIDGE OF ELDERSLIE PAISLEY **PAISLEY**
GREENOCK WEIR WEST **CANAL**

This 21 mile-long cycle and walkway is part of the National Cycle Network Route 75, an 114 mile-long route from Leith to Portavadie on the Cowall Peninsula in Argyle. The Paisley and Clyde Walkway follows the trackbed for almost the full distance of the former Glasgow & South Western Railway line from *Paisley Canal* to *Greenock Princes Pier* which was opened by the Greenock & Ayrshire Railway on 23 December 1869 and closed by BR on 10 January 1983.

PENICUIK TO MUSSELBURGH CYCLE-WALKWAY (7A/22A)

http://www.sustrans.org.uk/ncn/map/route/route-196

PENICUIK — AUCHENDINNY — BONNYRIGG — SMEATON
ESK BRIDGE ROSSLYN HAWTHORNDEN
CASTLE

This cycle-walkway follows most of the former *Musselburgh* to *Penicuik* line and forms part of the 26 mile-long National Cycle Network Route No.196 from Haddington to Penicuik. The 4.5 mile Penicuik branch was opened by the Penicuik Railway on 2 September 1872, closed to passengers by BR on 10 September 1951 and totally on 27 March 1967. The northern part, from *Musselburgh* to *Smeaton* was totally closed by BR on 24 May 1965.

PENCAITLAND RAILWAY WALK (7A)

https://ridearoundedinburgh.wordpress.com/east-lothian/pencaitland-railway-walk/

ORMISTON — SALTOUN
CROSSGATEHALL PENCAITLAND
HALT

The 7 miles-long Pencaitland Railway Walk utilises the trackbed of the former North British Railway branch to Gifford from *Crossgate Hall Halt* to *Saltoun*. The branch was opened throughout by the Gifford & Garve Light Railway on 14 October 1901, closed to passengers by the L&NER on 3 April 1933 and totally closed by BR on 24 May 1965.

ROB ROY WAY (10A)

http://www.robroyway.com/

LOCH TAY KILLIN JUNCTION BALQUHIDDER STRATHYRE CALLANDER
KILLIN GLENGOGLEHEAD KINGSHOUSE CRAIGNACAILLEICH
CROSSING PLATFORM

This walk, from Drymen on the West Highland Way [qv] runs north east to Pitlochry. Depending on which route is taken it is either 77 or 94 miles in length. The ex-Callander & Oban Railway line from *Callander* to just short of *Killin Junction*, which opened on 1 June 1870 and was closed by BR on 28 September 1965, forms a section of the walk as does the branch line from *Killin* to *Loch Tay* which was opened by the Killin Railway on 1 April 1886.

ST VIGEANS NATURE TRAIL (11A)

http://www.walkscotland.com/route8.htm

LEYSMILL ——————————— COLLISTON

The trackbed between *Colliston* and *Leysmill* stations forms the main part of this five mile walk. The line was opened by the Arbroath & Forfar Railway on 24 November 1838 and closed by BR on 25 January 1965.

SCOTTISH NATIONAL ROUTE (2A)

http://www.sustrans.org.uk/scotland/national-cycle-network

PALNURE ——————————— CREETOWN

There are approximately 2,371 miles of National Cycle Network routes in Scotland and part of the short section of trackbed between *Creetown* and *Palnure* stations is utilised in the route. This former Portpatrick & Wigtownshire Joint Railway line was opened on 12 March 1861 and closed by BR on 14 June 1965.

SPEYSIDE WAY (15A)

http://www.speysideway.org/

GILBEY'S
NETHY GRANTOWN- DALVEY COTTAGES
BRIDGE ON-SPEY FARM HALT BLACKSBOAT HALT
BALLIFURTH CROMDALE BALLINDALLOCH KNOCKANDO
FARM HALT KNOCKANDO
DUFFTOWN ABERLOUR CARRON HOUSE HALT
CRAIGELLACHIE DALVAINE IMPERIAL
HALT COTTAGES HALT

It was first opened in 1981, to run from Spey Bay to Ballindalloch, with a 15 mile-long spur to Tomintoul being added in 1990. A northern extension from Spey Bay to Buckie followed in 1999 and the route was further extended from Ballindalloch to Aviemore in April 2000. The Speyside Way is now 65 miles long and links the Moray coast with the edge of the Grampian Mountains, generally following the valley of the River Spey. Two of the sections mainly follow trackbeds, from *Buckie* to *Spey Bay*, which is also part of the Moray Coast Trail [qv] and *Craigellachie* to *Ballindalloch*, plus some sections of the line between *Dalvey Farm Halt* and *Nethy Bridge*, which was opened by the Strathspey Railway on 1 July 1863 and closed by BR on 4 November 1968.

WATER OF LEITH WALKWAY (7A/22A)

http://www.waterofleith.org.uk/walkway/

CURRIE COLINTON CRAIGLEITH
BALERNO JUNIPER HAILES MURRAYFIELD
GREEN HALT

This 12 miles-long walkway opened in 2002 and follows the Water of Leith from Balerno to Leith utilising the former Caledonian Railway trackbeds between *Balerno* and to the east of *Colinton* and between *Murrayfield* and beyond *Craigleith*. The Balerno branch was opened by the Caledonian Railway on 1 August 1874 and closed by BR on 4 December 1967 whilst the Murrayfield to Craigleith section opened on 1 August 1879 and was totally closed by BR on 21 June 1965.

WEST FIFE CYCLEWAY (10A/11A)

http://www.sustrans.org.uk/

FOREST MILL BOGSIDE OAKLEY
CLACKMANNAN EAST DUNFERMLINE
ROAD GRANGE UPPER

The 11 mile-long West Fife Cycle Way starts just to the northeast of Clackmannan and follows the course of the former Stirling & Dunfermline Railway between *Dunfermline Upper* and *Clackmannan Road* which opened on 28 August 1850 and was closed by BR on 7 October 1968.

WEST HIGHLAND WAY (10A)

http://www.west-highland-way.co.uk/

KILLEARN ——————————— DUMGOYNE

The 96 miles long route starts at Milngavie and finishes at Gordon Square in Fort William. A short section of trackbed of the former Blane Valley Railway from *Dumgoyne* to just north of *Killearn* forms part of the route. This line opened on 12 August 1880, was closed to passengers by BR on 1 October 1951 and totally on 5 October 1959.

SIGNAL BOXES

Despite ongoing modernisation programmes many signal boxes still remain, either operational, disused, preserved (or "listed") or in private use. The following are a small selection of them

BARRHEAD

A 25-lever box built in 1894 for the CR. Viewed on 18 March 2017.

FORSINARD

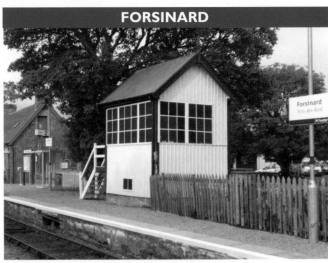

Built in 1894 for the HR with a Dutton frame and after closure it was in PW use. Viewed on 16 September 2015.

DALWHINNIE

A 20-lever box built in 1909 for the HR. Viewed on 15 September 2015.

PITLOCHRY

A 24-lever box with a Mackenzie & Holland frame, built in 1911 for the HR. ("Listed" 12 October 1994). Viewed on 15 September 2015.

ELGIN WEST

A 26-lever box built in 1951 for BR (Scottish Region). The upper section came from *Mosstowie Signal Box* and was placed on a new brick-built base. Viewed on 17 September 2015, it was demolished on 7 October 2017.

ROGART

Built in 1894 by Dutton & Co. for the HR, closed by BR in 1985 and subsequently used by the PW Department. ("Listed" 28 June 2013). Viewed on 16 September 2015.

STRUCTURES
A BRIEF SUMMARY OF THE HISTORY OF THREE OF SCOTLAND'S FAMOUS BRIDGES

FORTH BRIDGE (11A)

The origins of the Forth Bridge date back to 1863 when a joint project between the North British Railway and Edinburgh and Glasgow Railway appointed Stephenson and Toner to design a bridge for the Forth, but six months later the commission was given to Thomas Bouch who was already working on concepts and designs. He was also involved in the design and build of the Tay Bridge (qv) but when this collapsed in 1879 his reputation collapsed with it and his design was formally abandoned on 13 January 1881. Sir John Fowler, WH Barlow and TE Harrison, consulting engineers to the project, were subsequently invited to give proposals for a bridge

The design of a cantilever bridge offered by Sir John Fowler and Sir Benjamin Baker was accepted with construction commencing in 1882 and the formal opening on 4 March 1890. Approximately 4,600 workers were employed at the height of the construction, of which there were sadly 57 fatalities

It is 8,094 ft long and 361 ft above high water level with two 1,700 ft spans which at the time of completion made it the longest single cantilever span bridge in the world. The bridge, quite rightly, is considered as an iconic structure, a symbol of Scotland and a UNESCO World Heritage Site.

GLENFINNAN VIADUCT (13A)

Designed by Simpson & Wilson Engineers and built by Robert MacAlpine and Sons, the 100ft high viaduct crosses the River Finnan and was completed in 1898 as part of the Mallaig Extension Railway which opened on 1 April 1901. It has a curve of 792ft radius, is 460 yards long and consists of twenty one 50ft semi-circular spans constructed in mass concrete.

This method of construction, which has a high compressive strength but poorer tensile strength, was selected due to the difficulties in working the schist, a medium-grade metamorphic rock

TAY BRIDGE (11A)

THE FIRST TAY BRIDGE

The North British Railway (Tay Bridge) Act received the Royal Assent on 15 July 1870 and the foundation stone was laid just over a year later, on 22 July 1871 with construction commencing the following day. Thomas Bouch, a renowned engineer who had been engaged by numerous railways, designed the bridge, nominally based on his successful Belah Viaduct at Stainmore on the South Durham & Lancashire Union Railway.

The original design was for lattice girders supported by brick piers resting on bedrock shown by trial borings to lie at no great depth under the river. At either end of the bridge the single rail track ran on top of the bridge girder, most of which then lay below the pier tops. In the centre section of the bridge, the "high girders", the railway ran inside the bridge girder, which could then run above the pier tops to give the required clearance to allow passage of sailing ships upriver. To accommodate thermal expansion there were few rigid connections between girders and piers.

However it soon became apparent that as the construction progressed the bedrock was much deeper than first thought and would not be able to support the piers. This led to a major redesign of the structure including the substitution of iron piers for brick ones, a reduction in the number of piers and, consequently, an increase in spans between them.

The bridge was completed in February 1878 and following the Board of Trade Inspection, which recommended a maximum speed of 25 miles/hr, it opened to passengers on 1 June 1878. The bridge only lasted just over a year as at 19.15 on the night of 28 December 1879 it collapsed after the central spans gave way during high winter gales. A train with six carriages carrying seventy-five passengers and crew was crossing at the time of the collapse and all lost their lives.

The subsequent Court of Enquiry heard that the wind velocity that night, at right angles to the bridge, was estimated as Gale Force 10 or 11 (55 – 72 miles/hr) and it concluded that there was no explicit allowance for wind loading in the design and, from witnesses testimony, that there were other flaws in detailed design, in construction, in maintenance and in the quality control of castings, all of which were, at least in part, firmly Bouch's responsibility. Having been knighted on 26 June 1879 for his work on the bridge he died within eighteen months, his reputation utterly destroyed.

THE SECOND TAY BRIDGE

A proposal for a second bridge was formally incorporated in July 1881 and the foundation stone was laid on 6 July 1883. This was a double-track bridge designed by William Henry Barlow, sited some 59ft west of the first and running parallel to it. The contractors were William Arrol & Co. who used 24,600 tonf of iron and steel, 68,900 tonf of concrete, 10,000,000 bricks and 3,000,000 rivets in the construction which lasted nearly four years and on which 14 men lost their lives. It was formally opened on 20 June 1887, with many of the stumps of the original still visible above the water as a grim reminder.

PHOTOGRAPH CREDITS
FORTH BRIDGE: Andrew Shiva/Wikipedia, CC BY-SA 4.0, https://commons.wikimedia.org/w/index.php?curid=51291330
TAY BRIDGE: https://commons.wikimedia.org/wiki/File%3ATaybridge_from_law_02SEP05.jpg
GLENFINNAN VIADUCTby de:Benutzer:Nicolas17 (Self-photographed) [CC BY-SA 2.5 (https://creativecommons.org/licenses/by-sa/2.5)], via Wikimedia Commons

ACKNOWLEDGEMENTS
We would like to thank the following for their assistance in producing this book:
John Alsop, The late Ben Brooksbank, Alan Brown, The late Ken Fairey, Alisdair Campbell (Highland Railway Society), John Ledward, Andy Pegg (Caledonian Railway [Brechin] Ltd), Nick Pigott, The late WT (Bill) Stubbs, Keith Turner and members of the Engine Shed Society
The maps used in this publication were sourced from Cambridge University Map Library (Reproduced with thanks to the Syndics of Cambridge University) and the National Library of Scotland (Reproduced with thanks). Tickets were kindly supplied by Peter Waller
(Larger versions of the maps may be obtained from the National Library of Scotland website: https://maps.nls.uk/)

SAMPLES OF PRE-GROUPING TICKETS

G&SWR: Belfast to Glasgow (St Enoch)
via Stranraer (7 April 1903)

CR:
Edinburgh to Carlisle

Portpatrick & Wigtownshire Joint Railways:
Kirkcowan to Glasgow (St Enoch)
(Date Unknown)

Portpatrick & Wigtownshire Joint Railways:
Millisle to Edinburgh (23 December 1902)

CR:
Moffat to Glasgow (Central) (22 May 1902)

NBR:
Peebles to Glasgow (9 May 1902)

L&NER:
Melrose to St Boswells (Date Unknown)

CR: Bicycle Ticket
Blairgowrie to Glasgow (Date Unknown)

CR:
Oban to Loch Awe (17 July 1899)

NBR:
Fort William to Arrochar & Tarbet
(10 August 1899)

CR: Warrant Ticket
Crieff to Perth

CR:
Larbert to Kilsyth

HR: Parliamentary Ticket
Fortrose to Garve (Date Unknown)

HR: Forces Ticket
Fort George to St Germans GWR

Dundee, Perth, & Aberdeen Junction Railway:
Lochee to Dundee (c1865 - 1870)

Inverness & Perth Junction Railway: (Issued by HR)
Inverness to Dunphail (29 August 1901)

Invergarry & Fort Augustus Railway:
Gairlochy to Fort Augustus
(Date Unknown)

HR: Parliamentary Ticket
Achnasheen to Strome Ferry (Date Unknown)

HR: Parliamentary Ticket
Inverness to Achnashellach

NBR: First Class Guest Ticket issued to
NA Ellingsen esq. on 27 May 1902
North Leith to Glasgow (Queen Street)

BIBLIOGRAPHY

THE HANDBOOK OF BRITISH RAILWAYS STEAM DEPOTS
by Paul Smith. Platform 5 Volume 4: Northern England & Scotland. ISBN 1 872524 14 1 (1990)

THE DIRECTORY OF BRITISH ENGINE SHEDS & PRINCIPAL LOCOMOTIVE SERVICING POINTS
by Roger Griffiths & Paul Smith. Oxford Publishing Company
Volume 2: North Midlands, Northern England & Scotland. ISBN 0 86093 548 5 (2000)

RAILWAY ATLAS, THEN & NOW by Paul Smith & Keith Turner. Ian Allan Publishing
Second Edition. ISBN 978 0 7110 3833 2 (2015)

FORGOTTEN RAILWAYS: SCOTLAND by John Thomas. David & Charles ISBN 0 7153 8193 8 (1981)

RAILWAY PASSENGER STATIONS IN GREAT BRITAIN: A CHRONOLOGY by Michael Quick.
Railway & Canal Historical Society ISBN 978 0 901461 57 5 (2009)

ENCYCLOPÆDIA OF BRITISH RAILWAY COMPANIES by Christopher Awdry. Guild Publishing CN8983

CLINKER'S REGISTER OF CLOSED PASSENGER STATIONS & GOODS DEPOTS IN ENGLAND, SCOTLAND AND WALES 1830-1980
by CR Clinker. Avon Anglia Publications. Second Edition. ISBN 0 905466 91 8 (1988)

THE DIRECTORY OF RAILWAY STATIONS by RVJ Butt. Patrick Stephens Ltd. ISBN 1 85260 508 1

COMPLETE BRITISH RAILWAYS MAPS & GAZETTEER 1825-1985 by CJ Wignall. Oxford Publishing Company. ISBN 0 86093 294 X

NORTH BRITISH RAILWAY STUDY GROUP, Journal No.126, July 2016 Dr McGregor pp 37-42

WEBSITES ACCESSED

DISUSED STATIONS: http://disused-stations.org.uk/

ENGINE SHED SOCIETY: www.engineshedsociety.co.uk

GREAT NORTH OF SCOTLAND RAILWAY ASSOCIATION: http://www.gnsra.org.uk/

NATIONAL LIBRARY OF SCOTLAND: https://maps.nls.uk/

RAIL MAP ONLINE: https://www.railmaponline.com/UKIEMap.php

RAIL SCOT: https://www.railscot.co.uk/

UK GRID REFERENCE FINDER: https://gridreferencefinder.com/

WIKIPEDIA: https://en.wikipedia.org/